Advance Praise for *One Truth and One Spirit*

Keith Readdy has alchemically united his passion for Aleister Crowley's A∴A∴ and O.T.O. with his academic training in Western esotericism. He tackles the thorny question of whether Thelema is a religion, a spirituality or a philosophy. He summarizes the evolution of Thelemic doctrine in the teachings of both Crowley and modern-day exponents like J. Daniel Gunther and Fratres Shiva and Phanes. He recounts the convoluted history of Thelema since Crowley's death—no easy feat! And he analyzes the role of publishing as the vehicle for preserving and promulgating the message of Aleister Crowley as the prophet of Thelema. It's rare for a book to offer something for everyone, but *One Truth and One Spirit* packs in so many thought-provoking details that anyone with an interest in Aleister Crowley or Thelema will encounter valuable insights throughout its pages.
—Richard Kaczynski, author of *Perdurabo: The Life of Aleister Crowley* and *Forgotten Templars: The Untold History of Ordo Templi Orientis*

* * *

I have often maintained that for Thelema to be taken seriously, we need to develop a culture of rational discourse. The possibility of such discourse depends on Thelemites using scholarly methods to develop how we approach our history, doctrine, and practices as Thelemites. In other words, it turns Thelema into a contributing subject, rather than being merely an object of study. Keith Readdy has accomplished something very special with this book. It covers the doctrines, organizations, and the often problematic history that is associated with the Law of Thelema. I fully believe that in the future, this book will be regarded as one of the pillars that made rational discourse possible within our community. —Kjetil Fjell, Psy. D., Specialist in Neuropsychology.

* * *

Keith Readdy simultaneously untangles and harmonizes many seemingly contradictory forces within modern Thelema to yield a vision of unity long desired.—Daniel Pineda, author of *Book of Secrets*

***

By properly approaching Thelema as a New Religious Movement, Keith Readdy, in his study *One Truth and One Spirit*, sets the stage for a clear-sighted engagement with Aleister Crowley's spiritual legacy. While Crowley himself has been the subject of more than a dozen biographies, the doctrinal aspects of the system, of which he considered himself the Prophet, received much less hermeneutical treatment. The author, trained in the academic study of Western Esotericism, provides a solid theoretical overview of Thelema and traces the historical development of the system from its inception up to the present moment. It is in particular this latter aspect of the book, where the author attempts to distinguish between history and mnemohistory between facts and narratives, that is going to be controversial and challenging to some readers. The issue concerns legitimacy and authority among various factions within the Thelemic movement, and the author offers an erudite and convincing exposition of his views on the matter. The book will be of great interest not only to the adherents of Thelema, irrespective of their personal allegiances and persuasions, but to all interested in the history of Western Esotericism and New Religious Movements.
—Gordan Djurdjevic, Ph.D., author of *India and the Occult*

***

Everyone interested in Crowley's institutional and philosophical legacy—and especially members of Thelemic bodies—will benefit from reading Keith Readdy's extensive study. Its strengths lie in clarifying Thelema's growth as a religious movement, in expressing its peculiarities as religion, philosophy, and magical order, and in adumbrating Thelemic ethics, along with the tangled history of the A∴A∴ and O.T.O.

Readdy traces the development of Thelema as a system after its initial prophetic impulse in 1904, making helpful distinctions between "religion" and "spirituality." Above all, he delineates the fate of Crowley's two principal orders after his death in 1947 in the context of a discourse on "duplexity."

Thelema's reliance on its publishing history is clearly presented, as is the long battle for possession, or re-possession, of Crowley's institutional legacy—principally his copyrights—waged between Karl Germer's protégé Marcelo Ramos Motta and Crowley's intended successor to Germer, Grady McMurtry. Tensions and hostility between Jane Wolfe's former "pupil" Phyllis Seckler (representing A∴A∴ interests), and husband McMurtry (representing O.T.O. interests), receive detailed treatment, building on James Wasserman's autobiographical account *Into the Center of the Fire* (2012). The issue of A∴A∴ "lineages" is a primary interest of the book's latter part.

Readdy illuminates the disconcerting reality of schism in the O.T.O. and continuing vexation in the A∴A∴ system over adherence to Crowley's original intentions. Readdy's concise, lucid treatment of the O.T.O.'s internalized *Ecclesia Gnostica Catholica* is a boon to understanding the complex Thelemic synthesis as manifested in practice.

Above all, while the author writes as an infra-movement adherent and specialist—accepting Crowley's privileged spiritual authority—he issues a summons for a rational case for the extension of academic interest in Thelema from the burgeoning chapel of Western Esotericism, so to engage with mainstream philosophy, sociology, psychology, political science, behavioral and cognitive sciences, even environmental studies.

Thelema has apparently reached a new stage in its 114 year development, and Readdy's book is both symptomatic of this, and arguably vital to its continuance. The time-factor is interesting. Most lasting religious movements go through a century or so of inward, incubatory drama before emerging on the greater stage of life. Readdy presents Thelema as a system ready to take its full place in the world.
—Tobias Churton, author of *Aleister Crowley: The Biography* and *Aleister Crowley in America*

* * *

An essential account of the history of the O.T.O. in modern America. A compelling and well-researched book that rewards repeated reference.
—Paul Feazey, webmaster of *LAShTAL.com*

ONE TRUTH
AND ONE SPIRIT
Aleister Crowley's Spiritual Legacy

ONE TRUTH
AND ONE SPIRIT

Aleister Crowley's Spiritual Legacy

KEITH READDY

Foreword by

VERE CHAPPELL

IBIS PRESS
Lake Worth, Florida

Published in 2018 by Ibis Press
A division of Nicolas-Hays, Inc.
P. O. Box 540206
Lake Worth, FL 33454-0206
www.ibispress.net

Distributed to the trade by
Red Wheel/Weiser, LLC
65 Parker St. • Ste. 7
Newburyport, MA 01950
www.redwheelweiser.com

ISBN: 978-0-89254-184-3
Ebook ISBN: 978-0-89254-677-0

Library of Congress Cataloging-in-Publication Data
available upon request

Book design and production by STUDIO 31
www.studio31.com

Printed in the United States of America
[MP]

DEDICATED TO

ANGEL LORENZ
(1981–2015)
"THE BEETLE"

Who in our teenage years introduced
me to Aleister Crowley as we became friends.
Who later encouraged me to pursue the Great Work
and served as an early guide. And who, later still,
I would have the honor to officially call
"Brother" in every sense of the word.

I await meeting you again,
in this incarnation or the next.

Contents

FOREWORD

Do what thou wilt shall be the whole of the Law.

I FIRST ENCOUNTERED the works of Aleister Crowley when I was a college student many years ago. The introduction to *Magick in Theory and Practice* was exactly what I needed at the time. It convinced me that magick was a rational undertaking rather than a supernatural phenomenon, and I began to experiment with the practices and rituals set forth in the book. For two years I studied and practiced on my own, never imagining that there were actually organized groups of magicians following the same path. After all, the book had a copyright date of 1929, and Crowley had been dead for many years. I assumed that whatever he started had died with him, and I saw myself as a spiritual archaeologist, conjuring wisdom from the distant past.

When I finally met another ceremonial magician on the UCLA campus in 1989, to be perfectly honest I didn't take him seriously at first. I figured that he had read some of the same obscure books that I had, and was infected with a bit too much missionary zeal for my taste. But when he shared with me a few issues of the *Baphomet Breeze*, published by the Los Angeles Lodge of Ordo Templi Orientis, I was astonished. Not only did a secret cabal of Aleister Crowley's followers survive from the 1930s into the present day, but they had *newsletters*!

The first O.T.O. event I attended was a Gnostic Mass. It was staged in the cramped living room of a small house in a sketchy neighborhood near downtown L.A. I sat on a saggy sofa, shoulder-to-shoulder with a handful of other attendees. The high altar was the dining room table, and the priest had to enter the temple through the front door of the house, from the street. In spite of the makeshift conditions, I was literally spellbound by the ritual. To me, witnessing live magick for the first time was nothing less than a revelation. I signed up for membership on the spot.

The difference between being a solitary practitioner of magick and becoming part of a genuine magical order, working with and learning from experienced occultists, is like playing a video game versus learning to fly a real airplane. There is only so much that can be learned from books. To obtain a real sense of magick, to learn the subtle details of the techniques and truly understand their application, requires transmission of knowledge via person-to-person contact and development of skills through practice, with supervised mentorship. This is the fundamental purpose of a magical order. I felt like I had emerged from a black-and-white movie into a Technicolor world.

During this time I was fortunate to meet Phyllis Seckler, a member of the old Hollywood O.T.O. Lodge in the 1940s who knew Wilfred Smith and Jack Parsons. When she found out I was living in Playa del Rey, she told me how they used to go out to the dunes near my house to do initiations. After I founded L.V.X. Camp (now Star Sapphire Lodge in Los Angeles) I used to quip that we did our initiations on the *exact same spot* where Phyllis had done hers. On the 50th anniversary of her Minerval initiation into O.T.O., I became a student of Phyllis and remained a member of her original College of Thelema for the next eight years.

Bit by bit I learned more about the history of O.T.O. and the dissemination of Thelema. I heard a lot about Grady McMurtry, who had revived the Order from near extinction in the 1970s. These and other stories were circulated at Baphomet Lodge, which was the center of my O.T.O. experience. I took classes, attended Gnostic Masses, and underwent initiations into the degrees of O.T.O., all at the same Lodge. I knew there were other Lodges around the country, but I knew almost nothing about them. The Grand Lodge was something of an abstraction, a distant bureaucracy that I had little cause to think about. And there were also whispers of another organization known only by the enigmatic initials A∴A∴—a remote, mysterious, and seemingly unattainable phantasm. For a short time I even believed that A∴A∴ was reserved solely for the spirits of dead occultists!

This was of course before the internet, or at least, before the world wide web (I was an early adopter of e-mail in 1984, but had very few correspondents in those days). Everything I learned about O.T.O. and Thelema came either from books, or from my peers and teachers at the Lodge. The books provided much in the way of formal doctrine, and when the Arkana paperback of *The Confessions of Aleister Crowley* appeared in 1989, it provided ample history of the Thelemic movement during Crowley's lifetime. Beyond this, however, most of what I knew about the events that transpired after Crowley's death was pieced together from anecdotes and stories I picked up around the Lodge. At the time, I accepted it all unconditionally. I had no reason to question the words or motives of my teachers. In the beginning I was blissfully unaware of the hidden agendas and political maneuvering that was behind the particular worldview that was being imparted to me.

But as I matured in the Order, the Order was maturing as well. Publishing ramped up, and much more Crowley material became available. The U.S. Grand Lodge was established as a distinct entity in 1996, and a year later I was asked to serve as its Treasurer. I traveled to numerous O.T.O. bodies in other cities and encountered perspectives which differed from my own. As I broadened my horizons and did more of my own research, I came to realize that not necessarily everything taught by my old teachers was grounded in reality. I had to recognize that some had their own agendas, and history was sometimes altered or even invented to serve those agendas. I learned to critically evaluate the information I had, and assess the reliability of my sources. And in the process, I had to discard some cherished notions which I had previously never thought to question.

Things are very different today. In the 1980s it was not uncommon for people to come to the Order having never heard of Aleister Crowley or Thelema. These days, however, newcomers are just as likely to show up at the Lodge quoting Kenneth Grant and asking for directions to the nearest Abyss crossing. Rather than a scarcity of information, we have a plethora of information, not all of it having equal value. Searching for "Ordo Templi Orientis" on the internet can turn up everything from the most somber academic history to the most outlandish conspiracy theories. There is a minor industry of websites devoted to anti-O.T.O. propaganda written by disgruntled ex-members. Even Wikipedia suffers from a modern-day tragedy of the commons, presenting a version of history in which popularity replaces veracity. And worst of all, social media is awash with self-appointed "experts" who are eager to proclaim "the Truth" with great conviction but little, if any, substance. How are we to make sense of it all?

In this age of clickbait and fake news, it is now more important than ever to apply our powers of reason and critical thinking to evaluate the information we consume. To more fully understand the modern Thelemic movement, we need to understand its history. Numerous biographies have shed plenty of light upon the development of Thelema and the orders O.T.O. and A∴A∴ throughout Crowley's lifetime, the best of these being *Perdurabo: The Life of Aleister Crowley* by Richard Kaczynski (2010). Important insights can also be gained from the story of Agape Lodge in the 1930s and 40s, as related in *The Unknown God* by Martin P. Starr (2003). But until now, there has been no comprehensive history of the survival (and revival) of Thelema from the death of Crowley to the present day.

One Truth and One Spirit: Aleister Crowley's Spiritual Legacy finally provides this history. Drawing upon an impressive array of primary sources, many of which have never before seen publication, Keith Readdy weaves together a well-researched, reliable account of the significant events which have shaped the manifestation of Thelema today. Here at last, the facts have been clearly set forth in print. The myths, legends, and stories which I first heard in my O.T.O. youth have now been collected, corrected, and presented as they actually happened.

But this book is much more than just a collection of names and dates. History is always subject to interpretation, and to misinterpretation as well. Keith's goal is not merely to inform the reader, but also to help us develop a better understanding of the subject by providing context and critical analysis. He not only guides us through Crowley's vision of Thelema, A∴A∴ and O.T.O., he also places that vision within the context of current scholarship on new religious movements and occulture. Thus armed, we are better equipped to interpret and evaluate the significance of the events of our past and comprehend how they have contributed to our present.

This book is also certain to be controversial to some readers, particularly those who have a stake in alternative interpretations of events which favor the official narratives of other organizations to which they belong. Indeed, the facts presented here may challenge some of *your* long-held beliefs and assumptions. But this is not a bad thing. As scientific illuminists, we must be prepared to abandon those hypotheses which are not supported by the evidence, however attached to them we might have become. This book is not for "true believers," those whose minds have been immunized against accepting new information, but for genuine seekers of Truth.

Seek, and ye shall find.

Love is the law, love under will.

—Vere Chappell
Laguna Hills, California
September 3, 2018

PREFACE

THE FOLLOWING WORK IS the result of a mixture of elements that mingled in the cauldron of my own academic research on, and my personal experience with, the spiritual movement forwarded by mountaineer, poet, champion chess-player, and religious thinker Aleister Crowley (1875–1947). My interest in Crowley's work began in my late teenage years when I was introduced to him by a friend, an already well-read Thelemite. He was one year my junior but had been studying the Great Beast since he was eleven. Since then, due to my inquisitive approach into the realms of philosophy and religion, I have progressively gained more interest and experience with Crowley and his spiritual teachings on Thelema. On a broad level, this book is a result of my own two decades of navigation into this subject.

More specifically, *One Truth and One Spirit* is the result of two specific factors. In one sense, it has been produced out of the unquenchable thirst brought about by spiritual inquiry. That is, my own personal journey as a seeker has led me to write the book. It is the work of a student of Thelema, an initiate, and aspirant—at this point neither novice, nor yet what I call seasoned. Secondly and on another level, much of this work was initially consolidated for my professional aims in academia. A great deal of the content in the following pages was written during my tenure as a master's degree student at the University of Amsterdam's Center for the History of Hermetic Philosophy and Related Currents. It is the work of a young scholar in Western esotericism, history, and religious studies research. That said, I would like to make clear that this work is meant to be accessible to both the scholar and the seeker. It is meant for the researcher *and* the practitioner.

The bulk of Part II was originally written as my master's thesis in 2015, titled "The Style of a Letter: The Thelemic Movement and its

Culture of Publication (1962–1979)." It is historical in nature, and spans the developmental years of the modern O.T.O.

One Truth and One Spirit was initially the title of a short sixty-page essay that I had written under my O.T.O. motto, "Τέλειος." The essay generated some level of interest within the Thelemic community because it addressed one of the more sensitive contemporary topics known as "Duplexity." I remain humbled by the praise I received for the essay from all over the world. I am also appreciative of the criticisms— and have attempted to address some of the counter-arguments in the present work, and to elaborate further on some of the original points. After all, we could never strengthen our ideas without such dialectic.

The title *One Truth and One Spirit* requires some comment. A name such as "One Truth" may give the impression that I am trying to make claims to "Truth." I am not. The title is inspired by Crowley's own words on the spiritual essence of Thelema, the A∴A∴, which he described as "that illuminated community which is scattered throughout the world, but which is governed by one truth and united in one spirit." Much of what this work intends is not just a history in the academic sense of the term, but a *spiritual history* of Thelema and Aleister Crowley's spiritual legacy. In my opinion, this legacy is most identifiable in the two movements he forwarded in his lifetime, the A∴A∴ and the Ordo Templi Orientis.

Some readers may find this book too academic in its approach, while many academics will find it blurring the lines of etic research and emic exclusivity of the subject at hand. This book is not necessarily intended for academia, though I have utilized my university training throughout. This book is not necessarily intended for only practitioners, though I have used my experiential knowledge as a member of the O.T.O. and an instructor in the A∴A∴ system throughout. In short, I hope that I have satisfied both worlds and not profaned either.

The reader should know that I am not herein making any authoritative claims to Thelema, the O.T.O., the A∴A∴, or the work of Aleister Crowley. At the time of this writing, I hold no official offices in either order and the views expressed herein are simply my own. It is my hope that these pages will help shed light on the colorful tradition that has made up the movement we know as Thelema. It is a turbulent, yet intriguing story of how a handful of dedicated and impassioned individuals put the right energies in motion to create a growing and diverse culture that exists and flourishes to this day. This book is a work of Love, from the material to the spiritual, and I am honored to present it to you.

—Keith M. Readdy
August, 2018

INTRODUCTION

IT WAS QUITE THE HONEYMOON. It was spring and the newlyweds were celebrating in Cairo, Egypt. The husband thought it would be an endearing move to charm his new wife by demonstrating his knowledge of the occult arts. He recited to her a spell from a Greco-Egyptian papyrus known to nineteenth-century occultists as "The Bornless Ritual."[1] Novice to anything of the sort, she sat and listened. In the days that followed, Mrs. Rose Edith Crowley reportedly began exhibiting strange behavior, telling her husband she was receiving "instructions" from the Egyptian god Horus. The instructions commanded that he enter a room of their Cairo flat on a precise day at a precise hour and record what he heard. He did so at noon on April 8, 9, and 10 in 1904. The result was a manuscript, originally titled *Liber L vel Legis* or *The Book of the Law*.[2] This "Law" has a central tenet, "Do what thou wilt shall be the whole of the Law." It describes the closing of an old age and the beginning of a "New Aeon" for humanity, one in which the individual would be spiritually liberated from the shackles of the religions of the past.[3]

---

[1] Samuel MacGregor Mathers attributed this invocation to *The Lesser Key of Solomon*, or the *Goetia*. See Aleister Crowley (ed.) (1995) *The Goetia: The Lesser Key of Solomon the King, Clavicula Salomonis Regis*, Samuel Liddell MacGregor Mathers (trans.), 2nd ed., Hymenaeus Beta (ed.) (York Beach, ME: Weiser Books). The ritual actually originates from a Greco-Egyptian rite of evocation that was first translated in Charles Wycliffe Goodwin (1852) *Fragment of a Greco-Egyptian Work Upon Magic from a Papyrus in the British Museum* (Cambridge: Deighton, Macmillan and Co.).

[2] Its name was changed to *"Liber AL vel Legis"* after a doctrinal discovery about the original manuscript. It will herein be referred to as *The Book of the Law* interchangeably with *Liber AL vel Legis* or simply *Liber AL*. See Aleister Crowley (1938) *The Book of the Law* (London: O.T.O.).

[3] The account of this revelation is given in Aleister Crowley (1991a&b) *The Equinox of the Gods* (Scottsdale, AZ and New York: New Falcon Publications, and O.T.O. in association with 93 Publishing, Ltd.) and in Crowley (1997) *Magick: Liber ABA, Book Four* (York Beach, ME: Weiser Books).

While it has been difficult to evaluate the specific details of these events, apart from Crowley's surviving diary entries, the reality is that the authoring of this text marked the beginning of a new religious movement that is alive and growing around the world to this day.

Aleister Crowley (born Edward Alexander Crowley, 1875–1947) is a well-known name to occult practitioners and religious scholars in the twentieth and twenty-first centuries. His image as an esoteric figure and alternative spiritual thinker has also extended into popular culture. He has been famously referenced as one of the faces on the album cover of The Beatles' *Sgt. Pepper's Lonely Hearts Club Band*, and he has been a strong influence on Led Zeppelin's Jimmy Page, among others. Crowley has also been depicted in numerous novels and films since his death. His lasting legacy as an occultist has influenced esoteric religion for the last century. More than a dozen biographies have been written,[4] and academic work focused on him continues to grow.[5] Recently a primetime television series has brought Crowley into the spotlight again with the airing of *Strange Angel* in the summer of 2018. It offers a sensationalized biographical sketch of rocket inventor and co-founder of the Jet Propulsion Laboratory (JPL), Jack Parsons, a devoted follower of Crowley.

---

[4] The most well-known and earliest biography is by one of Crowley's literary executors, John Symonds. See Symonds (1951) *The Great Beast: The Life of Aleister Crowley* (London: Rider). The reader will especially benefit from consulting a number of biographies such as Lawrence Sutin (2000) *Do What Thou Wilt: A Life of Aleister Crowley* (New York: St. Martins Griffin), Martin Booth (2000) *A Magick Life: A Biography of Aleister Crowley* (London: Hodder and Stoughton), Richard Kaczynski (2010) *Perdurabo: The Life of Aleister Crowley* (second edition, Berkeley: North Atlantic Books) and several from Tobias Churton (2011), (2014), and (2017). The various biographical accounts of Crowley's life have been explored in Marco Pasi (2003) "The Neverendingly Told Story: Recent Biographies of Aleister Crowley," in *Aries: Journal for the Study of Western Esotericism*, 3:2. pp. 224–245. Crowley's own autobiography up to the 1920s is given in Crowley (1969a) *The Confessions of Aleister Crowley: An Autohagiography*, John Symonds and Kenneth Grant (eds.) (London: Jonathan Cape, and New York: Hill & Wang).

[5] See for example Henrik Bogdan and Martin P. Starr (eds.) (2012), *Aleister Crowley and Western Esotericism* (Oxford: Oxford University Press).

Despite his status as one of the most famous esotericists of the twentieth century, and regardless of the abundance of extant pop literature that has been published on the study and practice of his spiritual philosophy, Thelema, there remains very little published work that examines Thelema as a movement. The intent of the current work is to: (a) explain Thelema from a philosophical and theoretical standpoint, and (b) conduct a historical analysis of the movement since the death of its founder. One of the more significant ways in which this can be done is to place Thelema within the context of the study of religion.[6]

Thelema from a Theoretical Perspective

A purely historical work on Aleister Crowley would relay the sequence of events and his interactions with the personalities surrounding him. Such a study would not need to focus on the deeper levels of analysis about his philosophy, or why Thelema was organized the way that it was during his lifetime. This study, although primarily historical in its approach, attempts to explore Thelema as Crowley's spiritual legacy. It will describe it as a religious movement—from a philosophical, theoretical, and doctrinal standpoint. This will be helpful for the practitioner, in particular. By tracing Thelema as a movement, certain insights into key doctrinal elements of its spiritual philosophy will be provided. We will be able to see how this magical system evolved as Crowley underwent progressive stages of his personal initiation. A study of Thelema's theoretical development will also shed light on the rituals and structures of its associated organizations in a way that a purely historical work might not.

Thelema as a Case Study in the History of Religion

A modern history of Thelema should provide insights into how a religion in contemporary society functions. The history of the first cen-

---

6 By "religion," I use the term in a specific academic context. A more detailed discussion of this is found in chapter six, entitled "Thelema as a New Religious Movement."

turies of a religious movement is of particular importance because it examines the experiences of human beings as they lay the groundwork for a particular tradition. It may grant insights into the inner workings of how a religion develops and what factors contribute to its vitality. Assessed properly, a critical history of a religion's early years can offer insight into the very nature of the human experience, with which the phenomenon of religion is intricately intertwined.

The need for a study of the early period of a religious movement may best be illustrated by example. In 100 CE, it was questionable whether the various sectarian movements generally associated with Christianity would have survived the persecution of the Roman Empire.[7] Conversely, social theorists have debated for the last century whether the influence of Christianity on Western society will ever completely disappear.[8]

In 2018, Thelema is well into the second decade of its second century. By 1957, a decade after Crowley's death, there were only about a dozen living adherents and barely any formal organization in the Thelemic movement. Today, there are over 4,000 dues-paying members of Crowley's international co-fraternal organization,[9] the Ordo Templi Orientis ("Order of Oriental Templars," or "Order of the Temple of the East," hereafter referred to as "the O.T.O."). These figures do not include lapsed members, or members of other Thelemic groups; nor those who study Crowley's works and consider themselves Thelemites without being affiliated to any groups. There are also many solitary

---

[7] Early Christian persecution has been dealt with in Geoffrey Ernest Maurice De Sainte Croix (2006) *Christian Persecution, Martyrdom, and Orthodoxy*, Michael Whitby (ed.) (Oxford: Oxford University Press).

[8] I refer here to the "secularization thesis," which argues that religious authority in society has diminished since the period of the Enlightenment, followed by the emergence of scientific rationalism and industrialization. See David Martin (1979) *A General Theory of Secularization*, Mark Chaves (1994) "Secularization As Declining Religious Authority," and Steve Bruce (2002) *God is Dead: Secularization in the West*. (Full citations can be found in the bibliography.) There is some discussion on this topic offered in chapter six.

[9] By "co-fraternal," I mean that membership includes both sexes.

workers, some of whom engage in online forums either directly or indirectly related to the subject.[10]

That being said, what I refer to in the following pages as the "Thelemic movement" includes the modern efforts of individuals associated with both the establishment (and re-establishment) of the two main magical orders forwarded by Aleister Crowley in his lifetime: the O.T.O. and the A∴A∴.[11] This study focuses primarily on the contemporary development of these two orders since his death.[12] There are many other groups identifying themselves with Thelema that are not officially associated with the Thelemic movement as defined herein. (They will be referred to within a broader context using such terms as "Thelemic community" and "Thelemic occulture.") While they might deserve a study of their own, such an endeavor is not within the scope of this book.

Already in its short century plus of existence, Thelema has experienced a great deal of growth and development, as well as the challenges that come with these. For example, schisms have emerged resulting from disputed claims of authority, and differing opinions have produced offshoots and branches within the Thelemic community.[13]

Despite these growing pains, Thelema has been formalized in the secular sphere through incorporation and the acquisition of nonprofit status through its most visible and populated organization, the O.T.O. Furthermore, leaders within and those closely associated with the O.T.O. have developed Thelema's philosophy and theology

---

10 This is what I call the "Thelemic occulture," the milieu of interest in Thelema and Crowleyana including online communities such as podcasts, blogs, social media, as well as art collectives, writers, and publishers. For a discussion on the use of internet technology and social media with regard to Thelema, see chapter twelve.

11 A general overview of these two orders is given in chapter three, "The A∴A∴ and the O.T.O."

12 These two organizations are publicly accessible through the world wide web. The O.T.O. is found at O.T.O. International (www.oto.org) and the A∴A∴ is known publicly through its First Order, the Outer College (www.outercol.org).

13 Other Thelemic organizations have emerged in some cases quite naturally with regard to the organic process of how movements grow and branch out. Others have surfaced out of conflict and schism. This is discussed in some details in chapter eleven.

through extensive publications and editorial efforts.[14] The O.T.O. has grown exponentially in membership since its re-establishment in 1969, and has systematized its policies and guidelines for uniformity within its community. In short, the Thelemic movement, as it has been established by the magical orders of O.T.O. and A∴A∴, has become a recognizable—and recognized—religious entity in a relatively short period of time.

Thelema in Context: Western Esotericism[15]

As mentioned, we place Thelema in the context of the study of religion,[16] categorized as a sub-branch of the discipline of religious studies known as "Western esotericism." This will provide us with perspective on how to approach and understand it in greater detail.

What is Western esotericism? It is a seemingly simple question with no easy answer. Its history as an academic discipline is an exhaustive discussion in and of itself.[17] As far as the material that is typically

---

[14] The most important and comprehensive editorial efforts have been those of the current "Outer Head of the Order" (O.H.O.) of O.T.O., Hymenaeus Beta (ps. of William Breeze) and the various editions of Crowley's works that have been published under his supervision. Most notable is his edition of Crowley (1997) *Magick: Liber ABA, Book Four* (York Beach, ME: Samuel Weiser).

[15] The following discussion pertains to the academic study of Western esotericism as described in Wouter Hanegraaff (2013) *Western Esotericism: A Guide for the Perplexed* (London: Bloomsbury Publishing Plc). Also helpful is Antoine Faivre (1994) *Access to Western Esotericism* (Albany: SUNY Press) and Nicholas Goodrick-Clarke (2008) *The Western Esoteric Traditions: A Historical Introduction* (Oxford: Oxford University Press).

[16] See especially chapter six.

[17] Prior to 1965, scholarship in the areas of history now considered part of the Western esoteric discourse was confined primarily to niche specialist circles in various pockets of academia. Some of the earliest formations of the modern discipline of Western esotericism can be traced back to scholars of comparative religion, folklore, and classics in the 1930s. Noteworthy here are the Eranos conferences that were held annually in Lago Maggiore near Ascona, Switzerland. These conferences were intellectual discussion groups on subjects of humanities, religion and psychology (among other fields), and hosted a number of scholars whose research concerned various areas

covered in the field of Western esotericism, it is essentially multi-disciplinary, incorporating the fields of history, religion, psychology, philosophy, gender studies, sociology, and many more. Yet the criteria that may be classified as "Western esotericism" remain problematic, as the term itself implies a collection of disparate subjects grouped together under a single heading. As Wouter Hanegraaff notes, Western esotericism is:

> a radically pluralistic field of currents, ideas and practices that can be studied from late antiquity to the present day, *without* seeking to privilege any historical period or any particular worldview as "more truly esoteric" [...] than any other. From that perspective, there is no such thing as a "best example" of esotericism, and there are no prototypical "esotericists." But obviously, such an approach begs the question of definition and demarcation, for it still assumes that the field as a whole can be set apart as somehow different from other fields of inquiry.[18]

---

of esoteric religion. Among these figures were Gershom Scholem (Jewish mysticism), Henry Corbin (Islamic mysticism), Mircea Eliade (history of religion), Carl Gustav Jung (depth psychology), and Joseph Campbell (comparative mythology). Western esotericism as a discipline of study is a fairly recent phenomenon in academic discourse. It was first formally established as a post of study in 1965 at the École pratique des hautes études in Sorbonne, Paris, which in 1979 became the "History of Esoteric and Mystical Currents in Modern and Contemporary Europe" under its department chair, Antoine Faivre. In 1980, the Hermetic Academy was founded by Robert McDermott and operated as a research outlet for esotericism, participating in discussion panels as the annual American Academy of Religion (AAR). See Faivre (1994), ix–x. In 1999, scholars of the history of religion from the University of Amsterdam established the "History of Hermetic Philosophy and Related Currents," and in 2005 the "Exeter Center for the Study of Esotericism" was created by the University of Exeter in the United Kingdom. Although still relatively small, the field of Western esotericism only continues to grow, with conferences now held every two years by the European Society for the Study of Western Esotericism (ESSWE), as well as the Association for the Study of Esotericism (ASE) in North America.

[18] Hanegraaff (2013), 12–13.

How is it that we can propose to set the field of study apart from others? Hanegraaff argues that the topics of Western esotericism are characterized chiefly as the "casualty of academic specialization after the eighteenth century." That is, Western esotericism makes up currents that have been considered "rejected knowledge" since the Enlightenment: "it contains precisely everything that has been consigned to the dustbin of history by Enlightenment ideologues and their intellectual heirs up to the present, because it is considered incompatible with normative concepts of religion, rationality and science."[19] Subjects such as "magic," "alchemy," "astrology," "the occult," "secret societies," and "paganism" all share a similar thread: somewhere among the modern trends of the academy, they have become forbidden topics, or at the very least, marginalized and neglected by scholarship.

Thelemic "religion" is characterized as esoteric because of its content: currents of the occult, alchemy, astrology, secret societies, illuminist movements, magic, and mysticism, among others.[20] Its relationship to the field of Western esotericism is critical.

Thelema and Publication

Another theme that will be discussed in this book is the importance that publication has played in the history of Thelema. As S. H. Steinberg has noted, "[t]he history of printing is an integral part of the general history of civilization. The principal vehicle for the conveyance of ideas during the past five hundred years, printing touches upon, and often penetrates, almost every sphere of human activity."[21] It is more or less a given fact that Western culture is constructed through writing,

---

[19] Ibid., 13. For an in-depth study of how esoteric currents have been marginalized and placed outside of mainstream intellectual discourse, see Wouter Hanegraaff (2012) *Esotericism and the Academy: Rejected Knowledge in Western Culture* (Cambridge: Cambridge University Press).

[20] The reader may wish to refer to a compendium of essays on Aleister Crowley and his placement in the study of Western esotericism. See Bogdan and Starr (2012).

[21] H. S. Steinberg (1961) *Five Hundred Years of Printing* (Harmondsworth: Penguin Books, Ltd.), 11.

printing, and publication. The printing of ink on paper, and the ability to reproduce it in vast quantities, has become one of the most significant forms of disseminating knowledge between groups and communities across space and time. Furthermore, printing and publishing have become a way that knowledge and information are legitimized. Literature historian Suresh Canagarajah writes, "[w]hen something appears in print it is widely construed as constituting publicly acknowledged facts in a manner that oral communication cannot."[22] Writing, printing and publication are also the very fabric of our societies through written laws and contractual agreements.

The impact that writing has had on religious movements has been significant both before and after the advent of the printing press. One need only consider the First Council of Nicaea, when church fathers were beginning to determine which writings would be formally accepted into Christian doctrine.[23] A more specific example that is related to Western esotericism is the emergence of the Rosicrucian manifestos. About a century and a half after the appearance of the printing press, when the Thirty-Years War was about to engulf Europe in religious conflict, these early seventeenth-century publications created a furor of religious activity across Western Europe, generating widespread interest in mysticism and esotericism. Rosicrucianism has been appropriated by several initiatory organizations ever since, influencing esotericism to the present day.[24]

---

[22] Suresh A. Canagarajah (2002) *A Geopolitics of Academic Writing* (Pittsburgh: University of Pittsburgh Press), 4.

[23] This event occurred in 325 CE, when Christian doctrine was first becoming formalized, and it was decided which teachings would be accepted into the church, and which would be considered heresy. See Lewis Aryes (2006) *Nicaea and Its Legacy* (Oxford: Oxford University Press).

[24] A good introduction to this can be found in Christopher McIntosh (1997) *The Rosicrucians: The History, Mythology, and Rituals of an Esoteric Order* (York Beach, ME: Weiser Books). For a thorough analysis on the early history of Rosicrucianism, albeit in Danish, see Carlos Gilly (2004) *Adam Halmayr* (In de Pelikaan: Amsterdam). Research in isolated areas of Rosicrucianism may be consulted in Susanna Åkerman (1998) *Rose and Cross Over the Baltic: The Spread of Rosicrucianism in Northern Europe* (Leiden: Brill) and Christopher McIntosh (1992) *The Rose Cross*

Aleister Crowley knew the importance publication played in delivering a religious message. He considered books and publications as objects of significant spiritual import. As Crowley bibliographer Timothy d'Arch Smith has noted, "Crowley's hand can be seen at work in every stage of the book's production [...]" He continues, "the books themselves, the books as artifacts, that is—as physical objects, their paper, their size, their colour, their price (we can go so far)—reflect as much as their contents the author's magical philosophies [...]"[25]

Thelema is a favorable case study of the history of religion and publication, a movement arguably driven by literature. (Publications of works by Crowley and associates that are now out of print sell at increased rates every year. Even editions from the 1990s have unfortunately become scarce.)[26] The fact that publications are so important for this community tells us that there is a significant connection between a form of disseminating information (in this case, publication) and the development of the religious movement. The development, formalization, and organization of the Thelemic community exists today by virtue of the network of individuals associated with it, but also by the *material culture* of publication which plays so important a role.

For example, the legal recognition of copyrights has served to legitimize the establishment of religious organizations beyond the codifying effect of print referred to by Steinberg and Canagarajah. The acknowledgment of copyright ownership grants an organization more control over its message. In speaking on the subject of copyrights with

---

and the Age of Reason: Eighteenth-Century Rosicrucianism in Central Europe and its Relationship to the Enlightenment (Albany: SUNY Press). Finally, see Thomas Willard (1983) "The Rosicrucian Manifestos in Britain," in *The Papers of the Bibliographical Society of America* Vol. 77, Fourth Quarter: 489–495.

[25] Timothy d'Arch Smith (1991) *The Books of the Beast: Essays on Aleister Crowley, Montague Summers and Others* (Oxford: Mandrake), 10.

[26] See Crowley (1983) *The Holy Books of Thelema* (York Beach: Weiser Books) and Crowley (1996b) *The Commentaries on the Holy Books* (York Beach: Samuel Weiser, Inc., both of which are now out of print and sell for an average, of $100 USD for used paperback copies on Amazon.com as of 2018. (This situation is being corrected, as O.T.O. is reorganizing its publishing program.)

regard to Crowley's writings, a long-time Thelemite who will be one of the key figures in the following story, James Wasserman (b. 1948), said in a 2012 talk, "a religious movement has no chance of achieving doctrinal coherence unless it has control of its message. Without the exclusivity of copyright, anyone can claim to be representing the Order [the O.T.O.]."[27]

One Truth and One Spirit: Aleister Crowley's Spiritual Legacy

Thelema is a vast subject, and so a number of approaches will feature into this study, which is divided into three parts. Part I, titled "Thelema: The Law of a New Aeon," aims to introduce Thelema, and to outline its theory, philosophy, doctrine, and organization. Chapter one will present Thelema's basic principles and theoretical framework, discussing its spiritual roots and philosophical precepts. Chapter two includes a brief biographical sketch of Aleister Crowley that will focus on him as the prophet of a new religious movement, and on his spiritual and initiatory development. In chapter three, the reader will be provided with an explanation of the two principal Thelemic orders advanced in Crowley's lifetime, the A∴A∴ and the O.T.O. In chapters four and five a more in-depth doctrinal discussion is offered, exploring key developments of Thelema that coincided with Crowley's initiatory career. Chapter six places Thelema within the context of religious studies.

Part II, "The Thelemic Movement: History and Publication," is a careful look at the modern Thelemic movement since Crowley's death. This is not as straightforward as it may sound. The modern history of Thelema involves ebbs and flows and twists and turns that can leave even the seasoned historian baffled. In an effort to eschew confusion and present the story in the clearest way possible, I have incorporated a methodology that highlights the historical, cultural, and geographic factors that either constrained or facilitated events in a particular direction. I have also utilized many source materials—

---

27 James Wasserman (2013) "In the Center of the Fire: A Modern History of O.T.O.," Pompano Beach, Florida. YouTube (accessed February 24, 2018).

including previously unpublished documents—that will assist the reader in following the narrative. Chapter seven begins in the last decade of Crowley's life and traces events from 1935 to the death of his immediate successor, Karl Germer, in 1962. Chapter eight describes the "Interregnum," a period in which there was no clearly identifiable successor to the Thelemic movement, until 1969, when Grady Louis McMurtry shouldered the responsibilities with which Crowley had entrusted him. Chapter nine illustrates the importance that publication played in the revival of the Thelemic movement in the late 1960s and early 1970s, showing that the vitality of Thelema was directly correlated with the availability of its literature. In chapter ten, it will be seen that the events surrounding publication culminated in a heated battle for successorship and a subsequent drive towards legitimacy in the greater social sphere of secular society. Chapters eleven and twelve explore more contemporary developments of the movement, such as schisms and offshoots and the use of digital media and social networking within the Thelemic community.

Part III contributes some main discussion points on selected topics of inquiry. It provides more detailed analysis of the Thelemic movement's principal organizations: the A∴A∴ and the O.T.O., and introduces the third or ecclesiastical branch, the E.G.C. (Ecclesia Gnostica Catholica). Chapter thirteen examines again the doctrinal relationship between the A∴A∴ and the O.T.O., with an additional critical discussion on how this relationship manifests today. Chapter fourteen offers a brief historical overview of the E.G.C. and examines its principal ceremony, "The Gnostic Mass," along with an analysis of the doctrinal relationship of A∴A∴ and O.T.O. as found within the Gnostic Mass.

I conclude with a critical discussion of: (1) current and possible future developments of the Thelemic movement; (2) some comments on Thelema as a religious phenomenon in a broader context; and (3) showing that the contemporary orders of the A∴A∴ and the O.T.O. have developed into an identifiably singular Thelemic movement with its own unique tradition, while Thelema in the broader context continues to grow within ever-larger cultural spheres of influence.

Authority and Sources

A word should be said about any authoritative claims that may be present in this book, as well as the sources that have been used. This study is meant exclusively as a *descriptive* analysis of Thelema and its theory, structure, and history, with a few *suggestive* points of opinion added. The author is not in any authoritative position to put forth a *prescriptive* set of guidelines for how the movements should operate. The statements made herein are deduced from examining historical records and assessing administrative attitudes within the groups in question. Conclusions are drawn from historical and sociological perspectives on Thelema as a new religious movement.

With regard to Authority,[28] it is assumed that both the general reader and the esoteric scholar have understood certain precepts that are held by Thelemites in general. For example, the author accepts the position that Aleister Crowley formed a link to the Secret Chiefs[29] and became Their scribe. Through this, he manifested as the prophet of Thelema known as *To Mega Therion*. It is pertinent then to regard his writings about Thelema as "authoritative." When talking about the posthumous years of Thelema, it is also important to consider the thoughts and attitudes of those who represent the modern O.T.O. and A∴A∴, particularly in an administrative capacity. The reader should consider that both spiritual and administrative authority in the O.T.O., after Karl Germer's death, rests in its appointed leaders under Fratres Hymenaeus Alpha[30] and Hymenaeus Beta.[31] Terms such as "Caliphate O.T.O." will not be used, as these sorts of phrases are mostly understood as polemical and are used by dissident groups outside of the O.T.O. Such an approach might appear limited in scope when considering other groups who have to some degree incorporated Thelema into

---

28 When discussing certain concepts, I will, on occasion, make use of capital letters.

29 This concept is described in detail in the chapters that follow.

30 Grady Louis McMurtry (1918–1985).

31 William Gary Keith Breeze (b. 1955). See Part II, chapter ten for a discussion of his election to the office of Outer Head of the Order (O.H.O.).

their activities. While a thorough study of Thelema in a broader sense may be considered by the author to be a commendable endeavor, it is regrettably too vast a subject to encompass in this work.

Since the term "Thelemic movement" refers to the developments surrounding the modern A∴A∴ and O.T.O. particularly, this study examines these movements as they have developed to the present day. The person holding the position of O.H.O. (Outer Head of the Order, i.e., the *executive director*) of the O.T.O., Hymenaeus Beta, is considered the contemporary representative of Crowley's work in the O.T.O. The same approach is applied to the A∴A∴, which is governed by a triune administration equilibrated by one Præmonstrator, one Imperator, and one Cancellarius.[32]

As for sources, a bibliography has been prepared utilizing many previously unavailable references. Out-of-print publications, unpublished letters from archives and private collections, and online references to websites and social media constitute the majority of sources. The reader is encouraged to consult the extensive footnotes and citations for further reading.

---

[32] This is covered on a theoretical level in chapter three, with a discussion on its current manifestation in Part II, chapters ten and eleven, and in Part III, chapter thirteen.

PART ONE

Thelema

The Law of a New Aeon

CHAPTER ONE

A New Law for the World

The word of the Law is θελημα.

—The Book of the Law, Liber AL vel Legis I:39

LET US BEGIN BY ANSWERING the question: What is "Thelema"? The word derives from the Greek (Θέλημα) meaning "Will." In a religious context, it originates in the New Testament. While it may be taken broadly that Thelema refers to the "Will of God," this is not the case for every instance of the word. In some passages, Thelema is used for the "will" of persons.[1] It is also used to indicate the "will" of the devil.[2] Θέλημα arises from Θέλω ("to will, to wish") with its suffix μα attributed to the result, or the "thing willed."[3] Important to this discussion, Θέλημα is used in Biblical and Patristic Greek, but not in the Classical. One of its most well-known uses in the New Testament is Matthew 6:10:

Thy kingdom come, thy *will* be done, in earth as it is in heaven.[4]

The word "Thelema" is also found in the works of the sixteenth-century Franciscan and later Benedictine monk, François Rabelais

---

[1] See, for example, Luke 12:47, Luke 23:25, and Peter 1:21. KJV.

[2] 2 Timothy 2:26. KJV.

[3] Herman Cremer points out that while the word *Βολή* (Bolè) also means "to will" and is a synonymn for Θέλω, the latter indicates a more active resolution of "willing" or "urging" an action. Herman Cremer (1895) *Biblico-Theological Lexicon of New Testament Greek* (Edinburgh: T&T Clark), 145.

[4] Mathew 6:10, KJV. In the Greek, it reads, "ἐλθέτω ἡ βασιλεία σου· γενηθήτω τὸ **θέλημά** σου, ὡς ἐν οὐρανῷ, καὶ ἐπὶ τῆς γῆς·" Stephanus, *Novum Testamentum Editio Regia* (1550) [emphasis added by author].

(1494–1553). Rabelais is best known for his work *Gargantua and Pantagruel*[5]—which can be understood as a humanist satire on the religious oppression that helped spark the Huguenot Wars in France in the latter half of the sixteenth century.[6] Book one, chapters 52–57, of *Gargantua and Pantagruel* depicts a utopian society called "Thelemites" who reside in the monastery called the "Abbey of Theleme." Their time is "spent not in laws, statutes, or rules, but according to their own free will and pleasure [...] In the rule of their order there was but this one clause to be observed: DO WHAT THOU WILT."[7]

The "Thelema" developed by Crowley is similar to the Theleme of Rabelais in name only.[8] The word "Thelema" first surfaced in the writings of Crowley in *The Book of the Law*.[9] This text serves as our foundational "Holy Book"—the "Bible" if the reader will excuse a parochial term. *Liber AL vel Legis* states, "The word of the Law is Θελημα."[10] The text that follows this verse includes Thelema's famous, "Do what thou wilt shall be the whole of the Law."[11] While many Thelemites understand this injunction as a "greeting" to one another, it is much more than that. It may be understood as a *challenge* and a "giving of the Law" from a Thelemite to another person. The official response to this phrase is, "Love is the law, love under will."[12] This implies an *acknowledgement* of

---

[5] François Rabelais, *Gargantua and Pantagruel*, trans. Sir Thomas Urquhart and Peter Le Motteux (London : William Benton, 1922).

[6] For a history on the French wars of religion, see Robert Knecht (2002) *The French Wars of Religion: 1559–1598* (Oxford: Osprey).

[7] Rabelais (1922), 65.

[8] As the Grand Master General of United States Grand Lodge, O.T.O., Sabazius X° (ps. of David Scriven) has remarked on this, "Saint Rabelais never intended his satirical, fictional device to serve as a practical blueprint for a real human society [...] Our Thelema is that of *The Book of the Law* and the writings of Aleister Crowley." Sabazius X°, Sixth National Conference of the U.S. O.T.O. Grand Lodge, August 10, 2007, Salem, Massachusetts.

[9] *Liber AL vel Legis sub figurâ CCXX,* cited as "AL" with chapter and verse (i.e., AL: I, 44)

[10] AL: I, 39.

[11] AL: I, 40.

[12] AL: I, 57.

the Law of Thelema, which is guided by Love. It is, in fact, interpreted by Crowley and his followers that "Thelema" is a word espousing a new spiritual Law for humanity.

⊰❦⊱

Thelema: A Spiritual "Philosophy"

A rudimentary glance at Thelema might lead observers to think of the movement as a religion. They would not be incorrect, and this idea will be explored in some depth throughout this book. Whether or not Thelema is a religion or a philosophy has been a subject of debate within the modern Thelemic community. For example, some in the O.T.O. appear hesitant to call it a "religion." The website for the United States Grand Lodge (USGL) of O.T.O. states, "the label 'religion' fits Thelema awkwardly in some context—it is in other senses a philosophy and a way of life [...]"[13] In chapter six, however, I will argue that Thelema fits most appropriately within the academic context of what we know as "religion." For the present, it is necessary to discuss USGL's phrasing of Thelema as "a philosophy and a way of life."

While Crowley indeed referred to Thelema as a philosophy,[14] and while he often directed his readers to the works of philosophers such as Kant, Berkeley, and Hume, some academics would assert that Thelema *is not* a "philosophy" in *the traditional academic use of the term today*. This is probably due to two facts that have been pointed out by modern Thelemic thinker Kjetil Fjell. First of all, Crowley himself was not an academically trained philosopher, and should rather be considered a contributor to writings on esoteric religion. While Crowley may refer his readers to works in philosophy, he did not engage in the methodological rigors that are typically found within the discipline of philosophy. Fjell writes, "For all his pretensions to impact on the

---

[13] U.S. Grand Lodge, Ordo Templi Orientis website. "Thelema" (accessed February 24, 2018).

[14] "Thelema implies not merely a new religion, but a new cosmology, a new philosophy, a new ethics." Crowley (1969a), 398.

real world, it is clear that Crowley could not be bothered with the slow methodical construction of an ideology that one would expect a philosopher to be engaged in." Fjell argues that the same goes for scientific and political studies, two other areas that Crowley would often refer to in his writings. Fjell continues, "For him such disciplined endeavours that would lead to real contributions to these fields, were tedious distractions to his real goal in life, the prosecution of the Great Work. Within [the] occult however he was perhaps the most disciplined individual and original thinker in the history of Magick."[15]

Secondly, Thelema cannot be labeled "a philosophy" by academics because of the present lack of development from its first principles within the field of philosophy itself. Only very recently in 2018 has this been attempted with Antti Balk's comprehensive analysis of Thelemic philosophy.[16] Balk uses a philosophical methodology within an academic framework in an effort to explore themes such as ontology, epistemology, and ethics. Balk's work may very well be one of the first attempts at laying the ground for a "Thelemic philosophy," providing axioms and maxims, and discussing precepts, assumptions, tenets, and first principles.[17] It would be more appropriate to say that, up until Balk's work, Thelema has remained less *a philosophy* in the academic use of the term than a *philosophical system of thought.*

---

[15] Kjetil Fjell (2014) "The Vindication of Thelema," *The Fenris Wolf,* Issue 7. (Stockholm: Edda).

[16] See Antti P. Balk (2018) *The Law of Thelema: Aleister Crowley's Philosophy of True Will* (London: Thelema Publications, LLC.).

[17] "A philosophy" in this case involves a method of critical inquiry, raising fundamental questions pertaining to ontology, epistemology, or ethics, for example, and putting forth an argument in an effort to solve such problems by rational means. Philosophical methods have been proposed since the time of the Pre-Socratic Thales of Miletus (624–546 BCE). Methodology has varied, ranging from the dialogues of Plato, to the rationalists and empiricists of the Enlightenment period, to the phenomenologists of the twentieth century.

Modern Philosophy and Thelema

The following few sections will be an attempt to discuss Thelema in the context of traditional and formal academic philosophy. I beg the reader's patience with these technical terms and believe it will be rewarded with a better understanding of the conceptual and intellectual depth of Crowley's teachings. I, on the other hand, will do my best to keep in mind that Magick is *experiential*—and acknowledge that what follows in the next few pages will generally not be found in the pages of a grimoire!

There are many examples in which Crowley referred to previous philosophies. Thelema does include philosophy's three main branches: epistemology, metaphysics, and ethics.[18] Epistemology (from the Greek, ἐπιστήμη, "knowledge") is the inquiry into how we obtain knowledge. Metaphysics concerns the study of the principles of existence. (Ontology is a branch of metaphysics dealing with the nature of *being*.) Ethics pertains to questions concerning human action. While epistemology and metaphysics tend to be more descriptive of how, what, and why something is known or exists, ethics often implies directly or indirectly a set of proscriptive measures on how we should conduct our behavior within the world.

Let us look closer into Crowley's own philosophical influences. His early writings on his system of magick (as found in *The Equinox*, Vol. I) draws on a significant amount of modern philosophy. This would make sense, as Thelema can be considered a product of modernity.[19] Modern philosophers tried to discern how human beings arrive at knowledge

---

[18] With the discussion that follows on philosophy and Thelema, it is assumed that the reader has a basic understanding of these three branches. An introduction to philosophy and its branches is found in Bryan Magee (2001) *The Story of Philosophy* (London: Dorling Kindersley).

[19] "Occultism" and the currents that converged to produce Thelema have been labeled as such by many scholars. See for example Alex Owen (2004) *The Place of Enchantment: British Occultism and the Culture of the Modern* (Chicago: University of Chicago Press) and Egil Asprem (2014) *The Problem of Disenchantment: Scientific Naturalism and Esoteric Discourse 1900–1939* (Leiden: Brill).

about the world around them (epistemology) and what constitutes it (metaphysics).

Two schools of thought compose modern philosophy: Rationalism and Empiricism. Rationalists such as René Descartes (1596–1650), Baruch Spinoza (1632–1677), and Gottfried Leibniz (1646–1716) believed that knowledge about the world could be ascertained through the rational faculty of human reason, and by way of the inherent *a priori* phenomena existent in the universe such as mathematics, scientific laws, and "God."[20] By contrast, empiricists like George Berkeley (1685–1753) and David Hume (1711–1776) argued that knowledge was obtained primarily through *a posteriori* sensory experience.[21]

---

[20] Descartes' famous saying, "I think, therefore I am," followed a logical deductive reasoning beginning from the methodological approach of skepticism. He posited that all prior knowledge he held about the world was false. The single truth he was able to know for certain is that, above anything else which could be false, he was at the very least something that is thinking. "Mind" was a substance, like that of mathematical proofs that exist in the universe prior (*a priori*) to any physical matter. Spinoza and Leibniz followed similar conclusions, arguing that the universe was necessarily a rational mechanism that can be understood using the rational faculties of human reasoning to eventually arrive at the fundamental truth of the universe which is God. See René Descartes (1996) *Meditations of the First Philosophy with Selections from the Objections and Replies*, John Cottingham (trans.) (Cambridge: Cambridge University Press), Benedict de Spinoza (1996) *Ethics*, Edwin Curley (trans.) (London: Penguin Books, Ltd.) and Gottfried W. Leibniz (1991) *Discourse on Metaphysics and Other Essays*, Daniel Garber and Roger Ariew (trans.) (Indianapolis: Hackett Publishing Company, Inc.).

[21] For Berkeley, knowledge about anything in the world is not achieved by regarding material things. Rather it is the *idea* of any given thing. We must base our knowledge of the world on ideas about things and our mere perception of them. Berkeley's philosophy is known as "immaterialism" or "subjective idealism." Hume, on the other hand, utilized the same method as Descartes, but arrived at a different conclusion. Hume found that knowledge is not always based in rationality, but that we as humans gather knowledge in other ways (i.e., emotional through our passions). Hume also argued that our experiences do not always equate with what we expect when we rely purely on deductive reasoning to predict the outcome of events. Rather, our sense experience proves that often phenomena occur in ways that cannot be understood through reason alone. See George Berkeley (2004) *A Treatise Concerning the Prin-*

Immanuel Kant sought to reconcile these two approaches with his *Transcendental Idealism*, maintaining that knowledge is apprehended by both our sensory apparatus and the world of ideas. Yet, Kantian epistemology asserts that both of these faculties are limited—as all they can do at best is to *perceive* the *a priori* truths of the universe, or the "things-in-themselves," which ultimately cannot be fully grasped.[22]

The above-named writers have been introduced to give us some idea of their influence on Crowley. He expected his readers to be familiar with modern philosophy as a prerequisite to his system of "Scientific Illuminism"—a designation of Crowley's methodological approach to magick and mysticism, what Egil Asprem has identified as a kind of "naturalized magic."[23] In *The Equinox,* Crowley developed what he considered a scientific approach to spiritual attainment. In doing so, he often referred to the epistemologies of the aforementioned rationalists and empiricists. While rationalist philosophers were correct in using skepticism and the reasoning faculty to discover higher knowledge, Crowley proclaimed that experiential knowledge could bring the practicing magician to truth.[24] He encouraged students to experiment with different modalities of perception in order to break through normal consciousness and to discover the center of the self.[25]

---

ciples of Human Knowledge (Mineola: Dover Publications, Inc.) and David Hume (2007) *An Inquiry Concerning Human Understanding* (Oxford: Oxford University Press).

22 Immanuel Kant (2007) *Critque of Pure Reason*, Marcus Weigelt (trans.) (Oxford: Penguin Books, Ltd.).

23 See Egil Asprem (2008) "Magic Naturalized? Negotiating Science and Occult Experience in Aleister Crowley's Scientific Illuminism," in *Aries: Journal for the Study of Western Esotericism*, 8, (Leiden: Brill), 139–165.

24 The reader should refer to "The Soldier and the Hunchback: ! and ?" in Crowley (1909) *The Equinox*, Vol. I, No. 1, 113–136.

25 By referring to these modern philosophies, Crowley was paralleling his system with Eastern thought and practice. For example, he pointed to the Vedantic doctrine of the "sheaths" of the human soul and the Buddhist mindfulness exercise of *Mahāsatipaṭṭhāna*. See Crowley (1906) "Science and Buddhism" in *Collected Works*,

* * *

One of the most important philosophers in Crowley's thought is Friedrich Nietzsche (1844–1900). Nietzsche's philosophy can be considered part of the *zeitgeist* of the *fin-de-siècle* British intelligentsia. Hymenaeus Beta, Frater Superior of the O.T.O., has noted that by the end of the Victorian Era in England, "the most important intellectual stimulus was Friedrich Nietzsche [...] It was the appearance in English of *The Birth of Tragedy* in 1909 that opened the gates to the 'Dionysian' impulse so long suppressed in England."[26]

While it is unclear when Crowley was introduced to Nietzsche, it is likely that it was as early as his time at university. The wide reach of Nietzsche in England has been well-documented in David Thatcher's *Nietzsche in England: 1890–1914*.[27] Thatcher discusses many central figures who commented at length on Nietzsche's philosophy. These include those with whom Crowley had either direct contact or was very familiar: William Butler Yeats (1865–1939), Alfred R. Orage (1873–1934), and George Bernard Shaw (1856–1950) among them.

Nietzsche was named by Crowley as a "Gnostic Saint" of the Ecclesia Gnostica Catholica (the Gnostic Catholic Church).[28] Concepts such as *amor fati* (love of one's fate), the *Übermensch* (Superman), *eternal return,* and *master-slave morality*[29] all feature into Thelema. However, it is in the philosophy of the "Will" that we find the most salient

---

Vol. II. Also see J. Daniel Gunther (2014) *The Angel and the Abyss* (Lake Worth: Ibis Press), 198–206 for a discussion on the five sheaths of the soul.

[26] Typescript of Hymenaeus Beta, "One Hundred Years of the O.T.O. in North America: Inspirations and Lessons," "O.T.O. In North America Centennial Conference," May 16, 2015. On Nietzsche's mentioned work, see Friedrich Nietzsche (1999) *The Birth of Tragedy and Other Writings*, Ronald Spiers (trans.) (Cambridge: Cambridge University Press).

[27] David Thatcher (1970) *Nietzsche in England: 1890–1914* (Toronto: University of Toronto Press).

[28] The Ecclesia Gnostica Catholica is discussed in chapter fourteen.

[29] For an introduction into Nietzsche's writings, see Walter Kaufmann (trans.) (2000) *Basic Writings of Nietzsche* (Toronto: Random House, Inc.)

connection between the two figures. Nietzsche's "Will to Power" is an obvious precursor to Crowley's "True Will."

Philosophy ranging from Plato and Aristotle, to Saint Augustine, along with contemporary strains from thinkers like Sartre, Heidegger, and even Foucault can easily be incorporated into discussions on Thelema. Antti Balk's work is hopefully the start of what can, in the future, become a fully-developed discipline of the "Philosophy of Thelema."

Thelema, Philosophy, and Western Esotericism

It may be better to consider Thelema's philosophical basis within the contextual framework of the world's esoteric traditions. These have remained primarily within the discipline of religious studies[30] and are rooted in the religious syncretism of arcane thought. Gnosticism, Neo-Platonism, Hermeticism, and much of the Western mystical tradition, including Thelema, are syncretic spiritual disciplines which assert *experiential certainty* within their epistemologies; that is, *knowledge is acquired through experiential means.* Furthermore, Thelemites believe that the opportunity for spiritual knowledge is augmented by recent shifts in the state-of-being of the world—i.e., the liberty made possible by humanity's transition into the New Aeon.

The New Aeon

Crowley came to understand Thelema as a new form of spiritual direction. "Do what thou wilt" is a command for each person to find and to do nothing but his or her "true purpose" in life. For Crowley, this "Law" was a new spiritual message that would emancipate humanity

---

[30] As noted in the introduction, Western esotericism has been classified as a collection of historical currents of "rejected knowledge" that were marginalized and removed from academic discourse in the modern period. Until the discipline of Western esotericism extends beyond the field of the history of religion, it will be difficult to consider Thelema as a philosophy in the academic sense of the term.

from the restrictive religious dogmas of the past. *The Book of the Law* announces a New Aeon, governed by a Child divinity who has come to supplant the previous patriarchal age of the Father (which followed a prehistoric age of the Mother). From the Thelemic perspective, this "coming of age" theme is summarized in three successive stages: (1) The Aeon of Isis (the Mother Goddess or nature), (2) The Aeon of Osiris (the Father God, patriarchy, and catastrophe), and finally (3) The Aeon of Horus (the Child, the current age as the result of the two previous perspectives). As Crowley would later describe these vast epochs:

> In the history of the world, as far as we know accurately, are three such Gods: Isis, the mother, when the Universe was conceived as simple nourishment drawn directly from her; this period is marked by matriarchal government.
>
> Next, beginning 500 BC, Osiris, the father, when the Universe was imagined as catastrophic, love, death, resurrection, as the method by which experience was built up; this corresponds to patriarchal systems.
>
> Now, Horus, the child, in which we come to perceive events as a continual growth partaking in its elements of both these methods, and not to be overcome by circumstance. This present period involves the recognition of the individual as the unit of society.[31]

---

[31] "Introduction," *The Book of the Law* in Crowley (1938). The reader should note that, while Crowley described each "Aeon" as spanning 2000 years, it has been argued more thoroughly by Thelemic author J. Daniel Gunther that what is referred to in Thelemic literature as "Aeons" are the psychic spiritual developments of humanity since the dawn of existence of homo sapiens. As such, Gunther sees Crowley's demarcations as arbitrary and not consistent with empirical historical evidence. For example, the establishment of a male-dominant conception of divinity occurred much earlier than 500 B.C., and that of matrifocal religion spans back into our prehistoric past. See J. Daniel Gunther (2009) *Initiation in the Aeon of the Child* (Lake Worth: Ibis Press), 159–160 and 193–194; also specific examples are given in Gunther (2014), 23–29, and Episodes 1 and 2 of White Rabbit Podcast, http://www.whiterabbitpodcast.com (accessed May 8, 2018).

The theory of Aeons is intricately tied to the traditional religious elements of apocalypticism and millenarianism, and these are crucial points to understanding some of the core principles underlying Thelema's philosophy. As Crowley scholar Henrik Bogdan writes, these "aeons mark evolutionary leaps in the development of humankind, and each is ruled by certain magical formulas."[32] He continues that the "new Aeon of Horus was preceded by the Aeons of Isis and Osiris, and it will in the future be superseded by a fourth aeon, that of Maat (Ma / Hrumachis), also termed the 'Aeon of Justice.'"[33] The idea of developmental stages of spiritual development is not new to Thelema, Bogdan argues, and "despite the fierce anti-Christian nature of Thelema, the Thelemic millenarian view of history is in fact deeply rooted in a Western esoteric understanding of biblical apocalypticism, as well as in the dispensationalism of John Nelson Darby."[34]

To understand the progression of Aeons, we must not look for strict demarcations of time throughout history, but rather patterns in shifting attitudes of culture that indicate a change in humanity's psychic relationship to the divine. This is exemplified when we look at the first of these vast periods of time, the Aeon of the Mother or Aeon of Isis.[35] This relates to prehistory and the domination of the Goddess motif in the human psyche. This is the earliest period of our history,

---

[32] Henrik Bogdan (2012) "Envisioning the Birth of a New Aeon: Dispensationalism and Millenarianism in the Thelemic Tradition," in Bogdan and Starr (2012), 90.

[33] Ibid.

[34] Ibid., 89. John Nelson Darby (1800–1882) was an early nineteenth century Calvinist who founded the Plymouth Brethren, a fundamentalist evangelical Christian sect. Darby described a series of evolutionary periods called "dispensations" that would progressively reveal God's grace on earth, ranging from "The Fall" to "The Second Coming of Christ." Crowley's father was a member of the Plymouth Brethren, and Darby's ideas were influential on Crowley's early spiritual development.

[35] The "Aeons" exclusively take on Egyptian symbolism, and so Isis is the *Imago Dei* of the Mother *par excellence*. Gunther opines that the exclusivity of Egyptian symbolism is probably due to the fact that Crowley's reception of *The Book of the Law* occurred in Cairo. Egyptian deities were also part of the Hermetic scheme in the Hermetic Order of the Golden Dawn, in which Crowley received his early occult training. See again discussions on Episodes 1 and 2 of White Rabbit Podcast.

about which we still know little. It is figuratively marked by matrifocal religion,[36] or, more specifically, matrifocal conceptions of the divine. This entails the images, symbols, and representational objects of the Mother motif that have impacted our species' psyche over time, and have carried with them heavily charged psychic power in how our consciousness relates to the world. In the Jungian sense, we are talking about archetypes. As Jungian writer Erich Neumann noted, primitive cultures did not understand the mysteries of creation, that male seed

---

[36] The term "matrifocal" is a better descriptor than "matriarchal" given the vast amount of literature that has surfaced over the latter half of the twentieth century disproving the existence of a true instance of prehistoric matriarchal religion. The spectrum of debate on this subject ranges widely. The archaeological writings of Marija Gimbutas suggested an early human period ruled by women (termed *gynocentric*) before being supplanted by a patriarchy. Such literature emerging out of second-wave feminism in the mid-twentieth century approach became emblematic of the goddess movements epitomized in the work of figures like Starhawk. Later authors such as Joan Bamberger and Cynthia Eller have argued that prehistorical matriarchy was a myth, and that archaeologists have uncovered substantial evidence that patriarchal relations have almost always been present in the history of *homo sapiens*. Eller claims that such "fake history" has actually hurt the credibility of women's movements, opening them to criticism for holding onto irrelevant arguments based upon misunderstood historical facts. However, Max Dashu has criticized Eller's work, noting that, (a) little is still known about the jural relations amongst prehistoric humans, and (b) our terminology of "matriarchy" does not fully encapsulate what we *do* know about how these early humans interacted. Dashu further notes that, "We know of many societies that did not confine, seclude, veil, or bind female bodies [...] We know, as well, that there have been cultures that accorded women public leadership roles and a range of arts and professions, as well as freedom of movement, speech, and rights to make personal decisions. Many have embraced female personifications of the Divine, neither subordinating them to a masculine god, nor debarring masculine deities." See Max Dashu (2005) "Knocking Down Straw Dolls," 185. For prehistorical matriarchy, see Marija Gimbutas (1991) *The Civilization of the Goddess: The World of Old Europe* (San Francisco: Harper). Critiques of this are found in Joan Bamberger (1974) "The Myth of Matriarchy: Why Men Rule in Primitive Society," in *Women, Culture, and Society*, Michelle Rosaldo and Louise Lamphere (eds.) (Stanford: Stanford University Press). More recently see Cynthia Eller (2000) *The Myth of Matriarchal Prehistory: Why an Invented Past Won't Give Women a Future* (Boston: Beacon Press).

was needed for impregnation. Life appeared to come from woman alone. Neumann writes:

> The question about the origin, however, must always be answered by "womb," for it is the immemorial experience of mankind that every newborn creature comes from a womb. Hence the "round" of mythology is also called the womb and uterus, though this place of origin should not be taken concretely. In fact, all mythology says over and over again that this womb is an image, the woman's womb being only a partial aspect of the primordial symbol of the place of origin from whence we come. This primordial symbol means many things at once: it is not just one content or part of the body, but a plurality, a world or cosmic region where many contents hide and have their essential abode.
>
> Anything deep—abyss, valley, ground, also the sea and the bottom of the sea, fountains, lakes and pools, the earth, the underworld, the cave, the house, and the city—all are parts of this archetype. Anything big and embracing which contains, surrounds, enwraps, shelters, preserves, and nourishes anything small belongs to the primordial matriarchal realm.[37]

Where human life sprang from the womb of the mother, vegetable and plant life sprang from the earth. All life then died and returned to the earth, the universal womb, nature. It is from this psychic connection and experience of life that the archetype of the Mother emerged.

The Thelemic narrative of the progression of Aeons continues that our species gradually became less nomadic as hunter-gatherers and made settlements as pastoral-nomads. This is correlated with the advent of agriculture, and the fact that these early settlers began to focus their attention on the progression of seasonal changes, which entailed observing the sun's apparent travels around the earth over the course of a year. The discovery of the science of agriculture to yield large amounts of harvest made it possible to progressively settle and establish villages,

---

37 Erich Neumann (1995) *The Origins and History of Consciousness*, R. F. C. Hull (trans.) (Princeton: Princeton University Press), 13–14.

towns, cities, and empires. The necessity of seed for fertilization was also found to be the central ingredient in the mysteries of human procreation. Thus was the gradual decline of the Goddess archetype and the reign of the Father God was established. For the Western world, the motif of the Father God, and the slain and resurrected male god, stems back well into antiquity. Jehovah and Allah are the most typical examples of the Father God. As for the motif of the slain and resurrected god, Osiris of Egypt is a classic model—he was known as the father of agriculture before becoming a god. The slain god theme continues in the West in the Greek pantheons with Attis, Adonis, and Dionysus, and is, of course, epitomized in Jesus Christ of Nazareth.

The patriarchal period lasted for thousands of years, and spanned much of written history into the late modern period. Now, according to the philosophy of Thelema, this all changed right at the turn of the twentieth century, when the Aeon of the Child was ushered forth. Horus is the son of Isis and Osiris. Psychically speaking, he is the result of the previous periods. He marks the advent of *individuated spiritual expression*. His maxim is "Do what thou wilt shall be the whole of the Law."

Besides the millenarian concept of the "coming of a new age," Thelema carries a dispensational quality to its narrative that can be understood within the context of a lineal descent of messiahs or god-men. Crowley came to believe himself to be one of a line of seven prophets. All of these "Magi," as he called them—Lao Tzu, Siddhārtha Gautama Buddha, Kṛṣṇa, Tahuti, Moses, Dionysus, and Mohammed—brought to the world their own spiritual "word of Truth" to humanity when it was needed.[38] Crowley came to believe that *The Book of the Law* announced "Thelema" as the most recent word, the next spiritual precipice, and the harbinger of individual freedom. It is a message that announces spiritual liberation and the right to self-expression, a call for all people to seek out and discover their true purpose in life.

---

[38] See Crowley (1991c) *Liber Aleph*, 68–75. For example, Lao Tzu expressed "Tao" as the spiritual word of Truth, and Siddhārtha Gautama Buddha gave "Anattā." Jesus Christ was never listed by name, but was instead considered to be the epitomized aspect of the "slain god," depicted in a number of myths throughout the Western world.

Besides *The Book of the Law*, there are a number of other important Thelemic texts that need mention, particularly a collection of writings known as the "Holy Books of Thelema." As it came to be understood both by Crowley and within Thelemic tradition, these texts, like *The Book of the Law*, were authored not by Crowley but by a "praeterhuman" spiritual intelligence communicating with or through him. Many of the Holy Books were written in a white heat, each one in the span of a day or two, the first group in the latter half of 1907. Among these are "Liber Liberi vel Lapidis Lazuli sub figurâ VII" and "Liber LXV Cordis Cincti Serpente sub figurâ אדני."[39] Others include "Liber LXVI vel Stellæ Rubæ," "Liber Arcanorum," "Liber Porta Lucis sub figurâ X," "Liber Tau," "Liber Trigrammaton," and "Liber DCCCXIII vel ARARITA." The remainder of the writings classified as Holy Books were written in 1911. They are: "Liber B vel Magi," "Liber Tzaddi," "Liber Cheth," and "Liber A'ash." Crowley would later describe all of these texts in his autobiography, *The Confessions of Aleister Crowley*:

> I cannot even call them automatic writing. I can only say that I was not wholly conscious at the time of what I was writing, and I felt that I had no right to "change" so much as the style of a letter. They were written with the utmost rapidity without pausing for thought for a single moment, and I have not presumed to revise them.[40]

Crowley deemed these the Holy Books of Thelema and designated them as Class A publications to guarantee that there would be no confusion as to their import. These texts, along with a collection of visionary experiences between 1909 and 1918,[41] serve as the primary body

---

[39] Crowley (1983), 7–35 and 51–83. These texts are fundamental in that they describe two significant moments in the Thelemic path: 1) the mystical experience called the Knowledge and Conversation of the Holy Guardian Angel (*Liber LXV*) and 2) The Crossing of the Abyss and attainment as a Master of the Temple (*Liber VII*).

[40] Crowley (1969a), 559.

[41] Most important of these is *Liber CDXVIII*, also known as *The Vision and the*

of material through which he would develop the foundation of the doctrine of Thelema. (They will be further discussed in chapter four.) Anyone who desires to understand Thelema in any depth from a philosophical and doctrinal level must be familiar with the Holy Books and the revelatory literature spanning 1904 to 1920.

The Qabalah: Ontology and Cosmogony

In order to clarify Thelema's metaphysics, it is necessary to take another detour and discuss its ontology, which is grounded in the cosmogony of the Qabalah.[42] The Qabalah itself may have been influenced by the mystical currents of Gnosticism and Neo-Platonism which predate

---

Voice. It records Crowley's visionary experiences with his student Victor Neuburg in December of 1909. It may be understood as the "Book of Revelation" of Thelemic literature due to its apocalyptic symbolism. The reader should note that the visions outlined in *The Vision and the Voice* began preliminarily in Mexico in 1900, while the bulk of them followed nearly a decade later in Algeria. See Crowley (1998a), 45. There are other revelatory visions: "The Bartzabel Working" in 1910, "The Ab-ul-Diz Working" in 1911, "The Paris Working" in 1914, and "The Amalantrah Working" in 1918. Several of these are published in Crowley (1998a) *The Vision and the Voice and Other Papers* (York Beach, ME: Weiser Books).

[42] "Qabalah" or "Kabbalah" or "Cabala" derives from the Hebrew קבלה, meaning "received." Despite its universality, interpretations of the Qabalah vary greatly from one tradition to the next, especially when distinguishing between the Hermetic *Qabalah* in the occult tradition and the Hebrew *Kabbalah* in the Jewish faith [variant spelling used to differentiate]. One of the most influential figures, and probably considered the father of modern Jewish Kabbalah, was Isaac Luria (1534-1572). The reader will benefit from consulting the work of Gershom Scholem, whose contribution to scholarship on Jewish mysticism has been no less than substantial. [See Gershom Scholem (1946) *Modern Trends in Jewish Mysticism* (New York: Schocken Books)]. Despite Scholem's comprehensive study of Jewish Kabbalah, however, he subsequently "threw the baby out with the bath water" when he refused to acknowledge the modern trends during the Enlightenment and Romantic periods as "real Kabbalah." It is within the modern period that the Qabalah resurfaces, transforms, and becomes established in other esoteric currents, including that of occultism for which Thelema is indebted. For a study on these modern trends, see Boaz Huss, Marco Pasi, and Kocku von Stuckrad (eds.) (2010) *Kabbalah and Modernity: Interpretations, Transformations, Adaptations* (Leiden: Brill).

the book *Bahir* (c. 1185), believed to be one of the earliest Qabalistic texts. In an effort to simplify the interwoven currents from antiquity to the modern era, I will briefly discuss a few themes found within the Qabalah: (1) the distinction between *cosmotheism* and *monotheism*; (2) the mystic theology describing the creation of the universe from a primordial nothingness; and (3) the significance of the Pythagorean idea of mathematical numeration for the foundation of being.

Similar to much of the Western mystical and esoteric tradition, Thelema's cosmogenesis is grounded in a *cosmotheistic* rather than a *monotheistic* scheme (see figure 1.1).[43] One of the main distinguishing features of cosmotheism is that it asserts a pantheistic rather than a monotheistic view of God. Unlike the Abrahamic religions, cosmotheism does not insist on a personal, omnipresent, omniscient deity beyond the reach of the terrestrial human being. In a cosmotheistic view, the universe is a living, animated phenomenon which is not separate from the divine. "God," in this sense, has manifested on all planes—emanating through cosmic heavenly bodies such as galaxies, stars, and planets, and into the terrestrial spheres of humans, plants, and animals. It is here that we find "emanationism," to which we will return to in our discussion on Pythagorean mysticism.

Thelema's cosmogony (the theory concerning the origin of the universe) is espoused most clearly in the Hermetic Qabalah. Essentially, Qabalistic doctrine states that "God" and the known universe emerged from a primordial "nothingness." That is: before *anything* existed, there was only Non-Existence. This Non-Existence began to take form into a "Limitlessness" and eventually extended into a primordial "Light." The process of "unveiling" is described in the Qabalah as the "Three Veils

---

43 The distinction between these two types of religious ontologies has been discussed by Jan Assmann, who notes that the cosmotheism of ancient religions was suppressed after the rise in power of monotheistic cultures. "The opposition between cosmotheism and monotheism, or between nature and revelation, was never resolved, but merely suppressed in the victorious development of the church." Yet cosmotheism later resurfaced during the Enlightenment period as mystery religion, or, more specifically esoteric religion. See Jan Assmann (1997) *Moses the Egyptian: The Memory of Egypt in Western Monotheism* (Cambridge: Harvard University Press).

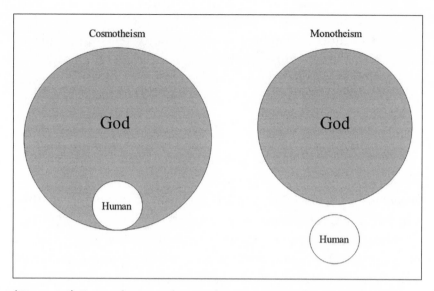

(**Figure 1.1**) **Cosmotheism and Monotheism.** In cosmotheism, God expands the breadth of the known universe and beyond, and the human being is not separate. In Monotheism, God is viewed as being set apart from humanity.

of Negative Existence" called "Ain" (אין), "Ain Soph" (אין סוף), and "Ain Soph Aur" (אין סוף אור), translated as "Nothingness," "Without Limit," and "Limitless Light." Crowley explains this in an early essay titled "Qabalistic Dogma":

> First is Nothing, or the Absence of Things, אין, which does not and cannot mean Negatively existing (if such an Idea can be said to mean anything) [...] Second is Without Limit אין סוף, i.e. Infinite Space. This is the primal Dualism of Infinity; the infinitely small and the infinitely great. The Clash of these produces a finite positive Idea which happens [...] to be Light, אור.[44]

---

[44] Crowley (1905), *The Collected Works of Aleister Crowley*, Vol I. (Des Plaines: Yogi Publication Society), 265. The "Third Veil of the Negative" is also known as אין סוף אור (The Limitless Light).

The Thelemic Holy Book, "Liber Trigrammaton," describes "an account of the cosmic process."[45] The opening line of the first verse says: "Here is Nothing under its three forms. It is not, yet informeth all things."[46] Author J. Daniel Gunther notes that this phrase can be acronymized into "N.U.I.T. forms"—which indicates the star goddess of the first chapter of *Liber AL vel Legis, The Book of the Law,* and implies the Three Veils of Negative Existence in Qabalistic Notariqon.[47]

Ideas pertaining to the primordial "nothingness" of the divine are new neither to Thelema nor Qabalah. Such mystical philosophy can be traced back to pre-Socratic antiquity in the work of Anaximander (c. 610–546 BCE), who like most of the pre-Socratics sought to identify the *archê* (ἀρχή), or the primary substance which constituted the universe. For Anaximander, this was called *apeiron*, a boundless, undifferentiated substance from which all matter came into being.[48] Later developments of "divine nothingness" found their way into Gnostic and Neoplatonic thought[49] and into some of the writings of early Christian Church

---

[45] Crowley (2007b) *The Equinox: The Official Organ of the A∴A∴, The Official Organ of the O.T.O.: The Review of Scientific Illuminism,* Vol. III, No. 1 (*The Blue Equinox*) (York Beach, ME: Weiser Books), 34.

[46] "Liber Trigrammaton," in Crowley (1983), 45.

[47] Nuit is considered to be the unbounded potentiality of the universe, and a principle of infinite expansion. See Gunther (2009), 176.

[48] A thorough investigation of this concept is in several works. See for example Charles H. Kahn (1960) *Anaximander and the Origins of Greek Cosmology* (New York: Columbia University Press) and Paul Seligman (1962) *The Apeiron of Anaximander: A Study in the Origins and Function of Metaphysical Ideas* (London: The Atholone Press University of London).

[49] Gnosticism, Neoplatonism, and Hermetism were three significant currents which became part of the discourse on the "ancient wisdom tradition." With regard to Gnosticism and Neoplatonism, these are mystical religious traditions that emerged out of the syncretic environment of Hellenist and Roman societies. Being steeped in Plato's cosmology in *Timaeus* (c. 360 BCE) and his theory of forms, these two currents developed into very rich mystical traditions. After the destruction of the Library of Alexandria by 642 CE, many of the original Gnostic, Neoplatonic, and Hermetic works were non-existent for centuries. During the failed attempt to reconcile the Eastern Orthodox and Western Catholic divisions of Christianity that took place in Florence between 1438 and 1439, these texts were rediscovered. The Byzantine

fathers. The apophatic theology of Pseudo-Dionysius the Areopagite (fifth–sixth century CE) sought a reconciliation with the Christian God and the Gnostic and Neoplatonist conceptions of the divine, by describing God not in the positive (i.e., properties actively attributed to God) but chronicling all characteristics that *are not* God.[50] Similarly, the ninth-century Irish mystic philosopher, John Scotus Eriugena (815–877 CE), an early commentator on Pseudo-Dionysius, developed a type of Christian Neoplatonism which asserted a transcendent unknown God that emerged out of a dark, formless non-being and into a being consisting of light.

The progression of creation in the Qabalistic scheme can also be explained in the Pythagorean concept of number. The highly influential pre-Socratic Pythagoras (c. 570–495 BCE) believed the *archē* (the foundation of the universe) was number, and that the truths of the operations of the universe could be known through mathematical equation. Pythagoras developed an entire mystery school which taught that spiritual truths could be arrived at through harmonies and intervals of number that he called the "harmony of spheres."[51] Similarly, Qabalistic doctrine describes a numerological progression of

---

philosopher Gemistos Plethon (1355–1452/1454) sought to preserve the sources from the possibility of destruction from an Ottoman invasion and the conquering of the Byzantine Empire. These writings became the platform for Renaissance esotericism and the revival of interest in magic, paganism, and mysticism. For a modern introduction to Gnosticism, see van den Broek (2013), and for the Neo-Platonic tradition George Luck (2000). For ancient Hermetism, see Fowden (1986). Finally, on Plethon, see Hanegraaff, "The Pagan Who Came from the East: George Gemistos Plethon and Platonic Orientalism" in Wouter Hanegraaff and Joyce Pijenburg (eds.) (2009) *Hermes in the Academy: Ten Years' Study of Western Esotericism at the University of Amsterdam* (Amsterdam: Amsterdam University Press), 33–49.

[50] Commentary on the work of Pseudo-Dionysius can be found in O'Rourke (1992) *Pseudo-Dionysius and the Metaphysics of Aquinas.* (Leiden: Brill), Paul Rorem (1993) *Pseudo-Dionysius: A Commentary on the Texts and an Introduction to Their Influence* (Oxford: Oxford University Press), and Eric Perl (2007) *Theophany: The Neoplatonic Philosophy of Dionysius the Areopagite* (Albany: SUNY Press).

[51] Thoroughly outlined in Thomas Stanley (2010) *Pythagoras: His Life and Teachings*, James Wasserman and J. Daniel Gunther (eds.) (Lake Worth: Ibis Press).

manifestation, by which the emergence of the divine is described in a mathematical progression from Nothingness (0) through a series of emanations (1–9), crystallizing in the physical world of matter (10).[52] Crowley described this in "The Naples Arrangement":

> "All this is evidently without form and void; these are abstract conditions, not positive ideas. The next step must be the idea of Position [...] Thus appears *The Point* [Kether, "Crown"], which has 'neither parts nor magnitude, but only position.'"[53]

Yet, without a corresponding position, there is nothing to which this singular point can be compared. Therefore, a plurality was necessary if consciousness and experience were to be present, and the point divided itself into nine separate aspects called the *sephiroth*. A second point (Chokmah, "Wisdom") and third point (Binah, "Understanding") produced a plane of divine existence, or a supernal trinity.[54] A fourth (Chesed, "Mercy') provided the definition of space, while a fifth (Geburah, "Strength") produced motion within space, or *space and time*. Sixth (Tiphareth, "Beauty"), the point produced consciousness of itself and became aware of its various attributes of "Being" (Netzach, "Victory"), "Thought" (Hod, "Splendor"), and "Bliss" (Yesod,

---

[52] There has been debate among scholars as to whether the *Sefer Yetzirah*, dating back to the third century CE can be considered a Qabalistic text. However, it is in this early manuscript that the idea of the ten sephiroth seems to be first laid out and would become the philosophical basis for the Tree of Life. It is the opinion of the author that historians of Jewish Kabbalah may not want to view the *Sefer Yetzirah* within the corpus of Kabbalah because of the overt Neoplatonic and Gnostic similarities to the ideas expressed in it. The best English translation is Aryeh Kaplan (1997) *Sefer Yetzirah; The Book of Creation in Theory and Practice* (York Beach, ME: Weiser Books). Rabbi Kaplan himself calls the *Sefer Yetzirah* "without question the oldest and most mysterious of all Kabbalistic texts." See Kaplan, ix.

[53] *The Book of Thoth*, in Crowley (2007a), 15. The "Point" here can be interchanged with the word "God."

[54] Known as the Supernal Triad of Kether (Spirit), Chokmah (Father) and Binah (Mother).

"Foundation").[55] The seventh, eighth, and ninth sephiroth were simply qualifications of the point's existence. Lastly, manifestation was finalized in crystallization in the number ten (Malkuth, "Kingdom") (see figure 1.2).

The above summary of the Naples Arrangement's description of the creation of the universe is a very brief overview of Qabalistic cosmogony. Please consult the bibliographical references in the footnotes within this section for more in-depth treatments of the subject. The next section will describe the reverse process by which the human being in Malkuth (the tenth sephira[56]) "ascends" the Tree of Life to reconnect with the source of Godhead. I parallel this with the "Path of the Great Return," which is the path of initiation.[57]

Knowledge and Ethics

It was stated above that Thelema can be considered to a large degree an *experiential* spirituality. This means that the path of Thelema places value on human experiences and how they bring individuals to knowledge of themselves and closer to their divine nature. As should be clear from the previous discussion, Thelema shares many syncretic elements of Gnosticism and Hermeticism. The human being is considered to be a microcosmic reflection of the macrocosmic universe. What this means is that Thelema is unlike traditional mainstream orthodox religion, which typically views God as above and separate from humanity, to which ethics are set down by authoritative edict. Similar to Gnostic, Neo-Platonic, and Hermetic currents, Thelema asserts that the human being has an inherent potential to unlock divine powers within him or herself, to experience apotheosis, and to self-regulate one's ethics in line with the divine Will.

When discussing the process of coming to knowledge of oneself

---

[55] It is worth noting that Crowley also writes that these three aspects refer to *Sat* (सत्), *Cit* (चित्), and *Ānanda* (आनन्द), the qualities of *Brahman* (ब्रह्मन्), the Ultimate Reality in Hinduism ("God").

[56] "Sephira" is the singular for sephiroth.

[57] Described in the works of J. Daniel Gunther (2009) and (2014).

(Figure 1.2) The Qabalistic Tree of Life. The Tree of Life is composed of ten emanations or "sephiroth." Beginning from the top is *Kether* ("Crown"), which manifested from the "Three Veils of Negative Existence." The cosmos and everything in it came into existence from this minute point.

and reaching Godhead, phenomenology determines epistemology.[58] In other words, the apprehension of spiritual knowledge is contingent on *experience*. Crowley remarks on the significance of experience for individual growth:

> The value of any being is determined by the quantity and quality of those parts of the universe which it has discovered, and which therefore compose its sphere of experience. It grows by extending this experience, by enlarging, as it were, this sphere [...] The real value of any new experience is determined by its aptitude for increasing the sum total of knowledge, or the degree of understanding and illumination it sheds on previous experiences.[59]

---

[58] Phenomenology is a branch of philosophy that is directly related to ontology. Phenomenology aims at studying and describing phenomena as it appears in consciousness. It is therefore intrinsically concerned with the study of consciousness and experience. Pioneer of the phenomenological method, Edmund Husserl noted that phenomenology "can also be called [the] 'science of consciousness,' if consciousness be taken purely as such." In contemporary philosophy, phenomenology has been employed as a method of inquiry into the study of consciousness in conjunction with the cognitive sciences. See Edmund Husserl (2001) *Logical Investigations*, Vols. I & II, J. N. Findlay (trans.) (New York: Routledge). Also a more contemporary figure in philosophical phenomenology, Shaun Gallagher and Zahavi (2008) *The Phenomenological Mind: An Introduction to Philosophy of Mind and Cognitive Science* (New York: Routledge). Within the modern study of religion, phenomenology has become problematic, being associated with "religionist" agendas (also known as "perennialist" or "essentialist" schools). Phenomenologists of religion have often sought after an essential element that underlies all religious experience. This approach has been criticized by scholars as defying the specificities of history and culture on their own merits, and therefore lacking the critical means for empirical research. Examples of the religionist school are Mircea Eliade (1959) *The Sacred and the Profane: The Nature of Religion*, Willard R. Trask (trans.) (London: Harcourt, Inc.), Rudolf Otto (1958) *The Idea of the Holy*, John W. Harvey (trans.) (Oxford: Oxford University Press), Walter T. Stace (1960) *Mysticism and Philosophy* (London: Palgrave Macmillan), and Robert Forman, "Introduction" in Forman (ed.) (1998) *The Innate Capacity: Mysticism, Psychology, and Philosophy* (Oxford: Oxford University Press), 3–41.

[59] Crowley (1998b), 172.

Crowley goes on to explain that at a certain point two beings may enter into disagreement with one another, and that at such moments it is important to welcome a divergent point of view and to assimilate it. Doing so will expand the individual star (the divine Self) to a greater capacity. The principles behind the theological ontology of this dynamic is in the trinity of the three deities that "speak" in *The Book of the Law*: the goddess Nuit (chapter I), Hadit (chapter II) and Ra-Hoor-Khuit (chapter III). In the 1938 publication of *The Book of the Law*, Crowley described these principles in his introduction:

> The elements are Nuit—Space—that is, the total of possibilities of every kind—and Hadit, any point which has experience of these possibilities [...] Every event is a uniting of some one monad with one of the experiences possible to it [...] Each one of us has thus an universe of his own, but it is the same universe for each one as soon as it includes all possible experience. This implies the extension of consciousness to include all other consciousness.[60]

Crowley further explains in *Magick in Theory and Practice*, "Infinite space is called the Goddess Nuit, while the infinitely small and atomic yet omnipresent point is called Hadit. These are unmanifest. One conjunction of these infinites is called Ra-Hoor-Khuit, a Unity which includes and heads all things."[61] The union of the Hadit principle, the individual monad's experience (i.e., the individual) with the boundless potentiality of infinite space—the principle of Nuit—is an act of "Love under will." Upon the embrace of this union, the apparent separateness, the illusion of division between "self" and "other," is dissolved in ecstasy. In other words, the dyad reduces to zero in yet another mathematical equation that Crowley expresses as "0=2," or $(+1) + (-1) = 0$ (i.e., two opposites combine and nullify one another).[62] The embrace of human experience then is a divine gift, and the perpetual movement

---

[60] "Introduction," in Crowley (1938).

[61] Crowley (1997), 137.

[62] See Crowley (1906) "Berashith: An Essay on Ontology" in *The Collected Works of Aleister Crowley*, Vol. II (Des Plaines: Yogi Publication Society), 233–243. Also,

towards growth and experience only increases our knowledge of self and our relationship to the divinely animated universe.

The religious ethos in this respect stems not from an all-powerful judging deity as in the monotheistic scheme of the Old Aeon; rather authority stems from within. Through the process of Initiation (discussed below), the sheaths of the profane self are slowly taken away, and the true self (the star) can freely and harmoniously revolve on its own unique orbit. In this sense, the Light of each star shines omnidirectional from within in self-governance in the world, being Light in Extension, or "Khabs am Pekht" (see figure 1.3).

To attain to such spiritual knowledge and realize the divine Will, there is neither an aimlessness to one's experiences, nor is there extreme attachment to any one goal. Crowley stated that the Thelemic phrase, "'Do what thou wilt' does not mean 'Do what you like.'" He continued that it is the most austere ethical precept ever uttered, and "is the apotheosis of Freedom; but it is also the strictest possible bond."[63] Here Crowley implies that an individual must diligently seek out her unique purpose in life, what is called the "True Will" (or "pure will").[64] Crowley continues:

> Thou must (1) Find out what is thy Will. (2) Do that Will with (a) one-pointedness, (b) detachment, (c) peace. Then, and then only, art thou in harmony with the Movement of Things, thy will part of, and therefore equal to, the Will of God. And since the will is but the dynamic aspect of the self, and since two different

---

Crowley (1986) "0=2" in *Magick Without Tears* (Tempe: New Falcon Publications), 52–63.

[63] Crowley (2007a), 41.

[64] See AL I:44. The reader should note that while it is commonly said among Thelemites that finding one's real purpose in life is the discovery of the "True Will," such a phrase is not found in *The Book of the Law* nor the Holy Books of Thelema. Crowley would only later expound upon the philosophy of Will and refer to the "True Will" in his epistle *De Lege Libellum*. See Crowley (2007b) *The Blue Equinox*, 99–125.

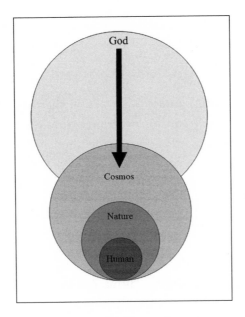

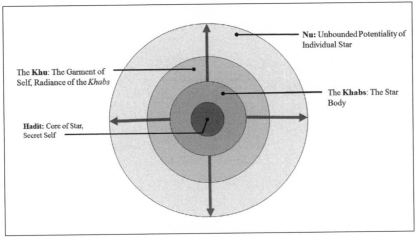

(Figure 1.3) Religious Authority in the Old Aeon and New Aeon. [ABOVE] In the monotheistic scheme that characterizes the Old Aeon, religious authority descends from an all-powerful, all-knowing deity. The cosmos, nature, and humankind must submit to the Will of God. [BELOW] In the New Aeon, our *ethos* stems from the Will of God, which is in each and every individual. It is through a rigorous process of Initiation that each person must volitionally peel away the mundane aspects of the self and discover the divine Will, each for himself. See also diagram and discussion in Gunther (2009), 61–73.

selves could not possess identical wills; then, if thy will be God's will, *Thou art That*.[65]

The path to "self-knowledge" is no easy task. It is through comprehensive developmental phases of Initiation that an individual comes to understand the self and his or her relationship to the world. The entire process entails a set of complex methods which blend practices from both Western and Eastern religious traditions: including prayer, ritual, yoga, meditation, and the elaborate ceremonial techniques of "Magick."[66] The initiate must then embrace a life of disciplined action and focused Will. The New Aeon makes it possible for each individual to free herself from a profane, uninitiated state of existence and into self-realized initiated life.

It is through the process of Initiation that Thelemic ethics takes root, and this is intimately tied to Thelema's soteriology (the doctrine of "salvation") and theodicy (the doctrine of "evil"). In terms of salvation, religions of the "Old Aeon" required either blood sacrifices, the cutting of one's flesh (as in the covenant between Abraham and Jehovah), or the restriction of one's actions to satisfy the vicarious atonement of sin (see figure 1.4). In Thelema, one is "saved" only by one's volitional effort to know oneself through the disciplined path of initiation—aiming to align with the divine Will. As J. Daniel Gunther has succinctly described the soteriology of Thelema:

> It is not accomplished by vicarious atonement and faith in the labors of another; within the crucible of each individual heart the coin must be redeemed by self-sustained effort. The price is paid with our own blood, not by faith in the blood of another.[67]

This immediately raises a philosophical problem. If each person has a unique "Will," what constitutes "right" and "wrong" when two

---

[65] Ibid., 42.

[66] Crowley added a "k" to the end of "magic" to distinguish it from stage magic. See Crowley (1997), 47.

[67] Gunther (2009), 124.

Aeon	Example	Soteriology
Isis (Goddess) **Nature** Neolithic	Egyptian Mayan/Aztec	Blood Sacrifice (Human or Animal)
Osiris (Dying God) **Catastrophe/Patriarchy** Bronze Age, Iron Age —▶ Modern Period	Jehovah/Allah (Father God) Dying Gods Motif: Osiris, Dionysus, Adonis, Attis, Jesus	Animal Sacrifice, Cutting of Flesh Vicarious atonement of Sin
Horus **Androgyne/Synthesis** 20th-century to Present	Dual-natured Heru-ra-ha Ra-Hoor-Khuit and Hoor-paar-kraat	Covenant of the Open Way* (i.e., Initiation)

(**Figure 1.4**) **Soteriology in the Aeons.** From human sacrifice, to the cutting of the flesh, to the elevation of the self through initiation, the path of salvation has been modified through the aeons. [*Gunther (2014), 226–233.]

"Wills" come into disagreement? Crowley points out in his essay titled, "The Message of the Master Therion," that "if every man and every woman did his or her will—the true will—there would be no clashing. 'Every man and every woman is a star,' and each star moves in an appointed path without interference. There is plenty of room for all; it is only disorder that creates confusion."[68] For Crowley, an initiate who has relinquished himself to the Will of God has the momentum of the universe behind him and would be in perfect harmony with the natural course of events, in a similar way a Taoist might move in harmony with nature. Right and wrong actions then are not defined in terms of "good and evil," but rather "balanced and unbalanced."

To further elucidate Thelemic theodicy (how or why evil exists), we must look once again to the Qabalah. In the Qabalah, the divine (i.e., God) divided itself into a dualistic world. We can deduce the reason for this from Qabalistic narratives which explain that in a world without distinction, there could be no possibility for experience. For example, without knowing pain, there would be no sensation to compare with

---

[68] Crowley (2007b), 41.

pleasure. Without sadness, happiness would be difficult to qualify. It is therefore for the sake of experience that a dualistic world exists.

The above, of course, admits that "wrong," "bad," and "evil" are necessary conditions to life. As unfortunate as this may seem, this is an objective description of the profane world at large. In the Qabalah, these "unbalanced tendencies" lie outside of the "balanced" Tree of Life and are called the "Qliphoth" (קליפות "shells," or "husks" in Hebrew). In the uninitiated, profane world of everyday life, the Qliphoth dominate our consciousness. It is where hatred, fear, and ignorance rule, and enable humans to commit crimes against one another. Salvation in this regard is achieved only through the path of initiation, one person at a time.

Thelema and Politics

One last point should be made regarding the ethics of Thelema and that is a brief discussion of the politically-charged document, "Liber LXXVII," also known as "Liber Oz."[69] It was published on the Winter Solstice of 1941 during the midst of World War II, yet it remains the most important ethical treatise for Thelemites today. This short and succinct statement is a positive assertion of "The Rights of Man." It is a declaration of individual freedom in thought, speech, and action. In 220 words, "Liber Oz" declares that each person has the right to live how and where she will, eat what she will, think, speak, and write what she will, and love whom she will. The most controversial phrase appears at the end: "Man has the right to kill those who would thwart these rights," implying a safeguard against tyranny and oppression, lest these rights not be recognized for all.

When we place "Liber Oz" into its historical context, we may understand that it expresses some rather radical statements, especially when one considers the level of atrocities besetting humanity at the time. Yet, the precepts in "Liber Oz" mean just as much today, politically speaking, as they did in 1941. With the superstructures of government imposing control and regulation on its citizenship as much

---

[69] See a copy of its original publication in chapter five.

as it is able, and with innocents being killed daily from various acts of violence, be they from terrorist attacks or disturbed individuals, "Liber Oz" continues to serve as an antiodote to despotism and compulsion. In short, "Liber Oz" stands as one of the clearest examples in history of a declaration of individual freedom.

Lastly, there is an essay entitled, "Duty" written by Crowley in the 1920s.[70] More suggestive in tone than the assertive declaration of "Liber Oz," "Duty" lays out a set of four aspects to performing one's actions in accordance with the Law of Thelema: (1) "Your duty to yourself," (2) "Your duty to other individual men and women," (3) "Your duty to mankind," and (4) "Your duty to all other beings and things." What is interesting to note about this essay is that it suggests that part of doing one's Will is to respect the business of others. With regard to its second point, the "duty to other individual men and women," Crowley says to "Abstain from all interferences with other wills," remarking that to seek "to dominate or influence another is to seek to deform or to destroy him." While Thelema involves active participation in discovering one's own Will, it theoretically embraces a philosophy of "non-interference" with others. Crowley elucidated upon this in his epistle to his student Charles Stansfeld Jones in *Liber Aleph* writing, "the most dangerous Man (or Woman, as has occurred, or I err) is the Busybody." He continues:

> My Son, there are Afflictions many and Woes many, that come of the Errors of Men in Respect of the Will; but there is none greater than this, the Interference of the Busy-Body. For they make Pretence to know a man's Thought better than he doth himself, and to direct his Will with more Wisdom than he, and to make Plans for his Happiness.[71]

The ethics of Thelema could be summarized as follows: Thelema is a spiritual philosophy that espouses tenets of individual freedom and self-reliance. Thelemites find solace in the world by disciplining their minds

---

[70] First published in Crowley (1998b), 135–144.

[71] Crowley (1991c) *Liber Aleph vel CXI*, "On Malign Fools," 148.

and bodies with yoga, meditation, and various ritualistic practices that aim to discover who they are and what their purpose is. We consider minding one's own business to be a virtue worthy of esteem. To help others in their ailments is a noble aim, but it is not always achievable. If something or someone is threatening the life, well-being, or livelihood of a Thelemite, it is understandable that they would defend themselves by whatever means necessary.

Thelema's relationship to politics has become an ongoing discussion, and the subject is much too large to cover fully in this short exploration of Thelemic ethics. It is the opinion of the author that Thelema, as a spiritual philosophy, extends beyond the dichotomies that divide people over political positions. What will be said on this point is that an exhaustive study of Thelemic ethics and politics has yet to be put forward in a critically and well-researched format. Such an effort will be a most appreciated contribution to the existing literature.[72]

The activities of the Thelemic movement, both during Crowley's lifetime and after, were motivated by the ideas and beliefs outlined in this chapter. Embracing the Law of Thelema and acting as an agent of the Crowned and Conquering Child is to welcome the possibility and reality of Freedom, not only in a mundane political sense, but in a spiritual sense. It is the opinion of the author that this philosophy is what Crowley sought to put forward, and it is what those who followed believed enough in to carry Thelema forward into its next incarnations. Let us now become briefly acquainted with the man known as Aleister Crowley, "The Great Beast," the Prophet of the New Aeon.

---

[72] Two collections of essays by O.T.O. initiates on Liber Oz and Liberty are worthy of note: Jack Parsons (1989) *Freedom Is a Two-Edged Sword* (New York and Las Vegas: Ordo Templi Orientis and Falcon Press) and James Wasserman (2004) *The Slaves Shall Serve* (New York: Sekmet Books).

CHAPTER TWO

Aleister Crowley: The Great Beast 666

Now ye shall know that the chosen priest & apostle of infinite space
is the prince-priest the Beast; and in his woman called the Scarlet
Woman is all power given.

—*The Book of the Law, Liber AL vel Legis* I:15

As mentioned in the Introduction, several biographies of
Crowley already exist. A number focus on the details of specific periods and themes.[1] This chapter is intended to highlight his role as the
prophet of Thelema. What follows is thus a very broad overview of his
life that will highlight some of the more important of his initiatory
experiences and efforts to forward Thelema.

Aleister Crowley is known as The Great Beast 666, but this title
is often misleading to those who are only marginally familiar with
this literature. He often employed such imagery as The Beast and the
number 666 in an effort to take an idea that was culturally accepted
as negative and turn it on its head. He believed that by identifying the
natural opposite to any idea, a person could break through to a greater
understanding of the world. He considered this to be part of the Great
Work, the "mingling of the contradictory elements in a cauldron,"

---

[1] See, for example, the work of Tobias Churton, who has covered Crowley's German
period (1930–1932) in Churton (2014) *Aleister Crowley The Beast in Berlin: Art,
Sex, and Magick in the Weimar Republic* (Rochester: Inner Traditions), and, more
recently, his earlier American period (1915–1919) in Churton (2017) *Aleister Crowley in America: Art, Espionage, and Sex Magick in the New World*. Crowley's alleged
involvement with the British Secret Service has been explored in Richard Spence
(2008) *Secret Agent 666: Aleister Crowley, British Intelligence and the Occult* (Port
Townsend: Feral House). An in-depth look at Crowley's history with politics may be
found in Marco Pasi (2014) *Aleister Crowley and the Temptation of Politics* (Bristol:
Acumen Publishing, Ltd.).

further describing it as "the satisfaction of the desire of the incomplete element of one kind to satisfy its formula by assimilation of its equal and opposite."[2]

At the same time, his "anti-Christian" imagery is easily explained when we look at his early childhood and upbringing. His youthful religious training played a considerable part in his recalcitrant views towards Christianity, yet left him with a sort of spiritual fervor that needed to be launched in an altogether different direction. That trajectory would see him evolving from a student of the occult into the prophet of a new religion.

⚜

Born Edward Alexander Crowley on October 12, 1875, in Warwickshire, England, to Edward Crowley (1829–1887) and Emily Bertha Bishop (1848–1917), his father was a shareholder in railways. The family wealth, however, came from a lucrative brewery business owned by his uncle and grandfather. Edward Crowley was also a devoted member of a fundamentalist Christian sect known as the Plymouth Brethren,[3] and little Alick received a strict Christian education from a young age at a school for sons of the Brethren. The school was supervised by Reverend Henry d'Arcy Champney (1854–1942), a sternly pious headmaster with a Master of Arts degree from Corpus Christi College in Cambridge. Historian Richard Kaczynski describes the horribly oppressive environment that Crowley must have experienced every day as a young boy:

> Extracurricular activities at the school were rigorously religious. Although the boys played cricket, scoring was forbidden lest they commit the sin of emulation. Prayers, ceremonies, meetings, Bible readings, and sermons filled each Sunday, with only two hours

---

[2] Crowley (2007a), *The Book of Thoth* (Newburyport, MA: Weiser Books), 103.
[3] See Peter Embley (1966) *The Origins and Early Development of the Plymouth Brethren*, Ph.D. Dissertation (Cheltenham: St. Paul's College).

allocated for other activities, such as reading books sanctioned for Sundays. On Monday nights, "Badgers' Meetings" opened the big schoolroom to feed and proselytize the residents of Cambridge's slum, Barnswell; alas, the visitors often left a bit of themselves behind, resulting in epidemics of ringworm, measles, and mumps at the school. Champney regarded illness among the boys as God's punishment for some undisclosed sin.[4]

Despite his harsh religious indoctrination by the Brethren, Crowley held his father in high esteem. Edward Crowley was a devoted father and a successful businessman. The young Alick was devastated when, at age eleven, he lost his father to cancer. He reacted to this trauma by rebelling against the authority figures around him, namely his mother and the headmaster Champney. His misbehavior was, of course, met with severe punishment by Champney, who would administer an increasing number of lashes for each instance. These experiences led the boy to develop an intense hatred for Christianity and a substantial level of distrust for Christians.[5] His skepticism was only reinforced upon entering the free-thinking and libertine environment of the university when he enrolled at Trinity College in Cambridge. The freedom he experienced to study and explore his passions in the arts, poetry, and literature couldn't have contrasted more with the puritanical climate of his upbringing.

The Making of a Magician

During his college years, Crowley developed an interest in mysticism. A tavern discussion on alchemy between himself and analytical chemist Julian Baker (1873–1958) in August of 1898 led to his becoming acquainted with George Cecil Jones (1873–1960) in October of the

---

[4] Kaczynski (2010), 27.

[5] Crowley's "Anti-Christianity" has been explored in detail in Marco Pasi (1998) "L' anticristianesimo in Aleister Crowley (1875–1947)," in *Aleister Crowley: Un Mago a Cefalù*, PierLuigi Zoccatelli (ed.) (Rome: Edizioni Mediterranee).

same year. It was through Jones that on November 18, 1898, at the age of twenty-three, Aleister Crowley was officially introduced into the secret magical society known as the Hermetic Order of the Golden Dawn.[6]

Crowley advanced quickly through the Golden Dawn's initiatory system. Reaching the peak of the Outer Order grades by May of 1899, he sought entrance into the "Inner" Second Order and the grade of Adeptus Minor (5°=6°), which could only be obtained with the approval of his Superiors in the London Lodge. However, schism was stirring within the Golden Dawn. Senior members began to quarrel with regard to the order's leading authority, Samuel MacGregor Mathers, who was living in Paris at the time. This was made worse when the London Lodge refused Crowley's admittance to the Second Order; he instead bypassed their authority and traveled to Paris, where Mathers was willing to initiate him on January 16, 1900. Tensions between London members and Mathers worsened over the following months, resulting in a formal decision by senior-ranking members in London to remove Mathers as head and expel him from the order. Thus ended the original conception of the Hermetic Order of the Golden Dawn.

Re-establishing the Link

Having become disenchanted by the political quagmires that erupted in the Golden Dawn, Crowley was, for a period, disheartened with magical societies. He traveled for some time beginning in 1900, going first to Mexico via the United States. There he took part in mountain climbing, one of his favorite pastimes, with his friend Oscar Eckenstein

---

[6] The Hermetic Order of the Golden Dawn was one of the most well-known initiatory societies that taught practical occultism in the nineteenth century. It was founded in 1887 by William Robert Woodman (1828–1891), William Wynn Westcott (1848–1925), and Samuel Liddell MacGregor Mathers (1854–1918). It would last in its original form until 1900, when it fell into schism. For a history of the Golden Dawn, see bibliography for Ellic Howe (1978), R. A. Gilbert (1983, 1986, and 1998), Mary K. Greer (1994), and Alex Owen (2004).

(1859–1921). He then traveled to the Far East and began studying Buddhism and Hindu yoga in India under his former Golden Dawn colleague, Allan Bennett (1872–1923). Arriving back in the UK in 1903, Crowley met and married Rose Edith Kelly (1874–1932).

The details of the writing of *The Book of the Law* in 1904 have been recounted in numerous places. What is important to note in this discussion is that Crowley seems to have either paid no mind to the experience in Cairo, or he was genuinely so troubled by it that he set the book aside, only to revisit it at a later date. Two years later, in 1906, he was reacquainted with George Cecil Jones, who encouraged him to pick up his magical practices again.[7] Upon revisiting the manuscript of *Liber AL*, he came to the understanding that his receiving *The Book of the Law* may have indicated that he had re-established a link to the Secret Chiefs—which had been lost with the downfall of the Golden Dawn. Therefore, on November 15, 1907, barely two weeks after penning *Liber VII* and *Liber LXV,* mentioned earlier, Crowley and Jones, along with John Frederick Charles Fuller (1878–1966), would found a new magical order.[8] It would be modeled after the structure of the Golden Dawn, being governed by a triune authority of officers. The new order would be called the A∴A∴.[9]

The Magician Becomes a Prophet

Crowley was engaged in publishing his poetic work and preparing a biannual publication called *The Equinox* to promote the A∴A∴. It was also around this time that he met and befriended Victor Benjamin Neuburg (1883–1940).[10] Neuburg shortly thereafter became an

---

[7] Kaczynski (2010), 165.

[8] Ibid., 179.

[9] See chapter three for a discussion on the structure and organization of the A∴A∴.

[10] Victor Benjamin Neuburg was an already published poet when he and Crowley met in 1907 at Trinity College in Cambridge. Impressed with the mystical leanings of his writing, Crowley introduced him to the curriculum of the A∴A∴ in 1908 and accepted his request to become a Probationer. Victor was of a middle-class Jewish family, though he rejected those conventions, instead embracing the free-thinking

aspirant to the A∴A∴, and, in December of 1909, the two magicians traveled across the North African desert of Algiers. It was on this expedition that Crowley and Neuburg worked the Enochian angelic magical system and produced what would come to be known as *The Vision and the Voice*. As we will see in chapter four, *The Vision and the Voice* marked a significant point in Crowley's magical career. Its text may be considered one of the most important milestones of both his personal work and the development of Thelemic doctrine. Israel Regardie noted that the experiences in the Algerian desert were a turning point for Crowley:

> Whatever the North African experience is finally reckoned to be, there is little doubt that it had a tremendous effect on the whole course of Crowley's subsequent life. One of the most immediate results was that he was able to lay claim firmly to the formerly achieved grade of 8°=3□, and soberly assume the responsibility relating to it. He came to accept the mission involved in The Book of the Law of disseminating a new moral code for mankind, and also became more willing to assume the role of teacher it had urged upon him.[11]

Drawing from Regardie's biography, Marco Pasi has identified two distinguishing phases of Crowley's life, transitioning in 1909:

> His life in fact appears to have been divided into two distinct phases. The first consisted of a striving for mystical and initiatory achievement: a more individualistic phase, characterized by what we might call a "search for the absolute." The second phase consisted of his complete identification with his religious "call." It was

---

and progressive ideals of a young college student in Trinity at the time. Nevertheless, he was predisposed to mystical experiences since childhood. His biography can be found in Jean Overton Fuller (1990) *The Magical Dilemma of Victor Neuburg: A Biography* (Oxford: Mandrake).

[11] Israel Regardie (1982) *The Eye in the Triangle: An Interpretation of Aleister Crowley* (Las Vegas: Falcon Press), 414.

the mission he felt invested with as a prophet: the propagation of the religion of Thelema.[12]

The event that marks this distinction is, in fact, Crowley's initiation into the A∴A∴ grade of Master of the Temple. This process will be described in more detail later; for the time being, it is important to note that this initiation indicated his arrival into the third and final tier of the system of the A∴A∴. Here he entered the spiritual community of the Secret Chiefs. In the years that followed, he would accept his role as prophet and make his primary task that of promulgating Thelema.

As biographer Richard Kaczynski notes, "Crowley kicked into high gear" upon returning to England in January of 1910, preparing for another issue of *The Equinox* in the spring. He had already authored several A∴A∴ documents and published them in 1909, including ΘΕΛΗΜΑ (The Holy Books of Thelema) which now included "Liber LXI vel Causæ," an account of the breakdown of the Golden Dawn and the subsequent re-established link with the Secret Chiefs. Also a few copies of the "Oaths and Tasks" of the grades of the Outer College, "Liber Collegii Sancti," were available, printed on vellum and bound with silk ties and a green cord.[13] One feature of *The Equinox* worth mentioning is the serial installment, "The Temple of Solomon the King."[14] The portion that ran in Volume I, Numbers 2–3, made available the rituals of the Golden Dawn. MacGregor Mathers attempted to keep No. 3 from publication, and Crowley was served with a writ for a court appearance on the matter. Mathers lost, but the trial generated attention from the press, with headlines like "Rosicrucian Rites: The Dread Secrets of the Order Revealed," and "Secrets of the 'Golden Dawn': Quaint Rites of the Modern Rosicrucians." According

---

[12] Pasi (2014), 25.

[13] See Gerald Yorke and Clive Harper (2011) "A Bibliography of the Works of Aleister Crowley," in *Aleister Crowley, the Golden Dawn, and Buddhism: Reminiscences and Writings of Gerald Yorke*, Keith Richmond (ed.) (York Beach: The Teitan Press), 51.

[14] "The Temple of Solomon the King" was a series that ran through most issues of *The Equinox*.

to Kaczynski, several initiatory societies took notice of Crowley, "all of whom conferred upon him membership in their organizations."[15]

Later that year, he gained less favorable attention from the press. He sought to promote the A∴A∴ beyond the publication of *The Equinox* with a series of public dramatic rituals, "The Rites of Eleusis."[16] The Rites were performed and open to the public every Wednesday from October 19 to November 30, 1910, at Caxton Hall in London.

The Rites however had the opposite effect of that intended. As Crowley recalled, "There was, however, another side of London life which till that time I had hardly suspected: that certain newspapers rely for their income upon blackmail."[17] Rather than attract members, the Rites generated considerable negative attention from the press, drove people away, and alienated the other two co-founders of the A∴A∴. J. F. C. Fuller distanced himself for fear that their association would affect his military career. George Cecil Jones attempted to sue the yellow press newspaper, *The Looking Glass,* for libel. The case was closed with Jones on the losing side, and his relationship with Crowley was irreparably damaged.

Ordo Templi Orientis

One of the more significant events that took place after the journey through Algiers was Crowley's introduction to the Ordo Templi Orientis. He was made a VII° by Theodor Reuss in March of 1910 because of the aforementioned newspaper articles following the trial with Mathers. However, when Crowley later published *The Book of Lies*, Reuss believed Crowley was unknowingly revealing secrets of the O.T.O. Reuss subsequently conferred upon him the highest degree of IX° in an effort to bind him to secrecy by oath so that he would not divulge the Order's mysteries. Soon after, he was made a X°, with the administrative title of Supreme and Holy King over "Ireland, Iona, and all the Britons."

---

[15] Kaczynski (2010), 208.

[16] See chapter four for more on this.

[17] Crowley (1969a), 638.

As will be discussed in the next chapter, the O.T.O. secret concerns the practice of sexual magic. It would seem that upon discovering the efficacy of this secret, Crowley would in time opt for the methods of the O.T.O. over the ceremonial magic that he learned in the Golden Dawn. While the methods of ceremonial magic and sexual magic differed, Crowley found that their ends were spiritually compatible. It just so happened that the sexual magic of the O.T.O. was more straightforward and was not entrenched with overly-elaborate and cumbersome rituals.

It was through the implementation of these methods that Crowley gained further initiatory insight into the A∴A∴ and the O.T.O. in "The Paris Working," a series of homosexual rites performed with his previously-mentioned magical partner, Victor Neuburg, in 1914. Crowley would continue to experiment with heterosexual, homosexual, and auto-erotic methods of sex magic in the years that followed.

American Magus ... and Spy?

With the onset of the Great War and his personal fears that the survival of the knowledge of initiation was at risk from a possible holocaust, Crowley left for America in October of 1914. This was an important period for his magical career and the growth of Thelema. Having fully attained to the A∴A∴ grade of Magus by 1915, he took steps to orientate the O.T.O. as an exclusively Thelemic organization. This meant that the O.T.O. would no longer be solely an *academia masonica,* which was one of its initial purposes, but that it would serve as a fraternal social engine to carry out his mission and promulgate his message. Armed with the publishing organ of the A∴A∴, *The Equinox,* and the coordinating abilities of a fraternal order guided by the Law of the New Aeon, Thelema could theoretically be established throughout the world. His efforts are evident in the publication of *The Blue Equinox* (Volume III, Number 1) in 1919 featuring: an outline of the curriculum of the A∴A∴; documents that cover the principles and organization of the O.T.O.; and the text of an ecclesiastical ceremony known as "The Gnostic Mass."

Crowley also spent his American period attempting to undermine the German war efforts. He wrote for *The International* and *The*

Fatherland, two pro-German journals founded by George Sylvester Viereck (1884–1962). Crowley's involvement with these journals has been the subject of debate and attempts were made by his contemporaries to label him anti-British. Nevertheless, the story would contain a twist. As Tobias Churton notes, Crowley understood the role that active pro-German propaganda played in encouraging America's willingness to financially assist England in the war:

> [The] German government [...] quickly perceived that the Allies had most to gain from American liberty to sell, and therefore gal-vanized their propaganda effort to demand strict neutrality from the United States as regards loans and matériel. Propaganda in America was not therefore a minor policy sideline either to the Germans or to the Allies; German propaganda was on the fore-front of British intelligence concern with regard to America. With German propaganda in the States went German spying in the States. German exasperation over what it came to perceive as hostile anti-German U.S. policy (permitting loans and arms sales) would lead to precipitous acts of espionage [...] that opened the road to America's finally entering the war [...] Crowley played a role in unbalancing the formerly fine-tuned German propaganda effort [...][18]

As Crowley explained it, he wrote for *The International* and *The Father-land* in an effort to subvert the German propaganda efforts by publish-ing outlandish articles to show the absurdity of the German cause and to urge America into the war to help the British. "It makes me weep for Germany when I think that Viereck published such hideous and transparent irony without turning a hair!" he later remarked in *Confes-sions*.[19] While he knew well his own sly and sarcastic sense of humor, he anticipated that American sentiments would not grasp such sub-tlety. As he recollected, his plan succeeded when he wrote an article on Count von Reventlow's *The Vampire*, in which he suggested England

---

[18] Churton (2017), 175.
[19] Crowley (1969a), 751.

was no more than a German colony and advocated an "Unrestricted Submarine Campaign." "I secretly calculated, rightly as the gods would have it, that so outrageous a violation of all law would be the last straw, and force America to throw off the burden of neutrality."[20]

The above description is intended to provide the reader with an example of the complexity of Crowley's personality and exemplify how difficult it is to pinpoint his motives, despite the negative attention and relentless criticism he received both in his lifetime and in popular media since his death. Still, by the time he left America in 1919, his reputation had taken a downturn with the "Mess in the Press" scandal that arose surrounding the publication of *The Blue Equinox* in Detroit.[21] It would only worsen in the 1920s.

We will revisit some of the doctrinal developments of Thelema during his American period in chapter four. For the moment, it is important to review his Thelemic communal experiment at the Abbey of Thelema.

The Abbey of Thelema (1920–1923)

Crowley's prior runs-in with the press followed him when he returned to Europe in late 1919. The yellow press tabloid *John Bull* reported with the headline, "Now we hear that the traitorous degenerate, Aleister Crowley, is anxious to sneak back to the land he has sought to defile."[22] Crowley was at the time in Paris. Taking notice of the not-so-warm welcome home to England, he decided there must be better places to take refuge. After consulting the *I Ching*, he determined he should go to Sicily. It was in the small village of Cefalù that he would establish the

---

[20] Ibid., 754. Crowley's war time efforts to serve the British cause are complex, and the details of his meetings with associates of British intelligence are fascinating. The interested reader will find an exhaustive analysis of this in Churton (2017).

[21] These events are laid out in details in Kaczynski (Spring 2006) "Panic in Detroit: The Magician and the Motor City" and also in Kaczynski (2015) in *Success Is Your Proof* (West Palm Beach: Sekmet Books), 85–100.

[22] "Another Traitor Trounced: Career and Condemnation of the Notorious Aleister Crowley" in *John Bull*, January 10, 1920. Quoted in Churton (2011), 247.

Abbey of Thelema in a five-roomed eighteenth-century villa amongst rocky cliffs facing the Mediterranean Sea.

The initial company who joined him at the Abbey in the spring of 1920 included his Scarlet Woman, Leah Hirsig (1883–1975, known magically as Soror Alostrael), and her son, Hans. Leah arrived with Crowley's infant daughter, Anne Leah (nicknamed Poupée), who had been born in France at the end of January.[23] Also included in the group were Crowley's lover, Ninette Shumway (1894–1990), and her son, Howard. Other notable students who came to the Abbey were Jane Wolfe (1875–1958), Frank Bennett (1868–1930), Cecil Frederick Russell (1897–1987), and Raoul Loveday (1900–1923), among others.

The living conditions at the Abbey were harsh, with no plumbing, electric, or gas. Fresh water had to be fetched and food gathered from the local village. Bathing was probably less frequent than desired by most. However, despite the hardships experienced at the Abbey, it was in principle what Crowley was intending for his disciples. Daily life consisted of the studies and practices of Thelema, including solar salutations in the manner prescribed in "Liber Resh vel Helios" and shared meals being blessed with the observance of "Will."[24] When time was not spent in study of Thelemic literature or performing rituals, there were outdoor excursions to be had, trekking around the beautiful rolling hills of Cefalù in the Sicilian countryside.

Pertinent to the current discussion are Crowley's magical experiments at this time. The Cefalù period can be seen broadly as his attempt to confront "the shadow." Later described by his student Norman Mudd as Crowley's engagement with the "Mystery of Filth," he partook in unrestrained sexual acts with Leah, Ninette, and others, and in drug-induced rituals. However, not all of these experiences were self-indulgent pleasures; some were even acts that disgusted him. The experiences ranged from humiliating and shameful circumstances resulting from masochistic practices to submitting himself to Leah in an act of coprophagia. Crowley believed that by performing such

---

[23] In bad health since birth, Poupée passed away in a hospital in Palermo in October later that year.

[24] Kaczynski (2010), 361.

despicable deeds, one could transcend the impressions of shame and disgust and pass on to higher levels of awareness.[25] As Gerald Yorke once noted, "Crowley didn't *enjoy* his perversions! He performed them to overcome his horror of them."[26] Crowley had written earlier on this subject in an epistle to Charles Stansfeld Jones (Frater Achad):

> Yet know this, that every Opposition is in its Nature named Sorrow, and the Joy lieth in the Destruction of the Dyad. Therefore, must thou seek ever those Things which are to thee poisonous, and that in the highest Degree, and make them thine by Love. That which repels, that which disgusts, must thou assimilate in this Way of Wholeness.[27]

Pushing himself to exceed his magical potential in such a way led to Crowley taking his final Oath, that of Ipsissimus ($10°=1^\square$), in May of 1921. It was the absolute pinnacle of the initiatory system of A∴A∴, described in "One Star in Sight" (written two months later in July of 1921) as a grade "beyond all [grades] and beyond all comprehension of those of lower degrees." The Ipsissimus "has no relation as such with any Being; He has no Will in any direction, and no Consciousness of any kind involving duality, for him all is accomplished [...]"[28] Crowley never spoke of taking the Oath of Ipsissimus, remaining silent on the matter for his entire life.

Although attracting several students to the Thelemic commune,

---

[25] There has been some parallel made between Crowley's practices at Cefalù and the antinomian practices espoused in Indian Tantra. The Aghorīs, in particular, note the efficacy in acquiring spiritual power by overcoming stimuli typically considered negative. See Gordan Djurdjevic (2012) "The Great Beast as Tantric Hero: The Role of Yoga and Tantra in Aleister Crowley's Magick," in *Aleister Crowley and Western Esotericism*, Henrik Bogdan and Martin P. Starr (eds.) (Oxford: Oxford University Press), 107–140, and Richard Kaczynski (2011) "Taboo and Transformation in the Works of Aleister Crowley," in *Lucifer's Rebellion: A Tribute to Christopher S. Hyatt, Ph.D.* (ed. Shelley Marmor), 75–86.

[26] In Fuller (1990), 231. Quoted by Kaczynski (2010), 363.

[27] "On the Mystical Marriage," in Crowley (1991c) *Liber Aleph*, 23.

[28] "One Star in Sight," in Crowley (1997), 490–491.

Crowley's tenure at the Abbey would meet a bitter end. In early 1923, one of his devoted and most cherished students, Raoul Loveday, fell fatally ill after drinking contaminated water from a spring (despite the Beast's warning to him not to drink the local water). Raoul's condition worsened over the next few weeks and he died on February 16. Having been already agitated by their experience at the Abbey, Loveday's wife, Betty May, returned to London and reported Crowley to the press, who were by now eager to present him as a murderous criminal. Before long, the Abbey was painted as the headquarters of an evil, perverse cult that engaged in lascivious orgies and human sacrifice. Mussolini's fascist regime had taken power six months earlier and Crowley would be issued a deportation notice on April 23, 1923.

Exile in France: Pour l'amour de l'exil et de l'amour

Crowley and Leah arrived in French Tunis on May 2, 1923. He would live on French soil, at one location or another, until 1929. It was a period of great difficulty for the prophet. He was struggling with an addiction to heroin (which had been prescribed to him by his doctor for asthma). His relationship with Leah began to break down, and he had been falsely accused of the death of one of his more promising students and friends. After the expulsion from Sicily, he was unsure of his mission. The Ipsissimus Grade was creating strange impressions within him. He was feeling like he was no more a person, just the embodiment of the Word, a message. But was this message even worth anything to humanity?

Crowley was in a rut. His feelings for Leah soured and she turned her attention to his student Norman Mudd (1889–1934). Crowley distanced himself from both. By the closing weeks of the summer in 1924, he was living just outside of Paris, and had found a new romance that would again inspire him. Dorothy Olsen, known as "Soror Astrid," was a thirty-two-year-old woman from Chicago. She was touring Europe when she met him that September in Chelles. Leah, although broken from her separation from Crowley and the loss of her office as Scarlet Woman, accepted the reality and attempted to interpret the appearance of Olsen as the result of her and the Beast's magical operations. While Leah remained in Paris scraping for funds and working odd jobs in kitchens, washing dishes for thirteen hours a day, Crowley took his new love and Scarlet Woman off to Tunis. There, they began newly energized operations which resulted in a document called "To Man," also known as "The Mediterranean Manifesto." It was an effort to ride the coattails of the current campaign initiated by the Theosophical Society through Annie Besant (1847–1933) and Charles Leadbeater (1854–1934), who were putting forth Jiddu Krishnamurti (1895–1986) as the next Messiah and "World Teacher."[29] Crowley's interest in this status will be explained shortly.

Another document written at this time, which holds some relevance, is the "Constitution of the Order of Thelemites." Plans to formulate this organization were outlined to Mudd in 1924. The initiatory structure was to be along the lines of the O.T.O., with the Man of Earth being called "Zelator," the Lovers, "Adeptus," and the Hermit, "Magister." Within the Order of Thelemites, there was some crossover membership expected in the A∴A∴. For example, "Zelators" in the Order of Thelemites were given preliminary A∴A∴ Class D documents to study and practice, and the Adepti were expected to be "Lords of the Paths."[30] A Magister was to be at least a Babe of the Abyss, the liminal stage in the A∴A∴ system between Adeptus Exemptus and Magister Templi.[31]

The aims of the Order of Thelemites seem very similar to how Crowley envisioned the O.T.O.: functioning as a social machine to carry through the Law of Thelema. He wrote Mudd: "Our overt object, which is the real one, is a reconstitution of Society aimed at averting the

---

[29] A critical account of Krishnamurti's experiences in the Theosophical Society is given in Russell Balfour-Clarke (1977) *The Boyhood of J. Krishnamurti* (Chetana: Bombay) and Roland Vernon (2000) *Star in the East: Krishnamurti, the Invention of a Messiah* (New York: Palgrave).

[30] See "The Robe of a Dominis Liminis" in "Liber Vesta vel פרכת sub figura DCC," Crowley (1996b), 56.

[31] "The Constitution of the Order of Thelemites," points 2(a) and 2(b). UC.

catastrophe of Bloody Revolution."[32] Yet, it is clear that once Crowley became the O.H.O. of the O.T.O. in the same year, all discussion of the Order of Thelemites ceased. In reality, the Order of Thelemites was never actually instituted. It can in large part be understood as Crowley's backup plan for a social initiatory structure in the event that he would not assume the leadership of the O.T.O. The reader should bear this in mind for a later discussion in Part II. As will be seen, the "Constitution of the Order of Thelemites" confused some later leaders of both the O.T.O. and the A∴A∴ because of its associative terminology, such as "Man of Earth" and "Zelator."

The Weida Conference: O.H.O. and the World Teacher Campaign (1925)

Theodor Reuss died in 1923, leaving the office of Outer Head of the Order of the O.T.O. vacant. It is clear from correspondence with Reuss that Crowley had considered he would fill that position as early as 1921. Reuss had written him in November demanding he keep the teachings of Thelema outside the O.T.O. Crowley took the order as an abdication of Reuss' leadership and a sign that he should assume the role of O.H.O. Tobias Churton interprets the exchange as follows:

> What Crowley meant by Reuss' abdication was that Reuss by his actions and words manifestly did not count himself bound to any obligation to the secret chiefs, without whom no truly Rosicrucian order could be regarded as genuine. As he, Crowley, had not broken his obligations to serve the chiefs, he, Crowley, was therefore O.H.O.[33]

In other words, in Crowley's mind, when Reuss rejected the Word of the New Aeon, he automatically relinquished his position to Crowley,

---

[32] Crowley to Mudd, May 27, 1924. GYC.

[33] Churton (2014), 58. Martin P. Starr points out that Reuss never abdicated his role of O.H.O. to Crowley. Rather it was simply the story Crowley provided. Yet those to whom the succession may have mattered at one time had little concern. See Starr (2003), 111–113.

whether he was conscious of it or not. The O.T.O. was the medium to promulgate Thelema. The process only worked one way, and never the other way around.

Crowley's official succession to the position of O.H.O. was agreed upon as early as 1924 with the support of two other existing X° members, Charles Stansfeld Jones (Frater Achad) in Canada and Heinrich Tränker (1880–1956) (Frater Recnartus) in Germany. By this time, neither of these two had any interest in becoming the O.H.O., and so the succession naturally fell to Crowley who was more than willing to accept the role. As the Outer Head of the Order, Crowley assumed the magical name, "Phoenix," the mythical bird who is reborn from the ashes of its predecessor. As we will see in chapter four, Crowley may have taken this name with magical intention, knowing that he held the office of Imperator of A∴A∴, the governing officer whose weapon is the phoenix wand.

Now that Crowley had secured administrative leadership of the O.T.O., he sought to widen the scope of Thelema. In the summer of 1925, at a meeting in Germany called the Weida Conference, held in Thuringia at Tränker's estate, Crowley sought to bring leaders of a number of extant magical societies under the fold of Thelema. One of these groups was a German-based occult organization known as the Pansophical Society in which Tränker held membership.

Prior to the meeting, Crowley's student and later successor, Karl Germer, and his friend, Oskar Hopfer, had published *Ein Zugnis der Suchenden* ("The Testament of the Seeker"). This tract was written by Crowley and translated into German. It asserted the need to replace Theosophy with Thelema. The Weida Conference, in a certain sense, can be understood as Crowley's push to forward his own "World Teacher campaign" in response to the Theosophical Society's aims with Krishnamurti. Many members of the German O.T.O. were supportive of Crowley. Several were not. The disagreement between them effectively brought the Pansophical Lodge into schism.[34] One member, Eugene Grosche (1888–1964), opted to found his own occult organization,

---

[34] These events eventually led the Pansophical Society to end its activities by 1926.

the Fraternitas Saturni. It developed its own flavor of masonry and Crowleyan occultism.[35]

In the end, Crowley's desire to further Thelema at the Weida Conference was largely unsuccessful, with the attendees divided. Some followed Crowley. Others distanced themselves. The German-based occult organizations were later effectively dismantled by the Nazi regime less than a decade later. As for the World Teacher campaign, Krishnamurti came to reject the title forced upon him by Besant and Leadbeater by late 1925. Crowley would eventually also lose interest in the matter. His final push may be considered his 1926 writing of *The Heart of the Master,* published a dozen years later.[36]

The Comment

There is another significant development of this period that should be mentioned. In November of 1925, Crowley would pen the "Comment" prophesied in *The Book of the Law*.[37] Also known as the "Short Comment," it was an inspired "Class A" document.

"The Comment" appears to have been precipitated by the contentious relationship that formed between Crowley and his acting Cancellarius, Norman Mudd, known magically as Frater O. P. V. ("Omnia Pro Veritate," "All For Truth"). There had been tension building between the two men since 1923. After Crowley's exile from Sicily, Mudd and Leah had developed affections for one another. Upon

---

[35] Years later, the Fraternitas Saturni along with what remained of the O.T.O. were suppressed by the Nazi regime during World War II. The F.S. was later re-established by Grosche. See Stephen E. Flowers (2018) *The Fraternitas Saturni* (Rochester, VT: Inner Traditions) and Starr (2003). Also, Alexander Popiol and Raimund Schrader (2007) *Gregor A. Gregorius: Mystiker des dunklen Lichts* (Esoterischer: Verlag) and Thomas Hakl (trans.) (2014) "The Magical Order of the Fraternitas Saturni," in *Occultism in a Global Perspective*, Bogdan and Djurdjevic (eds.) (New York: Acumen), 37–56.

[36] Khaled Khan (ps. of Aleister Crowley) (1938) London: O.T.O., new edition, ed. Hymenaeus Beta (1992) Scottsdale, AZ: New Falcon.

[37] "But the work of the comment? That is easy; and Hadit burning in thy heart shall make swift and secure thy pen." AL, III: 40.

discovering this, Crowley decided Mudd was falling out of discipline with the Great Work and allowing his emotions for the Scarlet Woman to cloud his judgment. This resulted in Crowley administering an "Act of Truth" for Mudd, which included him denouncing his love for Hirsig. Over time, Mudd's estrangement with Crowley increased. In October of 1925, he began a campaign asserting that Crowley had been largely unsuccessful with regard to Thelema over the twenty years of its existence. According to Mudd, *The Book of the Law* should never have been given to the world at large. As Mudd would later remark, Crowley instead was, "exploiting the Word which was entrusted to you in confidence [...]"[38] Furthermore, Mudd claimed Crowley failed the program simply because he had not yet received "The Comment" prophesied in *Liber AL vel Legis*.[39] It was in the midst of this exchange that Crowley wrote "The Comment," described in AL, III:39–40.

Do what thou wilt shall be the whole of the Law.

The study of this Book is forbidden. It is wise to destroy this copy after the first reading.

Whosoever disregards this does so at his own risk and peril. These are most dire.

Those who discuss the contents of this Book are to be shunned by all, as centres of pestilence.

All questions of the Law are to be decided only by appeal to my writings, each for himself.

There is no law beyond Do what thou wilt.

Love is the law, love under will.

The priest of the princes,

Ankh-f-n-khonsu

---

[38] Norman Mudd to Crowley, October 29, 1925. GYC.

[39] "The urgent and vital necessity to your Work of establishing the Law is to obtain the true Comment [...] Given this, complete success will follow, and quickly. Not having it, your position for a full XVI years has been radically and intrinsically false— even, in actual fact, treacherous." Norman Mudd to Crowley, October 30, 1925, GYC.

The Comment is a short and succinct statement. Being "Class A," it has long been held as a safeguard against the type of tyrannical dogmatism to which spiritual movements can so easily fall prey. With the Comment, the Thelemite is ensured that each person will have a unique relationship with *The Book of the Law.*

⬩⚕⬩

In 1929, Crowley would see the publication of two important works. The first was his exhaustive magnum opus on his system of Magick. Called *Magick in Theory and Practice* (being Part III of Book IV), it is one of his most important attempts to outline Thelema's entire framework. The book went to press in 1929, privately printed by Lecram Press with the assistance of Gerald Yorke, an important figure in the history of Thelema as we will see later. In the same year, the first two volumes of Crowley's autobiography (or, as he called it, "autohagiography")[40] were published as *The Spirit of Solitude, subsequently anti christened The Confessions of Aleister Crowley* by Mandrake Press in London. A massive, but expurgated, posthumous version of the entire work was published in 1969 as *The Confessions of Aleister Crowley.*

Crowley's literary career slowed in the first years of the 1930s. Much of his attention in the beginning of that decade was given to his artwork. Then, he returned to England and continued what Mandrake had started with *The Legend of Aleister Crowley:* namely, trying to rehabilitate his name. He sued a bookseller for saying *Diary of a Drug Fiend* had been withdrawn from publication; he sued Ethel Manin over her slanderous characterization in *Confessions and Impressions;* and he tried unsuccessfully to sue Nina Hamnett/Constable & Co. over her *Laughing Torso.* The downside to all this litigious activity was that he wound up in legal straits himself, charged with receiving stolen letters in the Hamnett case, and coming to the attention of creditors and the Official Receiver, resulting in him becoming bankrupt. Yet, by 1936, he at last produced the final Part IV of *Book 4, The Equinox of the Gods,* which became *The Equinox,* Volume III, Number 3. This completed

---

[40] "Hagiography" is the biography of a Saint.

his twenty-five year project of publishing *Book 4*. *The Equinox of the Gods* included *The Book of the Law* with its facsimile, along with an exhaustive account of how the book came about.

The erudite short epistle *The Heart of the Master* and the cogent writings in *Little Essays Toward Truth* followed in print a year later in 1938. A series of successful lectures Crowley delivered on the topic of yoga was published in 1939, called *Eight Lectures on Yoga*. Finally, one of his greatest literary masterpieces, *The Book of Thoth*, was printed in 1944. *The Book of Thoth* by far demonstrates not only a comprehensive look into the Tarot deck he developed with artist Frieda Lady Harris, but shows a fully matured and evolved system laid out with his in-depth analyses on Tarot, Qabalah, Magick, and the systems of the A∴A∴ and the O.T.O.

⁓⊛⊷

Aleister Crowley's level of intelligence, ingenuity, and drive—as well as the historical and cultural conditions in which he was situated—have embedded him deep within modern culture. In the pages that follow, the religious philosophy he put forth, and its subsequent history, will be elaborated upon in greater detail.

CHAPTER THREE

Two Orders in the New Aeon
A∴A∴ and O.T.O.

WHILE THELEMA STANDS ON ITS OWN as a unique spiritual movement—apart from any group or organization that has adopted its teachings—its overall message is elucidated and its mysteries are disclosed in the two magical orders forwarded by Aleister Crowley in his lifetime. The first of these, as we have seen, is the A∴A∴,[1] officially established on November 15, 1907.[2] Like many of the aspects of Thelema, the A∴A∴ is a complex subject. The most esoteric of Thelema's associated organizations, the A∴A∴ has its physical and structural roots in late nineteenth-century British occultism,[3] while its spiritual roots extend beyond time.

For convenience to the reader, the following discussion on the A∴A∴ will outline three significant characteristics: (1) the A∴A∴ is connected with the spiritual teachings—and is therefore considered to be the spiritual source—of Thelema; (2) the A∴A∴ was established as a school to instruct students into the mysteries of Thelema and test them by empirical methods of "scientific illuminism"; and (3) the

---

[1] Generally referred to as the "Eternal and Invisible Order that hath no name among men," there is much discussion about what the letters, A∴A∴ mean. One interpretation is "Argentum Astrum," Latin for Silver Star, of which its topmost triad is defined in "One Star in Sight." See Crowley (1997), 488–498.

[2] Kaczynski (2010), 165.

[3] By "occultism," I refer to those historical currents which have their basis in modernity. Many scholars agree that this begins in the early nineteenth century with Éliphas Lévi, otherwise known as Alphonse Louis Constant (1810–1875). Occultism is a form of esotericism characterized by a systematic approach of negotiating religion and science, placing much emphasis on the discovery of arcane wisdom and individual liberation. See Faivre (1994), 86–90. More recent overviews are given in Pasi (2005) and Bogdan and Djurdjevic (2013).

A∴A∴ became visible to the world at large primarily through the publication and printing of literature.

The second Thelemic organization of importance is the Ordo Templi Orientis (O.T.O.). It is a fraternal organization[4] that has its roots in Freemasonry and is structured along the lines of a similarly freemasonic initiatory development. Although Crowley was not an original founder of the O.T.O., he was chartered as the leading authority in Great Britain in 1912. He officially took over the leadership of the entire organization in 1924–1925, at which point he officiated the O.T.O. as a "Thelemic" order. The O.T.O. is significant in this discussion because it has served as one of the primary engines by which Crowley's spiritual legacy has persisted to the present; it holds the copyrights to his literary estate; and it is the most populous Thelemic organization.

There is a third group related to both the A∴A∴ and the O.T.O. that will feature throughout this analysis, albeit to a lesser degree. That is the ecclesiastical branch of Thelema known as the Ecclesia Gnostica Catholica (the E.G.C.). Although never truly formalized in Crowley's lifetime, the E.G.C. has taken a much larger role in recent decades as a medium to promote Thelema and to build the Thelemic community. The E.G.C. operates under the auspices of the O.T.O., and performs clerical work in the traditional form of a church—administering sacraments to a congregation of adherents, and providing outlets amongst O.T.O. members and the public at large to experience communal fellowship and share fraternity. The E.G.C. and its central ritual are discussed in chapter fourteen.[5]

In this chapter, I will examine the A∴A∴ and the O.T.O. in some depth, offering a brief review of their respective histories and their overall general structure and purpose in relation to Thelema. While

---

[4] "Fraternal" includes "Sororal," with a focus on the principle of "universal brotherhood" or "sisterhood."

[5] A thorough historical account of the Ecclesia Gnostica Catholica as well as its functions and operations have been outlined by Grand Master Sabazius X° of the United States Grand Lodge, O.T.O. in (2014) *Mystery of Mystery: A Primer of Thelemic Ecclesiastical Gnosticism* (Berkeley: O.T.O.).

this discussion may appear rudimentary for the well-read Thelemite, this background information is important for what follows.

⁂

Although only having a lifespan between the years of 1887 and 1900, the popularity of the Hermetic Order of the Golden Dawn can be understood as the harbinger for what has come to be known by historians as the "occult revival of the fin-de-siècle."[6] The success of the Golden Dawn was in large part due to its highly systematized and beautifully elaborate initiation rituals, along with its complex system of teachings in the "Hermetic tradition."[7] Hermeticism was believed to originate from a legendary Egyptian priest, known as Hermes Trismegistus, and became synonymous in the Western esoteric tradition with the Egyptian god Thoth. The ancient wisdom of Hermes was believed to have continued throughout the centuries, protected by non-temporal divine intelligences overseeing the spiritual evolution of humankind.[8] These

---

[6] Surviving groups of the Hermetic Order of the Golden Dawn continue to function despite the collapse of its founding Temple.

[7] From a critical historical perspective, it is easier to talk about a "Hermetic reaction" than to point to any singular unbroken movement linking the Hermetism of antiquity to the revival of the *Corpus Hermeticum* in the Renaissance and Enlightenment periods. As Joscelyn Godwin argues, the nineteenth century witnessed a phenomenon in which esoteric discourse began attempting to locate the "ancient wisdom" in the Far East, in India and Tibet, for example, especially in the Theosophical current advanced by Helena Petrovna Blavatsky (1831–1891) and Henry Steele Olcott (1832–1907). Godwin describes a "Hermetic reaction" in fin-de-siècle occultism (i.e., the Golden Dawn, among others). Its proponents argued that the ancient wisdom originated in the West, particularly in Egypt with Hermes Trismegistus. See Joscelyn Godwin (1994) *The Theosophical Enlightenment* (Albany: SUNY Press), 333–362.

[8] This concept of a chain of initiated adepts has a long tradition in esotericism, most prevalently since the century of Enlightenment. While these beings have been referred to by various names (in Theosophy, for instance, they are called "Mahatmas"), they are called "Secret Chiefs" within the milieu of Rosicrucianism. The earliest mention of Secret Chiefs originates from a 1767 Rosicrucian document entitled *Rosenkreuzerey* reproduced by I.A. Fessler between 1805 and 1806. See Christopher McIntosh (1997), 70–72. See also the mid-seventeenth century Gold-und Rosenkreuz Order

Light Bearers were, perhaps, once-living adepti who have transcended physicality and now functioned in the spiritual realm.

According to the story, a set of "cipher manuscripts" were discovered by masonic scholar Adolphus Frederick Alexander Woodford (1821–1887) within the pages of a book at a second-hand bookstore. Woodford gave the mysteriously coded manuscripts to his colleague William Wynn Westcott (1848–1925), who deciphered the papers and found outlines to rituals for a secret society, along with contact information for a mysterious German Rosicrucian Adept, "Sapiens Dominabitur Astris of Nuremberg," also known as Anna Sprengel.[9] Upon writing to "Fräulein Sprengel," Westcott was granted permission by her to establish a secret occult order of Rosicrucian Adepts to teach the science of spiritual attainment.[10] Along with Samuel Liddell

---

in Germany and its teaching of Hidden Masters. The concept of super-human entities of spiritual wisdom would serve as the foundation for many nineteenth century initiatory and occult organizations, and is an important aspect for the Golden Dawn.

[9] The narrative of the discovery of the cipher manuscripts has been contested by historians, who claim that the story is by and large a fabrication on the part of Westcott to legitimize the Golden Dawn. Yet, the story is far too complex to be hastily dismissed. Following the trail of evidence through a plethora of esoteric figures during the nineteenth century will reveal that the cipher manuscipts and their origin travels through a list of individuals, including Robert Wentworth Little (1840–1878), Frederick Hockley (1809–1885), William Robert Woodman (1828–1891), Kenneth Mackenzie (1833–1886), Éliphas Lévi (1810–1875), Edward Bulwer–Lytton (1803–1873), and Hans Heinrich Ecker und Eckerhoffen (1750–1790). It is doubtful that this list is complete with regard to the cipher manuscripts that led to the formulation of the rituals of the Golden Dawn. Many of these figures were Freemasons who participated in various currents associated with Masonry and Rosicrucianism. Their activities can be linked to organizations such as Societas Rosicruciana in Anglia (S.R.I.A.), the Fratres Lucis, the Asiatic Brethren and even the Gold-und Rosenkreuz, among many others. The reader should note that critical histories written about the origins of the Golden Dawn have been written by masons who, with their own biases and predispositions toward dismissal, have viewed the Golden Dawn as a clandestine fringe masonic organization. One must therefore read their scholarship with some degree of skepticism.

[10] More recently, Christopher McIntosh has identified discrepancies in the use of gender pronouns in the cipher manuscripts and has thus hypothesized with good

MacGregor Mathers (1854–1918), the two formed a "spiritual link" to the hidden community of Rosicrucian adepts (referred to hereafter as the Secret Chiefs) and set the foundation for what would later be called the Hermetic Order of the Golden Dawn. Joined by the third officer of the founding Triad, William Robert Woodman (1828–1891), they formally launched the Golden Dawn on March 1, 1888. As we will see, it is this tradition of secret transmitted spiritual wisdom that would influence Crowley and his teaching system the A∴A∴.

The Golden Dawn system of initiation was based upon the Qabalistic Tree of Life (see figure 3.1). The student began her initiatory path outside the Order's fold as a Neophyte ($0°=0^\square$), and subsequently progressed in an upward trajectory to Malkuth on the Tree of Life at the grade of Zelator ($1°=10^\square$), through the Outer Order to the grades Theoricus ($2°=9^\square$) in Yesod, Practicus ($3°=8^\square$) in Hod, and Philosophus ($4°=7^\square$) in Netzach. The initiation rituals associated with these grades were highly elaborate undertakings designed to give the candidate insight into Hermetic and Qabalistic mysteries. At each stage, initiates would be given study materials and practices to prepare them for entry into the Second Order.

The Second Order, known as the Order of the Rosæ Rubæ et Aureæ Crucis (Red Rose and Golden Cross) were the Rosicrucian grades and began with the initiation ritual of the Adeptus Minor ($5°=6^\square$). Here one would enter the Vault of Initiation and become an Adept. According to the legend, upon entering into the Vault of the Mountain of Abiegnus (the Mountain of Initiation), the tomb of the Rosicrucian adept Christian Rosencreutz was discovered. And herein lay the mystery of redemption.[11] Furthermore, the candidate would swear to "purify and exalt my Spiritual Nature so that with the Divine Aid I may at length attain to be more than human, and thus gradually raise and unite myself

---

evidence that the author of the manuscripts was not female, but male. If that is the case, then this brings a new level of inquiry into the identity of the author of the manuscripts. See McIntosh (2011).

[11] This legend is outlined in numerous historical sources, including McIntosh (1997), and Goodrick-Clarke (2008), 107–130.

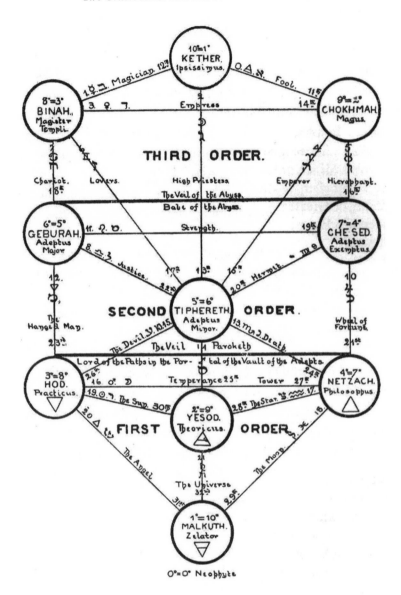

(**Figure 3.1**) **The Hermetic Order of the Golden Dawn** initiatory structure was based upon the Tree of Life of the Qabalah. The candidate began outside the Order's fold as a Neophyte (0°=0°) and then advanced into the First Order, or Outer Order. If candidates proved themselves worthy, they were admitted to the Second (Inner) Order and underwent the Initiation of the Adeptus Minor, by which they were instructed in the mysteries of the Rosicrucian Adept, Christian Rosencreutz.

to my Higher and Divine Genius."[12] The experience of knowing one's "Higher Divine Genius," or "Augoeides" is what Mathers would later identify as the result of the magical operation of "the Sacred Magic of Abramelin the Mage," an epistolary grimoire supposedly dating from the fourteenth or fifteenth century, originally translated into English by Mathers himself.[13]

It was in the Second Order that the Golden Dawn's administration was localized, traditionally governed by a trinity of officers: Præmonstrator, Imperator, and Cancellarius. They handled the affairs of the order in instruction, government, and record-keeping, respectively.[14] The Second Order was separated from the Third by the "Abyss," a chasm that made crossing into the Supernal Triad a human impossibility. It was in the Third Order that the Secret Chiefs themselves resided.

As was alluded to in the previous chapter, the original manifestation of the Hermetic Order of the Golden Dawn eventually broke apart due to schism and discrepancy in authority. By 1897, two of the three founding members, Woodman and Westcott, had either died or resigned, leaving S. L. MacGregor Mathers solely in charge.[15] Over time, members of the Golden Dawn's Isis-Urania Lodge in London became critical of Mathers' leadership. After his representative in London, Florence Farr, resigned, a general meeting was held by the remaining London members, who resolved to remove Mathers from the order.

---

[12] Quoted in Ellic Howe (1972), 87.

[13] See Georg Dehn (2007) *The Book of Abramelin: A New Translation* (Lake Worth: Ibis Press) for a discussion on history and recent translation of this text.

[14] These offices are discussed below in the section entitled "The Governing Triad."

[15] Westcott was apparently forced by his employer to resign the order when his membership was discovered. See Howe (1978).

The Great White Brotherhood

What exactly then is the A∴A∴, first and foremost? It was described by Crowley as the "Eternal and Invisible Order that hath no name among men," and that, "The Name of the Order and those of its three divisions are not disclosed to the profane."[16] His explanatory essay on the A∴A∴, entitled "One Star in Sight," is referred to as a "glimpse of the structure and system of the Great White Brotherhood."[17] Elsewhere, Crowley describes the A∴A∴ as an "illuminated community which is scattered throughout the world, but which is governed by one truth and united in one spirit." He continues:

> From all time there has been an exterior school based on the interior one, of which it is but the outer expression. From all time, therefore, there has been a hidden assembly, a society of the Elect, of those who sought for and had capacity for light [...] All that any external order possesses in symbol, ceremony, or rite is the letter expressive outwardly of that spirit of truth which dwelleth in the interior Sanctuary [...] this Sanctuary, composed of members widely scattered indeed but united by the bonds of perfect love, has been occupied from the earliest ages in building the grand Temple (through the evolution of humanity) [...][18]

By "illuminated community," Crowley is referring to all of the aforementioned Secret Chiefs, the various adepts in history who have transmitted spiritual wisdom to humanity over the span of our species' existence on the planet. The mission of this interior Sanctuary (known as the A∴A∴), is to deliver a universal Truth intended to liberate humanity. What is this message of Truth? It is transmitted through its line of prophets and their respective Words as discussed in chapter one.

---

16 "One Star in Sight," in Crowley (1997).

17 Ibid.

18 "An Account of the A∴A∴," in Crowley (1996b), 25–26.

The Book of the Law, and the subsequent corpus of "Class A" literature, is a continuation of this agelong process.

The Curriculum for Attainment

Having established a new link through Crowley, the Secret Chiefs of the interior Sanctuary were reliant on him to promulgate their message and help humanity to attain to the next spiritual summit. Crowley therefore set up a school designed to instruct students through a rigorous curriculum—involving, among other practices, meditation, astral exploration, yoga, Qabalah, ceremonial Magick, and devotional exercises. While the demands of the grades of A∴A∴ are strenuous, and the challenges of the ordeals are unique to each individual, Crowley devised the curriculum in such a way that by following a universal (and what he considered "scientific") method, it was possible for each person whose aspirations are genuine, and efforts diligent, to advance.[19] If they could endure the burden of attainment through the grades, they would eventually speak directly with the divine in their own unique way and be reborn as a Master of the Temple, giving selfless service to humanity in the Light of the Holy One, who is described in the Holy Books of Thelema:

> I who comprehend in myself all the vast and the minute, all the bright and the dark, have mitigated the brilliance of mine unutterable splendour, sending forth V. V. V. V. V. as a ray of my light, as a messenger unto that small dark orb.[20]

---

[19] A thorough discussion on Crowley's naturalistic approach to occultism with his methods of "Scientific Illuminism" can be found in Asprem (2008) "Magic Naturalized? Negotiating Science and Occult Experience in Aleister Crowley's Scientific Illuminism," in *Aries: Journal for the Study of Western Esotericism*, 8, (Leiden: Brill), 139–165.

[20] "Liber Porta Lucis sub figurâ X," 2. In Crowley (1983), 39. Readers who are unfamiliar with such terminology are directed to study the corpus of "Class A" Thelemic literature as well as the *Vision and the Voice*. It would also benefit the reader to consult

While modeled on the original grades of the Hermetic Order of the Golden Dawn, Crowley made several revisions to that order's original initiatory scheme. He eliminated all the seemingly extravagant and convoluted rituals and sought to "re-establish the ordeals, in spirit and in truth."[21] This also meant that students were not to meet in groups or in lodges, since it was social prestige, politics, and spiritual pedigree that caused schism in the Golden Dawn. Instead, the "Outer Order" grades (see figure 3.2) were intended to prepare the fledgling aspirant through a solitary journey of the student-teacher dynamic, until he or she would partake in the mystery called "The Knowledge and Conversation of the Holy Guardian Angel." This experience granted the individual a direct communication with divine consciousness whereby the true spiritual guide became manifest.

The experience of Knowledge and Conversation of the Holy Guardian Angel marks the student's entry into Adepthood and the "Inner" Second Order of the "Rosæ Rubæ et Aureæ Crucis." Advancing to the grade of Adeptus Major ($6°=5^{□}$) and the sephira Geburah, the adept must further consolidate all he has attained thus far along the path, working in isolation, acquiring complete self-reliance, and demonstrating his comprehension of the use of the spiritual forces which his grade has granted him. Upon reaching the grade of Adeptus Exemptus ($7°=4^{□}$), situated in the Qabalistic sephira of Chesed, the adept then prepares a thesis that exemplifies his knowledge of the universe and shows himself capable to be a leader in a school of thought. He furthermore becomes wholly devoted to serving humanity in line with the principles of the order. When sufficient time has passed in which the Exempt Adept has prepared himself as a "pure vehicle for the influence of the order to which he aspires," and has decided upon the necessary steps to divest himself of all of his attachments, he becomes a Babe of the Abyss and must pass through the "Ordeal of Crossing

"An Account of the A∴A∴" in Crowley (1996b) for a general understanding of the subject.

21 *Confessions*, Crowley (1969a), 561.

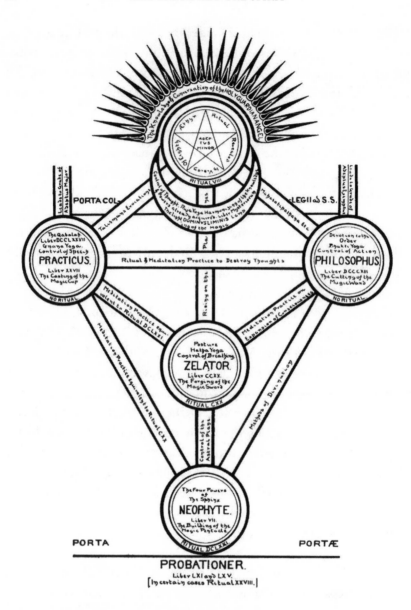

(Figure 3.2) The "Outer College" Grades of the A∴A∴ (referred to as the
G∴D∴, "Golden Dawn") consist of a series of prescribed solitary practices
intended for the student to work in private and experience individually, without
disturbances arising from the group dynamics of a lodge. (Illustration from
Liber XIII vel Graduum Montis Abiegni. First published in *The Equinox*, Vol I,
No. 3, 3–8.)

the Abyss." *All* attachments with the world must be relinquished.[22] If successful in this endeavor, the adept enters into the Third and final Triad becoming a Master of the Temple in the Order of the A∴A∴, or the S.S. ("Silver Star").[23] It is not until one successfully passes through the Ordeal of the Abyss that one enters the spiritual community of the Secret Chiefs, essentially becoming a living expression of the divine on earth.

The Governing Triad

Authority in A∴A∴ derives directly from the Secret Chiefs of the Third Order of the Silver Star above the Abyss. Referring to figure 3.3, we see that the first officer is Aiwass (as Cancellarius), the second officer Therion (as Imperator), and the third officer V. V. V. V. V. (as Præmonstrator). They serve in the sephiroth of Kether, Chokmah, and Binah, respectively. They are then reflected into the Second Order or Inner College of the Rose and Cross. Here the Præmonstrator functions in Chesed as the first officer, the Imperator is in Geburah as second officer, and the Cancellarius is in Tiphareth as the third officer. Descending to the First Order, the Outer College or Golden Dawn, the officers are reflected once again. Here, the Imperator is the first officer in Netzach, the Præmonstrator becomes the second officer in Hod, while the Cancellarius remains in the Middle Pillar as the third officer in Yesod.

Each officer further corresponds to an elemental attribution and the Mother Letters of the Hebrew Alphabet. Thus, the Cancellarius is Air (א Aleph), the Imperator is Fire (ש Shin), and the Præmonstrator is Water (מ Mem). These attributions remain constant through the three Triads.[24]

---

[22] Crowley's own initiatory experience of this is found in *The Vision and the Voice*, published in Crowley (1998a).

[23] "One Star in Sight," in Crowley (1997).

[24] An editorial footnote in Crowley (1998b), 37 reads, "the Imperator governs, the Præmonstrator teaches, and the Cancellarius records." The reader should note that, while the office necessitates the grade, the grade does not confer the office. In other

Despite the mistaken opinions of many within the Thelemic community today, there is no singular temporal "Head" of A∴A∴. Rather, all three officers govern the Order in commensurable balance. While they each have distinctive roles, they are equal to one another. The concept of a trinity of officers, and the names of their offices, follows the tradition of the Hermetic Order of the Golden Dawn.

Note again, that the positions of the three officers on the Tree of Life have no bearing on their respective status or importance (they all govern equally), but are constituted by the nature of the sephira they reflect. Finally, the roles of the officers never change. The Imperator is always the Commander-in-Chief and Governing Officer, the Præmonstrator is always the Instructing Officer, and the Cancellarius is always the Record-Keeper and Communicating Officer.

The Præmonstrator, Latin for "prophesier" or "forth-speaker," oversees all matters of doctrine and teaching as they are transmitted by the Chiefs of the A∴A∴, and observes that they remain genuine and without corruption. The Imperator, "commander" or "leader," oversees and officiates Order policy, handles the affairs of the Order in secular matters, and acts with authority to govern the Order. The Cancellarius, or "record keeper," maintains records of all Order activities and members. The Cancellarius also acts as the official contact between the Inner and Outer Orders, and performs the role of Guardian between the two.

Each of the three officers balance one another in their stations in each of the Three Orders. For example, while the Imperator acts as Second Officer in the Second Order, and oversees the general governance of the entire system, he is also responsible to keep steadfast the *Logos* of the Aeon, which is "Thelema" as it emanates from the second sephira in the Third Order, Chokmah. Likewise, he sits as the First Officer in Netzach in the Outer Order, overseeing its Temple of Initiation and appointing officers as he sees fit.[25] The Præmonstrator

---

words, one may be an Exempt Adept, but not be the Præmonstrator. However, one must be an Exempt Adept to be the Præmonstrator.

[25] Refer to "Liber Collegii Sancti sub figure CLXXXV," under "The Task of the Dominus Liminis." Crowley (1996b), 51.

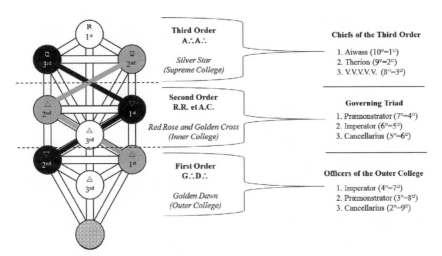

(Figure 3.3) The officers of A∴A∴ and their stations are reflected in each of the Three Orders. The positions of the officers are based upon the reflection of the Three Primary Elements as they are positioned in the Supernal Triad on the Tree of Life, along with one of three "Mother Letters" of the Hebrew alphabet (Aleph [א], Mem [מ] and Shin [ש]). Hence, in Kether is Element Air (△, א), in Chokmah is Element Fire (△, ש), and in Binah is Element Water (▽, מ).

holds chaste to his link with the Third Order with the message as embodied in V. V. V. V. V. in Binah,[26] while maintaining the bounty of his natural position in Chesed through the Splendour that is the reflective on his station in Hod in the Outer Order. The Cancellarius maintains a strict balance of force on the Middle Pillar between Kether, Tiphareth, and Yesod.

The Imprimatur and Publication

The final element of the A∴A∴ that warrants discussion is that, since it is a secret organization of aspirants and adepts who work in solitude, its primary channel of visibility to the world is through the publication of its teachings. After its official formation in 1907, the A∴A∴ was publicly announced in 1909 in *The Equinox*, a massive periodical,

---

[26] See chapter four for a discussion of V. V. V. V. V.

originally published semi-annually, that would grow to ten issues in five years.

Official Order documents bear an "Imprimatur" (see figure 3.4) labeling the publication as an "A∴A∴ Publication," followed by a designated letter to denote one of five "classes." Any publication that does not bear the Imprimatur is not considered official. "Class A" documents have already been mentioned. They are considered divinely inspired writings penned not by Crowley, but "represent the utterance of an Adept entirely beyond the criticism of even the visible Head of the Organization."[27] "Class B" are designated works of "ordinary scholarship," while "Class C" are to "be regarded rather as suggestive than anything else." "Class D" documents are reserved for official instruction for ritual practice according to the A∴A∴ curriculum. A designation of "Class E" was added later and is intended for promulgation in the format of "manifestos, broadsides, epistles, and other public statements."[28] In an effort to eschew pretension and fraudulence (common traits that Crowley claimed were often found amongst occultists), *The Equinox* periodicals were initially sold only at the cost it took to produce them. Crowley insisted that the A∴A∴ would never ask for monetary gain for its tutelage:

> The Brothers of the A∴A∴ have set their faces against all charlatanism, whether of miracle-mongering or obscurantism; and all those persons who have sought reputation or wealth by such means may expect ruthless exposure, whether of their vanity or their dishonesty; for by no gentler means can they be taught.[29]

Although Crowley often sought financial assistance from his supporters, especially in the last two-thirds of his life after he depleted his inheritance, he always tried to keep his need for money separate from

---

[27] See "Introduction," in Crowley (1983), 262.

[28] Ibid.

[29] *The Equinox*, Vol I, No. 1, in Crowley (1972a), 2.

A∴A∴   Publication in Class B

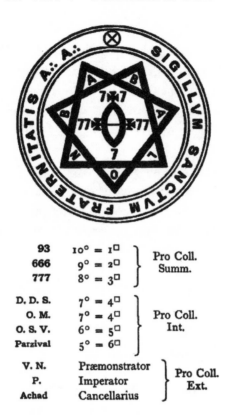

93	10° = 1▢	
666	9° = 2▢	Pro Coll. Summ.
777	8° = 3▢	
D. D. S.	7° = 4▢	
O. M.	7° = 4▢	Pro Coll. Int.
O. S. V.	6° = 5▢	
Parzival	5° = 6▢	
V. N.	Præmonstrator	
P.	Imperator	Pro Coll. Ext.
Achad	Cancellarius	

(**Figure 3.4**) **The A∴A∴ Imprimatur** used by Crowley and his successors to designate official publications includes the Seal of the Order, in addition to the document classification (Class A–E) for the benefit of the adherent. Thus there should be no confusion as to the various levels of interpretation available to the aspirant. In the "signature area," the various initials and numbers identify the grade and position of the officer on the Tree of Life. "O.M.," for example, is Crowley's magical motto for his grade of Adeptus Exemptus (7°=4°) and "O.S.V." his motto for Adeptus Major and role of Imperator. "Pro Coll. Summ." indicates "From the Supreme College" (Third Order). "Pro Coll. Int." means "From the Inner College" (Second Order). "Pro Coll. Ext." implies "From the Outer College" (First Order).

teachings related to the A∴A∴. In "One Star in Sight" (1921), he proclaimed that all spiritual teaching must be free from monetary gain:

> There is however an absolute prohibition to accept money or
> other material reward, directly or indirectly, in respect of any ser-
> vice connected with the Order, for personal profit or advantage.
> The penalty is immediate expulsion, with no possibility of rein-
> statement on any terms soever.[30]

The important role that publications played for Crowley, and particularly for his A∴A∴ movement, have been mentioned in the introduction. Books and literature were not only of significant spiritual value to get his message out, but publication is of monumental worth for a religious movement in general. As we will see in Part II, the literature surrounding the Thelemic movement became the single driving force in the Outer that influenced the Thelemic movement as it functions today.

A Temple from the East: the Ordo Templi Orientis

The Ordo Templi Orientis is the most visible organization attached to Thelema today.[31] It was started by Austrian industrialist Carl Kellner (1850–1905), and German singer and journalist Theodor Reuss (1855–1923). As mentioned earlier, the O.T.O. originally began as an attempt by Kellner to form an *academia masonica* in Germany with the intention that a number of different Masonic rites would be collected into one system. O.T.O. historian Richard Kaczynski points out that this was not surprising for its time, but rather that the concept of a "college of rites" was a growing trend in the Masonic world.[32] However, such a college had not yet been operated in German Freemasonry.

---

[30] "One Star in Sight," in Crowley (1997), 495.

[31] For a complete history of the O.T.O. up to Aleister Crowley's lifetime, see Kaczynski (2012) *Forgotten Templars: The Untold Origins of Ordo Templi Orientis* (Self-published by Author).

[32] A "Grand College of Rites" was opened, for example, in the Grand Orient de

It would appear that Kellner's O.T.O. was only an idea in 1895, but by September of 1902, Theodor Reuss was given a charter by English Freemason and occultist John Yarker (1833–1913) to establish "The Sovereign Sanctuary 33°–95° etc., in and for the Empire of Germany." Yarker authorized him to work the Rite of Memphis and Misraïm, and the Ancient and Accepted Scottish Rite.[33] Yarker was considered a powerful force in the Masonic world of his day, and was responsible for the growth of Freemasonry by issuing charters to a number of aspiring budding masons.

The O.T.O. would develop into an initiatory society that placed an emphasis on sexual magic. It was not surprising that a sexual element featured into the symbolism and practices taught within the O.T.O. For one, Kellner was genuinely familiar with Eastern practices of Indian yoga, and it appears that tantric yoga philosophy may have influenced his leanings towards incorporating sexual teachings into the O.T.O.[34] He is also thought to have been either a member of, or in some way close to, the Hermetic Brotherhood of Light, an occult organization that appropriated the sexual magic teachings of African-American spiritualist and occultist Paschal Beverley Randolph (1825–1875).[35] Theodor Reuss made sex central to the O.T.O. system, designing its upper degrees to instruct its members in the sexual secret of the universe. The focus on sex would later be openly acknowledged in the

---

France, Scotland already had a Supreme Council of Rites, and Arthur Edward Waite was seeking a "Secret Council of Rites." Kaczynski (2012), 185.

[33] Ibid., 196.

[34] See Carl Kellner (1896) *Yoga Eine Skizze über den psycho-physiologischen Teil der alten indischen Yogalehre* (Munich: International Congress of Psychology), shown in Kaczynski (2012), 79. It is not clear however whether the sexual element in the O.T.O. came from Kellner or from Theodor Reuss. See Kaczynski (2012), 245.

[35] For a biographical sketch of Paschal Beverley Randolph, see Patrick Deveney (1997) *Paschal Beverley Randolph: A Nineteenth-Century Black American Spiritualist, Rosicrucian and Sex Magician* (Albany: SUNY Press). A history of the Hermetic Brotherhood of Luxor is found in Godwin, Chanel, and Deveney (1995) *The Hermetic Brotherhood of Luxor: Initiatic and Historical Documents of an Order of Practical Occultism* (York Beach: Samuel Weiser, Inc). For Kellner's involvement with the H.B. of L., see Kaczynski (2012), 249–250.

1912 Jubilee edition of the Order's publication, *The Oriflamme*, which stated that the O.T.O. holds:

> the KEY which opens up all Masonic and Hermetic secrets, namely, the teaching of sexual magic, and this teaching explains, without exception, all the secrets of Nature, all the symbolism of Freemasonry and all systems of religion.[36]

It was around this time that Aleister Crowley came into the fold of the O.T.O. because of his publication of *The Book of Lies*, as mentioned. Reuss essentially approached Crowley, accused him of publishing the central secret of the Order, and bound him to secrecy by initiating him into the IX°, the "Sovereign Sanctuary of the Gnosis." Crowley was chartered as Grand Master General in England, and would succeed Reuss as the "Outer Head of the Order." Under Crowley's authority, the Order would adopt the principles of *The Book of the Law* and serve as the social device to promote Thelema.[37]

It was Crowley's original idea that the O.T.O., "would be a sort of training ground for the A∴A∴," claiming that, when people become "ripe, they are joined to the chain."[38] He wrote that, "the Law cometh from the A∴A∴, not from the O.T.O.," however the O.T.O. "is but the first of the great religious bodies to accept this Law officially, and its whole Ritual has been revised and reconstituted in accordance with this decision."[39] The O.T.O. proved to serve a function that the A∴A∴ could not. It was able to make a more public outreach to a larger number of people to the end of further establishing Thelema as a religion. As Crowley historian Marco Pasi describes it, "[b]etween

---

[36] English translation originally quoted in Francis King (1970) and referenced in Bogdan (2006), 215.

[37] A comprehensive overview of the O.T.O. is found in Pasi (2005) "Ordo Templi Orientis," in *Dictionary of Gnosis & Western Esotericism*, Wouter J. Hanegraaff (ed.) (Leiden: Brill), 898–906.

[38] Crowley to Charles Stansfeld Jones, dated July 2, 1919, O.T.O. Archives.

[39] Crowley (2007b), 179.

the individualist A∴A∴ and an O.T.O. which, at least according to Crowley's intentions, could reach the 'great mass,' the latter had to be given preference."[40] However, Crowley never seemed to prioritize the O.T.O. over the A∴A∴, as will be shown later when we examine his American period between 1915 and 1919. Yet, due to the terms of Crowley's will regarding his literary estate, nearly forty years after the Beast's death it would appear that the O.T.O. would take immediate precedence when the Thelemic movement established its copyright ownership in the U.S. in 1985.[41]

The Path in Eternity

While the O.T.O. is rooted in traditional Freemasonry, it has also developed into its own unique system, replete with Thelemic symbolism. The spiritual framework of the O.T.O. is distinct from the A∴A∴. Where the A∴A∴ follows "The Path of Return,"[42] the O.T.O. is referred to as "The Path in Eternity."[43] The A∴A∴ offers a curriculum designed for practical instruction and solitary initiatory work in spiritual terms.[44] The O.T.O. initiates the candidate in the natural world; instructs its members through a system of *karma yoga* (i.e., service and duty in the world); and provides tools that encourage self-sustenance and responsibility alongside principles of fraternity and community. In short, O.T.O. initiations aim to refine individual members into efficient and functional members of society. Like A∴A∴, the O.T.O. is divided into three "Triads," each including several degrees symbolizing

---

[40] Pasi (2014), 27.

[41] This history is explored in Part II.

[42] "The Path of the Great Return" implies the initiate moving upward along the Tree of Life, from the material plane of Malkuth back to the spiritual source of the Divine. While this is an oversimplification, please see Gunther (2014) for an in-depth analysis.

[43] Crowley (1986) *Magick Without Tears*, 123.

[44] By "spiritual," I refer to the individual, internal, and mystical comprehension of one's relationship to the divine.

various stages of life. In his autobiography, Crowley described the initial scheme of the O.T.O. initiations:

> The main objects of the instruction were two. It was firstly necessary to explain the universe and the relations of human life therewith. Secondly, to instruct every man how best to adapt his life to the cosmos and to develop his faculties to the utmost advantage. I accordingly constructed a series of rituals, Minerval, Man, Magician, Master-Magician, Perfect Magician and Perfect Initiate, which should illustrate the course of human life in its largest philosophical aspect.[45]

The above description outlines the third (or beginning) triad of the O.T.O., the "Man of Earth" or first series of M∴M∴M∴ (*Mysteria Mystica Maxima*). The candidate begins his or her initiatory journey as a soul seeking incarnation. Through subsequent lessons of birth, life, and death, the initiate is brought to a point of "annihilation" in the degree of "Perfect Initiate."[46]

Any person "of full age, free, and of good report" is entitled to the Man of Earth degrees; however, subsequent degrees require invitation, as they lead the candidate into the second or "Lovers Triad." These later initiations are described by Crowley as elaborations of the Second degree, which represents "Life."[47] He writes, "since in a single ceremony it is hardly possible to sketch, even in the briefest outline, the Teaching of Initiates with regard to Life. The Rituals V°–IX° are then instructions to the Candidate as to how he should conduct himself; and they confer upon him, gradually, the Magical Secrets which make him Master of Life."[48] Crowley here uses his usual style of employing ambiguous language to veil what he is truly saying. He is of course referring to a technique concerning the central magical secret of the O.T.O., which is sexual in nature. Its practical import is reserved for initiates of the

---

[45] Crowley (1969a) *Confessions*, 700.

[46] Crowley (1986) *Magick Without Tears*, 123.

[47] Ibid.

[48] Ibid., 123–124.

IX° in the "Sanctuary of the Gnosis," the pinnacle of the O.T.O. system which lies in the third and final triad called "The Hermit."[49]

The central secret and what it entails will not be covered in any depth here. However, it is worth noting that the entirety of the O.T.O. system can be summarized as follows: the entering candidate is first prepared with a set of allegories through dramatic ritual in the Man of Earth degrees (0°–P∴I∴). These degrees are intended to assist the candidate to govern himself within the world according to his own unique nature. Upon demonstrating the necessary proclivities towards enthusiasm, inspiration, love, and service to the Order, the member may be invited into the bridging degree of Knight of East and West (K.E.W.), where he is expected to "devote his life to the Establishment of the Law of Thelema."[50] Next, the candidate is invited into the Lovers Triad (V°–VII°). Here she is required to dedicate a substantial portion of her time in selfless service to further the cause of the O.T.O. While all this groundwork is laid, usually over the course of decades, the initiate is being prepared through a process of *karma yoga*—learning patience, discipline, devotion, and temperance—so that he or she may effectively understand and execute the central secret, which is formally introduced on a practical level in the VII°, expanded upon in the VIII°, and disclosed fully in the IX°.

The Structure of O.T.O.'s Government

The way in which the O.T.O. is intended to function as a Thelemic organization is outlined in several source documents. In "Liber CXCIV: An Intimation with Reference to the Constitution of the Order," first published in *The Blue Equinox* in 1919,[51] it is implied in the introductory paragraph that the O.T.O. is meant as a model for a Thelemic society:

---

[49] There is a X°, but it is an administrative title, as discussed below.

[50] Crowley (2007b) "Liber CXCIV: An Intimation with Reference to the Constitution of the Order," in *The Blue Equinox*, 242.

[51] Ibid., 239–246.

This is the Constitution and Government of our Holy Order; by the study of its Balance you may yourself come to apprehension of how to rule your own life. For, in True Things, all are but images one of another; man is but a map of the universe, and Society is but the same on a larger scale.[52]

The members of the lowest tier, the Man of Earth "take no share in the Government of the Order." Members in the Man of Earth operate almost exclusively at local levels, participating in events where their degree is not restricted, learning about Thelema and the O.T.O., and incorporating the lessons from their initiations into their personal lives with the aim of functioning in a higher capacity.

It is at the V°, the first degree of the Lovers Triad, that the welfare of the Order in general is expected to become a concern for members. Initiates of the V° form councils that aim to extend beauty and harmony among members and facilitate fraternity within their local groups.[53] It is at this point that a person is eligible to take part in the government of the Order and join the Senate. An administrative body called the Electoral College consists of a council of members holding the degree of Knight of the Red Eagle. They oversee the operations and well-being of the Man of Earth degrees; charter local O.T.O. Camps, Oases, or Lodges; appoint local Masters of such bodies; approve the advancement of members to the V°; and appoint two IX° Revolutionaries.

Above this is the VI° and Grand Inquisitor Commander, who may sit on another council called the Grand Tribunal which deals with formal disputes within the Order.

Next lies the VII°, which is a transition between the Second and First Triads of the O.T.O. VII° members act as Sovereign Grand Inspectors General. They travel and report on the activities of local Lodges to the administrative head, the National Grand Master General, also known as the Supreme and Holy King of the X°. Members of the

---

[52] Ibid., 241.

[53] O.T.O. groups are known as "Camps," "Oases," and "Lodges." Such designations imply frequency of activity among other characteristics and requirements.

VII° are also given episcopal duties in the Ecclesia Gnostica Catholica, and may administer clerical ceremonies such as marriages, baptisms, confirmations, and ordinations of clergy.

The VIII° is described as a "Philosophical Body," with its members "being fully instructed in the Principles of the Order save in one point only."[54] These members of the Areopagus meet on a regular basis to discuss Order business and are concerned with executive functions concerning the Order as a whole.

The IX° initiates, being at the culmination of the O.T.O. system, are said to "move unseen and unrecognized [...] subtly and loftily leading us into the mysteries of the True Light," and that their primary duty is to "practice the Theurgy and Thaumaturgy of the grade."[55]

The Grand Master General, or Supreme and Most Holy King, holds the X°. He or she is the administrative head of any country with a "national section," called a "Kingdom."[56] The X° is therefore mostly an administrative title.[57] A Kingdom is established when there are enough members within a given country to fill the aforementioned governing bodies and the member base is large enough to operate on a national scale. The Grand Master is appointed by the International Head of the Order, called the "Outer Head of the Order," O.H.O., or "Frater Superior." The O.H.O. oversees all Order business and is the administrative head for the international section, or the areas that are not yet instituted as Kingdoms.[58]

---

[54] Ibid., 243.

[55] Ibid., 244.

[56] For example, as of this writing (2018), the O.T.O. has established five national sections in these countries: the United States, the United Kingdom, Australia, Italy, and Croatia, each with a presiding X°, "Grand Master General" or "Supreme and Holy King."

[57] It should not be considered as purely administrative, as the Supreme and Most Holy King of the X° is granted initiatory authority by the O.H.O. to conduct initiations from 0° to VII° under his or her own name within his or her Kingdom.

[58] Countries that are not yet Kingdoms are under the jurisdiction of "International Headquarters" (IHQ). Such a country may have a designated supervisor called "Frater Superior's Representative" (FSR).

⁂

These first two chapters have been necessary to lay both historical and theoretical groundwork for the discussion that follows. What I have sought in these opening pages is a clarification of key terms. It is often the case with writing history that the narratives and the figures associated with them become so interwoven that a clear story of events becomes nearly impossible to trace without background details.

The next two chapters of Part I will further illustrate the theoretical dimension of Thelema as developed in the A∴A∴ and the O.T.O. Looking more closely at some of the doctrinal developments that were informed by Crowley's visionary revelations will help clarify his original concept of the functions of the A∴A∴ and the O.T.O., as well as their relationship with each other.

CHAPTER FOUR

In the Name of the Secret Master

*The Unveiling of Thelemic Doctrine in the
Magical Workings of Aleister Crowley*

In V. V. V. V. V. is the Great Work perfect.

Therefore none is that pertaineth not to V. V. V. V. V.

In any may he manifest; yet in one hath he chosen to manifest; and
this one hath given His ring as a Seal of Authority to the Work of
the A∴A∴ through the colleagues of FRATER PERDURABO.

—*The Book of Lies,* "Corn Beef Hash"

A COMMONLY OVERLOOKED ASPECT about the emergence of Thelema as a comprehensive system of magical development is that, while
The Book of the Law serves as its benchmark, there is a great deal of
source literature to suggest that its philosophy and doctrine evolved
over the course of time. This would make sense since Crowley had not
yet attained to the pinnacle of his own initiatory development until
some years after the reception of *Liber AL*.[1] Therefore, we must think
of Thelema as a spiritual path *beginning* in 1904, but going through
stages of doctrinal development, even as Crowley progressed to the
apex of the A∴A∴ system.[2] We must consider that the writings of

---

[1] By "pinnacle," I refer to his initial entrance into the last three grades of the A∴A∴.
Crowley's full comprehension of Crossing the Abyss and attaining to the Grade of
Magister Templi (8°=3□) occurred in 1909. He would become a Magus (9°=2□) in
1915. It would not be until the closing months of 1923 and through February 1924
that Crowley would complete his initiation into the topmost grade of the A∴A∴,
Ipsissimus (10°=1□). See Kaczynski (2010), 407.

[2] Although Ipsissimus is the highest grade, the Adept's function as such seems to be
beyond matters associated in any way with the lower grades, whereas the Magus has

the first group of Holy Books in 1907, the visionary experiences in the Algerian desert in 1909, the next group of Holy Books in 1911, the magical workings between the years 1911–1918, and the publication of his spiritual writings throughout the remainder of his life were all parts of his own initiation. In other words, he was receiving more doctrinal insight into Thelema as time passed.[3] The majority of the literary corpus of Thelema's teachings was produced in the second decade of the twentieth century. The bulk of this material is explored in the following chapter and will help substantiate Crowley's belief that a link had been established with the Secret Chiefs.

After Liber AL vel Legis

Aleister Crowley was initially shocked and confused by the Cairo experience. Although he found himself rather flattered by his own magical abilities, he considered a great majority of the commands given in the text—such as translating it "into all tongues" and fortifying an island with weaponry—to be not only unrealistic, but absurd. Unsure of what to make of Liber AL vel Legis he set it aside for the time-being and went on with married life.

Rose gave birth to their daughter, Nuit Ma Ahathoor Hecate Sappho Jezebel Lilith in July of 1904,[4] and Crowley spent the remainder of the year concerned with his writing and poetry and vacationing in Switzerland. In May of 1905, he traveled to the Far East, where he would set off on the ambitious endeavor to climb Kangchenjunga, a Himalayan mountain that is the third highest peak in the world.[5] The climb ended in a bitter failure, with several climbing comrades perishing on the

---

specific duties such as proclaiming a spiritual Law to humankind. See "One Star in Sight," in Crowley (1997) Liber ABA, 490–492.

[3] Crowley's magical experiments throughout this period are too many to be detailed. Only the more significant workings that demonstrate the development of Thelema will be explored in this chapter.

[4] Kaczynski (2010), 138.

[5] Ibid., 145.

journey, and Crowley on the receiving end of blame for not attempting a rescue. He sojourned with Rose and their daughter in Calcutta, and the family then traveled throughout China for the remainder of the year. In March of 1906, he sent Rose and Lilith back home across the continent, while he continued with his travels in Asia and into North America, across Canada, landing in New York on May 15. He then sailed back to England, arriving in Liverpool on June 2, albeit with the most awful news a father could receive—his daughter Lilith was dead. Bearing the burden of her daughter's premature death due to typhoid, the devastated Rose Crowley coped less than constructively. She sank into alcohol abuse, and Crowley became neglectful of their marriage by retreating into his writing and magical studies. The event of Lilith's death spawned problems for the couple that would ultimately end their marriage.

⋖⋗

Forming the "Chain"

Later in that same month of June 1906, Crowley was visited by former Golden Dawn colleague George Cecil Jones, who encouraged him to take up his magical practices once again. Over a series of discussions about the Work, the two men began formulating plans to found a new magical order on July 29, 1906.[6] While Crowley sensed he had become an Exempt Adept ($7°=4^{\square}$) during his travels through China, thus reaching the pinnacle of the Second Order of the Golden Dawn, his meetings with Jones seem to have reinforced this feeling. He was now about to make the leap into the Third and final Triad, the Silver Star, to become a Magister Templi ($8°=3^{\square}$).

His magical practices were back in full swing and were producing positive results. Then on Sunday, March 17, 1907, almost three years to the day after the Cairo experience, Crowley recorded the following in his diary:

---

[6] Ibid., 164–165.

Received from V. V. V. V. V. the Word of ☉ in ♈: Catena. This is alike the Chain of Penance and that of Power. it shall therefore be my task to form a chain of brethren by *tapas*.[7]

As alluded to above, "Catena" translates from Latin to "Chain." The "Chain of Penance" in this instance may refer to a link formed from the Secret Chiefs through a chain of adepts, who are in service to the Great Work to teach humanity methods of spiritual attainment. This diary entry is significant for two reasons. First, this is the "Word of the Equinox," a phrase of spiritual significance divined biannually on each Equinox and delivered to Neophytes in the A∴A∴.[8] Given that this entry is dated to the Spring Equinox prior to the official establishment of the A∴A∴ (which occurred later that year in November), this diary note can be understood as an intimation of the founding of the new magical order.

Secondly, Crowley remarks that he received the Word "*from* V. V. V. V. V." (emphasis added). This abbreviation has been understood by many authors to refer to Crowley's 8°=3□ magical motto, "Vi Veri Vniversum Vivus Vici."[9] However, the diary entry cited above states that he received the Word *from* V. V. V. V. V., an intelligence other than his own mind. This is a matter of great significance, as it pertains to a key doctrinal element that will be examined throughout this chapter. The fact that he makes this entry so early on in the development of his system suggests that he was already aware of a higher intelligence attempting to make contact with him. Furthermore, the praeterhuman intelligence from whom he received the Word was none other than the Chief Adept he would later consider to be the "Secret Master," whose words are revealed within the Holy Books of Thelema. As it is written in *Liber Porta Lucis sub figurâ X*:

---

[7] AC Diary, March 17, 1907. O.T.O. Archives.

[8] The Word of the Equinox was received after Crowley composed himself in Holy Meditation.

[9] *Latin*, "By the power of Truth, I, while living, have conquered the universe." See Kaczynski (2010), 172–175.

I who comprehend in myself all the vast and the minute, all the bright and the dark, have mitigated the brilliance of mine unutterable splendour, sending forth V. V. V. V. V. as a ray of my light, as a messenger unto that small dark orb.[10]

Crowley would only occasionally make references to V. V. V. V. V. in writings outside of the Holy Books, and usually in a messianic context. It is thus a mistake to assume that V. V. V. V. V. refers exclusively to Crowley's motto as a Master of the Temple. A close reading of the Holy Books of Thelema and an observance of the Order teachings suggests that V. V. V. V. V. is an independent divine intelligence altogether, or rather *the* divine intelligence who communicates with His disciples.[11] Crowley would later describe this Adept, who resides in the spiritual community called the A∴A∴, in *The Equinox*, Volume I:

This society is in the communion of those who have most capacity for light; they are united in truth, and their Chief is the Light of the World himself, V. V. V. V. V., the One Anointed in Light, the single teacher for the human race, the Way, the Truth, and the Life.[12]

The year 1907 served as a significant turning point for the development of Thelema. The bulk of the Holy Books were written between

---

[10] "Liber Porta Lucis sub figurâ X," 2, in Crowley (1983), 39.

[11] The motto of a Master of the Temple is intrinsically linked to the Secret Name given to the aspirant upon attaining to the Knowledge and Conversation of the Holy Guardian Angel. This Name is first given at the grade of Adeptus Minor (Within). The true consummation occurs between the Adept and the Angel after the Master of the Temple has crossed the Abyss, entered the Holy community of the Third Order, and established a final unification with the Angel—to the end that he or she becomes indistinguishable from God. Above the Abyss, all is one without distinction. While V. V. V. V. V. may have been an abbreviation of a Latin phrase that Crowley chose as his motto as a Master of the Temple, he was also thence united with the Chief Adept V. V. V. V. V. See Gunther (2014), 350–351.

[12] Crowley (1972a) Vol. I, No.1, 8.

October and December, seven months after the first Word of the Equinox was received. Not only was the A∴A∴ officially established as a teaching order, but it was the beginning of what would evolve into a fully developed religious movement.

Announcement Through Publication: The Equinox (1909)

Being assured that he had formed a link to the Secret Chiefs—and then subsequently establishing a school for the A∴A∴ by which students were taught the methods of attaining to the next spiritual precipice— Crowley now had to somehow reach the general public to get his message out. As previously mentioned, the A∴A∴ is not composed of physical lodges and its members do not meet. It does not charge dues and is operated solely by private communication between instructor and student. The way in which it could announce itself as a presence to the public was through publication. Crowley therefore began to print a biannual periodical called *The Equinox* to promote the Order.

The Equinox featured articles, poems, short stories, and official instructive documents. These documents ranged from the "Class A" holy literature to official ritual instruction in "Class D." *The Equinox* therefore served as the official journal for the A∴A∴, making publication the primary means to recruit new aspirants. The ten numbers of Volume I contain some 4,000 pages.

The Thelemic "Book of Revelation": The Vision and the Voice (1909)

One of the most fascinating magical accomplishments of Aleister Crowley was a collection of visionary experiences he recorded and later published as *The Vision and the Voice (Liber CDXVIII)*.[13] These workings adopted the Enochian system of Angelic magic first discovered by sixteenth-century seer Edward Kelly (1555–1597) and mathematician, astronomer, and philosopher John Dee (1527–1609).[14] *The Vision*

---

[13] Crowley (1998a).

[14] John Dee was an advisor to Queen Elizabeth I. He devoted a great deal of his

and the Voice can be understood, among many things, as the Thelemic "Book of Revelation." Crowley himself considered its importance second only to *The Book of the Law*.[15] The subject matter deals with highly elaborate apocalyptic visions revealing core doctrinal tenets, including the millenarian advent of a New Aeon, the initiatory experience of Crossing the Abyss, and the complex principles associated with Babalon and her consort The Beast. In December 1909, Crowley journeyed across the Algerian desert in North Africa accompanied by his student Victor Benjamin Neuburg. On each consecutive day, he called the Enochian Æthyrs one by one, placing a shew stone against his forehead and entering into a revelatory vision occupied by Angels and spiritual beings. Each Æthyr housed imagery and messages of immense initiatory insight.

The Vision and the Voice is significant to this discussion for two reasons. First, it gives the reader an insight into Crowley's own initiatory path and understanding of himself. Second, *The Vision and the Voice* outlines several important doctrinal aspects about Thelemic spirituality and the shifting paradigms of the New Aeon.

---

life to studying alchemy and Hermetic philosophy. After becoming acquainted with Edward Kelly, who impressed Dee with his abilities in spirit mediumship, the two men began experimenting with summoning angels using a magic mirror. The results produced a discovery in an Angelic language called Enochian, along with a highly complex method codified by Dee to call upon such Angels. Numerous works have been written on Dee's system, and readers must be cautious with some of the more unreliable sources on the subject. For academic work on Dee, see Deborah Harkness (1999) *John Dee's Conversations with Angels* (Cambridge: Cambridge University Press), György E. Szönyi (2004) *John Dee's Occultism* (Albany: SUNY Press), Nicholas Clulee (1988) *John Dee's Natural Philosophy* (London: Routledge), and Stephen Cluclas (ed.) (2006) *John Dee: Interdisciplinary Studies in English Renaissance Thought* (Dordrecht: Springer). Egil Asprem has more recently released work on the Golden Dawn's and Crowley's use of Enochian in Asprem (2012) *Arguing with Angels: Enochian Magic and Modern Occulture* (Albany: SUNY Press). For those interested in learning the system itself as a practitioner, see Geoffrey James (1998) *The Enochian Magick of Dr. John Dee: The Most Powerful System of Magick in Its Original, Unexpurgated Form* (St. Paul: Llewellyn Publications).

[15] Crowley (1998a) *The Vision and the Voice*, "Editor's Introduction," ix.

The Vision and the Voice is paramount to understanding Crowley's magical development and thus the development of the spiritual movement of Thelema. The visions display Crowley's confrontation with the self in terms of magical and spiritual enlightenment. As historian Alex Owen has said:

> In mundane terms, however, it is clear that Aleister Crowley's magical work was intrinsically bound up with the articulation of what we have come to understand as a modern sense of self. Certainly, one reading of his North African experience is that advanced ritual magic invited a radical "modernist" decentering of the subject, even as it pursued the occult goal of repairing a split and divided self.[16]

In order to interpret Crowley's ideas about Thelema after the experiences in Algiers, it is crucial to understand how he viewed his initiation and what that meant for his own awareness about himself as a vessel for the Secret Chiefs and their message.

The attainment to the grade of Master of the Temple changed the way he understood his purpose. The revelations produced from his experiences in Algiers further intimated that he had a mission to communicate a spiritual directive to humankind. Further, with regard to Thelema in general—and not just for Crowley's sake—the prophetic message contained in the text significantly advanced the doctrines of the New Aeon, which had been ushered in with the reception of *Liber AL vel Legis* in 1904. But Crowley had already been given intimations of this as early as 1900 in Mexico, when he scryed the first two Æthyrs.

---

[16] Owen (2004), 219. Owen is skeptical of Crowley's success, believing that he failed to cross the Abyss, that "Crowley's work was fatally flawed," and even concluded that he "decorated the left-hand Path with the forbidden names of dark power to produce an influential demonic Magick." While Owen echoes the common procrustean interpretations of Crowley with which many readers are so familiar, her analysis at least succeeds in identifying Crowley's experience in Algiers to be situated within the modernist approach to confronting and re-evaluating the self that typifies contemporary esoteric thought.

In the 29th Æthyr, for example, we see the Old Aeon of the patriarchal slain god exclaim:

> No! no! no! All is changed, all is confounded; naught is ordered: the white is stained with blood: the black is kissed of the Christ! Return! Return! It is a new chaos that thou findest here: chaos for thee: for us it is the skeleton of a New Truth![17]

This chaos, this "skeleton of a New Truth" was later revealed in the North African desert on November 25, 1909, as a new paradigm for humankind, "And there comes a voice: It is the dawn of the æon. The æons of cursing are passed away. Force and fire, strength and sight, these are for the servants of the Star and the Snake."[18]

The Vision and the Voice did more than announce the dispensational coming of a new age for humanity. It also delivered key doctrinal points that would be further elucidated by Crowley for years to come. While most of these cannot be explored in any detail here, it will help to briefly outline two examples.

Upon reaching the 10th Æthyr, Crowley was confronted by an embodiment of evil at the frontier of the Abyss. He described this entity later in his *Confessions*:

> The Abyss is empty of being; it is filled with all possible forms, each equally inane, each therefore evil in the only true sense of the word—that is, meaningless but malignant, in so far as it craves to become real. These forms swirl senselessly into haphazard heaps like dust devils, and each such chance aggregation asserts itself to be an individual and shrieks, "I am I!" though aware all the time that its elements have no true bond; so that the slightest disturbance dissipates the delusion [...][19]

---

[17] Crowley (1998a), 43.

[18] Ibid., 61. These words are reminiscent of *Liber AL*, II:20–21.

[19] Crowley (1969a) *Confessions*, 622.

In other words, the Abyss is a collection of the impressions of the faculty of reason, all the constructs created in us by the ego and personality, coalesced in the form of a demon called Choronzon. Doctrinally speaking, "crossing the Abyss" requires initiates to divest themselves of all attachments: materially, intellectually, and spiritually. Upon passing successfully through the Abyss, one annihilates the "old" self, and enters into equilibrium with the course of nature. Success in this Ordeal places the Adept in the sephira of Binah, the Supernal Mother, and the Third Order of A∴A∴, becoming a Master of the Temple. The Adept is newly born in the "City of the Pyramids" under the "Night of Pan." The Master of the Temple swears to "interpret every phenomenon as a particular dealing of God with my soul,"[20] rendering the Adept one with the divine as a living god incarnate on earth. Those who refuse to relinquish themselves at the frontier of the Abyss when confronted with Choronzon are thrown backward onto the Tree of Life and become a Brother of the Left-hand Path, condemned to self-aggrandizement and isolation.

Another key doctrinal point revealed in *The Vision and the Voice* sheds light on the principle of Babalon, the Whore of Abominations. She is described in the 5th Æthyr:

> And a voice cometh: Thou didst seek the remedy of sorrow; therefore all sorrow is thy portion. This is that which is written: "God hath laid upon him the iniquity of us all." For as thy blood is mingled in the cup of BABALON, so is thine heart the universal heart.[21]

The powerful imagery of the "Whore Babylon" is ingrained in the psyche of most Westerners as the harbinger of the coming of an evil Anti-Christ, the destroyer of the world, as depicted in the biblical *Book of Revelation*. In *Liber CDXVIII*, however, Babalon embod-

---

[20] Ibid., 590.
[21] Crowley (1998a), 205.

ies the divine feminine, the Great Mother of all living things.[22] Here "whoredom" represents her willingness to indiscriminately take all living beings into her fold. Those who dedicate their lives to the Great Work in selfless service have given every drop of their blood to fill her chalice, the Holy Grail.[23] Here, *The Vision and the Voice* incorporates a *mysterium oppositorum* by which a symbol commonly portrayed as negative is inverted to be reinterpreted as a sacred and positive thing.[24]

The above descriptions of the Abyss and Babalon are merely brief overviews of a number of very deep, comprehensive subjects of Thelemic doctrine unveiled in *The Vision and the Voice*.

Recruitment for a Magical Order: The Rites of Eleusis (1910)

Having attained significant insights through his explorations of the Enochian Æthyrs in Algiers, Crowley returned to England and sought to place the A∴A∴ front and center on his agenda. *The Equinox* had already been in publication since the spring of 1909, and the third issue of Volume I was due in spring of 1910. In addition to other efforts, Crowley wrote a series of dramatic rituals to help promote the A∴A∴. "The Rites of Eleusis," as mentioned in chapter two, were ceremonial plays associated with the planetary spheres meant to be invoked in sequence.[25] Crowley intended these to show that the A∴A∴ didn't exist solely on paper, but that it was an organization of serious and dedicated students of Magick and mysticism. The Rites were open to the public and performed for seven weeks at Caxton Hall in London.

---

[22] The variation in the spelling of Babylon/Babalon is explained in *The Vision and the Voice* in the 12th Æthyr, Ibid, 148–153.

[23] The cup frequently represents a feminine symbol in magical literature.

[24] This "mystery of opposites" is a common theme within Thelema and is crucial to understanding its philosophy as well as its practical application. A thorough discussion on this topic is found in Gunther (2014) *The Angel and the Abyss*.

[25] The Rites can be found in *The Equinox* I, 5 and Crowley (1990) *The Rites of Eleusis* (Thame, Oxon: Mandrake).

After the performance of the Rites of Eleusis backfired in the yellow press, they were never performed again in Crowley's lifetime, but they have been widely incorporated into the modern O.T.O. They have been executed in several different ways, from rock opera variants by the performance group Eleusyve Productions, to more traditional stagings of the original plays by The Heart of Blood, an organization devoted to Thelemic education. A contemporary history of the Rites of Eleusis performances has been traced by long-standing O.T.O. member Lita-Luise Chappell in recent years.[26] Chappell has uncovered many archived photographs of these performances, reflecting the colorful and festive character that often typifies O.T.O. functions.

Summer (1911)

The summer of 1911 was a prolific one for the prophet. Much of the Class B, C, and D materials were written and later published in *The Equinox*. Class B books of "ordinary scholarship, enlightened and earnest," included "Liber Israfel" and "Liber Viae Memoriae vel ThIShARB," while the "Official Rituals and Instructions" of Class D books consist of works such as "Liber NV," "Liber HAD," "Liber Yod," and "Liber Resh vel Helios," among others. These form the bulk of the official A∴A∴ literature issued by Authority and intended for adherents of the system.

Most important to note here is that the remaining "Class A" Holy Books were also received in the summer of 1911. These works include "Liber B vel Magi" (a text describing the function of a Magus, 9°=2□), "Liber Tzaddi vel Hamus Hermeticus" (describing the path of Initiation), "Liber A'ash vel Capricorni Pneumatici" (outlining a particular magical formula), and "Liber Cheth vel Vallum Abiegni" (which details the Crossing of the Abyss and describes the nature of Babalon).

The remaining points of discussion for this chapter include three later magical workings: "The Ab-ul-Diz Working," "The Paris Working,"

---

[26] Lita-Luise Chappell, "A Historical Overview of the Rites of Eleusis," in O.T.O. (2015) *Success is Your Proof*, 177–188.

and "The Amalantrah Working." While these may be considered peripheral when compared to the Holy Books and *The Vision and the Voice*, they provide important insight. We also look closer at Crowley's elevation in O.T.O.

The Magician's Book: Ab-ul-Diz and the Holy Books of Thelema (1911)

One of the single most important publications related to Thelemic doctrine is the book known as *Book 4*.[27] Outlining the basic theory behind Crowley's philosophy of "Magick" and its practice, *Book 4* may be considered to be Crowley's *magnum opus*. The work is divided into four parts, (1) "Mysticism," (2) "Magick: Elemental Theory," (3) "Magick in Theory and Practice," and (4) "Thelema, The Law: The Equinox of the Gods."[28] The publication did not complete for 24 years, but it began with a visionary working by Crowley and a new magical partner, Mary d'Este Sturges (1871–1931).[29]

Known as the "Ab-ul-Diz Working,"[30] it has merit for several reasons. First, it was the first major magical ceremony that Crowley performed with a different "Scarlet Woman." Crowley's first wife, Rose, was the primary source behind the Cairo Working, the reception of *The Book of the Law* in 1904. Crowley believed Rose to be his magical consort and that she "held the title" of "Scarlet Woman." However, the breakdown of their marriage in 1910 and Roses' subsequent spiral into alcoholism convinced him that she had abandoned her position. He realized that the Scarlet Woman was "an officer replaceable as need arises."[31] He met Soror Virakam (Mary d'Este Sturges) in the fall of 1911, a woman he recalled having "possessed a most powerful

---

[27] The most recent and comprehensive edition of this is titled *Liber ABA*, Crowley (1997).

[28] See Crowley (1997).

[29] Born Mary Dempsey, she was known as Mary d'Este Sturges to Crowley. For a summary of their association, see Hymenaeus Beta, "Editor's Introduction," in Crowley (1997), xlviii–lvi.

[30] Published in Crowley (1998a).

[31] Quoted by Hymenaeus Beta in "Editor's Introduction," Crowley (1997), xlvii.

personality and a terrific magnetism." On the night of November 21, soon after their relationship began, Sturges reportedly began acting strangely, behaving in a manner that reminded him of Rose in Cairo. This precipitated the events known as the "Ab-ul-Diz Working," with Sturges acting as seer and Crowley as the magician guiding the effort.

The purpose of the working, as the two participants were told, was to instruct them to write a treatise on Magick. A series of magical sessions ensued over the following month into December, and Crowley and Sturges found themselves settled in Villa Caldarazo, in Naples, Italy, where Parts I and II of *Book 4* were authored over the course of a few weeks. Their relationship ended not long after.

The contents of Parts III and IV took much longer to produce, and their history is much more complicated. Ordeals often arose for Crowley when it came to the publication of his important works. Nevertheless, Part III finally went to press some eighteen years later in 1929 and Part IV in 1936.

The Adept and the King: The Book of Lies and the O.T.O. (1912)

As mentioned in chapter two, Aleister Crowley was given the title of Grand Master General of the British O.T.O. in 1912 by Theodor Reuss. Crowley wrote in the *Confessions* that Reuss approached him and pointed out that he had exposed the O.T.O.'s highest secret in his recent publication *The Book of Lies*.[32] The book is one of his most demanding literary works. Even its obtuse subtitle, *Falsifications of the One Thought ...* , leaves one to ask whether to take its contents seriously or to consider the text a joke. It consists of short poems in aphoristic style, writing with puns, and qabalistic word puzzles. While it may sometimes look like nonsense on the surface, *The Book of Lies* contains some of his most important writings concerning Thelema. It is one of the best examples of the technique of teaching in humorous riddles.

---

[32] Crowley (1981). The publication itself is deceptively listed as being printed 1913, perhaps a subtle example of Crowley's attempt to play the trickster and the book's intended aim to make the reader pause and reflect on the nature of truth and falsity.

As Crowley biographer Richard Kaczynski recounts the meeting, Reuss approached Crowley in London:

> Crowley answered the door to his flat at 124 Victoria Street to find Herr Reuss peering at him [...] "You have published the secret of the IX°," he claimed, referring to the innermost secret of Ordo Templi Orientis, "and you must take the corresponding oaths." [...] He protested, "I have done nothing of the sort. I don't know the secret, and I don't want to know the secret." "The magical secret of sex? But of course you do." Reuss stepped across the room to Crowley's bookcases and retrieved a copy of the newly printed *Book of Lies*."[33]

The Book of Lies thus serves as an example of the important role that publication played for Crowley. The book displayed Crowley's initiated acumen to his contemporaries and started a series of events that would transform the O.T.O. into what it is today. Upon receiving the honorary degree of X°, Supreme and Most Holy King, Crowley subsequently revised the rituals of the O.T.O.—particularly the first triad called the Man of Earth—to fit within the framework of Thelema. We will later see that in the years that followed, a crossroads between the A∴A∴ and the O.T.O. would emerge when the two orders were placed front and center on his agenda to promulgate Thelema.

Jovial Mischiefs: The Paris Working (1914)

"Liber CDXV: The Paris Working" was performed in 1914, just shy of two years after Crowley was granted the title of X° in the O.T.O. Named so because it was performed in Paris in the first two months of the year, "Liber CDXV" consisted of a series of homosexual magical rites involving Crowley and Victor Neuburg, his magical partner from the 1909 Enochian workings in Algiers. Intended to invoke the expansive and beneficent spirits of Jupiter and Mercury, "The Paris Working"

---

[33] Kaczynski (2010), 251–252.

proved not only to grant bounty in the magicians' temporal existences, but established meaningful advances in Thelemic doctrine. The rites produced insightful connections into the theories of both A∴A∴ and O.T.O., and generated visions that continued in a similar character to the ecstatic imagery given in *The Vision and the Voice* and the Holy Books.

"The Paris Working" is significant because it serves as a dual working of both the A∴A∴ and the O.T.O. Crowley performed these ceremonies as O.S.V.,[34] his motto as an Adeptus Major (6°=5□) and Imperator (Governing Officer) of A∴A∴. He also noted in the introduction that he had been "initiated by Fra. M.[35] into the Greater Mysteries, and been by him inducted into the Throne of the Order of the Temple"—and so "it is fitting to reconstitute this Order in its splendor [...]"[36] As Frater V.V., the current Imperator of the A∴A∴, has noted, techniques used in "The Paris Working" "pertain to both the grade of Adeptus Major in A∴A∴ and the IX° and XI° of O.T.O.," showing that the two orders, "though distinct and independent, closely intersect at this grade and these degrees in matters of magical technique."[37] In "One Star in Sight," one of the techniques of the Major Adept is described as "The Beast Conjoined with the Woman." When we reference the "A∴A∴ Curriculum" reading list for the grade of Adeptus Major, we are advised that "aspirants to this grade should have attained to the 9th degree of O.T.O."[38]

Given the results produced from "The Paris Working"—and the dual nature of the respective A∴A∴ grade and O.T.O. degree—it can reasonably be assumed that at these levels the two orders have significant doctrinal and technical similarities. "The Paris Working" also revealed intimations of the grade of Magus (9°=2□) that Crowley would attain to in a year's time.

In addition, these workings produced results Crowley described as

---

[34] Ol Sonuf Vaoresaji, Enochian for "I reign over you."

[35] Merlin Peregrinus, Theodor Reuss.

[36] Crowley (1998a), 352.

[37] "Editor's Introduction," in Crowley (1998a) *The Vision in the Voice*, x.

[38] Crowley (1997), 458.

"spiritual illumination." One example was the "certain identification of Christ with Mercury." While he would have already been familiar with the association of Mercury and Jesus from the Hermetic Order of the Golden Dawn,[39] the doctrinal development coming from this connection is particularly evident in "The Paris Working." There is also continuity between earlier writings in the Holy Books of 1907, and visions obtained in 1909, that bear upon the messianic association with the eight-pointed star of Mercury in "The Paris Working" of 1914.

To illustrate, in October of 1907, Crowley wrote in "Liber VII":

> Also I read in a great Book.
> On ancient skin was written in letters of gold: Verbum fit Verbum.
> Also Vitriol and the hierophant's name
> V. V. V. V. V.
> All this wheeled in fire, in star-fire, rare and far and utterly lonely—even as Thou and I, O desolate soul my God![40]

Similarly, the Holy Book "Liber Porta Lucis," written later in December of 1907, opens with:

> I who comprehend in myself all the vast and the minute, all the bright and the dark, have mitigated the brilliance of mine unutterable splendour, sending forth V. V. V. V. V. as a ray of my light, as a messenger unto that small dark orb.
> Then V. V. V. V. V. taketh up the word, and sayeth:
> Men and women of the Earth, to you am I come from the Ages beyond the Ages, from the Space beyond your vision; and I bring to you these words.[41]

---

[39] For example, see in Israel Regardie (1984) *The Complete Golden Dawn System of Magic* (Tempe: New Falcon Publications), 61–63. The "Vision of the Universal Mercury," was fundamental to the teaching in the Golden Dawn.

[40] "Liber VII," IV:40–43, in Crowley (1983), 23.

[41] "Liber X," 1–4 in Ibid., 39.

Later in 1909, in the 6th Æthyr of *The Vision and the Voice*, he has a vision of an eight-pointed star he likens to the Vision of the Universal Mercury of the Hermetic Order of the Golden Dawn:

> [...] above me appears the starry heaven of night, and one star greater than all the other stars. It is a star of eight rays. I recognize it as the star in the seventeenth key of the Tarot, as the Star of Mercury [...] And in the heart of the star is an exceeding splendour,— a god standing upon the moon, brilliant beyond imagining. It is like unto the vision of the Universal Mercury.[42]

This theme continues in "The Paris Working," in "Opus VIII" (the number eight being attributed to Mercury):

> With one foot on this crest stands Mercury again, around him soft flames of orange, and green, and purple. And these words spake he from golden mouth: "Thou art mine. Thou comest always unto me. Always in every grade am I thy guide; and even at this hour do I burn up thy dust. Moreover, thou shalt behold a certain earnest of thy work, and that right early." [...] I now see the eight-fold star of Mercury suddenly blazing out, it is composed of four *fleur-de-lys* with rays like antlers, bulrushes in shape between them. The central core has the cipher of the Grand Master, but not the one you know. Upon the cross are the Dove, the Hawk, the Serpent, and the Lion. Also one other symbol, yet more secret.[43]

The connection between the Vision of the Universal Mercury, Christ/ Messiah, and Mercury/Hierophant throughout the Thelemic corpus has been examined in depth by J. Daniel Gunther. He notes that there is a common motif in religious literature that likens the coming of a Messiah to a star, a symbol of hope. Gunther argues this same theme finds its way into Thelemic literature, but in a way different from past religions.

---

[42] Crowley (1998a), 191–192.

[43] Crowley (1998a), 373.

(Figure 4.1) The Vision of the Star of the Messiah. Artwork by Elena Bortot for "Path in Eternity," Grand Lodge O.T.O. Italia, Florence, October 11–12, 2014.

"The appearance of our Messiah was not intended to evoke the exoteric worship of men or to be openly known as the anointed one. His mission was to bring to man the Word that would intoxicate the inmost, not the outermost." Gunther continues that in the Holy Books, Crowley acknowledges "that by his work, he will not be acknowledged by men as the Redeemer, but that the coming of the Messiah V. V. V. V. V. will be manifest in the one word, which is Thelema."[44] Indeed, Gunther points to an early document in *The Equinox*, Volume I, Number 1 (1909) entitled "An Account of the A∴A∴," where Crowley quoted nearly verbatim from *The Cloud Upon the Sanctuary* by Karl von Eckartshausen. In von Eckartshausen's work, Jesus Christ is referred to as the "Light of the World himself," and "the One Anointed in light, the single mediator for the human race, the Way, the Truth, and the

---

44 J. Daniel Gunther, "Christeos Luciftias: Messianism in the New Aeon," lecture delivered in London, United Kingdom, June 4, 2017.

Life [...]"[45] In "An Account of the A∴A∴," Crowley clearly interprets
V. V. V. V. V. as the Messiah:

> This society is in the communion of those who have most capacity
> for light; they are united in truth, and their Chief is the Light of
> the World himself, V. V. V. V., the One Anointed in Light, the
> single teacher for the human race, the Way, the Truth, and the
> Life.[46]

The Wizard and the Beast: Amalantrah (1918)

The "Amalantrah Working" was performed with a new female partner,
Roddie Minor (1884–1979), nicknamed "The Camel,"[47] who took the
magical name of "Soror Ahitha." Around the time of Minor's involvement with him, Crowley was beginning another productive literary
streak. He wrote *Liber Aleph: The Book of Wisdom or Folly*, a collection
of spiritual writings set in epistle format addressed to his closest student
at the time, Charles Stansfeld Jones (Frater Achad) (1886–1950). During the evening of January 14, Roddie had some visions that Crowley
found significant enough to pull him away from his task. As he recalled
the event:

> I was sitting at my desk, working. To my surprised annoyance, the
> Camel suddenly began to have visions. I shut off my hearing in the
> way I have learnt to do; but after some five minutes babbling she
> pierced my defences by some remark concerning an egg under a
> palm tree. This aroused me instantly, for the last instruction given
> to myself and Soror Virakam was to go to the desert and look

---

[45] Karl Von Eckarthausen (1896) *The Cloud Upon the Sanctuary*, Isabel de Steiger
(trans.) (San Diego: The Book Tree), 16. Quoted by Gunther (2017).

[46] "Liber XXXIII—An Account of the A∴A∴," in Crowley (1996b), 26.

[47] Named so because the Hebrew letter Gimel is attributed to the High Priestess of
the Tarot, whose divine influence emanates from the topmost point of the Tree of
Life, Kether.

for just that thing. I saw then a kind of continuity between those
visions and these. It was as if the intelligence communicating were
taking up the story at the point at which it had been dropped.
[...] The Camel said that someone, whom she called "the Wizard,"
wished to communicate with me.[48]

The Wizard who became the prevailing figure of Ahitha's visions identified himself as "Amalantrah." The importance of this communication
was soon evident. Crowley received an answer to a perplexing problem
concerning the nature of his O.T.O. motto, Baphomet,[49] and the mystical numeration of his A∴A∴ title as Magus, To Mega Therion ("The
Great Beast"). More indirectly, he received a confirmation concerning
the validity of Aiwass, the messenger who delivered *Liber AL vel Legis*
in 1904.

Crowley claimed that for nearly six years prior, when he took the
name "Baphomet" as Grand Master General of the British O.T.O.,
he was baffled when trying to find its numerical significance through
gematria—a mystical system used in the Qabalah to find deeper meaning
in words by their enumeration.[50] In an effort to test Amalantrah for
authenticity, he asked how to spell the name Baphomet so as to reveal
its inner meaning. Without hesitation, the Wizard replied through
Ahitha, BAFOMIThR (באומיעתר),[51] which added up to the Wizard's

---

[48] Crowley (1969a), 832.

[49] Upon being given the title of Grand Master General of the X° in the United Kingdom by Theodor Reuss in 1912, Crowley adopted the magical name of "Baphomet,"
the goat-headed figure worshipped by the legendary Knights Templar, at least according to some occult authors of the nineteenth century. See for example the work of
Éliphas Lévi, born Alphonse Louis Constant (1810-1875), where he refers to "the
Baphomet of the Templars, the bearded idol of the alchemist, the obscene deity of
Mendes, the goat of the Sabbath." Lévi (1896), 307.

[50] In languages like Hebrew, Greek, and Arabic, the letters do double-duty as numbers. Therefore, a combination of letters can be read as either (or both) a word and a
number.

[51] "[...] taking Vau as Ayin (70 instead of 6); this is legitimate Cabbala." Grant and
Symonds (1969a), 935.

(Figure 4.2) Éliphas Lévi's famed image of the secret Lord of Initiation, Baphomet, the alchemical, androgynous, reputed god of the Templars.

own name of 729. Crowley discovered that the Greek word "χηφας" ("rock")—the name given to Peter by Christ as representative of the cornerstone of the Church—added to the same value. He was amazed, believing that the Wizard "had cleared up the etymological problem and shown why the Templars should have given the name Baphomet to their so-called idol. Baphomet was Father Mithras, the cubical stone which was the corner of the Temple."[52] This revelation would

---

[52] Crowley (1969a), 833.

echo the previous insight from "The Paris Working" of 1914, when Crowley realized it was the 600-year anniversary of the execution and martyrdom of Jacobus Burgundus Molensis and the disbanding of the Knights Templar Order.[53] "The Paris Working" therefore marked the occasion to "reconstitute this Order in its splendor."[54] Amalantrah's key supported the idea that Crowley as Baphomet was to serve as the cornerstone of the Temple.

The next development in the "Amalantrah Working" came under mysterious circumstances. It would not only reinforce Thelema as the new Truth to the world, but further emphasize Crowley as its prophet. Upon attaining to the grade of Magus in 1915, he took the name To Mega Therion, "The Great Beast." On February 24, 1918, Crowley asked Amalantrah if he could enumerate this name for further meaning. The Wizard replied that he could by using only the word "Therion." Crowley then attempted to devise a way to add the values of the letters to yield something mystically meaningful, initially failing to come up with anything. The following Monday morning, a letter was received at his office at *The International*. The letter was from a Samuel A. Jacobs, who was responding to Crowley's essay entitled "The Revival of Magick," published three months earlier. Jacobs had discovered the appropriate spelling and numeration of Therion. In his letter, he explained that when placing the Hebrew letters together "תריון" (ThRIVN), the value adds up to 666, the number of the Beast of Revelation. Jacobs then signed the letter with his full given name, "Shmuel bar Aiwaz bie Yackou de Shirabad."[55] Stunned by seeing the name "Aiwaz," Crowley wrote:

---

[53] Jacobus Molensis, also known as Jacques de Molay (1243–1314), was the last Grand Master of the Order of the Knights Templar. A history of the mysterious order of knight-monks can be found in Malcolm Barber (1994) *The New Knighthood: A History of the Order of the Temple* (Cambridge: Cambridge University Press) and their trial and disbanding in Barber (2001).

[54] Crowley (1998a), 352.

[55] Kaczynski (2010), 325–326.

Till that moment I had had no idea that Aiwass was anything but an artificial name, like Ahitha. I had tried to find a spelling for it, having never seen it written except in the English in The Book of the Law, but only heard it. I had decided on AIVAS [סאיא] = 78, the number of Mezla, the influence from the highest unity, and therefore suitable enough as the title of a messenger from Him.[56]

When Crowley wrote to Jacobs inquiring about the correct spelling of his name, he was shocked to find that the Hebrew variation, "OIVZ" (צייון) added to 93, the numeration of Thelema in Greek (θελημα). This was stunning, to say the least! The New Law and the name of its Messenger held the same value. Crowley would henceforth not merely believe Aiwaz to be his Holy Guardian Angel, but he would consider Aiwaz to be an independent being outside himself. He would conclude that the fact that "Aiwaz should have, so to speak, signed himself with His Law, was irrefutable proof of his existence."[57]

Having confirmation of his duty to serve humankind, to promulgate Thelema as a Magus of the A∴A∴, and to resurrect the Templar Order under command of the Secret Chiefs as Grand Master General of the O.T.O., Crowley arranged for one of his most important books. *The Equinox* Volume III, Number 1, would put both orders in the public sphere together. Although obstacles abounded with this project as well,[58] *The Blue Equinox* was published in spring of 1919 and featured writings pertaining to the A∴A∴ and the O.T.O., providing the reader with a fully-developed and integrated system intended to proselytize Thelema to the world.[59]

---

[56] Crowley (1969a), 835.

[57] Ibid.

[58] See a discussion in Kaczynski (Spring 2016).

[59] Chapter five of this book discusses the importance of this work in more depth.

The O.H.O. and the Imperator

One more doctrinal point remains to be addressed in this chapter. It concerns Crowley's 1925 succession of Theodor Reuss as Outer Head of the O.T.O. There is some indication that Crowley assumed this position keeping in mind his role as the commander-in-chief of the A∴A∴ (i.e., Imperator), and that he believed the roles of Imperator and O.H.O. would be held by the same person.

One reason for this connection is the name he took as O.H.O., "Phoenix."[60] Like his motto as Grand Master X° (Baphomet), Crowley would have chosen this word with extreme care. The Phoenix Wand is a symbol of the adept who holds the administrative role of Imperator in A∴A∴.

Grand Master General Shiva X° of the Grand Lodge of Australia has pointed out in his lecture, "Aspiring to the Holy Order," that Crowley may have taken the name Phoenix because of the myth of the phoenix rising from its ashes. It was Crowley's will to "reconstitute the [Templar] Order in its splendor,"[61] as discussed above. As "Baphomet X°," he would serve as "the cornerstone of the Temple." As "Phoenix," O.H.O., he would fully establish the Order in line with the principles of the New Aeon of Thelema.

As we have seen, the 1914 "Paris Working" revealed important doctrinal connections between O.T.O. and A∴A∴. Furthermore, as mentioned in chapter two, by 1921 Crowley was already considering himself for the position of O.H.O. because Reuss had written to him demanding he keep Thelema out of the teachings of the O.T.O. Crowley interpreted this as proof that Reuss was abdicating the role of O.H.O. by revealing he had not established a link to the Secret Chiefs. In other words, by virtue of rejecting Thelema, Reuss had automatically relinquished his leadership to Crowley, the Magus of the New Aeon.

Grand Master General Phanes X° of the Grand Lodge of Italy has stated that Crowley (who was in Cefalù in 1921) "would come to shape

---

[60] Crowley (1998b), 217.

[61] Shiva X°, "Aspiring to the Holy Order," Florence, Italy, October 11, 2014.

his will to succeed Reuss as O.H.O." Phanes notes that it was at this time that Crowley "went public on this among his disciples, and more importantly in 'One Star in Sight,'"[62] where he wrote that the Adeptus Major "must exert his whole power and authority to govern members of the lower Grades [...] he must employ to those ends the formula called 'The Beast conjoined with the Woman' [...]" Furthermore, "He must set up this ideal for the *orders* which he rules" [emphasis added].[63] Phanes elaborates:

> The formula called "The Beast conjoined with the Woman" can be taken also as a direct reference to the Sovereign Sanctuary of the Gnosis: so basically, he's speaking here of a very specific example of major Adept, one who is also IX° of O.T.O. and in a ruling position. This of course relates precisely to the Commanding Adept, since in the Outer College of A∴A∴, the Imperator is the First Officer, his symbol being the sword. As Second Officer in the Inner College, his symbol is the bennu-headed [phoenix] wand. As such, he helps the Chief Adept or Præmonstrator to govern.[64]

Phanes continues by implying that "orders" is given in the plural because it refers to the roles of both Imperator *and* O.H.O. "[W]hy is the word 'order' being here written plural? I believe this is to be a direct reference to the Order of the Oriental Templars, ruled by the Outer Head of the Order, who is the Commanding Adept representing the authority of The Beast."[65]

This will all be of increasing concern as we continue. In the next chapter, we will discuss Crowley's original design for unity between the two orders. What has been discussed here is their crossover on an administrative level.

---

[62] Phanes (2015) "Gathered into Their Fold" in O.T.O. (2015), 80.

[63] "One Star in Sight," in Crowley (1997), 494.

[64] Phanes (2015), 81.

[65] Ibid.

⚜

We have seen the evolution of Thelema as a comprehensive new spiritual philosophy. It was not the teachings of the Golden Dawn—saturated in Christian dogma with its membership falling into fissure—nor was it the fatigued rite of Freemasonry—long profaned, and which failed to initiate people into the Mysteries. The Secret Chiefs had a new message for humanity, the writings of the New Aeon of Horus enshrined within the words of the Secret Master, the author of the Holy Books of Thelema and this mysterious being's scribe, Aleister Crowley: To Mega Therion in the A∴A∴ and Baphomet and Phoenix in the O.T.O.

CHAPTER FIVE

The War-Engine

Crowley's Vision of Thelema, A∴A∴, and O.T.O.

Choose ye an island! Fortify it! Dung it about with enginery of war! I will give you a war-engine. With it ye shall smite the peoples; and none shall stand before you.

—The Book of the Law, III: 4–8.

"THE PARIS WORKING" had been deemed a success by Crowley and Neuburg. This series of rituals was intended to invoke the magnanimous and benevolent energies of Jupiter and they indeed produced favorable outcomes. On the material plane, Crowley was cured of his bronchitis, and Neuburg found himself in charitable and delightful company immediately following the working.

> We ourselves became identified with Jupiter, but in different aspects. Frater L.T. [Neuburg] was, for some months following, the personification of generosity, though himself with the most meagre resources. All sorts of strangers planted themselves on him and he entertained them. In my own case, I became that type of Jupiter which we connect with the idea of prosperity, authority, and amativeness. I received numerous occult dignities; I seemed to have plenty of money without quite knowing how it happened; and I found myself exercising an almost uncanny attraction upon every woman that came into my circle of acquaintance.[1]

---

[1] "The Paris Working," in Crowley (1998a), 350.

"The Paris Working" provided more than these mundane prosperities. In addition to the insights we have discussed about the grades of Adeptus Major ($6°=5^{\square}$) and the IX°, there were allusions to the A∴A∴ grade of Magus ($9°=2^{\square}$). Crowley began to meditate fervently on the hints he had received about the Magus grade, as well as upon the sexual working of the IX°. In the autumn of 1914, he wrote several instructive papers pertaining to the sexual magick of O.T.O., entitled "De Nuptiis Secretis Deorum Cum Hominibus," "De Arte Magica," and "De Homunculo Epistola."[2] He would soon begin to experiment with these techniques exclusively.

On October 24, 1914, with the Great War starting to rage in Europe and Crowley beset with financial difficulties, he set sail for America, far away from the conflict. He arrived in New York City on November 1, having voyaged on the famous *Lusitania* only half a year before German U-boats would sink the vessel, dragging the United States into the war.[3] Aleister Crowley was about to begin one of the more colorful and fruitful periods of his life, which included sexual magick, espionage, and "business-way" promulgation of Thelema.

While these events are far too extensive to explore in depth here, they have recently been covered in Tobias Churton's *Aleister Crowley in America*.[4] What I will look at in the time period between 1915 and 1919 is how Crowley came to envision Thelema as a movement that could change humanity for the better, and how his ideas about the A∴A∴ and the O.T.O. could help carry out these aims. By reviewing some clues in Crowley's diaries and letters, we see some interesting developments with regard to how Thelema would be put forth.

---

[2] Kaczynski (2010), 275.

[3] Ibid.

[4] Kaczynski (2010), 277–354. More recently Crowley's American period is examined in great depth in Churton (2017).

Sex Magick and the Birth of the Magus

> "There is also, of course, the secret of the IX° which is so to say, the
> weapon which they may use to further these purposes."
>
> —Aleister Crowley to Karl Germer, September 16, 1946

As noted, Crowley had been shown in "The Paris Working" the connection between Mercury the messenger and Christ the redeemer. Known to the Greeks as Hermes and to the Egyptians as the ibis-headed Tahuti or Thoth, the mercurial god of wisdom and communication represented the transmitter of the Logos of the New Aeon to Crowley. In this sense Hermes/Thoth was identified with the second sephira of the Tree of Life, Chokmah ("Wisdom"), and the A∴A∴ grade of Magus, 9°=2□.[5] This all played out in his thought as he journeyed to America in late 1914. In a journal, written at the time of his arrival in New York City, *Colloquy of V.V.V.V.V. that is to be a Magus 9°=2□ with the God ΘΩΘ*, he wrote, "I came to the Conclusion that ☿ [Mercury] was Lord of New York, and I began various invocations of this as best I could, notably by the O.T.O. method. I shall refer here, and after to the record 'De Arte Regia' [The Royal Art]."[6]

Rex de Arte Regia ("King of the Royal Art") details his employment of the sexual technique of the IX°. He found this method so thoroughly sublime that once he landed in America, he experimented with it exclusively with various partners, sometimes for mundane matters such as acquiring money, and other times for more spiritual means.

While *Rex de Arte Regia* reveals that when he aimed for material gains he came up with mixed results, it does show that he made some profound spiritual discoveries. Remember his initial epiphany in 1912 when Reuss pointed out that the secret of the O.T.O. is sexual in nature, the magical formula of the *Hieros Gamos* ("Holy Marriage").[7]

---

[5] See table of correspondences in Crowley (1997), 548 and 553.

[6] GYC, OS20, quoted from Churton (2017), 238.

[7] This topic is explored in more depth with its connection to the Gnostic Mass in chapter fourteen.

Also referred to as the formula of the Rose and Cross, a short detour is required here to place all this in context.

The Rose and Cross can be understood as a psychic powerhouse of symbolism.[8] Aleister Crowley claimed that the Rosy Cross is the "supreme mystery of practical Magick."[9] Noting the many forms of its iconography, he claimed the Rosy Cross was:

> the uniting of subject and object which is the Great Work, and which is symbolized sometimes as this cross and circle, sometimes as the *linga-yoni*, sometimes as the *ankh* or *crux ansata*, sometimes as the spire and nave of the church or temple, and sometimes as a marriage feast, mystic marriage, spiritual marriage, "chymical nuptials," and in a hundred other ways. Whatever form chosen, it is the symbol of the Great Work.[10]

The Rose and Cross can then be understood as an essential element in the initiatory journey of the individual, a formula by which the human being unites with God. In Thelema, this mystery is gradually revealed in both the A∴A∴ and the O.T.O. While the mystery of the Rose and Cross is encapsulated in the grade of Adeptus Minor (5°=6□) in the A∴A∴ curriculum—and signifies the entrance into the Inner Order of the Rosæ Rubeæ et Aureæ Crucis (R.R. et A.C.)—it is first intro-

---

[8] The Rose and Cross, as a symbol of spiritual significance, has a long history. It is possible that it developed from symbols as far back as the Neolithic period of prehistory, as well as hieroglyphs from Egyptian civilization of the ancient world. The "sun cross" ($\oplus$), being an equilateral cross within a circle has been identified as a solar symbol in prehistoric religion. See Martin Persson Nilsson (1950) *The Minoan-Mycenaean Religion and Its Survival in Greek Religion* (New York: Biblo & Tannen Publishers), 421. It has also been argued that the Egyptian Ankh, (☥) was used as a symbol for life and as a symbol for the union of male and female. See Thomas Inman (1875) *Ancient Pagan and Modern Christian Symbolism*, 2nd edition (New York: J. W. Bouton). The symbol of the Rose and Cross is most developed in the early modern period with the advent of Rosicrucian symbolism and the seventeenth century "Rosicrucian manifestos," for which see Christopher McIntosh (1997).

[9] Crowley (1997), 208.

[10] Ibid., 51.

duced in the Ordo Templi Orientis at the V° and fully disclosed in the IX°, the Sovereign Sanctuary of the Gnosis. Furthermore, it is revealed in dramatic form in the Ecclesia Gnostica Catholica during the performance of "Liber XV," The Gnostic Mass.

Within the curriculum of the A∴A∴, the formula of the Rose and Cross is first introduced to the Zelator, albeit only in theory. It is important for the Zelator to begin its study, as this grade is located in the sephira Yesod ("Foundation"). As one ascends the Tree, Yesod is the last grade of the First Order (the Outer College) to be situated on the balanced Middle Pillar. Aspirants there begin to build the foundations of their own being with the study of the Rose and Cross and *The Book of the Law*. The Zelator is also expected to master āsana (physical posture) and prāṇāyāma (breath control), to discipline the physical body and control the flow of subtle energy. It is imperative that the Zelator is well-acquainted with these practices because he or she will need to control and direct the life force (i.e., magical force) in a disciplined manner when it comes time to make contact with the Holy Guardian Angel. At the liminal stage between the Outer College and the Inner Order—wherein is the experience of Knowledge and Conversation of the Holy Guardian Angel—the aspirant is given practical instruction in the formula of the Rose and Cross when the title of Dominus Liminis is conferred upon the Philosophus by Authority. The Dominus Liminis must fortify him or herself by applying the Rose and Cross as taught, so as to consolidate all that has been learned in the Outer College. Mastery is disputed at every turn. When the Dominus Liminus has sufficiently demonstrated such ingenium, the candidate proceeds to the grade of Adeptus Minor (without) and swears to attain to Knowledge and Conversation of the Holy Guardian Angel. This experience marks the True and Most Holy aspect of the Rose and Cross: the union of the candidate with the Angel.

In the teachings of the O.T.O., the Rose and Cross takes on a specifically sexual symbolism. The degrees of Minerval (0°)–VI° are designed in such a way as to gradually prepare the candidate for an initial glimpse of the IX° technique. It is not until the V° that the mysteries of the Rose and Cross are hinted at to the Sovereign Prince(cess) of the

Rose Croix. We are, at present, more concerned with the final degrees leading up to full disclosure of the central secret—the instructions of VII°, VIII°, and IX°. As Frater Superior Hymenaeus Beta has noted, the VII°–IX° of O.T.O. can be understood as a series that completes the natural cycle of human sexual development. He writes:

> The first stage is infantile, undifferentiated, and of course gener-
> ally chaste. The second stage narcissistic, usually corresponding
> to adolescence, and masturbatory. In the third, the phallic as they
> [psychoanalysts] chose to call it, the individual psychology is so
> organized as to integrate the psyche, the genital consciousness and
> its associated instincts, and is then prepared to enter the world, to
> have intercourse [...] Incidentally, these three psychological stages
> of genital organization correspond exactly to the Seventh, Eighth,
> and Ninth Degrees of O.T.O.[11]

Just as the natural development of the human's sexual life begins with virginity and matures into intercourse to produce a child, so too is the initiate carefully prepared to harness the magical force within, local-ized in the sexual center.

The universality of the Rose and Cross for Crowley was so magnificent, he believed its application could liberate humanity. Returning to his journal, *Rex de Arte Regia*, we see that he recorded his reflections about the nature of the technique on November 21, 1914, not long after arriving in America:

> Although this record is that of an investigator, and it is hoped
> that the results may be of value to my most holy colleagues, the
> allied Kings of the Nations of the Earth, and to my children, the
> thrice holy, thrice illuminated and thrice illustrious Initiates of
> the Sanctuary of the Gnosis, yet it is also that of a Magus bent on
> the accomplishment of a Work; and the details of that achieve-

---

11 Hymenaeus Beta (Fall 1997) "Women's Conference Address," in *The Magical Link*, New Series No. 1, 9.

ment in their event and policy should prove as instructive as an arid, though more rigid, skeptical demonstration. I wish further to add that I see no reason to suppose that the Elixir is miraculous in the sense that sceptics would like it to be taken.[12]

The "Elixir" was the key ingredient, the result of the operation that housed the creative power of the divine. It could be used as a talisman for magical means to produce a "magical child" or another intended result. Crowley would later write, "To me [the secret of the IX°] is (a) convenient in various practical ways, (b) a machine for carrying out the orders of the Secret Chiefs of A∴A∴, (c) by virtue of the Secret a magical weapon of incalculable power."[13]

The Mystic Marriage of A∴A∴ and O.T.O.: "Duplex"[14]

Crowley's American period beginning at the end of 1914 was later described by him as the "Chokmah Days," which he associated with his Initiation into the grade of Magus.[15] As we know, the IX° featured prominently in: (1) his magical practice, (2) his understanding of himself as the prophet of Thelema, and (3) the function of the A∴A∴ and the O.T.O. In a 2004 article written by O.T.O. member AISh MLChMH, a significant journal entry of *Rex de Arte Regia* was analyzed to give evidence of this.[16] AISh MLChMH shows that in March of 1915, Crowley prepared to divine the Word for the upcoming Spring Equinox as had become tradition for the A∴A∴. His journal

---

[12] Crowley (1972c), 7.

[13] *Magick Without Tears*, in Crowley (1986), 427.

[14] See chapter thirteen for a more complete discussion on this topic.

[15] Crowley (1969a) *Confessions*, 795.

[16] See Frater AISh MLChMh, entitled "Duplexity: A cursory glance at the relationship existing between the Orders O.T.O. and A∴A∴," The Laughterful Caress: The Journal of Leaping Laughter Oasis, O.T.O., Vol. V, No. 1, Spring Equinox 2004 Anno IV: xii (Minneapolis: Leaping Laughter Oasis, O.T.O.), 7–11.

reveals that he did this by using the O.T.O. masturbatory technique and obtained a rather remarkable result:

> 21 March 11.30 p.m. Weather cool and cloudy. Lights of temple (four small).
>
> The true moment of the Equinox was 4.51 p.m.
>
> *Frater Perdurabo in manu illius.* [Brother Perdurabo in his hand]
>
> Object: To obtain The Word of the Masters for this Equinox following.
>
> The Operation was most extraordinary, being done in full open Temple of Neophyte A∴A∴ in the Ceremony of the Equinox.
>
> The orgasm and ejaculation were double, as it were twins, and in the instant between the two, the word DUPLEX was placed in my mind with a clarity and certitude that I have never previously known. The Elixir was abundant and excellent.
>
> Result: As above recorded, great success. Very remarkable all this; it is a word of mystic marriage of A∴A∴ and O.T.O.[17]

AISh MLChMH notes in a more recent article that, "the O.T.O. was radically transformed with Crowley's Magus initiation, into being a vehicle for promulgating his Law, which comes from the A∴A∴."[18] The reader will recall that Crowley had already received impressions of the crossover between the two orders in "The Paris Working" only a year before. As Phanes X° notes, "The Paris Working confirmed something Crowley had in mind in the context of the *Hieros Gamos* formula, and was therefore instrumental to the levels of intersection between both orders."[19] This intersection was indeed practical and direct with regard to the two systems.

Crowley later noted in his journal in June of 1915 that "Duplex"

---

[17] In Crowley (1972c), 20–21.

[18] AISh MLChMH, in O.T.O. (2015), 121.

[19] Phanes X°, in O.T.O., (2015), 77.

was clearly the right word. It was immediately understandable to him, and the idea of a closer alliance between the two orders was quite clear and matter-of-fact. He told his closest A∴A∴ student, Frater Achad, in July that a person reaching the pinnacle of the O.T.O. system (the IX°) could become "a very fine and balanced 6°=5□."[20] Crowley wrote Achad again in October about his intention to place O.T.O. within the framework of the A∴A∴.; that is Crowley was laying O.T.O.'s foundation solidly within the context of Thelema:

> Now I must tell you a far more important thing. I have got my A∴A∴ grade which I didn't think it possible to get in this life, and that, too, exactly at the time prophesied. Soror H[ilarion—Jeanne Robert Foster] thinks, however, that it will be another year before that becomes fully manifest. Nevertheless, I must do my duty (Vide Liber I) and that is to preach my Law. Therefore this is the Word of Baphomet to all the members of O.T.O.
>
> ΘΕΛΗΜΑ.[21]

It is evident from the years of correspondence with Jones (Achad) that Crowley began to believe that the A∴A∴ and the O.T.O. had definite, albeit different, methods to accomplish the same goal, which was to promulgate Thelema. The next year, he explained to another disciple, Frank Bennett:

> It was my original idea that the O.T.O. would be a sort of training ground for A∴A∴.. It was still in my mind that the A∴A∴ was the only thing worth doing. But recent initiations have changed my mind considerably. I had not paid sufficient attention to the statement in Liber XXXIII. To the effect that when people become ripe, they are joined to the chain. But the O.T.O. has a perfectly definite function in connection with the New Aeon. At a time like the present, when individual liberty is threatened in

---

[20] Crowley to Charles Stansfeld Jones, July 10, 1915. O.T.O. Archives.

[21] Crowley to Charles Stansfeld Jones, October 29, 1915. O.T.O. Archives.

a way to which history offers no parallel, a strong and vigorous order is required to guard humanity. The A∴A∴ does this, it is true, but in a manner so beyond even your present conception, that I think it only fair to give even the most commonplace of men the chance to co-operate actually.[22]

The Secret Chiefs, it seemed, had a plan to execute by experimental design. The teachings of Thelema and its mysteries were guarded by the most austere measures of initiation. Aspirants to the A∴A∴ were forbidden to know the identity of one another lest the sacred become profaned—like the Golden Dawn, with its politics and outward spiritual pedigrees. Crowley had even seen the effects of this in the early days of the A∴A∴. He recalled to Achad:

> I should like to remind you of my experience in London. Although I was doing my work very strictly according to the programme of the A∴A∴, it was not very long before I found out that people were meeting each other. This of course is most undesirable [...] Now if you cannot prevent people from meeting, the only solution is to treat them as groups, and to avoid trouble by discipline. It is principally for this reason that the O.T.O. seems so valuable, and there is no doubt in my mind that the head of the organization was sent to me at the right time by the right people.[23]

In Crowley's mind, the spiritual work of the A∴A∴ would unfold gradually within the hearts of aspirants and continue to present itself to the world through publications. The O.T.O. would be the social machine to carry out the overall mission of the A∴A∴—to promulgate Thelema. He wrote Frank Bennett in Australia, to "distinguish carefully between A∴A∴ and O.T.O. The latter is a practical organization devoted to the establishment of the work of the former."[24]

---

22 Crowley to Frank Bennett, December 1916. O.T.O. Archives.

23 Crowley to Jones, February 7, 1919. O.T.O. Archives.

24 Crowley to Bennett, December 23–25, 1916, in Keith Richmond (ed.) (2009) *The*

THE EQUINOX

THE OFFICIAL ORGAN OF THE A∴A∴

Do what thou wilt shall be the whole of the Law.
Love is the law, love under will.
The word of the law is
Θελημα

THE OFFICIAL ORGAN OF THE O.T.O.

Deus   Homo.

est

THE REVIEW OF SCIENTIFIC ILLUMINISM

The method of Science; the aim of Religion.

An XV   Vol. III. No. I.   ☉ in ♈

MARCH MCMXIX E.V.

THE UNIVERSAL PUBLISHING COMPANY
DETROIT, MICHIGAN

(**Figure 5.1**) **Blue Equinox title page** (1919) encapsulates Duplexity for the first time in a publication.

The Blue Equinox (1919)

The first overt instance of the cooperative relationship between the two orders was exemplified in the publication of *The Equinox*, Volume III, Number 1, *The Blue Equinox*.[25] It opened, "The world needs reli-

---

Progradior Correspondence: Letters by Aleister Crowley, Frank Bennett, C.S. Jones, and Others (York Beach: The Teitan Press), 55.

[25] See Crowley (2007b), *The Blue Equinox*. "Volume II" never existed in print. The

gion. Religion must represent Truth, and celebrate it. The truth is of two orders: one concerning Nature external to Man; two, concerning Nature internal to Man [...] The Law of Thelema offers a religion which fulfills all necessary conditions." It continued, "The A∴A∴, or Great White Brotherhood, through Whom this Law was obtained, is a Body of the highest Initiates pledged to aid mankind [...] The O.T.O. is the first of the great religious Societies to accept the Law."[26] *The Blue Equinox* contained a dual Imprimatur, giving both the A∴A∴ sigil of the illuminated Eye in the Triangle, along with the O.T.O. lamen, its first appearance in *The Equinox*.[27] *The Blue Equinox* featured a number of documents pertaining to the A∴A∴ such as the Class A Holy Book, "Liber Cordis Cincti Serpente," Class E literature meant for promulgation, and an outline of its curriculum. Also included were several papers elucidating the principles and structure of the O.T.O., and the full text of "The Gnostic Mass."

⁂

Jumping ahead some two decades, we observe that, despite the wishes of his predecessor in the O.T.O., Crowley would formulate a close alliance between the two orders as he envisioned them throughout the remainder of his life. He would keep them separate in their respective functions, however, maintain that they were both Thelemic orders. He wrote to his eventual successor, Karl Germer in September of 1946, just a year before his death:

> The difference between the A∴A∴ and the O.T.O. is very clear and simple. The A∴A∴ is a sempiternal institution, and entirely secret. There is no communication between its members. Theoretically, a member knows only the superior who introduced him, and any person whom he himself has introduced. The Order is

---

A∴A∴ traditionally alternated between periods of five years of "Speech" and five years of "Silence."

26 "Khabs am Pekht," in Crowley (2007b), 9–10.

27 Refer to the symbols on the front cover of this book.

run on purely spiritual lines [...] The O.T.O. has nothing to do
with this, except that *The Book of the Law* and the Word of the
Aeon are essential principles of membership. In all other respects,
it stands by itself as a body similar to Freemasonry, but involving
acceptance of a social and economic system which is intended to
put the work on its feet [...] To show you the difference, Theodor
Reuss was the Supreme Head of the O.T.O., but was not even probationer of the A∴A∴.[28]

Another Look at Liber Oz

Five years earlier in 1941, with World War II raging across Europe and
Japan, millions of people were being killed. Crowley initiated his own
"War Aims of Thelema." He was in correspondence with Frieda Lady
Harris, with whom he was working to produce the *Thoth Tarot* images.
He wrote that he would "settle finally the 'war aims' of Thelema. I
shall ask you to let me use one of the coloured cards for the Banner of
the Manifesto. This will serve as an official O.T.O. New Year Card."[29]
Crowley was talking about a postcard he would distribute to as many
people as he could. It proclaimed in a concise 220-word document (the
same number as the verses of *The Book of the Law*) the message of Thelema in the midst of wartime atrocities. "Liber Oz," is also known as
"The Rights of Man." "Oz" is Hebrew for "goat" and so it was appropriate that Atu XV, "The Devil" accompanied the message.

"Liber Oz" warrants attention again in this chapter, as it serves as
the political program of Thelema. It asserts that each person has the
right to choose his own way in life without compulsion. Its concluding
clause, "Man has the right to kill those who would thwart these rights,"
ensures a defense against tyranny. Grand Master Shiva X° has remarked
about the document:

Although Aleister Crowley never specifically referred to it as such,
in my opinion Liber Oz could be and perhaps should be consid-

---

[28] Crowley to Karl Germer, September 16, 1946. O.T.O. Archives.
[29] Crowley to Frieda Harris, November 7, 1941. UC.

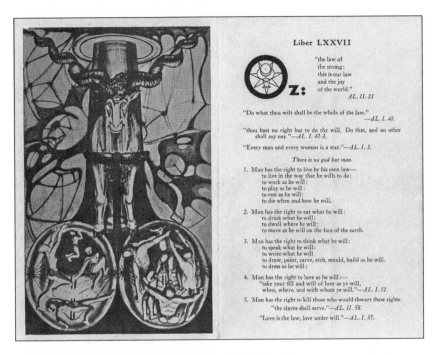

(Figure 5.2) An example of the postcard for "Liber Oz" sent to Crowley's contemporaries in early 1942.

ered an OTO Commentary to *The Book of the Law* [...] Keep in mind here, that what you now know as "Liber Oz" was initially a private instruction from an O.T.O. initiation ceremony.[30]

Shiva notes that "Liber Oz" is the key to freedom—not just *political* freedom but also *spiritual* freedom. In the New Aeon, each and every person has the inclination towards this unwavering liberty latent within, but it is not a privilege and must be realized through initiation:

> We must root out our own fears and ignorance, our complexes and prejudices, and our destructive tendencies and desires. We must emancipate ourselves before we can in any lasting manner

---

[30] Grand Master General Shiva X°, "Aspiring to the Holy Order," lecture delivered September 3, 2011, Tokyo, Japan.

emancipate others. And in order to achieve this we must recognize the light as well as the dark aspects of ourselves. In short, we must seek the wholeness of Initiation in order to commence an Initiation of wholeness. Not a one-sided view of ourselves, of Initiation, of the OTO, or of Thelema coloured by our egos and desires, our wants and whims, but a holistic view capable of awakening the Spirit.[31]

Many contemporary Thelemites have tried to appropriate Thelema into one political ideology or another. The wide spectrum of Crowley's political views have been discussed by scholars, who argue that his ambivalence proves not that he was necessarily less concerned with the political sphere—that he wanted, above all else, to establish Thelema in the world by whatever means necessary. As Marco Pasi points out, regardless of Crowley's various political opinions throughout his life, his occasional idiosyncrasies regarding race and gender, and his ambiguous activities during the interwar period, "it appears that he more or less consistently endeavored to keep these personal attitudes separated from the universal value of his religious message."[32] Despite his colored associations with figures from various political persuasions, Crowley's primary mission always lay with his efforts to put Thelema into the world. He believed it was a message of freedom, the emancipation of humanity through "Light, Life, Love, and Liberty, the Word of whose Law is Thelema,"[33] which was to be achieved by means of the systems of the A∴A∴ and the O.T.O.

---

[31] Ibid.

[32] Pasi (2014), 137.

[33] See "The Creed" in "Liber XV: The Gnostic Mass."

CHAPTER SIX

Thelema as a New Religious Movement

Spirituality in the A∴A∴,
Religiosity in the O.T.O., and Occulture

AFTER THIS BRIEF HISTORICAL OVERVIEW of Thelema during Crowley's lifetime, it is necessary to place the movement within the broader context of religion. Although labeling Thelema as a religion is a subject of debate, especially among some in the contemporary Thelemic community, setting defined parameters on such a complex topic will aid the reader as we move forward. Thelema shares many of the common elements that a scholar would identify as "religion," and is best understood within a religious context. The following chapter will therefore examine Thelema, the A∴A∴, and the O.T.O. within the framework of religious studies.

Thelema: A Religion?

Is Thelema a religion? This may be a difficult question with no easy answer. Thelema is, among other things, a highly complex set of practices. At times, Crowley was reluctant to label it a religion, and claimed that in doing so, one "might easily cause a great deal of misunderstanding, and work a rather stupid kind of mischief."[1] He continues by saying that "[t]he word does not occur in *The Book of the Law*."[2] As I alluded to in chapter two, there is a reluctance by many to call Thelema a religion. The United States Grand Lodge (USGL) O.T.O. website describes it as follows:

[1] *Magick Without Tears*, in Crowley (1986), 219.

[2] Ibid.

> [I]t is very difficult to make blanket statements about its [The-
> lema's] nature or (still more so) the natures of its adherents. Even
> the label "religion" fits Thelema awkwardly in some contexts—it
> is in other senses a philosophy and a way of life, while also over-
> lapping with the set of practices and symbols commonly called
> "Magick."[3]

While a number of modern Thelemites insist on a naturalistic, psychological, or secular interpretation instead of a religious one,[4] what
does Crowley say of the word "religion"? In *Magick Without Tears* he
notes that the term derives from the Latin, *religio*, and means "piety."
He writes, "But it also implies a binding together, i.e., of ideas; in fact,
a 'body of doctrine.' Not a bad expression. A religion, then, is a more
or less coherent and consistent set of beliefs, with precepts and pro-
hibitions therefrom deducible."[5] As long-standing O.T.O. member
William Heidrick has noted, the reluctance to characterize Thelema
as a "religion" is most likely due to the baggage associated with the
term rather than any objection on Crowley's part to label Thelema as
such. Heidrick writes "the only reason for such hesitancy would be the
abuse and limitation of the word 'religion' by others."[6] Indeed, Crowley expressed such a sentiment, writing in *Book 4*, "[w]hat is the curse
upon *religion* that its tenets must always be associated with every kind
of extravagance and falsehood?"[7] It is clear however from the letter in
Magick Without Tears quoted above that he did not consider the term
exclusively negative. In fact, he associated Thelema with religion when

---

[3] "Thelema," U.S. Grand Lodge, Ordo Templi Orientis website (accessed April 4,
2018).

[4] The attempt to negotiate religion with science is a common characteristic of pop
esotericism in the modern era, especially in the post-Chaos magick paradigm of contemporary occultism.

[5] *Magick Without Tears*, Chapter 31, in Crowley (1986), 218.

[6] Heidrick (1992), "From the Outbasket," in *Thelema Lodge Calendar*, November
1992, e.v. (Berkeley: O.T.O.).

[7] Crowley (1997), 30.

he commented on *The Book of the Law* writing, "Our *religion* therefore, for the People, is the Cult of the Sun."[8] Similarly he noted "the Law of Thelema definitely enjoins us, as a necessary act of *religion*," and "*religious* ecstasy is necessary to man's soul."[9] Finally, in 1919 he opened *The Equinox* Volume III, Number 1, with the words, "THE WORLD NEEDS RELIGION."[10]

If Thelema is going to be defined within the framework of religion, it is important that we first investigate the term. Grand Master General of the United States, Sabazius X°, reminded members recently in his keynote address to the national O.T.O. conference (NOTOCON) in America that "[t]he Latin word *ligare* means to tie, bind, or unite; and to reestablish such a bond, to reunite after separation or division, is *re-ligare*, from which we ultimately derive our word religion."[11] Indeed, most scholarly sources on the etymology of the word agree that this is its root, which can be traced back to the Roman philosophical poet, Lucretius (c. 96–55 BCE).[12] In this sense, *religion* refers to the bond created between humans and gods. However, all the works that have analyzed the ways in which the word "religion" has been used throughout human history, its etymology, and its definition, could probably fill the contents of several large libraries. More pertinent to the current discussion is how the word is used to describe the phenomenon in the world that we understand today as religion, and to briefly outline how I intend to use the term to apply to Thelema. For this, I will incorporate the work of social theorists and historians who have identified the shifting cultural attitudes towards religion since the late modern period. I am referring here not to how religion has been understood throughout the past centuries, but rather to religion as it has been affected by modernity.

---

[8] Crowley (1996a), 163. Emphasis added by author.

[9] Ibid., 85, Emphasis added by author.

[10] Crowley (1972b), 9.

[11] Sabazius X°, NOTOCON XI Keynote Address, August 12, 2017, Orlando, Florida.

[12] Sarah Hoyt (1912) "The Etymology of Religion," in *Journal of the American Oriental Society*, Vol. 32, No. 2., 126.

When approaching the subject of religion in contemporary society, it is important to discuss specific changes that religion has undergone since the Enlightenment. Social processes have been set in motion by the advancement and influence of scientific rationalism and industrialization, which further led to the bureaucratization and corporatization of Western society. Today, we call this phenomenon "secularization."[13] The secularization thesis has been considered by many social theorists as a way to explain the decreasing influence of religion in society. Some scholars have even suggested secularization will lead to the complete disappearance of religion, or at least they believe it has lost its social significance in the world.[14] Others have maintained that, while the world has become disenchanted due to the modernization of Western culture,[15] it is more probable to say that

---

[13] Four different typologies of secularization have been identified: *disappearance*, *differentiation*, *de-intensification*, and *co-existence*. In short, the *disappearance* thesis claims that religious interpretations about reality will inevitably disappear due to the secularizing processes in Western culture. Such processes include, for instance, the increasing tendencies to explain how the world works through a scientific understanding. As Western culture began to comprehend the world through scientific discovery rather than religious authority, *differentiation* has pushed religion out of the social sphere, and religion shifted primarily into the private domain. Although religion has remained in society, it has witnessed a *de-intensification*, becoming much less influential in the world than in previous centuries. Finally, religion's *co-existence* as a social phenomenon is evidence that it persists as a vital force in some degree. These four typologies have been identified and discussed by Linda Woodhead and Paul Heelas (eds.) (2000).

[14] For arguments defending secularization, refer to Mark Chaves (1994) "Secularization as Declining Religious Authority," and Steve Bruce (2002) *God is Dead: Secularization in the West* in the bibliography.

[15] Max Weber noted that "mysterious and incalculable forces" once held in religious belief became dispelled in such a process, leading Western culture into a disenchanted paradigm, or what Weber referred to as *Enzauberung*. See Weber (1922), "Wissenschaft als Beruf," *Gesammlte Aufsaetze zur Wissenschaftslehre* (Tubingen), 524–55. Translation found in H.H. Gerth and C. Wright Mills (trans., eds.) (1946) *Max Weber: Essays in Sociology* (New York: Oxford University Press), 129–156. The discourse on how disenchantment can even be described has gained some recent attention within religious studies scholarship. Contrary to what many sociologists have

religion has simply changed in form, and that it will never actually go away.[16] How has religion changed? I will get to that shortly. However, I would first like to offer a clear definition of the term "religion" as it will be used here.

"Religion" vs. "Spirituality"

I have selected a definition of religion that has been carefully considered and applied using sources from scholarship within religious studies as well as the sociology of religion. Additionally, the definition of religion by Wouter Hanegraaff (see below) has been utilized within the study of Western esotericism, with which we may approach the subject of Thelema and Aleister Crowley in particular. Finally, the proximate interpretation of the term religion also includes within it a distinction between religion and an even more elusive term, "spirituality."

Religion is defined by Professor Wouter Hanegraaff of the University of Amsterdam as "any symbolic system which influences human action by providing possibilities for ritually maintaining contact between the everyday world and a more general meta-empirical framework of meaning."[17] This definition should be compared with Hanegraaff's

---

defined as a *process*, Egil Asprem has shown that the "process-focused" terminology is problematic for critical historical research; rather the phenomenon of disenchantment is better approached from a "problem-focused" approach. For example esotericists in the twentieth century sought to solve this "problem" by offering scientific interpretations of religion, such as is the case with Aleister Crowley's "Scientific Illuminism." See Asprem (2014) *The Problem of Disenchantment*. The reader may also wish to consult Olav Hammer (2004) *Claiming Knowledge: Strategies of Epistemology from Theosophy to the New Age* (Leiden: Brill). Hammer shows that late modern esotericism has utilized various discursive methods to legitimize its practices, using scientific language in its narratives. In this latter example of narrative and legitimacy, see also chapter eleven in Part II, "Hydra Lernaia."

16 See Rodney Stark (1999), "Secularization, R.I.P."

17 Hanegraaf (1999), 372. In his essay, Hanegraaff examines definitions offered by many prominent scholars of religion such as social theorist Emile Durkheim, anthropologist Clifford Geertz, and scholars of religion Rudolph Otto and Mircea Eliade among others. Hanegraaff's definition therefore incorporates considerations on

interpretation of "a religion," which is "any symbolic system, *embodied in a social institution*, which influences human action by providing possibilities for ritually maintaining contact between the everyday world and a more general meta-empirical framework of meaning."[18] Where *religion* in general refers to a complex system of symbols to aid a human being to make contact (or "create a bond," i.e., see above etymology) with a source beyond empirical boundaries, *a religion* is the same albeit a set of practices *embodied in a social institution* (i.e., a church or fraternal organization).

With these definitions in mind, let us further consider a similarly elusive term, "spirituality." The Oxford dictionary gives only an ambiguous definition: "The quality of being concerned with the human spirit or soul as opposed to material or physical things."[19] Similarly, Merriam-Webster describes spirituality as "the quality or state of being concerned with religion or religious matters: the quality or state of being spiritual."[20] While neither definition is satisfactory, the reader should recall the previous mention of secularization, disenchantment, and the aforementioned changing landscape of religion since the late modern period.[21] This "shift" has been well-documented by scholars of religion to refer to a decrease in traditional, congregational forms of religion and an emerging presence of personal, individualized forms of religion. This distinction helps to explain the growing cliché sentiment, "I am spiritual, but not religious."[22]

---

religion from many sides of the academic podium. The reader would benefit from consulting this reference for a sufficient overview of the discourse in defining religion.

[18] Ibid. Emphasis added by author to show distinction.

[19] Definition, "Spirituality," Oxford Dictionary website. (accessed November 16, 2016).

[20] Definition, "Spirituality," Merriam-Webster Dictionary website. (accessed November 16, 2016).

[21] C.f. previous section.

[22] See Paul Heelas (1996) *The New Age Movement: Religion, Culture, and Society in the Age of Postmodernity* (Cambridge: Blackwell Publishing) and Heelas and Linda Woodhead (2005) *The Spiritual Revolution: Why Religion is Giving Way to Spirituality* (Malden: Blackwell).

"Spirituality" therefore refers to an individualized form of religion. This was first identified by sociologist Ernst Troeltsch, who distinguished between regular "religion" and "mystical religion."[23] "Religion," Troeltsch argued, referred to groups in the traditional sense of a "church" or "sect,"[24] while "mystical religion" applies to a personalized set of beliefs. He described "mystical religion" as:

> [...] that of a religious individualism which has no external orga-
> nization, and which has a very independent attitude, with widely
> differing views of the central truths of [religion].[25]

More recently, Paul Heelas and Linda Woodhead have noted an increasing "individualization" in religious behavior occurring in the latter half of the twentieth century, a phenomenon they refer to as the "subjective turn." It is marked by what they call "subjective-life spirituality," the sacred localized within the individual believer. This stands in direct distinction to "life-as-religion" characterized by traditional congregational activity. The group-based "life-as-religion" identifies the sacred in an external source of authority (i.e., God) whose message is delivered to laity by a priest, rabbi, or imam in a church, synagogue, or mosque.[26]

To understand fully the distinctions being made here between group-focused religion and individualized spirituality, we must compare Wouter Hanegraaff's previous definition of "a religion" with what he calls "a spirituality." The latter is defined as "any human

---

23 Troeltsch noted as early as 1912 that certain aspects of religion were becoming more individualized, and labeled this phenomenon "mystical religion." See Troeltsch (1992) *The Social Teaching of the Christian Churches*. 2 Volumes (Westminster: John Knox Press).

24 The fundamental difference between church and sect is the size of the group, which will dictate other qualifications of the groups' activities.

25 Troeltsch (1992) Vol. I, 381.

26 Heelas and Woodhead (2005), 13–23. While the authors make a clear case, their distinctions remain reductionist, and seem to devalue group-focused religious activity, while favoring individualized spiritualities. Still, their data is compelling evidence of growing sentiments towards individualized forms of religion.

practice which maintains contact between the everyday world and a more general meta-empirical framework of meaning *by way of the individual manipulation* of symbolic systems."[27] Hanegraaff here provides a clear and simple distinction between a personalized set of beliefs and practices called "a spirituality" and "a religion" which has a more social dimension.

It is my opinion that the definitions offered by Hanegraaff meet the criteria to place Thelema within the context of religion. Like all spiritual and religious messages, those who have accepted Thelema have a very deep personal connection to it. Thelema indeed has a structure that relies heavily upon symbolic systems of meaning intended to establish contact between the adherent and a reality beyond the material world (e.g., "praeterhuman intelligences").[28] When we talk about Thelema as a *movement*—insofar as there is a growing network of people who have incorporated the ideas and practices set in place by the religion's founder, Aleister Crowley, and have organized themselves into one or more recognizable bodies—then we may define any institution that embraces Thelema (i.e., the O.T.O. and E.G.C.) as *a religion*. Finally, if we consider the discussion in chapter two of the A∴A∴, then *a spirituality* might best fit to describe the A∴A∴.

A∴A∴: The Spiritual Dimension of Thelema

The A∴A∴ is primarily concerned with spiritual and mystical matters. That is, the A∴A∴ concerns the teachings of the Secret Chiefs and the spiritual development of the individual to the end of making contact with these Chiefs. In *Magick Without Tears*, Crowley describes the system of the A∴A∴ in a letter to one of his students:

the A∴A∴ concerns the individual, his development, his initiation, his passage from "Student" to "Ipsissimus"; he has no con-

---

[27] Hanegraaff (1999). Emphasis added by author.

[28] The reader should note I used "material" world, and not "natural," "phenomenal," or "empirical" world.

tact of any kind with any other person except the Neophyte who introduces him, and any Student or Students whom he may, after becoming a Neophyte, introduce. The details of this "Pilgrim's Progress" are very fully set forth in *One Star in Sight* [...][29]

The above description of the A∴A∴ defines it primarily as the teaching order put in place by Crowley for individual attainment. Indeed, one of his primary goals was to encourage each and every man and woman to discover his or her own individual unique nature or "True Will."

The reader will recall my assertion that the A∴A∴ is the transmitter of Thelema—the spiritual message of the Secret Chiefs—to Aleister Crowley. He became the prophet of the New Aeon, To Mega Therion, because of this.

Crowley called the training curriculum in the A∴A∴ system "scientific illuminism," claiming that anyone disciplined enough, and pure of intention, could make fruitful strides toward spiritual development. It is for this reason that when an individual "aspires to the A∴A∴," he or she is fulfilling the spiritual element of Thelema. In fact, whenever an individual performs a Class D ritual or practice from the curriculum, he or she may be understood as in some way seeking after spiritual contact with the A∴A∴. Hymenaeus Beta has recently noted the efficacy of the system, even for those who are solitary practitioners, saying: "there are kids out there in their bedrooms just using the internet for this information who are really doing this stuff, and they are getting places with it, and that is the most encouraging thing about it."[30] We can see from this understanding of the A∴A∴ that the above definition of spirituality as an individualized, mystical form of religion is sufficient to describe the A∴A∴.

---

[29] Crowley (1986), 122.

[30] William Breeze, speaking on a panel for the New York University Steinhardt art exhibition, "Language of the Birds: Occult and Art," moderated by curator Pam Grossman, 80WSE Gallery, New York City, February 10, 2016.

O.T.O.: The Religious Dimension of Thelema

The O.T.O. serves a different function than that of the A∴A∴. As we saw in chapter three, its aim is to promulgate and help establish Thelema in the world at large. I will here discuss the O.T.O. as a group-based Thelemic organization that fulfills the "religious" element of Thelema. However, it is first important to present the spiritual aspect of the O.T.O. so that readers are aware that the distinctions made between the two systems are not hard divisions but fluid.

The difference between subjective spirituality in the A∴A∴ and group-based religion in the O.T.O. is admittedly reductionist to some degree. This differentiation is made for convenience to help demonstrate the social element that characterizes O.T.O. activities, and to remember that the system of the A∴A∴ is primarily an individualized path to attainment. It is worth mentioning that the classification of the O.T.O. as group-based is *not* the same as claiming that there is not a personalized, *spiritual* element to the O.T.O. system. In fact, the initiatory system of the O.T.O., beginning with the degrees of Man of Earth, is designed to be an intensely personal experience for its members. The fundamental difference in the initiatory paths of the O.T.O. and the A∴A∴ is that the former instructs candidates to externalize their spiritual center of awareness in the world at large, to govern themselves in society and among their peers through the lessons they learn, and to establish bonds of fraternity with their fellow members. By contrast, the A∴A∴ brings the candidate on an inward journey of self-discovery, to understand who one truly is, and for what purpose we have come into existence.

The above description of the initiatory differences between the O.T.O. and the A∴A∴ was expounded upon in November of 2016, when J. Daniel Gunther presented a series of lectures in Belgrade, noting the "twin phases of the Path" of Thelema: the rites of passage "from Life unto Death" in the O.T.O. system, and "from Death unto Life" in the A∴A∴. These "Two Ways of Going" were described by Gunther as the "Path of Day," in the O.T.O. or "Initiation in the Natural World." The "Path of Night," by contrast, is the A∴A∴ or "Initiation in the

Spiritual World."[31] Gunther later remarked, "each order has a different approach, each order has a different methodology. Our goal, on the other hand, is essentially the same [...] Our job is to try to manifest the Law of Thelema to the world [...] and we need to work hand-in-hand— and we do work hand-in-hand—to bring this to pass."[32]

Returning to the social dimension of the O.T.O. as group-based religion, we may recall from the earlier discussion that *a religion* was defined within the context of being *embodied in a social institution*. The O.T.O. may then be understood as operating within the *religious* dimension of Thelema. It fulfills the social need for spiritual fellowship amongst a group of people. The O.T.O. includes group functions— such as initiation rituals and the performance of public ceremonies like the Gnostic Mass. Many O.T.O. groups around the world hold other social events—including workshops, classes, fundraisers, celebrations, and dinner parties. The O.T.O., then serves a function for adherents to Thelema that the A∴A∴ does not. The O.T.O. serves the basic human need for fellowship and community for a group of people with like interests.

The nature of the business handled by the O.T.O. is also different from that of the A∴A∴. The exclusively personalized characteristic of the A∴A∴ is such that it brings the student through a rigorous system of disciplinary practices so that he or she experiences union with God and, in turn, assists others to accomplish the same mystical experiences under their tutelage. The O.T.O. instructs its members how to operate in the world through a series of allegorical ceremonies that represents one's journey in life. It therefore deals with groups, and functions under guidelines and policies which promote unity in diversity through the principles of fraternity. In short, O.T.O. aims to create a society that operates on Thelemic principles, a "Thelemic culture" so to

---

[31] J. Daniel Gunther, "The Order that Hath No Name Among Men," Belgrade, Serbia, November 12, 2016.

[32] Interview J. Daniel Gunther by Frater Puck (p.s. Peter Seals), Thelema NOW! 2015.

speak. Advancement in the Order is conferred by one's aptitude and willingness to devote oneself to the service of his or her fellow brothers and sisters. In this way, the spiritual dimension of the O.T.O. is present in the refining process of a mundane person into an initiate through dedication and the selfless service of *karma yoga*.

⚬⚭⚬

Before concluding this chapter and bringing Part I to its close, it is important to provide a brief analysis of the academic development in the sociological study of the occult. This synopsis will prepare the reader for the discussion on the Thelemic movement in Part II, particularly when we arrive at the pivotal period of the 1960s counterculture and the emergence of "Thelemic occulture."

The Sociology of the Occult: From the Cultic Milieu to Occulture

Esoteric and occult currents gained serious scholarly attention in sociology following the counterculture years of the 1960s.[33] In the 1970s, social theorists drew heavily from Troeltsch's aforementioned distinctions between religion and mystical religion, the latter of which was now referred to as "cultic religion."[34] Cultic religion is defined as being individualistic and inclusive (or syncretic) by nature, and as having a loose and unstable structure. Characterized by a tolerant religious pluralism, cultic religion is composed of various diffuse spiritualties that make up a general cultural ethos described by Colin Campbell as the

---

[33] Most notable is Edward Tiryakian (1972) "Toward the Sociology of Esoteric Culture," in *American Journal of Sociology,* 78:3 (November), 491–512. For a survey on sociological work on esotericism and the occult, see Kennet Granholm, "Sociology and the Occult," in Christopher Partridge (ed.) (2015) *The Occult World* (New York: Routledge), 720–731.

[34] For clarification on the usage of the term "cultic religion," see Roy Wallis (1974) "Ideology, Authority, and the Development of Cultic Movements," in *Social Research*, Vol. 41, No. 2, 299–327.

"cultic milieu."[35] According to Campbell, these cultic groups have no clear boundaries and are highly transitory:

> Given that cultic groups have a tendency to be ephemeral and highly unstable, it is a fact that new ones are being born just as fast as the old ones die. There is a continual process of cult formation and collapse which parallels the high turnover of membership at the individual level.[36]

Despite this heterogeneousness, Campbell claims that this cultural ethos is composed of a single milieu that can be characterized by deviant religious beliefs:

> At the basis of the unifying tendencies is the fact that all these worlds share a common position as heterodox or deviant items in relation to the dominant cultural orthodoxies. This fact gives rise to a common consciousness of deviance and the need to justify their own views in the light of the expressed ridicule or hostility of the larger society.[37]

The quality of "deviance" is important to note, as it implies that these diffuse spiritualties are divergent from traditional forms of religion.[38] In this sense, esoteric and occult currents of the subcultural and countercultural underground are oppositional to mainstream society.[39]

---

[35] See Colin Campbell (1972) "The Cult, the Cultic Milieu, and Secularization" in M. Hill (ed.) *A Sociological Yearbook of Religion in Britain*, Vol. 5, 9–36. Also Colin Campbell (1977) "Clarifying the Cult." In *The British Journal of Sociology*, Vol. 28, No. 3, 375–388.

[36] Campbell (1972), 121.

[37] Ibid., 122.

[38] For a discussion of what is meant by "deviance" in culture, refer to Howard Becker (1963) *Outsiders: Studies in the Sociology of Deviance* (London: Collier-Macmillan, Ltd.).

[39] See Jeffrey Kaplan and Heléne Lööw (2002) *The Cultic Milieu: Oppositional Subcultures in an Age of Globalization* (New York: Rowman & Littlefield Publishers, Inc).

Campbell claims that the cultic milieu includes "the worlds of the occult and the magical, of spiritualism and psychic phenomena, of mysticism and new thought, of alien intelligences and lost civilizations, of faith healing and nature cure."[40]

More recently, scholars have equated the cultic milieu with the highly elusive term, "New Age" religion.[41] As Wouter Hanegraaff notes, "the New Age is either synonymous with the cultic milieu or that it represents a specific historical stage in the development of it."[42] Like Campbell's cultic milieu, Hanegraaff classifies New Age religion as a phenomenon combining various loosely structured religious currents that hang together insofar as they are unlike normative orthodoxy. Paul Heelas and Linda Woodhead have similarly grouped the myriad branches of New Age religion under the previously discussed "subjective life spirituality," defining it as "multifarious forms of sacred activity which are often grouped together under collective terms like 'body, mind, and spirit,' 'New Age,' 'alternative' or 'holistic' spirituality, and which include (spiritual) yoga, reiki, meditation, tai chi, aromatherapy, much paganism, rebirthing, reflexology, much Wicca and many more."[43]

More recently, scholarship on esoteric religion has further developed the discourse on the cultic milieu, utilizing the neologism "occulture." The term is a portmanteau of "occult" and "culture," and refers to occult currents that underlie and even saturate Western society. "Occulture" was originally coined by industrial music pioneer Genesis P-Orridge (born Neil Andrew Megson, 1950) to describe the formation of an occult counter-identity through the use of art, media and occult practices. As an academic phrase, occulture refers to a phenomenon that strides the currents of a deviant counterculture

---

[40] Ibid.

[41] See Wouter Hanegraaff (1998) *New Age Religion and Western Culture: Esotericism in the Mirror of Secular Thought* (Albany: State of New York University Press) and Paul Heelas (1996) *The New Age Movement: Religion, Culture, and Society in the Age of Postmodernity* (Cambridge: Blackwell Publishing).

[42] Hanegraaff (1998), 16.

[43] Heelas and Woodhead (2005), 23.

and a normative mainstream, wherein occult and esoteric streams of art and music penetrate popular culture. Christopher Partridge argues that "occulture is ordinary," implying that occult currents have become a common element in Western society as a whole.[44] Partridge draws heavily upon the sociological concept of the cultic milieu, along with the work of Raymond Williams, to help explain occulture.[45] However, Partridge distinguishes occulture from the cultic milieu, arguing that occulture comprises common elements of *mainstream* popular culture rather than that of the *deviant* sub-cultures of the underground. In this case, occulture is a sort of "mystical collective" that is part and parcel of contemporary society:

> [W]hilst mystical religionists are individualistic, they are aware that they belong to a wider community of like-minded religious individualists, the mystic collectivity [...] those belonging to the mystic collectivity often feel a sense of duty to serve that spiritual community through, for example, fairs, publications, or workshops, thereby leading, on the one hand, to a greater sense of fellowship and, on the other hand, often to the establishment of external organizations, centres and groups.[46]

Partridge argues that interest in the occult has become so widespread in popular culture that it can be regarded as an ordinary phenomenon. Furthermore, Partridge claims that occulture is: (1) an expression of a way of life, and (2) describes the creative processes of constructing meaning—two fundamental (and ordinary) processes of culture. Not only has traditional religion declined, but there is a parallel rise in individualized forms of religion, while popular culture has increasingly

---

[44] See Christopher Partridge (2013) "Occulture is Ordinary," in Asprem and Granholm (2013), 113–133.

[45] See Raymond Williams (1958) "Culture is Ordinary," in *The Everyday Life Reader*, Ben Highmore (ed.) (London: Routledge).

[46] Christopher Partridge (2004) *The Re-enchantment of the West: Alternative Spiritualities, Sacralization, Popular Culture, and Occulture*, Vol. I. (London: T&T Clark International), 65.

disseminated the esoteric and occult through art and media. From best-selling novels like *The Da Vinci Code* to prime time television shows like *Ancient Aliens*, Partridge argues that new meanings and ways of life related to the occult are common phenomena, and hence a basic aspect of our culture. Finally, the increasing popularity of alternative religious practice and their widespread dissemination are evidence of a society that has become "re-enchanted" despite the processes of secularization.

It should be clear that the on-going discourse on the study of religion is complex. I have devoted so much time to this subject because by distinguishing loaded concepts such as "religion" and "spirituality"—two terms that have historical, cultural, and social baggage—we are able to define our topic, Thelema, more clearly. By categorizing the differences between "a religion" and "spirituality," we can better understand Thelema, which partakes of both.

The term "occulture" is also important for our future discussions, because it can be used as a methodological phrase to indicate the various Thelemic currents that are becoming increasingly salient in contemporary culture. From this perspective, Thelemic occulture can refer to Thelemic publications that were present throughout the 1960s and 1970s, as well the various digital platforms that appropriate Thelema through online channels today.

⚜

Let us now explore some history of how Thelema was put out into the world, how it became nearly extinguished, and how it has resurfaced as a lively and diverse movement of individuals today. The subsequent pages will show the complex dynamics involved in the development of a new religious movement in contemporary society.

PART II

The Thelemic Movement

History and Publication

(1962–1998)

CHAPTER SEVEN

A Prelude:

The Sun Sets on the Beast and in the West

Agape Lodge and Crowley's Closing Decade
(1935–1950)

WE NOW ENTER A HISTORY of the Thelemic movement since the death of Aleister Crowley. For nearly four decades, spanning the years from 1947 to 1985, Thelema underwent a series of events during which it nearly disappeared. The following chapters will show that the survival of the movement was contingent on both the publication efforts to print Crowley's literary corpus and a handful of dedicated followers who strove to keep the two orders alive. The story that follows is a complex one—with a twisting and complicated series of events that can leave even the historian perplexed. A number of specific historical, cultural and geographic factors both constrained and facilitated Thelema's growth in a variety of ways, presenting a fascinating narrative of how a new religious movement claims its place in modern culture.

Let us begin with a look at the last decade of Crowley's life and the state of the movement at the time of his death. In the United Kingdom, Crowley had established relationships with a few disciples, even though the O.T.O. was not functioning in any lodges. Almost all of the fraternal activity of the O.T.O. in the closing years of the Beast's life was centered in California in Agape Lodge, an overview of which will now be presented.

America Revisited: Agape Lodge (1935–1949)

The Thelemic movement weakened after Crowley's death. This was due in part to the activity, or rather inactivity, of his successor, Karl Johannes Germer (1885–1962). Germer's lack of urgency to continue the O.T.O. was a result of his dealings with intragroup conflicts in Agape Lodge, as well as the trauma he suffered in Germany in WWII and subsequently in post-war America. As we will soon see, it would be the remaining members of Agape Lodge and Germer's student, Marcelo Ramos Motta (1931–1987), who would be the few who would care enough to pick up the pieces.

Even in 1925, when Crowley succeeded Theodor Reuss as the Outer Head of the Order,[1] activity associated with the O.T.O. was losing momentum worldwide. The attempt to form a Supreme Grand Council of O.T.O. in Detroit, Michigan, between 1918 and 1919 proved to be a failure from the start.[2] Agape Lodge of North Vancouver, formally British Columbia Lodge No. 1, held its last meeting in February of 1922.[3] There had been no lodge activity in England since the raid of O.T.O. headquarters by London police in 1917.[4] While Crowley

---

[1] Refer to chapter two for a discussion of this event.

[2] The problem began with attempts to publish his periodical *The Equinox*, the distribution of which was originally agreed to be handled by Albert Winslow Ryerson (b. 1872) through his company, Universal Book Stores. Ryerson, along with a number of other masons, signed a pledge form for O.T.O. in April of 1919. However, the agreement to establish an O.T.O. headquarters in the U.S. failed the following November when several of the Freemasons objected to O.T.O. parameters, such as the admission of women, and a disagreement concerning the ritual of the Gnostic Mass published in *The Equinox* Vol. III, No. 1. A scandal also arose due to this publication, with the local press inciting concern from the authorities of the existence of a devil-worshipping love-cult in Detroit in January and February of 1922. This is discussed in detail in Kazcynski (2010), 331–354; Starr (2003) 95–103; and in more depth in Kaczynski (2006), and again in O.T.O. (2015) *Success Is Your Proof*, 85–100.

[3] O.T.O. had its first existence in North America in British Columbia, Canada. British Columbia Lodge No. 1 was established on April 17, 1915 by Crowley's student Charles Stansfeld Jones (1886–1950). Jones was later appointed a Grand Master (X°) for North America by Reuss.

[4] Pasi (2014), 16.

continued to instruct students in the A∴A∴ and promote Thelema through his publishing efforts,[5] it became increasingly difficult to realize a functioning O.T.O. group in Europe during the turbulent time of the interwar period.

Agape Lodge in America was the most successful and longest running O.T.O. lodge in Crowley's lifetime. It was re-established in southern California in September of 1935 by Wilfred Talbot Smith (1885–1957). Smith had joined the Canadian Agape Lodge in 1915, and began informal activities in Los Angeles as early as 1922 when he moved to the United States.[6] Membership included a handful of other figures such as Thelemic refugee from Cefalù and actress Jane Wolfe (1875–1958), opera singer and voice teacher Regina Kahl (1891–1945), and Smith's work colleague Oliver Jacobi (1894–1974), among others. As the California Thelemites began to congregate, they formed a community. Smith and Kahl began the first public performance of "Liber XV: The Gnostic Mass" in March of 1933.[7] Regular celebrations of the Gnostic Mass followed at Agape Lodge's temple on Winona Boulevard in Hollywood, and Smith established "The Church of Thelema," placing the Mass at center stage. Membership grew quite significantly, attracting some who will later become key players in our story, including Phyllis Seckler, Grady Louis McMurtry, and John Whiteside (Jack) Parsons.

Although Agape Lodge was quite active, it was also fraught with difficulties. Smith caught the sharp criticism of Crowley, who was made aware of seemingly questionable behavior concerning Smith and female members. According to Lodge member Max Schneider, Agape had developed an atmosphere of open adultery amongst its members, which led to personality conflicts, jealously, and discord. These reports

---

[5] Some of the more notable works of these included *Magick*, published by Lecram Press in Paris in 1929, followed by *The Equinox of the Gods*, published privately in 1936 and limited to 250 copies. It was an ongoing struggle, even in Crowley's lifetime, to get his works into print. See Hymenaeus Beta's editor notes in Crowley (1997).

[6] Smith had emigrated from England to Canada in 1907, living for some time in British Columbia before finally settling in California in the spring of 1922.

[7] Starr (2003), 193.

were shared with Germer, who had relocated to the United States to escape his home country of Germany under the Nazis.[8] Crowley came to believe that Smith's "sexual acrobatics tended to give the Order the reputation of being that slimy abomination, a 'love-cult'."[9] Many of the allegations were probably embellished by jealous members like Schneider, but there was undoubtedly some truth to them. Smith was eventually forced to resign as Lodge Master and required to take a compulsory "Magical Retirement" in the summer of 1943.

With Smith sequestered away, Agape Lodge was taken over for a short period of time by Jack Parsons (1914–1952).[10] This, however, proved to be only temporary, as Jack would be led away by his own escapades less than three years later. He began to perform the so-called "Babalon Working"[11] with L. Ron Hubbard in January of 1946. Parsons and Hubbard then entered into a business relationship. They agreed they would purchase yachts in Florida, sail them to California, and sell them for a profit. However, Hubbard attempted to swindle Parsons by taking his money (and his girlfriend), and sailing off with a yacht purchased in Miami. Parsons followed Hubbard to Florida and recovered whatever losses he was able. Upon his return to Pasadena, Agape Lodge languished for a time. Parsons decided to take the Oath of the Abyss in 1949 and sold off all his assets. Tragedy struck on June 17,

---

[8] Germer suffered imprisonment in a Nazi internment camp for a time, and subsequently came under investigation by the FBI after relocating to New York.

[9] Crowley to Wilfred T. Smith, November 11, 1943, GYC.

[10] John Whiteside Parson was an American engineer, pioneering the development of rocket propulsion. His involvement with O.T.O. amid the cultural climate of McCarthyism in the United States found him accused of espionage, resulting in his inability to continue working with rocketry. He was also an early influence on the founder of Dianetics and Scientology, L. Ron Hubbard. See Carter (2004) and Pendle (2005). On his involvement with Hubbard specifically, see Corydon and Hubbard, Jr. (1987) and Miller (2014).

[11] The events that took place between Parsons and Hubbard has been outlined in Henrik Bogdan (2016) "The Babalon Working 1946: L. Ron Hubbard, John Whiteside Parsons, and the Practice of Enochian Magic." In *NVMEN: International Review for the History of Religions*, Vol. 63 (Leiden: Brill), 12–32.

1952, when he was killed in an explosion in his home. The remaining members attempted to revive the Lodge, but with Crowley dead and Germer's lack of leadership, activities ceased shortly thereafter.

⊰⧉⊱

Succession: Karl Germer

> There are some small spirits who proclaim their folly that Thelema is dead, and that nothing is happening. The Gods, however have Their own Timetable.
>
> —Karl Germer to Marcelo Motta, December 9, 1958

Aleister Crowley died in Netherwood, Hastings, on December 1, 1947. Karl Germer,[12] known by his magical name of Frater Saturnus, assumed leadership of both the A∴A∴ and O.T.O. as intended by Crowley. He had sent Germer a legal document on July 18, 1941, granting Germer authority in both orders:

> By these Presents, I, Edward Alexander Crowley, otherwise known as Aleister Crowley, or as To Mega Therion, chief of the A∴A∴, or as Baphomet, Frater Superior and O.H.O. of the O.T.O. (Ordo Templi Orientis) do appoint Mr. Karl J. Germer, now residing [...] to be my personal agent and representative in the United States of America.
>
> I hereby authorize and empower him to initiate, carry through, and conclude any contracts that he may see fit to make

---

12 Born in Germany, Karl Germer spent most of his childhood in his home country and later studying in Paris at Sorbonne University. In the 1920s he worked at Barth Publishing House with O.T.O. member Heinrich Tränker (see chapter two). It was within this milieu in 1925 that he met Crowley during the Weida Conference in Thuringia. He became a devoted follower of Crowley, and would later become his representative in the United States to help oversee Agape Lodge and ultimately succeed the Beast in the O.T.O. and the A∴A∴.

on my behalf especially as concerns my work as a writer and lecturer.

All persons in authority under me in connection with the A∴A∴ and O.T.O. are to recognize him as their chief.

This present document is to be regarded as Equivalent to a Power of Attorney, and is to be valid until further notice.

Witness my Hand
Edward Alexander Crowley   Aleister Crowley
To Mega Therion 666 9°=2□ A∴A∴
Baphomet O.H.O. X° 33° 90° 97°[13]

While the idea of Germer succeeding him never wavered to his dying day, we will see later that Crowley had in mind a "successor's successor" to follow Germer. For the moment, it is important to explore in more depth what the years of Germer's headship entailed.

As might be expected for a religious movement in the first years after the death of its founder, the early posthumous years of Thelema were little more than "transitional." It is evident that Germer was not particularly interested in advancing the O.T.O., and instead put his aims in the A∴A∴, at least with regard to publication. He admitted to Jane Wolfe in March of 1948, "The trouble is that Agape Lodge has not produced anyone with the Tiphareth stage or beyond (5°=6□ of the A∴A∴) it seems." He continued, "What I am concerned with is the A∴A∴ material, etc. for which I want a safe place, over which I have some sort of control, so that I need not worry constantly that it might be falling under control of people who have not even a faint glimpse of the lofty higher grades."[14] He expressed his lack of interest in the O.T.O. later to his student Marcelo Motta when he wrote, "the O.T.O. does not interest me too much; mine is only in the A∴A∴."[15] Germer's main

---

[13] Crowley to Germer, July 18, 1941, O.T.O. Archives.

[14] Karl Germer to Jane Wolfe, March 8, 1948. In Shoemaker, Ferrell, and Voss (eds.) (2016), 158.

[15] Karl Germer to Marcelo Motta, September 20, 1957. GMC.

prerogatives then would lie in securing Crowley's literary estate and publishing either out-of-print books or previously unavailable works. It was an arduous task that was not undertaken alone. Crowley's last will and testament left these materials to the O.T.O. His literary executors, John Symonds (1914–2006)[16] and Louis Wilkinson (1881–1966), compiled the extensive collection of diaries, letters, and manuscripts, while Gerald Yorke (1901–1983) consolidated much of the literary remains that were in existence in the United Kingdom.[17] Yorke and Germer arranged to send one another materials that the other was missing. Once Yorke gathered the corpus in its entirety, he placed the archives in the Warburg Institute of the University of London, where they exist today. Once Germer secured the literary remains, he placed them in storage in his house in Hampton, New Jersey.

O.T.O. Under Germer

As alluded to above, little O.T.O. activity developed under Germer's authority. What effort he put forth was toward the designation of higher degrees. He did, however, make some attempts to further the Order in Europe. Germer authorized Frederic Mellinger (1890–1970)[18] to give Hermann Metzger (1919–1990) the IX° in Hamburg, and a charter to formulate an O.T.O. Lodge in Switzerland. Kenneth Grant (1924–2011) was initiated into the IX° by Germer on October 5, 1948, and

---

[16] Symonds would be one of the last people in close proximity to Crowley before his death. As Crowley's literary executor, Symonds would gain access to much of the raw materials and publish in 1951 the first biography of Crowley, *The Great Beast*. See Symonds (1951).

[17] Gerald Yorke had been a student of A∴A∴ under Crowley, and had taken a magical oath to preserve the Beast's work as early as 1928. He eventually parted from Thelema in 1932 to study Buddhism and later Hinduism, though the two men retained a friendship and Yorke kept his Oath.

[18] Frederic Mellinger, IX° O.T.O., was a Jewish refugee from Germany who had occult leanings and came into contact with Wilfred T. Smith in 1940 during his residency in California. Upon his acquaintance, Mellinger was introduced to both the A∴A∴ and the O.T.O. by Smith. See Kaczynski (2010), 546–547.

issued a charter to operate a Camp of O.T.O. in England in March of 1951. Both of these efforts failed, however. Germer fell into disagreement with Metzger over his German translations of Crowley's works.[19] In 1955, Grant published a document entitled, "Manifesto of the New Isis Lodge O.T.O.," an eight-page treatise announcing a "new and compelling influence" that was enveloping the earth, transmitted from a "transplutonic" planet he called Isis.[20] Grant identified this planet with the speaker of the first chapter of *The Book of the Law*, the star goddess Nuit. Germer did not approve, claiming that Grant was blaspheming the Thelemic Holy Book. "Isis = a planet = Nuit!! It is utterly crazy, as a planet is a mere satellite, then part of the Sun. The Sun with all its planets, is a mere mite in the system of our galaxy of stars. There are thousands or millions of galaxies. And Nuit embraces them all."[21] Germer subsequently expelled Grant in July of 1955 for "making false and misleading statements therein, printing outright lies, and generally sailing under false pretenses."[22]

Grady Louis McMurtry made an attempt to convince Germer to re-establish the O.T.O. in the United States, but this attempt was met with failure. Given that McMurtry was associated with the now-defunct and ill-reputed Agape Lodge, Germer had no interest in working with McMurtry, or any of the other California Thelemites, in re-establishing the O.T.O. Any effort to activate the O.T.O. aroused

---

[19] Starr (2003), 343.

[20] See Bogdan, (2014).

[21] Karl Germer to Jane Wolfe, June 27, 1955. In Shoemaker, Ferrell, and Voss (eds.) (2016), 335.

[22] Letter to Kenneth Grant, signed "Karl Germer X° and Frater Superior O.T.O., Hampton, New Jersey," July 20, 1955. Grant was a primary exponent of Crowley's legacy in the latter half of the twentieth century. He would administer his own Thelemic organization, first known as the Typhonian Ordo Templi Orientis and later the Typhonian Order. Grant has contributed a great deal to disseminating the works of Aleister Crowley. He also published works by occultist Austin Osman Spare, considered the forefather in the narrative of the Chaos Magick tradition emerging in the 1960s. A proper biography of Grant has yet to be written, although a bibliographical history has been treated in Bogdan (2003), and a collection of essays, Bogdan (ed.) (2018) *Servants of the Star & the Snake* has been announced by Starfire Publishing,

Germer's suspicions. As McMurtry later recalled, Germer, "saw this as 'treason' and 'plotting against me.'"[23]

Germer's recalcitrant attitude to further O.T.O. is not difficult to understand. He lived within a wartime culture. Suspicions abounded; he was a foreigner from Germany; and cold-war tensions were aflame in 1950s America.[24] Germer had suffered five months of imprisonment by the Nazi regime in 1935 on the allegations of being an associate of the "High Grade Freemason Aleister Crowley."[25] Later, on May 10, 1940, he was captured by French authorities in Belgium and sent to a concentration camp in Le Vijean, where he stayed until February 1, 1941. When his wife at the time, Cora, secured a visa for him, he was freed and moved to New York City in March of 1941. Germer soon came under the suspicion of the F.B.I. His New York City apartment was searched, and he himself was interrogated and interviewed about his German background and correspondence with Aleister Crowley.[26]

The reader will recall the frustrations and annoyances with the California Thelemites and the social quagmire at Agape Lodge. Germer was expected to handle these matters as Crowley's representative in the United States. However, his lack of interest in Lodge work was only compounded by his past traumatic experiences, which reinforced his proclivities towards reclusiveness. It is no surprise that he turned his sights to the publishing world of Thelema.

Early Posthumous Publications and the A∴A∴

While the O.T.O. languished under Germer—and it would be nearly twenty years before the Templar Order would see any significant activity—Germer must be understood as an indispensable figure during the early post-Crowley period. His securing of the Crowley library alone was incalculably important for the future of the Thelemic movement.

---

[23] Letter from Grady L. McMurtry to Phyllis Seckler, December 19, 1968. GM-PSC.

[24] A short introduction to the cultural paradigm is offered in the following chapter.

[25] Martin P. Starr (2012), 227.

[26] Starr (2003), 284–285.

Yet, it is apparent from a 1942 letter to Jane Wolfe that he never went through any of the technical curriculums of either order, "I have never in the outer formality, been initiated into the A∴A∴, nor the O.T.O. for that matter. It seemed to make a difference to me years ago; but no longer."[27] Germer believed Crowley stopped keeping track of all the tedious grade work by the end of his life. He felt that, in terms of the path of the A∴A∴, people had to initiate themselves through the grades. He would remark years later to his student, Marcelo Motta, of his personal approach to the system:

> Yours is the magical and intellectual field, and we have no one here whose feet fit into A.C.'s shoes, as far as that part of the Work goes. As you know, my field is entirely different; I have not read much of the occult literature; I have not done the practices; my mind and memory doesn't encourage it.[28]

While Germer may have been nearsighted about the practical import of grade work, his mundane business sensibilities allowed him to consolidate the Crowley library and publish some of the Beast's work. One of his earliest publications would be *The Vision and the Voice* in 1952. He was assisted by former Agape Lodge member and later mistress Phyllis Seckler, née Pratt (1917–2004),[29] who retyped the work from a typescript with Crowley's commentary. *The Vision and the Voice* was printed in October on mimeographed sheets and bound in a thirty-two-ring spiral notebook, limited to around 100 copies, and published by Germer's own "Thelema Publishing Company" in Barstow, California.[30]

---

[27] Karl Germer to Jane Wolfe, September 15, 1942. UC.

[28] Karl Germer to Marcelo Motta, February 15, 1957. GMC.

[29] While her last name may be listed as Pratt, Seckler, Wade, or McMurtry, depending on the period of her life, she will be referred to herein as Phyllis Seckler.

[30] *The Vision and the Voice* had only previously been available in the original periodical, *The Equinox*, Volume I, Number 5, published in 1911. See Crowley (1909–1913). Many of these original copies of the 1952 edition described above remained unbound until they were reissued by Helen Parsons Smith sometime in the 1970s.

Phyllis Seckler

It is appropriate here to introduce Phyllis Seckler in more detail. She was a significant figure in the modern development of the O.T.O. and it is through this early correspondence with Germer that she begins to step into more light for our narrative. Phyllis had been initiated at Agape Lodge into the Minerval degree in 1939. An extremely strong-willed individual, Seckler had developed a reputation for clashing with the people around her, even in the early days of Agape Lodge. Jane Wolfe once remarked to Karl Germer that Phyllis had "an amazing capacity for upsetting the house."[31] Wolfe later described Phyllis' demeanor:

> At times she looks like an angel straight from heaven, but there is a hard cold side like marble, and calculating. Always knew better than anyone else: stubborn and unyielding. She is my probationer, has been for 1½ years. I think the suffering she has gone through with [sic] has been necessary to soften up some of these hard spots.[32]

Despite her combative and high-strung personality, which may have typified some others in Agape Lodge as well, her timeline as this story progresses will show that she had a keen sense of being in the right place at the right time, or at least being in contact with the right people at the right time.

The correspondence between Phyllis and Germer, initiated in 1952, sheds light on other developments at that time. Before Germer wrote to Phyllis in February to inquire about assistance with *The Vision and the Voice*, he mused to Jane Wolfe, "I know well about Roy having played the 'spark-plug' for Phyllis' growth to Tiphareth [...]

See Crowley (1952a). Some pictures of the re-issued edition by Helen Parsons Smith can be found at 100th Monkey Press, an online source for antiquarian esoteric literature (www.100thmonkeypress.com, accessed April 4, 2018).

31 Wolfe to Germer, October 11, 1942. Quoted in Starr (2003), 279.

32 Jane Wolfe to Karl Germer, September 9, 1943. UC.

Incidentally, I feel sometimes as if Phyllis focused her imagination too much on me as an object of love."[33] Or maybe Germer was feeling flattered. Regardless, as the publication project ensued, so too did their relationship. Correspondence during this time reveals not only the project regarding the publication of *The Vision and the Voice*, but also contains seemingly amorous exchanges, as well as a developing A∴A∴ student-teacher relationship. Phyllis sent Germer poems that "were inspired by love"[34] and earnestly discussed her purported experience with the Holy Guardian Angel. Germer often replied with fawning statements towards Phyllis and offered guidance in A∴A∴ work. In several letters, he wrote to her believing she had made illuminating achievements: "Dear child, [...] you have risen to or above Tiphareth where the voice of the Secret Chiefs is gradually taking over and begins to speak to your soul."[35] As we will later see, this early correspondence between Seckler and Germer will play a significant role in the construction of her A∴A∴ narrative of legitimacy.

The Odd Couple: Karl Germer and Marcelo Ramos Motta

It is now necessary to turn our attention to another major figure who makes his appearance at this time. Germer was in the midst of publishing another significant work. In the late 1940s, Crowley had intended to publish a book known as *Aleister Explains Everything*. It was a collection of some eighty personal letters sent to his students, discussing a number of varied subjects—ranging from ceremonial magic to philosophical topics on morality, marriage, and death. This work was consolidated and finally published by Germer in 1954, again by Thelema Publishing Company, and entitled *Magick Without Tears*. It was copy-

---

[33] Karl Germer to Jane Wolfe, January 5, 1952. Shoemaker, Ferrell, and Voss (eds.) (2016), 259.

[34] Seckler to Germer, 1952. Exact date not given. Seckler (2012), 214.

[35] Germer to Seckler, July 7, 1952. Quoted by Seckler (2012), 277. Many have interpreted this to mean that Germer recognized Seckler as an Adeptus Minor, the grade of 5°=6□, wherein the student attains to the "Knowledge and Conversation of the Holy Guardian Angel."

righted under Germer's name and address in Hampton, and included a forward by Germer himself.[36]

Germer needed a promising student who could aid him in his publishing endeavors. Enter a young Brazilian by the name of Marcelo Ramos Motta (1931–1987), then a student at Louisiana State University in Baton Rouge.[37] Upon their initial meeting in 1953, Motta recounts that, when Germer gave him the option of choosing O.T.O. or A∴A∴, he chose the latter without hesitation.[38] Germer accepted Motta as his only formal student in A∴A∴, Motta taking *Adjuvo* ("I help") as his magical motto. It is clear from their correspondence that Germer and Motta were a strange, yet complementary, match. Their mutual dispositions towards paranoia may well have suited each other, as they had in common a relatively dysfunctional proclivity towards being overly suspicious. Yet, they also shared similar meticulous and calculating attitudes that probably aided their cooperation in future publishing endeavors.

Germer's inclination towards paranoia has been mentioned above. He and his wife Sascha came to believe that their phones had been tapped and that they were under constant surveillance. Motta, on the other hand, seemed to suffer from social anxieties and self-image concerns. His early letters to Germer describe a sincere, yet troubled, student who confides in his teacher about his shyness with women and working through his tendencies towards homosexuality. He had complained that his dominating mother had caused him difficulty in

---

[36] See Crowley (1954).

[37] Motta had been raised in Rio de Janeiro, and had been exposed to occultism from a young age. As a teenager, he was initiated in August of 1948 into the Fraternitas Rosicruciana Antiqua, a Rosicrucian fraternity founded by Arnold Krumm-Heller. In his autobiography of his early occult life, Motta recalls meeting Krumm-Heller's son, Parsival. Upon their meeting, Motta inquired as to the relationship between Krumm-Heller and Aleister Crowley, of whom he initially had not received a good impression. Parsival reportedly urged Motta to take up a more careful study of Crowley, which he did. In a year's time, Motta would be directed by Parsival to continue his studies under a more advanced initiate, Karl Germer. See Motta (1962).

[38] Ibid.

talking to women and led him to masturbate compulsively. Germer would sometimes offer Motta guidance in these early letters, suggesting that his young student needed discipline:

> The danger for those who possess [the extremely passive side of genius] is that they are liable to be mentally disturbed and upset, because they perceive too much and are constantly hurt by coarser nature [...] Now yours is a sensitive soul, and you should go about doing the type of mental discipline—I would add that all these people, men or women, who are so constituted suffer much anguish; the sooner they recognize the root of the trouble, the sooner they begin to do practices, the quicker they obtain the necessary balance and insight.[39]

What can be said of the extensive correspondence between Germer and Motta is that the two men certainly shared a close, sometimes fatuous, and other times disquieted, relationship. Germer would at times express admiration for his student, saying "I have with pleasure seen your devotion, your loyalty. I accept them gladly as devoted to the Great Work."[40] Yet Germer would also frequently point out to Motta his errors: "one of your defects is your vanity, and conceit—mostly, I think, because you were aware too much of your intellectual superiority."[41] Still, Motta's passion for Thelema inspired Germer, while Germer's practical and observant approach would often display the wisdom Motta needed to be reflective of his experiences. In short, their nine years of regular correspondence reveals a genuine magical relationship that evolved, and demonstrates both men's level of erudition regarding Thelema.

As Motta asked more questions, Germer encouraged him to come visit West Point, California, where Germer had recently relocated. He wrote:

---

[39] Karl Germer to Marcelo Motta, April 29, 1953. GMC.

[40] Karl Germer to Marcelo Motta, May 26, 1956. GMC.

[41] Germer to Motta, November 13, 1959. GMC.

I'll admit, I can teach but not in the normal way as your type, the intellectual type, expects [...] I am totally different from the usual Hierophant or teacher of the occult. [...] And as for your own situation, truly, I can't see that I can give you any positive advise or direction. I expect much from you in the future, for you have qualities. If I can convey something to you, I have felt for months that it could only be done by a close series of personal discussion, with the library at hand for references.[42]

Motta subsequently arranged to visit with Germer later that year in December of 1956. Germer then suggested Motta meet with some of the remaining Thelemites. "We can always take a trip to L.A." But he was more concerned with speaking with Motta in person. "What I have in mind is to show you some manuscripts and things you cannot see elsewhere. It is about time that you make a step forward."[43]

Motta arrived in California on December 13. According to Germer, the visit seemed foreboding for his student. Motta met many of the California Thelemites and had what appears to have been insightful discussion with his A∴A∴ instructor. Germer reminded Motta upon his return, "if you firmly implant and practice the viewpoint of considering every event ... as a particular dealing etc. you will find that the two months on the West Coast have been fruitful for you."[44] To "consider every event as a particular dealing of God with your soul" is a clause taken directly from the Oath of the Master of the Temple.[45] Germer reiterated to Motta shortly after, "Your re-formulation of your oath (to give all you are and have to the G.W. [Great Work]) is significant. It may land you in severe and hard ordeals. If so, don't forget cause and effect then."[46] One wonders what conversations these two men had while driving down to Los Angeles that winter. But from this correspondence, it could imply Germer was instructing Motta,

---

[42] Germer to Motta, May 26, 1956. GMC.

[43] Germer to Motta, November 27, 1956. GMC.

[44] Germer to Motta, Februrary 10, 1957. GMC

[45] Refer to chapter four and the description in *The Vision and the Voice*.

[46] Germer to Motta, February 15, 1957. GMC.

and encouraging his student to take the great leap forward towards the Supreme Attainment of the Master of the Temple.[47]

Germer and Motta in Publication

Pertinent to this discussion are the publishing efforts between Germer and Motta. As early as 1956, Germer had expressed his plans about publishing to Motta. He wrote, "I believe I have mentioned to you: the next phase of 'Speech' of the A∴A∴ begins March 21, 1959, a period of 5 years." Germer was anticipating that it would be a fruitful and productive time for printing and wanted Motta as his partner. "This includes that I hope to be able to count on much collaboration from you."[48] In the meantime throughout the rest of 1957 and 1958, Germer and Motta were trading books back and forth by mail, including several Crowley works such as *Tao Teh King* (Liber CLVII) and *Across the Gulf* (Liber LIX), among other Crowley works. Germer would send typescript copies of publications such as *Magick Without Tears* and Motta would put them in bindings and send them back.

Yet, as the Spring Equinox of 1959 came, both parties were strapped for cash, and life seemed to get in the way. Motta was struggling financially with a newborn son, Krel, and the demands of academia kept him psychologically preoccupied. Germer wrote him, "many outer things kept me very busy and physically exhausted; 'Speech' has been forbidden to me for the moment."[49] Germer's latest project was to publish *Liber Aleph vel CXI: The Book of Wisdom or Folly*, a collection of over two-hundred epistolary writings on the philosophy

---

[47] Germer, perhaps, reveals here his lack of understanding of the need to follow the preliminary steps of the A∴A∴ Grade work. Not having gone through the Grades systematically himself, Germer's enthusiastic suggestion for Motta to "treat every phenomenon as a particular dealing of God with your soul" makes sense, and explains why he may have pushed his promising student to the Tasks reserved for higher attainments. It is also possible that the needs of the Great Order at this time simply outweighed any concerns for the apparent well-being of this particular Aspirant.

[48] Germer to Motta, November 1, 1956. GMC.

[49] Germer to Motta, March 20, 1959. GMC.

of Thelema by Crowley, intended for his student and "magical son," Frater Achad.[50] *Liber Aleph* had only been previously available in very limited typescript copies to members of Agape Lodge and was never published in Crowley's lifetime. Under Germer's supervision, it was edited and introduced by Motta, finally going to press in September of 1961. Noteworthy about this final publication of Germer's lifetime was that *Liber Aleph* bore the traditional A∴A∴ Imprimatur, listing Motta as Imperator with his motto initial, "φ." *Liber Aleph* was beautifully printed in hardback and featured a dust jacket with artwork by *Thoth Tarot* card artist Frieda Lady Harris (1877–1962).[51]

It was around the time that *Liber Aleph* was finalized and went to press that Motta's grandiose reflections on Thelema became overbearing on the now-aging and stern Frater Saturnus. His letters offer page after page of extravagant commentary on Thelema and his understanding of his initiatory Work. He wrote Germer on December 17, 1961, "Regardless of what you think of Marcelo Ramos Motta personally, he is, with approval of the Secret Chiefs, and of 666 and Aiwass, the Incarnated Beast, the Priest of the Princes, Head of the A∴A∴ and your Superior."[52] Germer could only assume Motta had blown out by attempting to cross the Abyss too early:

> I have seen and had to observe similar cases of Demonitis (includ- ing my own) but yours beats all records in our files. I saw the dis- ease creeping up months ago; it is good it broke out in the open. The most charitable interpretation I could put on it is that you prematurely took the Oath of the Abyss, without being prepared by previous initiation. If so, there is nothing I can do. You have to

---

[50] Given that Crowley acknowledged Charles Stansfeld Jones to be his closest stu- dent in A∴A∴ at the time, and that he was also re-writing the O.T.O. degrees to conform to Thelema, *Liber Aleph* may be considered one of the more important com- mentaries on the movement's philosophy. See Crowley (1962).

[51] Harris was in correspondence with Crowley about the creation of Crowley's Tarot deck, the Thoth Tarot. She painted an entire deck of seventy-eight cards under his direction in the 1940s.

[52] Motta to Germer, December 17, 1961. GMC.

be left alone until you either slay the demon once and for all, or be devoured by it.[53]

Karl Germer died on October 25, 1962. His last years were spent with his wife Sascha in West Point, California. Although he was living in the same state as most of the remaining Thelemites in the world—apart from Switzerland, England, and Motta in Brazil—he had grown isolated from everyone around him. According to Grady McMurtry, Karl and Sascha Germer only reinforced one another's suspicious attitudes about people. McMurtry recollected his attempt in November of 1959 to convince Germer about the possibility of putting the O.T.O. back together. McMurtry later recalled their conversation in a letter to Phyllis Seckler, telling her that it was impossible due to Karl's "mental condition."[54] McMurtry blamed Germer's suspicious disposition on "Sascha's continuous dripping of poison in his ear."[55] Nevertheless, Germer was successful in continuing the Thelemic movement through his publishing efforts, with the help of the few Thelemites he trusted. Despite his close correspondence with Motta, and his fondness for Phyllis Seckler, he named no successor, passing all of the Crowley library "to the Heads of the Order." Germer named his wife, Sascha, and Frederick Mellinger as his literary executors in his last will and testament. It seemed that, with the death of Karl Germer, the Thelemic movement was, for the time being, also laid to rest.

---

[53] Germer to Motta, December 23, 1961. GMC.

[54] Letter from Grady L. McMurtry to Phyllis Seckler, December 19, 1968. GM-PSC.

[55] Ibid.

CHAPTER EIGHT

From Ashes to Flame

Interregnum (1962–1969)

What must be done is to keep the little faithful group together, and not let them despair or become despondent, because there are no outward signs of growth. I feel that the Work, the Work of Thelema, is heading towards a crucial period, and that important events are not too far off. May-be a "dry spell" has to precede it?

—Karl Germer to Jane Wolfe, November 11, 1947

ALTHOUGH THE GERMER YEARS were pivotal for Thelema, the period that followed was even more crucial. Indeed, the first two decades following Crowley's death—the post-war years and the 1960s—marked a time of significant change all over the world. This chapter will take a few detours as we seek cultural and historical context for how events transpired. Let's begin by briefly discussing the general milieu of these two decades and explain how certain cultural attitudes emerged from the 1950s and laid fertile ground for the counterculture of the 1960s. We will then turn our attention back to the correspondence between Marcelo Motta, Phyllis Seckler, and Sascha Germer. Some discussion is also warranted of a small sect in California known as the Solar Lodge, a group that appropriated Thelema for a short period of time in the 1960s. Finally, this chapter will set the stage for the Thelemic revival by revisiting the subject of publication.

⛤

From the Post-war 1950s to the 1960s Counterculture

The post-war years of the 1950s found Europe in a reconstructive phase. Much of its industrial infrastructure had been destroyed. An economic downturn strangled the region with millions of people left homeless. Millions more were displaced and found themselves in hostile territories due to new borders being drawn by victorious nations. The partitioning of Germany by Western occupational forces and the Soviet Union became one of the contributing factors for the Cold War that would later ensue. In 1947, the United States government initiated the "European Recovery Plan" led by U.S. Secretary of State at the time, George Marshall. Lasting from 1948 to 1952, the "Marshall Plan," as it was also known, allocated $13 billion to reconstruct Europe.

The United States, by contrast, enjoyed an economic boom after World War II unmatched in the entirety of the twentieth century, accompanied by a period of rapid social transformation. On average, national production grew 250%, and per capita income was at a 35% increase from the decades preceding the 1950s.[1] Economic prosperity was marked by an expanding middle-class earning an increasing amount of disposable income. Marriage and fertility rates increased, while divorce rates were in decline, creating what has come to be known as the "baby boomer generation."

The nostalgic picture of 1950s American culture depicts a utopian vision of a cohesive family unit where children were respectful, adults held high moral values, and life was somehow better and more simple than the quotidian life of the average person today. However, beneath the myths of an ideal American society during the 1950s, there were plenty of social tensions. Poverty levels were at 25%, and domestic violence and alcoholism were not uncommon. Women's relegated roles to housewifery and motherhood were normally not freely chosen but expected, and male bachelors over the age of twenty-one

---

[1] Stephanie Coontz (2000) *The Way We Never Were: American Families and the Nostalgia Trap* (New York: Basic Books), 46–47.

were categorized as immature, infantile, and deviant.[2] In short, the expectations of family values and gender roles were contrived, and the "happy family" image often had a dark and grimy reality behind closed doors.

There were also political tensions with which America was grappling. The age of "McCarthyism"[3] shrouded society with Cold War anxieties. The U.S. Government and the media placed the everyday citizen on the front lines of the fight against the "Red Terror," with coercive propaganda suggesting that neighborhoods across the country be on the lookout for a permeating conspiratorial communist agenda. Many citizens and residents were subject to investigation by United States Intelligence agencies. Some people were imprisoned and thousands of others lost their jobs under the alarmist conjecture that they were cooperating with communist countries. There was an air of suspicion and paranoia throughout the cultural atmosphere.[4]

It was explained in the last chapter that some of these factors played a role in the Thelemic movement entering into a period of quiescence. Karl Germer was certainly affected by such conditions. Coincidentally, Germer's death in 1962 was accompanied by a cultural shift away from this political repression. The American citizens who would make up the next generation developed a sharp eye for hypocrisy amongst the social contrivances of the previous decade. A subculture would stir at the edges of the polished façade of the 1950s nuclear Christian family. There was a growing distrust of the U.S. government as militarization

---

[2] Ibid., 51–55.

[3] Named after U.S. Senator Joe McCarthy (1908–1957), McCarthyism is associated with the "Red Scare" during the first half of the 1950s, in which political repression was heightened in the United States by fears of an overarching communist conspiracy infiltrating American culture. See Fried (1997), Shrecker (1998), and Wax (2008) in the bibliography.

[4] On the other hand, one might investigate the following works for an alternate point of view about the "Red Scare." Evans (2007) *Blacklisted by History,* Haynes and Klehr (1999) *Venona,* and Weinstein (1997) *Perjury.* See bibliography for complete citations.

and Cold War anxieties increased. As the 1960s approached, many citizens, among them America's youth and fringe intellectuals within educational institutions, began to challenge social conventions.[5] Feminist and civil rights movements emerged, literature from the Beat movement stirred a rebellious air, and the use of psychedelics opened the door for introspection. These factors, along with a growing anti-establishment sentiment in music and art, created the environment of the 1960s counterculture.[6] This phenomenon was not exclusive to the United States. It was also quite dominant in the United Kingdom, and would spread throughout Europe in the 1970s.

In the midst of such cultural fervor, the practice of religion began to change, and a "cultic milieu" emerged.[7] The growth of "cultic religion" during the 1960s and 1970s in America and Britain has been referred to as the "Occult Revival."[8] The explosion of interest in the occult was apparent even in popular media. For example, the cover story in a 1972 edition of *Time* magazine featured an article on the

---

[5] A prime example of social critique at the time can be found in Paul Goodman (1956) *Growing Up Absurd: Problems of Youth in the Organized System* (New York: House). Goodman assesses that the troubled youth population is due to disproportion within society and a faulty educational system.

[6] The term, "counterculture" was first coined in Theodore Roszack (1969) *The Making of a Counter Culture: Reflections on the Technocratic Society and Its Youthful Opposition* (Garden City: Doubleday & Company, Inc). Roszack identifies the radicalism of this subculture to be localized in its rejection of "technocracy,"—the increasing mechanization that results from the growth of corporate and technological dominance over industrial society.

[7] Refer back to the discussion in chapter six on the "cultic milieu."

[8] More specifically, it is perhaps a second "Occult Revival." The term had been used to describe the prevailing interest in occultism during the *fin-de-siècle* of nineteenth century Great Britain and the number of initiatory societies active at the time. Publication during the nineteenth century Occult Revival has been covered in depth by Robert A. Gilbert (January 2005). On occultist periodical culture of that period and early twentieth century, see Morrisson (2008). Occultist performance art is explored by Lingan (2006). "Occult Revival" as it is used here refers to the phenomenon of the counterculture years of Western society as discussed in the then contemporary sociological journals. See Truzzi (1972) and Tiryakian (1972). A later discussion is given by Jorgensen (1982).

increased interest in occultism in popular culture, noting the growing sales of occult and New Age literature by bookstores and publishers across the United States and England.[9] The reader may also recall the growth in popularity of the occult in films such as Terrence Fisher's *The Devil Rides Out* (1968), based on Dennis Wheatley's novel by the same name; *The Dunwich Horror* (1970), based on Lovecraft's short story; Kenneth Anger's *Lucifer Rising* (1972); and Alejandro Jodorowsky's *The Holy Mountain* (1973). We discussed "occulture" in chapter six. The trends of occultism in art and media during this period are an example of this concept. It was within the occulture of the 1960s and 1970s that movements such as Gerald Gardner's[10] modern Witchcraft[11] and Anton Szandor LaVey's[12] modern Satanism were popularized. It is also within this social sphere that Thelema was revived.[13]

Intellectual Freedom from Copyright

In addition to cultural factors that would set the stage for the growth of the Thelemic movement, there was an intellectual space generated by a period I have called *open access*. In short, this open access period was marked by an absence of legally recognized copyright to Crowley's literary estate, resulting in the growing availability of Crowley's written

---

[9] [Author unknown], "The Occult: A Substitute Faith," (1972) *Time*, 99 (25), 68.

[10] Gerald Gardner (1884-1964) was the founder of modern witchcraft and was for a brief time an O.T.O. member under Crowley. In fact much Thelemic ideology would serve as an early foundation for Gardner's new movement of Wicca. For a biography of Gardner, see Philip Heselton (2012a-b) *Witchfather*, Vols. I and II.

[11] The modern Wicca movement is covered in depth by Ronald Hutton (1999) *The Triumph of the Moon: A History of Modern Pagan Witchcraft* (New York: Oxford University Press).

[12] Biographies are given by Burton Wolfe (1974) *The Devil's Avenger: A Biography of Anton Szandor LaVey* (Salem: Pyramid Books) and Blanche Barton (1990) *The Secret Life of a Satanist: An Authorized Biography of Anton LaVey* (Port Townsend: Feral House).

[13] For further sociological literature regarding alternative religiosity in the counterculture years, see Shepherd (1972), Hardwick (1973), Wallis (1974), and, more recently, Ellwood (1994).

material. At least this was the case in North America. Later we will see how this situation led to a race to establish copyrights on the Thelemic material, which would, in turn, help the O.T.O. become confirmed as a religious organization.

As mentioned in the last chapter, Aleister Crowley willed the rights to his work to the O.T.O. and named John Symonds and Louis Wilkinson as his literary executors. Karl Germer, who succeeded Crowley in the O.T.O. and the A∴A∴, inherited the literary remains. Also as previously noted, Germer consolidated what was left in his possession and what still remained in England with the help of Symonds and Gerald Yorke. In Germer's last will and testament, he directed that the property of the O.T.O. (i.e., Crowley's literary remains and belongings) be "passed to the Heads of the Order" and named his wife Sascha as executor along with Frederic Mellinger.[14] Unfortunately this never came to pass. Sascha, like her husband before her, became increasingly reclusive and alienated from the remaining Thelemites. Her disaffection and mistrust of the group was exacerbated by the robbery of the Crowley library in 1967, the details of which will be discussed shortly. Germer's misstep in not clearly appointing a successor, and Sascha's isolation and reluctance to perform the duties outlined in Germer's will, created a storm of confusion with regard to the library and the estate.

The copyright to Crowley's literature in the United Kingdom was different. The publication of Crowley's work was constrained to a greater extent in Great Britain, as it required the permission of John Symonds, Crowley's literary executor. According to Yorke, Symonds had "the right to authorize or forbid quotations and republications or fresh publications of A.C.'s work."[15] In one instance, The Aquarian Press of Northampton attempted to publish an anthology of Crowley's work that Israel Regardie organized, but the publication was restrained

---

[14] Typescript of Karl Germer's will, New York, December 4, 1951, in a letter from Gerald Yorke to Phyllis Seckler, July 2, 1969, Seckler (2012), 265.

[15] Seckler (2012), 255.

by a threat of court action invoked by Symonds.[16] Symonds became the first posthumous biographer of Aleister Crowley, publishing *The Great Beast* in 1951. Despite the fact that he developed an increasing hostility and skepticism toward Crowley, he would remain one of the most significant editors of Crowley's work in the United Kingdom, together with Kenneth Grant.

There is one more location worth mentioning before continuing with our story. That is the O.T.O. in Zurich, Switzerland, headed by Herman Metzger. As briefly covered in the last chapter, Metzger was given the IX° in Hamburg by Frederic Mellinger with the permission of Karl Germer in 1951. Metzger's group published a great deal of Crowley's work in German, however he would fall into a quarrel with Germer—just before the latter's death—over discrepancies in translation.[17] In January of 1963, Metzger proclaimed himself Outer Head of the Order based on a unanimous vote by his Swiss O.T.O. members.[18] On account of the literary remains passing to the "Heads of the Order," Sascha Germer's only attempt to act as literary executor of her husband's will was to consider sending Metzger the Crowley-Germer library. However, Frederic Mellinger, who had been designated by Germer to supervise Metzger's operations in Switzerland, invoked his right as co-literary executor to block the request in a letter dated September 25, 1963. Mellinger denounced Metzger as a fraud and claimed that he had failed the program of instruction. Metzger never secured the library and was never accepted as the Outer Head by anyone outside of his own group. Although he never contended nor cooperated with the O.T.O. as it was later established by Grady McMurtry, Metzger's Swiss O.T.O. continued to operate independently until the death of his successor, Annemarie Aeschbach, in 2008.[19]

---

[16] Ibid.

[17] Starr (2003), 343.

[18] "History: Interregnum," USGL O.T.O. website, (accessed April 4, 2018).

[19] Christian Giudice, "Ordo Templi Orientis," in Christopher Partridge (ed.) (2014) *The Occult World* (New York: Routledge), 280.

Interregnum

On October 25, 1962, Marcelo Motta received a cable from Sascha Germer reading, "THINK NOT O KING UPON THAT LIE." It was a quote from *The Book of the Law* about death. Sascha followed up with a letter five days later announcing Karl's death:

> Our beloved Master is dead. He succumb [sic] Oct. 25, 8:55 P.M. under horrifying circumstances. You are the Follower. Please take it from me as he died in my arms and it was his last wish. Who the heir of the library is I do not know up to now. My cable to you was a cry for help to save the Work and the Library and I hoped that you understand as he left everything open.[20]

Motta was, as usual, strapped for cash and could not afford a visit to California from Rio de Janeiro, where he was now living. He encouraged Sascha to stay strong and warned her to be on guard with anyone who could not be trusted. In his mind, this meant everyone. He wrote her, "If this 'follower' thing is what it seems to be, don't speak about it to anybody [...] I don't want such a thing to come out. I am not prepared. I am not anything. It will be many years yet before I am ready to do anything. I have much work to do on myself yet, and you know that better than anybody!"[21] Motta advised Sascha to place any valuable materials in a safety deposit box and to appeal to the authorities of law if there were any problems.

Motta was increasingly paranoid about the postal system being monitored in Brazil, and began to suspect that a high profile Thelemic contact might be monitored in the United States, as well. He initiated correspondence with Phyllis Seckler as an attempted go-between. Seckler was living in California as well, albeit at a distance from Sascha Germer. Motta stressed to Seckler the urgency of making sure Sascha's well-being was looked after and that securing the library was of

---

[20] Sascha Germer to Marcelo Motta, October 30, 1962. SWC.

[21] Motta to Sascha Germer, November 8, 1962. GMC.

tantamount importance. With his magical-mindedness and tendency towards being suspicious, Motta presciently warned Seckler that they were subject to magical or physical assault and that the library was now vulnerable. He wrote, "Have no doubts—you will be attacked, both of you."[22] Motta expressed his concern to Phyllis that his mail to Sascha may be scrutinized. He was writing her instead so his letters could be passed on to Sascha.

Seckler was annoyed at the inconvenience, and thought Motta's paranoia was unreasonable, writing him, "It is very foolish of you to think mail is monitored, which I assure you it is not here in America."[23] Because the intended letter to Sascha from Motta had been originally addressed to Seckler, Phyllis accidentally opened it. Upon delivering the opened letter to Sascha, Seckler reported, "she demanded to know to whom I had shown it [...] Then she intimated in a suspicious manner that I had shown it to some enemy of hers and of Karl."[24] Sascha was not fond of Phyllis. Historian Martin P. Starr noted that when Karl had been insistent on moving to California in 1957, "Sascha threw up endless roadblocks to prevent them moving from New Jersey. She had premonitions that they would come to a bad end in California; she was also suspicious of his desire to settle where virtually all the Sisters of the O.T.O. were located, and with just cause."[25]

Sascha was not far off the mark, as Phyllis and Karl explored their romantic attraction that had been initiated in their previously mentioned correspondence in 1952, and engaged in an affair for a short time upon Germer settling in California. This would have most certainly earned Phyllis the distrust of Sascha, and contributed to Sascha's reluctance to listen to Phyllis when it later came to the safety of the Crowley-Germer library. Phyllis explained to Motta, "I can no longer be of assistance if I am going to be suspected." She continued:

---

[22] Marcelo Motta to Phyllis Seckler, November 7, 1962. MSC

[23] Seckler to Motta, November 20, 1962. MSC.

[24] Seckler to Motta, November 20, 1962. MSC.

[25] Starr (2003), 333.

But Thelema and A.C.'s manuscripts hold such a fascination for me that I would gladly copy them one by one [...] Since you are probably the heir to the library from what Sascha says since she witnessed the will, and since she is the executor, I can do nothing without either of you asking me to so do. And I can do nothing if I am not trusted.[26]

It would appear that Motta and Seckler had not gotten along from the very beginning. Seckler recalled years later in her journal *In the Continuum* her impression of Motta when they first met in 1957, during Motta's California visit to Karl Germer:

He had very little of a sense of responsibility where women and children were concerned. This I noticed by the way he talked to the girls and by the way he treated me. He was so immature, even though he was 25 at the time. He displayed a contempt for his parents and mostly for his father and thought of them only in terms of the money he might inherit from them.[27]

Seckler continued by chiding Motta about his concern over magical attacks. Her opinion was that such attacks could only be possible if one was not in touch with the Holy Guardian Angel. She explained:

My extreme conviction is that ['attacks'] cannot occur when one obeys the Angel. I am also convinced that lack of strength occurs because Angelic guidance is far off or not heard, or turned away from. On this matter my first advice to anyone suffering from 'attacks' or suspicion of [the] same is to consult the Angel immediately.[28]

---

[26] Seckler to Motta, November 20, 1962. MSC.

[27] Seckler (1993), 42.

[28] Seckler to Motta, November 20, 1962. MSC.

She concluded this letter by implying that Motta's fears were the result of self-delusion, "I wish to leave you with your own point of view—if you enjoy them, who am I to say they don't exist for you? At least in your own imagination."[29]

The fact that the mail was delayed did not ease Motta's suspicions. Whether the delay in post was due to the holiday season as Seckler suggested, or Motta's mail was indeed being monitored as he believed, he did not receive Seckler's updates on Germer's will and Sascha's condition. He followed up with Seckler three weeks after his first letter to her. She responded with frankness, "please do not get alarmed when I run slow to answer you. Sometimes it may be a week or more before I get around to the answer as I find that careful thought makes a much better letter than impulse. So don't expect quick replies from me unless the matter is very urgent."[30] Yet, for Motta, the matter *was* urgent. He needed to know about the condition of the library and whether or not he was the heir to Crowley's literary legacy.

Once Motta finally received Seckler's chiding letters, he responded, "In the first place, if you were as high an Initiate as you think you are, it would be quite unnecessary to send me letters and things by mail; you could send them via a demon." He continued later, "If you were as true a Thelemite as you think yourself, you would try to encourage me—not give off with owlish-wisdom!" He continued at length:

> But what I can't understand is how all you people can be so blinded by your Egoes [sic], when the curriculum of the A∴A∴ is at your disposal and perfectly explicit! You think yourself, no doubt, at least a Minor Adept. Well, have you conquered Asana as A.C. described it, at least twenty times over in several different books? And have you done the practices in Liber HHH to the perfection—even in a lower plane, as He says clearly—demanded even of a full Zelator? Have you reached the Grade of Practicus, with the necessary symptoms. And Oh great Philosophus, how

---

[29] Ibid.
[30] Seckler to Motta, December 9, 1962. MSC.

do you measure your devotion the Great Order to which you aspire? In plain words: What have you done for the A∴A∴?[31]

Phyllis indeed later stated she had never done the Grade work of the A∴A∴ herself until after 1975.[32] In her correspondence with Germer in 1952, she even doubted the authenticity of her experience as constituting Knowledge and Conversation of the Holy Guardian Angel.[33] Some months later in 1963, Motta pointed out to Phyllis:

> You have mistaken the initiation in Tiphereth of Malkuth— which is the main Neophyte Initiation, where the Neophyte has the first vision of the Holy Guardian Angel—for the initiation in Tiphereth of Tiphereth, which is the Minor Adept Initiation, and which is very far as yet—if the letters you wrote me are any indication of your spiritual advancement at present.[34]

Motta never received a response from Phyllis, and the two would not speak again until 1976. Sascha Germer, however, remained widowed, paranoid, and isolated in her home in West Point. She maintained almost no contact with the Thelemic community, and what little she saw in it was in Motta. Her last letter to Motta for a number of years came to him in September of 1963. She mentioned that Karl had given a charter to Motta to run the O.T.O. in Brazil. She wrote, "You are young, you are the future of the Work, I did not believe when Karl said: It will take another 10 years to make Motta the heir! But spiritu-

---

[31] Motta to Seckler, January 13, 1963. MSC.

[32] "I retired from teaching and Grady and I parted in 1975 and I was now free and had enough time to go back and pick up the work in the A∴A∴ which had not been done." Seckler states a few pages earlier that her Probationary period had lasted 30 years. See Seckler (1996), 4.

[33] Seckler expressed to Germer that she felt she had not attained. "I do not at this time think I have attained to that point!" She would only later believe it to be the case once Germer told her. See Seckler (2010), 324–325.

[34] Motta to Seckler, October 1, 1963 MSC.

ally you are his Heir! You have to work on in Brazil [...] You fight [for] the Work! Fight with Ra-Hoor-Khuit!"[35] Motta would not hear from Sascha again for another four years.

The Robbery of the Library

As if confirming the worst of Motta's fears, Sascha Germer fell victim to a robbery at her home in West Point on September 3, 1967. A significant portion of Thelemic memorabilia once owned by Crowley and Karl Germer was stolen. In a letter to Motta dated October 7, 1968, Sascha wrongly accused Phyllis' daughter as the perpetrator: "I was the victim of a hold up by O.T.O. members. Stella Seckler (Phyllis' oldest daughter) came with 3 daughters [who] all call themselves O.T.O. and attacked me, bound and gagged me, Stella sprayed my eyes with acid and since this time my eyesight has lost 80%."[36] Sascha Germer by this time was not of sound mind, and she was mistaken as to the identities of the perpetrators. In reality, the thieves were members of an independently-run, self-identified Thelemic organization calling itself the Solar Lodge.[37]

The Solar Lodge

The Solar Lodge can in many ways be considered the stereotypical cult amidst the counterculture furor. Located in Los Angeles and the

[35] Sascha Germer to Motta, September 15, 1963. SWC.

[36] Sascha Germer to Motta, October 7, 1968. SWC.

[37] The most significant information available on the Solar Lodge is the alleged tell-all from an insider who calls himself Frater Shiva, and claims to have been a member since 1965. (It should be noted that this "Frater Shiva" is not to be confused with Frater Shiva X° O.T.O.) His personal account is outlined in Frater Shiva (2007). An expanded edition was later published, Frater Shiva (2012), and includes stories of the use of psychedelics in combination with their rituals of initiation extracted from Crowley's teachings.

deserts of southern California, they set up a Thelemic-based commune and combined magical practices with LSD. More importantly for this story, members of the Solar Lodge engaged in questionable and criminal activity.

The Solar Lodge began when former Agape Lodge member and initiate of the IX° Ray Burlingame (1893–1965) chose to initiate Georgina "Jean" Brayton in 1962, despite the fact that Burlingame did not hold a charter to initiate.[38] Throughout the 1960s, Brayton initiated others, and by 1967, the Lodge grew to over fifty members, owned several rental properties, a gas station, a bookstore, and land in the Sonoran desert dubbed the "Solar Ranch."

In 1967, at the time of the robbery, Grady McMurtry (later, Caliph Hymenaeus Alpha) had been living in Washington D.C. since 1959. His clashes with Karl Germer had nearly caused him to give up hope on the O.T.O. Rather than further incite Germer's wrath, he had left the state. Informed of Germer's death (which had been kept secret for some years) and the theft of the library, McMurtry returned to California in 1969, further encouraged by a romantic exchange of correspondence with his future wife, Phyllis Seckler.

In his role as a Sovereign Grand Inspector General (SGIG), so appointed by Crowley, McMurtry was now diligently attempting to ascertain the whereabouts of the Crowley Library, and identity of the thieves who stole it. He was in correspondence with Crowley's former secretary, biographer, and promoter of the Golden Dawn, Israel Regardie (1907–1985), whose library had also been robbed. He discovered that Jerry Kay, who had been an early Crowley publisher in the revival, knew the location of the perpetrators. McMurtry recounted to Regardie, "On Sept. 24, I was finally able to get Jerry to guide me, if I drove, to the place where the Braytons had had their 'temple,' he identified the house." Jerry Kay got cold feet when it came time to go in with McMurtry to confront the Solar Lodge, and so Grady "'went

---

[38] Without proper charter, the Solar Lodge has never been accepted as a legitimate O.T.O. group.

over the top' style like the sheriff in 'High Noon' by myself."[39] As Solar Lodge member Frater Shiva recounts:

> He [Grady McMurtry] later professed outrage at finding rare books, supposedly stolen from West Point, for sale at high prices in The Eye of Horus bookstore. While he was correct in his surmise that members of the Lodge had been responsible for the theft, he was quite wrong about any of the spoils being offered for sale in the bookshop.[40]

The Solar Lodge's Frater Shiva goes on to claim in his book that the materials found by McMurtry were "standard, older works that had been previously purchased from other stores." He continued that "all the West Point material had vanished in the Solar Ranch firestorm."[41] Shiva is referring here to a fire that took hold of the Solar Ranch, for which six-year-old Anthony Saul Gibbons was held accountable because he had been playing with matches.[42] A few months later, the mischievous boy was caught attempting to start another fire by Solar Lodge member Frater Dys. The boy's parents were away from the ranch at their respective jobs. When Frater Dys called the boy's father to report on his behavior, the father replied, "Do whatever you have to do to keep him under control, even if you have to chain him!" Frater Dys apparently took him literally and chained the boy inside a large wooden box room which had previously been used as a goat pen. When a disgruntled member informed police about problems at the Solar Ranch, an investigation took place and the boy was found by authorities.[43] As a result, thirteen members were arrested by police at the compound

---

[39] Grady McMurtry to Israel Regardie, October, 1969 [date illegible]. MRSC.

[40] Frater Shiva (2012), 210.

[41] Ibid.

[42] Ibid., 184.

[43] The press released an article telling of a boy who was locked in a box in the dangerous Sonoran Desert heat. See, "Six-year-old boy held prisoner in packing crate," *The Bulletin*. Bend, Oregon. (UPI), July 29, 1969, 7.

for the mistreatment of the young boy. Brayton and several others fled from the authorities. They were caught and pleaded guilty three years later. None of the members who were caught by authorities would serve a prison sentence, as it was determined their charges had been subject to entrapment laws. Solar Lodge ceased activity by 1972.

Other Agape Lodge Members, Reactivating the Order,
and the Robbery Investigation

California was one of the most well-known and prolific hubs of counterculture activity throughout the 1960s and 1970s. It was also the home of Thelemites Sascha Germer, Phyllis Seckler, Grady McMurtry, Helen Parsons Smith, several other Agape Lodge members, Israel Regardie, the cultists of the Solar Lodge, and a number of would-be publishers of Crowley material. In short, California was a hotbed of Thelemic activity.

Helen Parsons Smith (1910–2003), the widow of former Lodge Master, Wilfred T. Smith,[44] had earlier been married to Jack Parsons. Helen was born in Chicago, the eldest of three daughters. Her mother relocated the family to Pasadena shortly after remarrying, following the death of Helen's father in January of 1920. Helen met Jack Parsons in 1933 at a congregational church gathering and the two decided to marry in 1935. It was through Jack that Helen was first exposed to Thelema. She was initiated into Minerval and I° on February 15, 1941. She also became a student in A∴A∴, taking the name "Grimaud." It was shortly afterward, in 1942, that Helen and Jack's marriage dissolved, largely due to Jack's infidelity with Helen's half-sister, Sara Northrup. In the midst of the breakdown of her relationship, Helen found in Agape Lodge master Wilfred Talbot Smith a confidant and partner with whom she could heal. The two would remain devoted to one another, even during Wilfred Smith's forced exile, where Helen would tirelessly assist him during his magical retirement whilst raising their young son, Kwen.[45]

---

[44] The above biographical sketch is summarized with reference to Starr (2003).

[45] In later decades, at least in 1976, Helen always referred to Smith as "Frater," spoken

As we will see in the chapters that follow, Helen Smith remained devoted to the Thelemic cause and contributed by publishing some well-crafted editions of lesser-known works by Aleister Crowley. She was also an instrumental figure in the re-establishment of the modern O.T.O., playing a large part in electing the current Outer Head of the Order, William Breeze. This will all be covered in due time.

Phyllis Seckler, like many of the members in the days of Agape Lodge, had a reputation for engaging in a number of romantic escapades. Jane Wolfe once remarked to Karl Germer, "Phyllis. The kind that makes goo-goo eyes at practically all men: at 9 o'clock will take a man to her room, at mid-night another. This is not a criticism, it is her make-up."[46] While Wolfe quipped that Phyllis, "ardently believe[d] in the communion of saints,"[47] what can be said is that Seckler's charismatic propensity for attracting Thelemic partners and her devotion to the movement were significant factors in the reconstitution of the O.T.O.

As mentioned, through a romantic exchange of letters initiated in 1967, and, once again, love poetry, Phyllis motivated Grady McMurtry to move back to California from Washington, D.C. She wrote suggestively, "Since I possess the IX° secret do you know if there is any chance of starting a Lodge?"[48] Through their correspondence, Seckler discovered that Grady held emergency orders given to him by Crowley in 1946 to "take charge of the whole work of the Order in California to reform the Organization."[49] It was upon Grady's arrival in 1969 at Phyllis' home in Dublin, California, that the new couple began devising a plan to reorganize the O.T.O. The surviving members of Agape Lodge were invited to participate. McMurtry, along with Phyllis Seckler, Helen Parsons Smith, and Mildred Burlingame (1913–1981)[50] began

---

with a tone of respect. Interview, James Wasserman by author, June 25, 2014, Stuart, Florida.

[46] Jane Wolfe to Karl Germer, September 9, 1943. UC.

[47] Wolfe to Germer, April 5, 1943. Quoted in Starr (2003), 279.

[48] Phyllis Seckler to Grady McMurtry, April 6, 1967. Seckler (2012), 245.

[49] Crowley to Grady McMurtry, March 22, 1946, GYC.

[50] Widow to the aforementioned Ray Burlingame.

performing initiations. The O.T.O. was, at last, in its initial stages of reconstitution. McMurtry and Seckler were frustrated in accomplishing their full aim, however, because Sascha Germer, now a reclusive widow, was alienated from all of the remaining California members. And it was Sascha who was in possession of the entire Crowley-Germer estate. She further refused assistance from the few who offered help in her fragile condition. Seckler recounts that she had "warned [Sascha] from the very beginning to place the books and manuscripts in the hands of responsible persons connected with either the O.T.O. or the A∴A∴ [...] She evidently chose to ignore me."[51] In 1967, Seckler would learn of Sascha Germer's robbery and thus was set in motion the factors that led to her correspondence with McMurtry, his subsequent move to California, and his extensive investigation, which he shared with the FBI, the Riverside County Sheriff Department, and a popular author and researcher named Arthur Lyons.[52]

⚶

In addition to California being home to the surviving members of the O.T.O.—and a location for nefarious countercultural, cult-turned-criminal hideouts—it was also the place where several Crowley publications emerged. As mentioned above, copyright in the United States was essentially absent, so once the message was out that Crowley could be published without constraint, the "cultic milieu" of the 1960s and 1970s was happy to oblige. While many of these publications did not surface until the 1970s, Jerry Kay's Xeno Publishing Company printed *The Book of the Law* in 1967. According to O.T.O. member James Wasserman, this 1967 publication of *Liber AL vel Legis* opened the "Crowley floodgates."[53] Although it was a low-production stapled paperback

---

[51] Seckler to McMurtry, December 6, 1968. GM-PSC.

[52] Author of Arthur Lyons (1970) *The Second Coming: Satanism in America.* Lyons subsequently passed along Grady's research on the robbery to Ed Sanders for his tome, (1971) *The Family.*

[53] James Wasserman (2012) *In the Center of the Fire: A Memoir of the Occult (1966-1989)* (Lake Worth: Ibis Press), 24.

edition, it was one of the few new productions since Germer's death. Other California publishers would soon follow, and we will get to them in due time. It is however important at this moment to acquaint the reader with a publishing house that will take center stage for our modern history of Thelema: Samuel Weiser, Inc. of New York City.

Journey to the East: Samuel Weiser, Inc.

One of the most well-known publishers of occult literature of the twentieth century was Samuel Weiser. Weiser began with a storefront in New York City's famous Book Row, an area that housed a plethora of antiquarian booksellers. Samuel Weiser Bookstore opened its doors in 1926. Samuel, working alongside his brother, Benjamin, developed certain specialty areas, including New Age, occult, and Eastern philosophy. As Marvin Mondlin and Roy Meador stated, "Literature in the occult and related fields was vast, and those interested in such subjects turned out to be plentiful. The store gained a worldwide following among magicians, students of the supernatural, and many others intrigued about topics often dismissed elsewhere as curiosa."[54]

Samuel Weiser's son, Donald, took over the family business in the late 1960s, and expanded into the publishing field. By the mid-1970s, Weiser's combined publishing and distribution catalogue had over a thousand titles of esoteric literature offered for competitive prices. Samuel Weiser Bookstore and Publishing became one of the most successful companies in the niche market of the occult. In his memoir, James Wasserman recounts his time in the 1970s working for Weiser, "Weiser's Bookstore was a crossroads for the world, with visitors from every nation in which an occultist could read English. I met a whole litany of people there. Many of them are my friends today."[55] In an inquiry regarding the cultural climate of the so-called "Occult Revival" discussed above, I asked Wasserman what came to mind when he heard the phrase. He replied:

---

54 Marvin Mondlin and Roy Meador (2004) *Book Row: An Anecdotal and Pictorial History of the Antiquarian Book Trade* (New York: Carroll & Graf), 98.

55 James Wasserman (2012), 57.

For me what comes to mind is Samuel Weiser Publishing and Bookstore. I participated in that Occult Renaissance, which started I would say in 1969. I began working at Weiser in 1973, although I was a customer at the store in 1968. They and Llewellyn Publications put out a slew of books and it fueled an entire generation of occultists with knowledge.[56]

By 1969, Weiser was beginning to release Crowley material that was by this time difficult to find. Samuel Weiser answered (and stimulated) the burgeoning call for Thelemic literature with a high quality reprint of *The Book of Thoth*, a 1944 treatise on the tarot which the Beast wrote towards the end of his life. As this story unfolds, it will be shown how Samuel Weiser, Inc. became intimately involved with the storm that ensued between two contenders for leadership in the Thelemic movement—Grady Louis McMurtry and Marcelo Ramos Motta.

The Road to Revival

It can be argued that the Interregnum, which began with Germer's death in 1962, ended in 1969. This is the year Grady McMurtry began to re-establish the O.T.O. In the next chapter, we will see that it was also the year that publication of Crowley's work really began to kick into high gear. While the road to revival was well underway, there was a long way to go. What we have seen is that due to Germer's solitary disposition, there were few active members who could be turned to after he passed. Motta was a likely candidate according to Sascha Germer, but his location in Brazil constrained his ability to handle the library. As we are also aware from the correspondence between Motta and Phyllis Seckler, it was unlikely that any fruitful cooperation could transpire between them.

In this chapter, two factors have been discussed that facilitated Thelemic activity, and a third factor has been introduced. The first is the relationship that started between Grady McMurtry and Phyllis

---

[56] Interview, James Wasserman by author, June 25, 2014, Stuart, Florida.

Seckler. Between the two of them, they laid fertile ground in California to re-establish the O.T.O. Secondly, the robbery of Sascha Germer by the Solar Lodge generated an awareness about the importance of the library and how vulnerable it could be. As we continue, the reader will find that the Crowley library began to take on an ontology of its own, playing an active role in constraining and facilitating certain outcomes to events. Thirdly, I have presented an outline of the initial movement of Thelemic publication—significant because it provides empirical evidence that a Thelemic revival was indeed in existence from the late 1960s and onward.

CHAPTER NINE

A Reproduction of this Ink and Paper

Actors in Publication and the Thelemic Revival
(1969–1975)

NOW IT IS TIME TO VENTURE into new territory amidst the counterculture frenzy of the later 1960s and 1970s. It is here that the spark
of the revival is ignited through publication and a new generation of
inspired students of Thelema. I will present an overview of some significant publications released between the years of 1969 and 1975 and
provide a brief discussion of the publishers and their efforts. I will also
explore, more specifically, a singular publication that had a substantial effect on the Thelemic movement. I am referring here to Marcelo
Motta's *The Commentaries of AL* (1975). We will see an ever-increasing
problem surrounding leadership within the movement and the issue of
publication and legitimacy. The end result of these battles will coalesce
in events that have formed the contemporary O.T.O. as it exists today.

The counterculture years in North America were in full swing. The
legendary "Summer of Love" witnessed a gathering of 100,000 people in
San Francisco in 1967, signaling the flowering of the hippie movement.
The Beatles had just released their psychedelic rock hit, *Sgt. Pepper's
Lonely Hearts Club Band,* in June, and Timothy Leary delivered his
talks on the LSD revolution at Golden Gate Park in San Francisco in
September, coining his slogan, "tune in, turn on, and drop out."[1] Phyllis

---

[1] Timothy Leary (1920–1996), who should need no introduction, was an American
psychologist known for advocating the use of LSD in the counterculture years, asserting the psychedelic drug's therapeutic uses. He became an icon for generations that
followed, and can be considered one of the most significant figures within the milieu
of counterculture, psychedelics, and late-twentieth century esoteric discourse. He
released a number of works, but the interested reader should consult Leary (1968)
The Politics of Ecstasy (Oakland: Ronin Publishing). His biography can be found in

Seckler remarked to Grady McMurtry in April of 1967, "I must admit that with the aid of LSD and other such drugs America does not seem to be so entirely a spiritual desert as before. Some of the young people I meet actually understand what an expansion of consciousness means because they have been through it."[2] Indeed, the soil was fertile for an alternative spiritual outlook on life that deviated from the normative superstructure. The time was ripe for Thelema.

Before 1969, Thelemic publications[3] were scarce. Much of what had been published in Crowley's time was very limited and remained in the possession of rare book collectors or surviving O.T.O. members. In other words, the majority of Crowley's work was either unpublished or simply unavailable. As previously discussed, Karl Germer was able to publish a few works before his death. These included *The Vision and the Voice* (1952), *777 Revised* (1952), *Magick Without Tears* (1954), *Liber Aleph* (1961), and *The Book of Lies* (1962).[4] These titles, however, were also in limited supply, and difficult to find by the late 1960s, not to mention that many copies of these editions were lost in the aforementioned robbery of Sascha Germer in 1967. Much of what was available was not written by Crowley; rather the majority of accessible material was secondary literature written either about Crowley or the occultist milieu in which he was placed. For example, John Symonds' biography, *The Great Beast,* had been published in 1951. Israel Regardie had written and published writings on the Golden Dawn system of magic, like *The Golden Dawn* (1937) and *The Middle Pillar* (1938).[5] Regardie's work should not be considered part of Crowley's teachings,

John Higgs (2006) *I Have America Surrounded: The Life of Timothy Leary* (Fort Lee: Barricade Books, Inc.).

[2] Phyllis Seckler to Grady McMurtry, April 6, 1967. Seckler (2012), 245.

[3] By "Thelemic publications" I refer to works by Crowley, and the editorial work of his disciples.

[4] Please refer to the bibliography for a list of these works.

[5] Refer to Regardie (1937) *The Golden Dawn: An Account of the Teachings, Rites, and Ceremonies of the Hermetic Order of the Golden Dawn*, 4 Volumes (Chicago: The Aries Press) and (1938) *The Middle Pillar: A Correlation of the Principles of Analytical Psychology and the Elementary Techniques of Magic* (Chicago: The Aries Press).

but rather part of a collection of writings fitting into Crowleyan occultism (except, of course, for *The Tree of Life* [1932], in which Crowley's magic figures prominently). By the first half of the 1970s, on the other hand, Crowley's work was being published in Great Britain by Symonds and Grant, and most explosively throughout North America.

Kindling of the Fire: Trends in Publication and the O.T.O. (1969–1973)

The closing years of the 1960s marked the beginning of the revival of the Thelemic movement. In addition to *The Book of the Law* produced by Jerry Kay in 1967, Grady McMurtry formed an agreement with Carr Collins of the Sangreal Foundation in Dallas, Texas. They produced an unsatisfactory monochrome edition of the Thoth Tarot cards in 1968, limited to 250 decks, whose lack of color detracted from the quality of the paintings by Frieda Lady Harris. Symonds and Grant's edition of *Confessions* followed in England in 1969, and Samuel Weiser contributed to this trend in the same year with its elegant hardback edition of *The Book of Thoth*.

When I had the opportunity to visit with retired owner of Samuel Weiser bookstore and publishing, Donald Weiser, I asked how he made decisions on what to publish when it came to something as obscure as occult literature. He simply responded with, "We published works that people wanted."[6] Donald's straightforward response gives the impression that, despite the fact that the beginning of the Thelemic revival was off to a slow start in the early years of the 1960s, there was indeed an increasing demand for occult literature as the decade progressed. This is evident in the increasing number of titles offered by Samuel Weiser in their catalogues throughout the 1970s. With regard to Thelemic literature, for example, their winter catalogue of 1970 offered thirteen titles written by Crowley. By 1977, this number nearly doubled to twenty-four newly-published editions; and these were

---

6 Interview with Donald Weiser by author, Lake Worth, Florida, June 23, 2014.

the ones that were listed by Weiser and not capable of being ordered through other houses.

In the meantime, the O.T.O. in California was growing, and McMurtry and Seckler were initiating new members. McMurtry decided on a new outreach tactic. He had struck a deal in 1970 with Llewellyn Publications of St. Paul, Minnesota, to print another edition of the Thoth Tarot deck, this time in color.[7] In an effort to stimulate interest in the O.T.O., the deck featured a "Caliph Card," displaying a red O.T.O. logo and his address in Dublin, California. The cards even caught the attention of Hermann Metzger in Switzerland at this time. He supposedly wrote to McMurtry and Llewellyn contesting Grady as "Caliph," asserting that Karl Germer "put a veto on [Grady McMurtry's] authorization in my time." Yet, Grady's response was unconcerned, "It will be interesting to see what he can produce, since my documents are signed by A.C."[8] On December 28, 1971, McMurtry registered the Ordo Templi Orientis Association with the State of California, giving the Order its first legal precedent.[9]

By 1972, the trend in publication began to increase. Samuel Weiser produced a lavishly-produced full set of *The Equinox*, Volume I, as ten separate hardbacks, limited to 515 copies.[10] Weiser also published a hardback edition of *The Equinox*, Volume III, Number 1, (*The Blue*

---

[7] An early initiate under McMurtry who is worthy of mention is Llee Heflin, owner of Level Press in San Francisco. Heflin helped McMurtry with the original photographs of the Thoth Tarot paintings. He published several works by Crowley throughout the early 1970s, notably *Liber Aleph* (1972), *777* (n.d.), *The Book of the Law* (1973), *Cocaine* (1973b), and a small collection of works entitled, *On Magick: An Introduction to the High Art* (1974b). In 1974, Level also published Frater Achad's *Liber 31*. Heflin eventually broke with McMurtry and resigned from the O.T.O. in 1971, shortly before he claimed to have received a collection of eight "dialogues" from the Secret Chiefs. He published this bizarre collection in 1973 as *The Island Dialogues*. See Heflin (1973).

[8] Grady McMurtry to Israel Regardie, December 13, 1970. MRSC.

[9] "O.T.O. Under McMurtry," United States Grand Lodge O.T.O. website (accessed April 5, 2018).

[10] Crowley (1972a).

Equinox).[11] These would prove significant as the "Encyclopedia of Initiation" was previously only available in its rare, first edition printings. Israel Regardie, who was at the time living in New York, published a rather careless edition of *The Vision and the Voice* through the Sangreal Foundation in Dallas, Texas, which included an introduction by Regardie and explanations to the commentary. It was awkward because the reader could not distinguish between Crowley and Regardie's commentary. Regardie had published a much more important work in 1970 through Llewellyn, *The Eye in the Triangle,* his own biography of Crowley. *The Eye in the Triangle* was released early enough in the Thelemic revival to have helped stir further interest in Crowley. This work was important because Regardie had known Crowley on a personal level, much closer than John Symonds. Regardie was also a student of occultism and psychoanalysis, which would have given the reader the viewpoint of a practitioner. *The Eye in the Triangle* was a fresh perspective on the Beast.

It was at this time that Kenneth Grant began to develop his own magical system along the lines of Crowley's teachings, authoring a series of trilogies—referred to as the Typhonian Trilogies—beginning in 1972 with the publication of *The Magical Revival.*[12] It is from these books that Grant's "Typhonian O.T.O." emerged.[13] Grant would also continue to co-edit Crowley's work with John Symonds, publishing *The Magical Record of the Beast 666* in 1972 and *Magick* in 1973.[14] England witnessed another new book in 1973 with Francis King's *The Secret Rituals of the O.T.O.*, published in London by C.W. Daniel

---

[11] Crowley (1972b).

[12] Kenneth Grant (1973). See Bogdan (2014), 325. Also for a discussion on Grant, refer to Evans (2004) and (2007).

[13] The Typhonian O.T.O., later renamed in 2011 the Typhonian Order, was developed by Grant along the lines of Crowley's teachings and his own writings found within these trilogies. The Typhonian Tradition is greatly indebted to the teachings of Crowley, albeit a deviation from Thelema proper, combining a discourse on sexual magic, tantra, and extra-terrestrial beings. See Bogdan (2014), 326.

[14] Crowley (1972c) and (1973a).

Company.[15] It was later released in the United States through Samuel Weiser. King's book offered, for the first time in open publication, the secret initiation rituals and many degree papers of the Ordo Templi Orientis up to the IX°. King most likely acquired these through the documents given to the Warburg Institute by Gerald Yorke. This text is now long out of print, and will most likely only see reprinting if and when the copyrights to the rituals expire.

In North America, several small publishers in the early 1970s are also worth mentioning. The first is Peter Macfarlane (1946–2009) and his wife Linda of 93 Publishing in South Stukely, Quebec, an area just outside of Montreal. 93 Publishing was responsible for producing very high quality, often hand-bound, limited-edition copies of various obscure titles by Crowley, such as his poem dedicated to Leah Hirsig, *Leah Sublime* (1976), and the important small work, *The Heart of the Master* (1973).[16] The Macfarlanes also released editions of *The Book of the Law*. Peter Macfarlane was a member of Kenneth Grant's O.T.O. and worked with Grant on publishing *The Magical and Philosophical Commentaries on the Book of the Law* (1974).[17] Macfarlane eventually broke with Grant and hired as editor an important future figure in the Thelemic movement, William Breeze (b. 1955). An American occultist and musician, born in France, Breeze worked closely with Macfarlane at 93 Publishing in the late 1970s. He became involved with McMurtry's O.T.O. group in 1978, and is most well-known for having eventually succeeded McMurtry in 1985 as Caliph, and later Outer Head of the Order of the O.T.O., a role in which he continues to serve.

Another small publisher emerged in California in the first years of the 1970s. Former Agape Lodge member Helen Parsons Smith began publishing small, beautifully-made limited editions of lesser-known works by Crowley. She began Thelema Publications in Kings Beach, California, with *Shih Yi* (1971), introducing the text with her magical

---

[15] King (1973).

[16] Respectively, Crowley (1976) and (1973c).

[17] Crowley (1974c).

motto, *Soror Grimaud.*[18] She followed in 1973 with a hardback edition of *Khing Kang King,* and *The Soul of the Desert* in 1974.[19] Smith would continue to publish various limited edition works into the 1980s.

The above list of publications during this period is far from complete. Still, it should exemplify the fact that there was a resurging Thelemic movement that was surrounded by a culture of publication in the first years of the 1970s, and that it was primarily centered in North America. Among those publishing Crowley in England were, of course, Symonds and Grant, and publishers Duckworth, C.W. Daniel Company, Neptune Press, and Routledge & Kegan Paul in London. In North America, Israel Regardie seems to have chiefly published through Llewellyn and Sangreal Foundation in St. Paul and Dallas, respectively. With the Macfarlanes and William Breeze operating from Quebec, Helen Smith producing small quantities of works in southern California, as well as the efforts of Llee Heflin in San Francisco, we can see that there were a handful of individuals involved in initiating the Thelemic publishing revival. While all these publishers contributed to the growing interest in Thelema, it was the alchemical components of Samuel Weiser's publications and the efforts made by Marcelo Ramos Motta that caught the attention of both young and seasoned disciples involved in the Thelemic movement.

Marcelo Ramos Motta and The Commentaries of AL (1973–1975)

> The A∴A∴ is now in a Period of Speech, and I am bound by my Oath, like it or not, to serve.
>
> —Marcelo Motta to James Wasserman, October 26, 1974

On July 19, 1973, Donald Weiser received an inquiry at his publishing office at 734 Broadway in New York City from a Mr. Marcelo Motta, who was writing to see if Samuel Weiser, Inc. would be interested

---

[18] Crowley (1971).

[19] Crowley (1973d) and (1974d), respectively.

in publishing his latest project, *The Commentaries of AL*,[20] a series of commentaries that Crowley wrote on *The Book of the Law,* along with Motta's own secondary commentaries. Motta had sent his initial request some years before, however that inquiry had gone unnoticed. Motta renewed his request, surmising that "enough interest in Crowley has been aroused, I think, for profitability." Motta assured Mr. Weiser that he was a legitimate representative of Thelema. "You may not know that Mr. Germer, Crowley's 'spiritual heir,' nominated me in his will as <u>his</u> spiritual heir in turn. I am, to all effect, his successor, as he was Crowley's successor."[21] Motta further wrote of his intention to implement the "Imprimatur seal," designating the work as a formal "A∴A∴ Publication." In keeping with Crowley's tradition of alternating periods of speech and silence, Motta informed Weiser that the A∴A∴ was now in a period of Speech, claiming that it was "time that the world should know that the Order is alive, and at work, and that the Chain of Authority has not been broken or even temporarily interrupted in these seventy years since *AL* was received."[22]

Nearly a year passed, and on June 26, 1974, Motta received a reply from James Wasserman, an employee of Weiser's. He informed Motta that the manuscript for his *Commentaries of AL* had been received and was being reviewed. Donald Weiser was familiar with Motta, and remembered working with him and Karl Germer during the publication of *Liber Aleph* in 1961. At this time in 1974, Samuel Weiser was open to the idea, but it was contingent upon some other upcoming publications at the time. Peter Macfarlane of 93 Publishing was working with Kenneth Grant on *The Magical and Philosophical Commentaries to the Book of the Law,*[23] which had been announced to be released shortly. Llewellyn had also announced Regardie's edition, *The Law Is For All.* The commentaries, edited by Grant and Symonds,

---

[20] Crowley and Motta (1975) *The Commentaries of AL* (New York: Samuel Weiser, Inc).

[21] Motta to Donald Weiser, July 19, 1973. SWC.

[22] Motta to Weiser, June 21, 1974. SWC.

[23] Crowley (1974b).

were a collection of writings by Crowley on *The Book of the Law* during his time in Cefalù and Tunisia in the early 1920s, as was Regardie's. Motta's book would include a selection of these along with Motta's own insights into the Thelemic text. Wasserman informed Motta that their decision to publish his book would depend greatly on the similarity of content in the three works. Samuel Weiser was, however, not averse to the project based on the fact that the 93 Publishing edition was "not being done in this country and therefore does not hinder our publication desires." Also Weiser agreed with Motta "that their [Grant and Symonds] claim to a kind of 'holy authority' is, at best, spurious" while Motta's appeared more legitimate.[24] Finally, the Llewellyn publication of Regardie had already been long announced and delayed.

Motta was informed of an edition of *Liber Aleph* by Llee Heflin of Level Press in San Francisco. Heflin was using Karl Germer's 1961 edition for his own printing, which Motta had originally edited and introduced. This was one example of what Motta believed was the problem arising from "unauthorized" publications of Crowley's work. Motta was at this time not fully aware of everything that had transpired over the last six years. He had not been in correspondence with Mrs. Germer since she informed him of the robbery in 1968. Although he sent a letter in an effort to reach her, he received no reply from the reclusive widow. He was under the impression that Sascha Germer was heir to the Crowley library, and not merely the executor of Karl Germer's will. Furthermore, he initially assumed Kenneth Grant had been granted permission by Sascha when he claimed to be the Outer Head of O.T.O. He wrote Wasserman, "I may at any time rescind this of course, but up to now see no reason to do so."[25] Like his Superior, Motta was never formally initiated into the O.T.O., however he may have been certified as a IX°—and Germer implied he was eligible to run the O.T.O. in Brazil. Regardless, what is known is that Motta, like Germer before him, was certainly more concerned with the A∴A∴.. He claimed to have advanced to the grade of Zelator by the time of

---

[24] Wasserman to Motta, June 26, 1974. SWC.

[25] Motta to Wasserman, July 19, 1974. SWC.

Germer's death, of which he wrote that it was precisely "the moment when I became able to carry on alone, but was not completely prepared." Motta claimed to have continued to work through the grades of the A∴A∴ and that he "underwent the Crossing of the Abyss, first on the emotional, then on the intellectual plane."[26]

Motta received a letter from Wasserman on August 7, informing him of Weiser's decision to go ahead with the publication of *The Commentaries of AL*. Wasserman, a young aspiring student of Crowley's work, was intrigued by the fact that he was now in contact with someone who seemed to be a living Adept with an authoritative chain linking back to the Master. Over the next few months, Wasserman had gained Motta's trust enough to be given the honor to write the preface for the new book. In September of 1974, Wasserman officially inquired about joining the A∴A∴, writing Motta enthusiastically:

> I have sought to find a valid representative of these Teachings for some time [...] The actual possibility that you are of so exalted a Grade as Magister Templi demands that I ask you for more information about the work and structure of the Order [...] I would specifically like to know something more of the Oath and Task of the Probationer.[27]

However, this spark of inquiry was extinguished for the moment when Motta suddenly became enraged by a copy of Israel Regardie's edition of *The Vision and the Voice* (published by the Sangreal Foundation and distributed by Weiser) that he had ordered through Samuel Weiser. The editing and commentaries were careless in Motta's opinion, and his lambasting escalated into criticizing Regardie for his Jewish background:

> I suggest your House ponder very carefully what your behavior towards Aleister Crowley and his followers has been in these edi-

---

26 Motta to Wasserman, August 14, 1974. SWC.

27 Wasserman to Motta, September 28, 1974. SWC.

tions. You not only have paid no royalties to any one for your editions, you have also allowed a second-rate scholar to do something that no high-minded and honest Jew would ever do [...] If necessary, we will sink the entire Middle East under water for twenty thousand years, to teach the Jews that Heru-Ra-Ha is the Lord of the Aeon, and that Jehovah, as all other gods, bows before Him [...] for the sake of all Jews, try to give an example of honest manhood both in your personal and business lives from now on [...] do us the human courtesy of publishing [Thelemic material] intact, and not allowing it to be pawed by imbeciles, be they Jews or Gentile![28]

Underneath the hostility and abrasiveness, it can be seen from the above that Motta was impatient with anything falling below his standards when it came to publishing Crowley's work. One gets the impression that he was singularly focused on Thelema, and became caustically hostile to anyone or anything that did not represent it fairly. Nevertheless, his letter did not sit well with James Wasserman, who was brought up in Judaism. He responded with oppositional sentiments, "I despised the anti-Semitic diatribes you were spewing forth, while sympathizing and agreeing with your frustration at people not publishing Crowley correctly [...] You will find in the future that I respond better to reason than to threats of sinking Israel."[29]

On October 24, Motta informed Wasserman that Gerald Yorke had provided a copy of Karl Germer's last will and testament signed back in 1951. Once Motta realized that Sascha was merely the literary executor and not the heir to the library, his attitude began to shift. Although he had expressed several times that he was not interested in the "Lodge work" of the O.T.O., Motta had been operating the O.T.O. in Brazil for several years, working the first three degrees. This was done under the impression given to him by Sascha Germer in a letter informing him that Karl had issued him a charter. He denounced Grant as the Outer Head of the Order of O.T.O., and claimed himself

---

[28] Motta to Wasserman, October 12, 1974. SWC.

[29] Wasserman to Motta, November 21, 1974. SWC.

as the sole inheritor of Thelemic leadership. Motta proceeded to write to Wasserman, addressing him as a representative of Weiser, "All your publications of Crowley material will be done with the Imprimatur, granted by me," and that Weiser should "make all necessary efforts and take all necessary measures to stop publication of pirated editions from any source whatsoever in any language [...] In short, all stealing of Crowley material, and even 'authorized' stealing, has to stop!"[30] To a large publishing house that was in the business of making money, these outlandish demands might be considered laughable. On the other hand, if Motta's copyright claims were sustainable, the idea of legal exclusivity to Crowley's oeuvre was tantalizing. With Weiser's permission, Wasserman began exploring Motta's legal options. However, since the copyright situation on Crowley's work would not be resolved until a decade later, all these editions were considered to be legally publishable at the time.

Motta's irritability subsided over time, and correspondence became cordial again in the first months of 1975. *The Commentaries of AL* was now on its way to completion, and talks of publishing his commentary to another Thelemic Holy Book, *Liber LXV Cordis Cincti Serpente*, began. As Wasserman read over the galley proofs of the text and compiled the index, he once again became interested in pursuing the work of the A∴A∴ under the supervision of Motta. On March 18, he formally requested to be admitted as a Probationer, writing to Motta, "I do not believe this to be an ill-considered request; it is rather the necessary fulfillment of the course of my life to this point."[31]

In the meantime, there was a new development with the A∴A∴ in the southeastern United States. Around April of 1975, Samuel Weiser received a letter from someone operating out of Nashville, Tennessee, announcing affiliation with the A∴A∴. "Please inform all publishing companies who are occupied in the presentation of material relating to the A∴A∴ or the individual works of Aleister Crowley, that our organization is still operative [...]"[32] A regular patron of Samuel

---

30 Motta to Wasserman, October 24, 1974. SWC.

31 Wasserman to Motta, March 18, 1975. SWC.

32 "Frater N.A.S." to Samuel Weiser, Inc., Undated. SWC.

Weiser's bookstore and friend of James Wasserman, Richard Gernon ("Gurney," as he was known to his friends, 1950–1989) took interest in the mysterious group, though they were both initially suspicious. Wasserman, having just signed the Oath of the Probationer reported to his now formal Superior, Motta, on the group. It was agreed between Gernon and Wasserman that, while Wasserman kept in touch with Motta, Gernon would travel down to Nashville to investigate. Gernon soon made contact with a "Frater K.N.," known to the mundane world as James Daniel Gunther (b. 1950). In the early 1970s, Gunther had been traveling in a progressive rock band known as Wakefield. In 1971, he found himself motivated by a mystical experience to begin seeking out the A∴A∴ and working through its curriculum. He had initially attempted to make contact with the O.T.O. in Dublin, California, which was the only Thelemic community he could find at the time. When he received no response from California, Gunther set up a post office box in Nashville as a point of contact. He proceeded to reach out to known publishers of esoteric literature in an effort to announce the presence of Thelema in the United States.

Upon their meeting, Gurney found in Gunther a remarkable level of erudition about Thelema and the Work of the A∴A∴, and began to study under his supervision. Word of Gunther's operations soon reached Motta, and news of his upcoming publication with Samuel Weiser soon fell on Gunther's ears. Gunther subsequently wrote to Samuel Weiser, Inc., addressing the Brazilian representative specifically,

DO WHAT THOU WILT SHALL BE
THE WHOLE OF THE LAW

Marcelo Motta,

This letter is to inform you of the existence of the American chapter of A∴A∴ which was sanctioned in 1973 E.V. by the Supreme Chiefs of the Third Order.

This Order is established perfectly in every manner and is NOT a deviation from the Order as set forth by the Master Therion.

It is the desire of the present heads of this Chapter of A∴A∴, that our two Chapters work together in Harmony, coalescing in Spirit for the benefit of the Law of Thelema.

Any information desired will be sent upon request.

We are yours in this, the Great Work.

LOVE IS THE LAW, LOVE UNDER WILL

CANCELLARIUS A∴A∴[33]

Motta's initial response to the young novice was mocking in tone, but gentle: "I am surprised to be informed of the existence of a 'chapter' of the A∴A∴, since the A∴A∴ has never had and will never have any sort of organization on the physical plane." Further, he was "even more surprised to know that the 'chapter' has been sanctioned by the Supreme Chiefs of the Third Order, since I happen to be one of them, and do not recollect sanctioning anything." Motta also pointed out to the young aspirant that, "to open and close your letters by words from Liber AL in straight capitals falls under the heading of 'changing the style of the letters' of the Book [...] this is not to be done."[34] Recognizing Motta as a legitimate link to the Master Therion through Frater Saturnus (Karl Germer), Gunther submitted his journals and relevant material, and, after several months of review, Motta accepted Gunther as his student, writing: "I am willing to accept you as a Philosophus of the A∴A∴, if you will take the trouble of typing over and mailing to me the Oath and Task of the Grades from Probationer to $4°=7°$."[35] It is clear from the abundance of their subsequent correspondence that the two became very close, with Gunther becoming Motta's personal representative for the next several years.

The Commentaries of AL went to press on November 5, with Wasserman remarking, "I have great confidence that we shall receive back a beautiful book that will have a great impact on the lives of

---

[33] Letter addressed to Marcelo Motta, August 5, 1975.

[34] Motta to J. Daniel Gunther, August 12, 1975. SWC.

[35] Motta to Gunther, November 1, 1975. SWC.

many people." *The Commentaries of AL* arrived in early January 1976 and, with its release, the renewed A∴A∴ movement was formally announced:

> This edition of the Commentaries on the Book of the Law has been prepared by Marcelo Motta the Præmonstrator of the A∴A∴ during its current Period of Speech. Mr. Motta was the devoted disciple of Frater SATURNUS, Karl Germer [...] We are pleased to greet the voice of a man whose magical work for over twenty years has been identified with the unbroken line of the A∴A∴ and the OTO as described by Crowley himself, particularly in One Star in Sight and in the Equinox. There is a sense of continuity of transmission that one experiences with the reading of this book, the perception of harmony between the writings of Aleister Crowley and Marcelo Motta.[36]

Also within *The Commentaries of AL* was an "O.T.O. Manifesto," in which Motta claimed to be the sole heir of the Thelemic manuscripts. The publication received immediate responses. In an interview Gunther remarked, "The movement did not become alive until *The Commentaries of AL*. After that publication, I received letters from all over the world."[37] However, a storm was brewing. Four years earlier, Grady McMurtry and Phyllis Seckler had registered the O.T.O. as a legal entity within the state of California. What would follow in six short months was a battle not only for successorship in the Thelemic movement, but also for the rights to the literary remains—which were still at the Germer house in West Point, California. Perhaps foretelling of this battle is a letter from Israel Regardie to James Wasserman in January of 1976. In it, Regardie gives his own opinion of the new, self-identified A∴A∴ publication:

---

[36] Crowley and Motta (1975), preface by Wasserman.

[37] Interview with J. Daniel Gunther by the author, Murfreesboro, Tennessee, February 22, 2015.

I must confess that both your edition and Kenneth Grant's amuse the living hell out of me. Both are in competition to be the successor to A.C. and the head of the O.T.O. [...] the whole situation of leadership is in a beautiful state of confusion [...] All I can say is: it should be a lot of fun watching in the near future the battle of the "giants" claiming successorship![38]

As we have seen, the Thelemic movement was gaining momentum through the culture of publication surrounding it. In the next chapter we will trace the results of the contact between Motta's A∴A∴, McMurtry's O.T.O., and the legal system of the United States of America.

---

[38] Israel Regardie to James Wasserman, January 30, 1976. SWC

CHAPTER TEN

The Clash of the Titans[1]

The Thelemic Battle for Legitimacy (1976–1985)

WE HAVE NOW REACHED a climactic point in our narrative, wherein the paths of various Thelemic figures begin to intersect. By 1976, the O.T.O. had been registered as a legal association in the state of California and was gaining more traction. Grady McMurtry and Phyllis Seckler were initiating new members, due in part to the printing of the *Thoth Tarot* deck by Llewellyn. Meanwhile, in New York, *The Commentaries of AL* by Marcelo Motta was published by Samuel Weiser, Inc. announcing the presence of the A∴A∴. Thelemic publications were coming out of every corner of North America. Yet, a storm was brewing. Here we finally see two Thelemic giants come face-to-face—Grady McMurtry and Marcelo Motta. Those apparently on the opposing sides were either caught up in, or played their own hand, in the power struggles that ensued over the Crowley library. Here, the reader will see how the Crowley library took on an agency of its own, culminating in a fundamental dilemma surrounding a new religious movement and its relationship to publication and legitimacy—that is, the role that legitimacy plays with regard to religion in contemporary culture within the larger sphere of secular society. It is here that we see a necessary turn in the Thelemic movement's attitude towards publication, passing from the period of *open access* to that of *legitimization.*

---

[1] Referring to Grady L. McMurtry and Marcelo Motta, the phrase "Clash of the Titans" was used in an interview with Stephen J. King, Shiva X° Grand Master General of Australian Grand Lodge, O.T.O. See King (2014), 13.

The Calm Before the Storm (January–April 1976)

In the first months of 1976, James Wasserman and Marcelo Motta remained in frequent contact. The nature of their correspondence regards both Wasserman's instruction as a student of Motta in the A∴A∴, as well as Motta's continued interest in publishing his work as Præmonstrator through Samuel Weiser, Inc. Wasserman and his wife at the time, Marianne, visited Motta and his partner, Claudia, in Rio de Janeiro in early February. The trip seems to have been a combination of Wasserman hand-delivering advance copies of *The Commentaries of AL* to Motta, and Motta giving Wasserman practical instruction in the A∴A∴ curriculum.[2] Wasserman, however, left Brazil troubled by the visit. Among other things, Motta had claimed responsibility for the death of Donald Weiser's brother-in-law and partner, Fred Mendel. Wasserman recalled his conversation with Motta: "unless Weiser knuckled under to the publishing program he demanded, more deaths would follow."[3] Wasserman further recounts this as a moment of realization in his own personal life. "My conflict-of-interest dilemma had now gone into overdrive. I decided I would have to leave Weiser's. On the other hand, I believed I was spiritually on the right path as far as Thelema was concerned—although there had been some conversation about my continuing A∴A∴ work with Gunther because of concerns raised by Motta's record and the visit."[4]

Upon Wasserman's return to the United States, he and Motta continued discussing the possibility of future publications. In April, Wasserman was now at the final stages of working on Motta's manuscript of *LXV Commented*, and Motta was planning to put together a collection of works, which included *The Field Theory of Sex, Letter to a Brazilian Mason, Liber CCXXXI: A Personal Research*, and *The Visions of the Pylons*. All of these were works written by Motta with

[2] See Wasserman (2012), 74–81.

[3] Ibid., 81.

[4] Ibid., 81.

the exception of the last, which was a collection of recorded visions of J. Daniel Gunther describing the Pylons in the Egyptian Duat or netherworld.[5] All of these works would not see the light of day through Samuel Weiser's publishing house, and it would be years before they would be published. More important matters were, however, developing regarding the Thelemic library. News of Motta and *The Commentaries of AL* had fallen on the ears of the O.T.O. group in California. On April 19, 1976, Motta received a letter from Phyllis Seckler (then McMurtry), who initially recognized his claim as Præmonstrator:

> There is much to discuss with you. I have been reading THE COMMENTARIES OF AL put out by you and am pleased to see you have done this. However, the whole thing puts a very different picture on what I am doing at the present. Since you are now Præmonstrator of the A∴A∴ and since I am a member of this body, there are details to be worked out in regards to the work of promulgating Thelema. So far, I have founded the College of Thelema and am putting out publication three times in the year call[ed] IN THE CONTINUUM. I have been working with a very few students, but those of the finest I could find.[6]

Seckler had discussed with McMurtry her idea of creating a "college of the occult" as early as 1969, writing him that it was an "idea which is bugging me at present. To somehow found a Thelemic college."[7] When they began to initiate people into the O.T.O. in 1969, they did so under the auspices of the College of Thelema. In 1973, Seckler started putting out a pamphlet-style publication called *In the Continuum*, claiming that it was "Founded in service to the A∴A∴." The publication included several of Crowley's works, some of the material photocopied

---

[5] Over 40 years later, this has finally been published by Ibis Press in June of 2018. See Gunther (2018).

[6] Seckler to Motta, April 19, 1976. SWC.

[7] Seckler to McMurtry, January 26, 1969. GM-PSC.

in with other Thelemic-related writings, and artwork contributed by Seckler and others within her circle.

The matter at hand, however, was not how Seckler and Motta were going to promulgate Thelema. Their efforts to further the movement were contingent on the fate of the Thelemic library. Seckler wrote to Motta, "I would like to know if Sascha Germer is dead? And if so, did she leave you the remains of the library at West Point?"[8] It had been many years since Seckler and Motta had any contact with one another. To Motta's recollection, Seckler had broken contact after he questioned her position in the A∴A∴:

> At the time she last wrote to me, she believed herself a Minor Adept of the A∴A∴ (and Mr. Germer thought so too). In my opinion—and I wrote her so—she had mistaken the Vision of the H.G.A.[9] in the Neophyte initiation for the Knowledge and Conversation. After I wrote her stating this and pointing out my reasons for this judgement, she never wrote me again.[10]

As the reader is now well-aware, Seckler and Motta had a history of clashing with each other, so it is not surprising that the nature of their correspondence at this point would be much the same. Motta was immediately skeptical of Phyllis. The last he had heard from Sascha Germer was in 1968, when she had written him, falsely accusing Phyllis' daughter of perpetrating the robbery against her. He wrote alarmingly to Wasserman:

> Now she writes to ask me if Mrs. Germer is dead or alive, if she left the "remains" of the library to me, and touches on the robbery. In my opinion, she is merely fishing. If so, I suspect she fell under

---

[8] Seckler to Motta, April 19, 1976. SWC.

[9] Holy Guardian Angel.

[10] Motta to Wasserman, April 29, 1976. SWC.

the shadow of her Evil Persona. In this case, she is an extremely dangerous influence and must be curbed pitilessly.[11]

Motta knew little to nothing of the Solar Lodge and was under the suspicion that Phyllis had been the thief. He warned Wasserman that "If she is not [innocent], and McMurtry is under her influence, his Lodge is diseased and any movement he starts will be diseased also. In which case I will have to quarantine them."[12] Motta may have been wrong in suspecting Phyllis of the crime, though not altogether mistaken in being dubious about her intentions. As will soon be revealed, Seckler would find her own way to come into possession of the library.

Sascha Germer's Death and the Thelemic Library (Spring 1976)

Not long after Seckler had written her first letter in years to Motta inquiring about the library, she wrote again informing him that she and Helen Parsons Smith had traveled to West Point to investigate the situation. Seckler followed up with Motta, "We learned that she [Sascha Germer] had been dead since April 1 or 2 of 1975."[13] Seckler claimed that she and McMurtry had previously requested that state authorities inform them upon Mrs. Germer's death, but this after all had not happened. The Germer estate was now to be put up for sale in the near future, and the proceeds "used to pay various bills Sascha and Karl incurred."[14] All of the contents within the household, including the library, were to be sold along with the estate. Given Motta's proclamation of ownership over the library in his "O.T.O. Manifesto," Seckler for the time was willing to recognize Motta's claim, writing him, "You seem to be the one most interested in Crowley's literary remains. You perhaps should have the library but you may have to bid against competitors. As for me, it is not part of my Will to work with it. However,

---

[11] Ibid.

[12] Ibid.

[13] Seckler to Motta, April 28, 1976. SWC.

[14] Ibid.

I will lend some assistance within reason to the deserving person who might ask for my aid in the matter."[15] Motta wrote back to Seckler, informing her that he was not able travel to the U.S. at present, but suggested that she be assisted by J. Daniel Gunther in sorting through the materials:

> He is a young man, very dedicated, and well trained. His grade is 4°=7□. I think you will find him very willing to do whatever he can to be of assistance to a worthy member of the Order [...] He is very proud, but I suspect we can expect great things from him in the future regardless—or perhaps because of it![16]

Further communication opened between Helen Parsons Smith and James Wasserman in May. She wrote to Wasserman that Karl Germer's will "has been lost, has strayed, or is stolen. The Germer Library [...] has been pilfered and vandalized of those choice documents! Everything reverts to the State—of California."[17] Smith also had concerns regarding Motta's "O.T.O. Manifesto." On May 11, she inquired of Wasserman in a telephone conversation as to why Motta was now making all these claims about the O.T.O. when he had not been in touch with them since 1963. Motta wrote back hastily to Smith, "I expected you people to get in touch if you felt you needed me for anything. Since you didn't, I surmised Mrs. Germer's hostility towards me had led everybody to cut contact with me."[18] Motta suggested to Smith that the California Thelemites quickly get legal advice about the issue at hand, and informed her that James Wasserman would soon be flying out to assist, serving with Motta's power of attorney. In the meantime, Motta wrote Wasserman and Gunther to keep him informed of the situation, and to be on guard as it developed.

---

15 Ibid.

16 Motta to Seckler, April 29, 1976. SWC.

17 Smith to Wasserman, May 7, 1976. SWC.

18 Motta to Smith, May 11, 1976. SWC.

The frontlines for the battle ahead were being established. With the exception of the newcomers—James Wasserman, J. Daniel Gunther, and Richard Gernon—the parties now involved had known each other since the days of Agape Lodge. Motta had shared Karl Germer's strong criticism of Wilfred Smith, Helen's now-deceased husband, when he visited their home in Malibu in 1957. As Martin Starr writes, "In Motta's view, Wilfred Smith was ultimately to be blamed for the promotion of Agape over Thelema as the Word of the Law and thus leading members astray." Starr notes that Motta often echoed Karl Germer's contempt for the California Thelemites, noting Germer's words for Agape Lodge as "'A General Fucking Institute, Unlimited." Starr writes: "Brotherly love did not prevail, nor did any moral or social virtue cement the Thelemites."[19] It would not be a stretch of the imagination to surmise that Motta's sentiments about Wilfred Smith extended to a fairly low regard for Helen, although he generally spoke well of her in his correspondence with James Wasserman. Likewise, Seckler was certainly not fond of Motta, while he had nothing but contempt for her. Such history couldn't have possibly aided any effort of future cooperation. The sour grapes were now being harvested for the vintage, and only the bitter taste of vinegar would be shared amongst them.

The month of June passed without much development. Phyllis Seckler and Helen Parsons Smith attempted to enter the Germer house, but had no luck with the Calaveras County Coroner, Adolph Gualdoni.[20] Too busy to deal with individuals who seemed to him to be two old ladies inquiring about materials that seemingly didn't belong to them, Gualdoni referred Seckler and Smith to the lawyer who was handling the matter. They were told that admittance into the house was not allowed unless they could provide a will from either Karl or Sascha.

---

[19] Starr (2003), 339.

[20] Wasserman recalled Gualdoni as "a classically overworked bureaucrat who had been overwhelmed by a series of recent events, including a multi-vehicle accident that had claimed numerous lives and blocked off several roads." Wasserman (2012), 88.

Magical War (Summer 1976)

It was not until the last half of July that the situation reached a fever pitch. James Wasserman arrived on July 14, acting not only on Motta's behalf, but, in Gualdoni's eyes, as a legitimate representative for a large New York publishing firm of Crowley's work. Wasserman recalls the delicate situation, feeling as if he were "walking a tightrope in a hurricane." He remarks, "On the one hand, here was a psychopath taking credit for a magical murder. On the other, a credentialed authority was suggesting a very profitable partnership with the world's largest Crowley publisher."[21] Motta had warned Wasserman that he may be entering into a diseased Black Lodge, and that he would be subject to manipulation and fascination of all kinds. Upon meeting Phyllis and Helen, Wasserman recounts that this was an overreaction of Motta's, and that it would have made more sense for Motta to "calmly warn me about walking into a viper's nest rather than frantically projecting me into some Dennis Wheatley-style outpost of the Black Lodge."[22] More realistically, Phyllis and Helen gave Wasserman the impression of being the embodiments of Jan and Dean's 1960s song *The Little Old Lady from Pasadena*.

Under Gualdoni's supervision, Wasserman, Seckler, and Smith were admitted into the Germer house and began to organize the multitude of papers and documents strewn about the place. Wasserman remarks, "We found a treasure trove in the midst of complete chaos."[23] The documents included correspondence between Crowley and many of his disciples, as well as many manuscripts of his writings. The following day, July 16, Wasserman assisted Grady McMurtry, Phyllis Seckler, and Helen Smith with moving the library materials safely into storage. During his visit to Dublin, Grady shared with Wasserman what has come to be known as "The Caliphate Letters"—a collection of letters from Crowley to McMurtry recognizing McMurtry as a legitimate

---

[21] Ibid.

[22] Ibid., 90.

[23] Ibid., 92.

successor, subject only to the veto of Germer. Since Germer had never exercised a veto, Wasserman realized very quickly that McMurtry had a legitimate claim to the O.T.O.—and the library belonged to the O.T.O. Having this new information, the landscape was beginning to shift under Wasserman's feet. He recounted, "My escalating awareness of the disconnect between Motta's perceptions and objective reality was playing some havoc with me. What was my responsibility in the face of the fact that everything I thought I had known appeared to be wrong?"[24]

According to Wasserman, McMurtry stated he was completely willing to share the library with Motta. Wasserman negotiated with McMurtry to accept Motta as the legitimate authority in A∴A∴ if Motta would in turn recognize McMurtry as the authority in O.T.O.:

> Grady told me he was entirely committed to the idea of sharing the Germer finds with Motta in a fraternal manner. He made it clear that he did not claim A∴A∴ leadership and was happy to accept Motta's claims to A∴A∴ authority. He expected the same courtesy from Motta regarding his position in O.T.O.[25]

Wasserman's account is buttressed by a personal letter written later by Grady to Israel Regardie recounting the events. "Together, we wrote up my letter [...] in which, as best I could, I extended the hand of friendship and offered an accommodation that would, Jim [Wasserman] and I agreed, finally give us basis for getting our O.T.O/Thelema/A∴A∴, etc., trip together [...]"[26] McMurtry's letter to Motta, although recognizing his role in A∴A∴, asked Motta to renounce claim to O.T.O.:

> I propose that you write a letter to me personally [...] stating that you renounce all claim to becoming O.H.O. of the O.T.O., on the basis that you have assumed the grade of XI° O.T.O. Also that you refrain from publishing future manifestoes concerning the

24 Ibid., 96.

25 Wasserman (2012), 97.

26 Grady McMurtry to Israel Regardie, February 22, 1977. SWC.

O.T.O., since the O.T.O. and the A∴A∴ are entirely separate organizations.[27]

McMurtry included copies of the Caliphate Letters and explained his position within the O.T.O., at the same time recognizing that Motta had a different relationship with Karl Germer. McMurtry was, however, elusive about his membership in the A∴A∴, writing:

> When James Wasserman asked me my grade in the A∴A∴ I refused a direct answer, choosing to obey A.C.'s injunction that "Theoretically, a member knows only the superior who introduced him, and any person who he himself introduced." I am one who takes TO MEGA THERION's words at face value, and if he says I am not to discuss my position vis-à-vis A∴A∴ except with my superior and the person I have introduced, I <u>obey</u> that instruction.[28]

McMurtry, thus, did not claim an official grade in the A∴A∴ in his letter correspondence. It can be surmised from his letters from Crowley that Grady never held any grade in A∴A∴ during the Beast's lifetime. For example, Crowley suggested McMurtry practice the solar adorations in "Liber Resh vel Helios," not with any A∴A∴ Grade sign as the document instructs, but with the 0°–III° signs of the O.T.O.[29] This would indicate that Grady, indeed, was not officially involved in the A∴A∴ as far as Crowley was concerned. Grady's letter to Motta, thirty-two years later, however, was not ambivalent about his involvement. He stated quite clearly, "you may take it as patent that Karl would not have included me among the A∴A∴ members to be notified [...]

---

27 Grady McMurtry to Marcelo Motta, July 21, 1976. SWC.

28 McMurtry to Motta, July 21, 1976. SWC.

29 "*Liber Resh* gives 4 adorations (*Magick* pp. 425–6) with directions for facing [...] Use at start signs of grades, 0°–III° O.T.O. and Sign of Enterer, followed by sign of Silence, the 'Hail'—Damnit, you saw me do it!" Crowley to McMurtry, March 30, 1944. Excerpt of letter in *The Magical Link: The Quarterly Newsletter of Ordo Templi Orientis International*, Vol. 4, No. 4, Winter 1990–1991, 26.

were I not higher than Zelator Grade in A∴A∴. I look forward to receiving copies of material in your possession concerning the Order of Thelema."[30]

"The Order of Thelema" about which McMurtry was making inquiry was being confused with a document discovered at the Germer house concerning the "Constitution of the Order of Thelemites," introduced to the reader in chapter two. The confusion is easy to understand. In addition to the similarity of names, both mention the Zelator Grade of A∴A∴. The "Order of Thelema" was a phrase from the initiation ritual for the Zelator, "Liber CXX," by which the candidate was officially received into the "Order of Thelema." In the early 1960s just before Germer's death, Motta sought to establish an actual Order of Thelema, along similar social lines to O.T.O., with the requirement that members had to be of the Zelator Grade or higher in A∴A∴.[31]

The reader will recall from chapter two that the Order of Thelemites was a short-lived alternative plan created by Crowley to work M∴M∴M∴ outside of the O.T.O. in the 1920s, in the event that he did not succeed Theodor Reuss as O.H.O. in 1925. However, the Constitution of the Order of Thelemites merely substituted the "Man of Earth" in the O.T.O. system with the term, "Zelator," and was not necessarily implying the title for the second grade in the Outer College of the A∴A∴. Hymenaeus Beta noted the confusion in the 1980s. "The true history of this ritual ["Liber CXX"] was further clouded by less excusable editorial practices. Its publication with Crowley's 'Constitution of the Order of Thelemites' by a bootlegger in the UK [...] unfortunately created an artificial linkage between the ritual and the much later Constitution."[32] The fact that McMurtry was

---

[30] Ibid.

[31] Motta wrote Germer, "I have felt for a long time that there was something intrinsically wrong with the O.T.O. [...] If I live to do any work of promulgation of Thelema, therefore, I do not intend publicizing the O.T.O. [...] at all. I shall work exclusively with the initiatic work, and with the Order of Thelema (which, the Gods willing, I shall organize) for masonic, that is, social work. In short, the A∴A∴ for individual, the Order of Thelema for social work." Motta to Germer, December 30, 1961. GMC.

[32] See H.B.'s discussion on this, http://oto-usa.org/static/legis/legis3/legis3.pdf (accessed December 1, 2016).

not aware of these nuances implies that he was indeed not involved with the A∴A∴ under Germer.

In any case, McMurtry and Wasserman agreed that Wasserman would gather the materials in the library so that he could deliver them to Motta. Wasserman returned to New York on August 4, 1976, but not before being officially initiated into the O.T.O. degree of Minerval by Grady McMurtry on July 27. He left California believing a resolution had been reached between Marcelo and Grady. It would soon prove that he was naively hopeful. Motta, as one may suspect at this point, was not satisfied with the terms. As Grady recounted, "Motta bit off my hand of friendship right up about the elbow." Motta wrote back:

> It is obvious that you hold no Patent from Frater SATURNUS at all [...] It is also obvious that you intend, if you can, to bypass this fact, and are now very subtly holding your possession (not legal, as you know) of the Thelemic Library over my head in the hope that I will knuckle under you [...] Don't wave flags of A∴A∴ membership at me. Remember, I know you. I met you. As I know Phyllis ex-Wade-ex-Seckler-McMurtry [...] And in the A∴A∴ you are nothing. Phyllis, a long time ago, was a Neophyte dreaming that she was an Adept. What she is now, I do not know, and I do not care [...] I will rebate your proposal with a counter-proposal. I want xeroxes of all the unpublished material in the Thelemic Library without exception. If you refuse to provide these [...] I <u>will</u> take you to court eventually [...] I will never recognize you as Caliph, because only Mr. Germer had the authority to do so, as stated in the original documents, and he didn't.[33]

Motta subsequently cut contact with Wasserman and severed his business relations with Samuel Weiser, Inc., not before he directed Wasserman to deliver xeroxes of the library into Gunther's custody. He wrote Wasserman, "Whether he [Gunther] will be willing to accept you as Probationer or not, is up to him."[34] He then wrote directly to Donald

---

[33] Motta to McMurtry, July 29, 1976. SWC.
[34] Motta to Wasserman, July 26, 1976. SWC.

Weiser, informing him that he was terminating his business relationship with Samuel Weiser, Inc. under the assumption that Weiser had "as my Publisher" not defended "my rights and interests to the best of your capacity and ability."[35]

Thus, in one short month in 1976, a rift occurred within the Thelemic community that has affected relationships to the present day. This initial disagreement was only the beginning. Years later the battle would reconvene in a court of law. For the meantime, other troubles were stirring between McMurtry and Seckler in California, and James Wasserman in New York. Personal relationships and the fate of the library were becoming mixed business. Thelemites, after all, are still human beings making mortal mistakes, just like the rest of humanity.

The Seizing of the Library (Autumn 1976)

In the 1978 publication of In the Continuum, Phyllis Seckler recalls her impressions of the summer of 1976 when the Crowley library was being recovered with Helen Parsons Smith and James Wasserman:

> [T]hrough communications with J.W. [James Wasserman] we found that Gualdoni had promised him access to the Germer property to pick up all the remaining mess of papers on the floor and to see that they got into storage. H. [Helen P. Smith] and I were outraged! We had worked for months to get access to the property to do this and had been given the runaround by Mr. Gualdoni. Now here a man from New York and a representative of a publishing firm was going to be allowed to do it![36]

As can be surmised from an earlier discussion, there is some indication from Seckler's early letters with Motta in 1963 that she coveted the library back when Germer had first died. One can imagine her frustration when a newcomer came around and was given access to the materials after she had been trying to do the same for months. Despite

---

[35] Motta to Donald Weiser, July 26, 1976. SWC.

[36] Seckler (1978), 17–18.

her annoyance, Seckler, being an ever-dedicated Thelemite, assisted McMurtry and Wasserman with gathering the materials that July. Gualdoni first authorized the library to be placed safely into a nearby storage facility where the coroner's office could monitor it. In August, Grady and Phyllis were finally given permission to move the library from public storage to Phyllis' house in Dublin, where the couple were living and operating the O.T.O. Seckler and McMurtry, however, were beginning to develop a history of their own. Grady owed Phyllis a good deal of money, as Phyllis had been paying Grady's way since he had relocated to California. McMurtry was having trouble finding steady employment, had developed a drinking habit, and was allegedly keeping unscrupulous company. Phyllis became increasingly paranoid when Grady began to inform others that the library had been secured and placed at the headquarters in Dublin. She did not trust Grady's judgments of character, recalling that he "was often fooled by certain types of people" and that he was drawn to "certain types of 'rip off' artists."[37] Seckler felt she had good reason to be concerned, so she removed the materials from her home and placed them in an undisclosed location. She subsequently wrote to Wasserman in September:

> First, because of some serious failures on Grady's part, the whole of the Germer-Crowley library is in storage and no one knows where it is except myself. It will remain there until such time as there is an utterly safe place to put it. As agreed upon by the higher officers of this Lodge, there are certain parts of these archives which will not be open to the lower Grades; much of the correspondence is in this category [...] Therefore, you will not have access to the library at the present moment [...] it will be some years before I will be ready to discuss the possibility of giving xerox copies of any part of these archives to Gunther or Motta [...] Frankly, I am quite convinced that Motta is not what he says he is and that his claims are spurious [...] there was no agreement to furnish xerox copies of everything to Gunther. I think you have sadly scrambled the facts here [...] that you could suppose

---

[37] Ibid., 24.

something as you did is no doubt due to the effect that Neptune square your Sun has on your nature. You might study this a little bit? Neptune is also square Mercury and Venus.[38]

Paranoid proclivities and astrological ruminations aside, Seckler was making a power move for herself. Or was it that *she* was the only person trustworthy enough to handle the library? When Phyllis and Grady split up, she threw him out of her place in Dublin, claiming she had been "cruelly exploited" by him. McMurtry recalled later to Israel Regardie, "I woke up one morning to find she had rifled my keys to car, house, etc. [...] Her exact words, concerning my future living circumstance were, and I quote: 'I don't care <u>how</u> you get along.'" McMurtry already had a new partner, and according to him, Phyllis became enraged upon learning that he was living with his new girlfriend, and that the two were planning a summer vacation to New Mexico. McMurtry further wrote:

> "Phyllis laid down an ultimatum. 'Go to [New] Mexico with that _____, and SOMETHING will happen!' [...] And sure enough, something damn sure happened. No sooner was I back than she sequestered the books and files of the library (so called) in commercial storage where I could not get to them, because I 'am not reliable!' So she had decided."[39]

In reality, what appears to have happened is that Seckler was extremely resentful towards McMurtry, feeling she had been taken advantage of financially. According to Seckler, she had paid almost $18,000 towards McMurtry's living expenses and health costs since he had moved out to Dublin in 1969.[40] It is questionable whether Seckler subsequently seized the library and refused to disclose its whereabouts as a justification for her frustrations with McMurtry.[41] It is unclear at which point

---

[38] Seckler to Wasserman, September 24, 1976. SWC.

[39] McMurtry to Regardie February 22, 1977. SWC.

[40] Letter from Seckler to O.T.O. members March 9, 1977. Seckler (2010), 340.

[41] See Seckler (2010), 340–347.

the materials that Phyllis cloistered away were supposed to be turned back over to the O.T.O. It would seem that she still held them, judging by a letter of March 1977, where she recounts to O.T.O. members her story of the events as they transpired.[42]

At the same time this was happening, Grady was publishing a new edition of the *Thoth Tarot* deck through Samuel Weiser. McMurtry wrote hastily to Wasserman that "Phyllis has gotten into one of her 'periodic fits of insanity' and has sequestered the material."[43] He asked that the O.T.O. address on the Caliph card be changed from the Dublin address to his new address in Berkeley. In the midst of all this confusion, the O.T.O. address was not published on the Caliph card in the 1977 printing. As Wasserman recounts, the conflict between Grady and Phyllis, as relayed to Donald Weiser by fellow publisher Helen Smith, resulted in Donald, "simply throwing up his hands and telling me to yank the address altogether."[44]

S.O.T.O. and Thelema Publishing Company (1977–1979)

The disagreements with McMurtry pushed Motta in a new direction. He turned his sights to his representative in the United States, J. Daniel Gunther. In November, he informed Gunther that he was now formulating plans to assume his right to the library in court, and instructed him to arrange official court proceedings. By the autumn of 1977, Motta began devising a new organization called the Society Ordo Templi Orientis (S.O.T.O.), appointing Gunther as director. Along with the help of Richard Gernon, and the financial backing of Jelks Cabannis, Motta wrote initiation rituals for S.O.T.O., and set plans for publishing efforts in Nashville, Tennessee, with his newly-established Thelema Publishing Company. S.O.T.O., however, was a rather unsuccessful attempt by Motta to form a "new O.T.O." As former Motta student Martin P. Starr remembers it, "S.O.T.O. existed solely on paper as a collection agency to pay Motta's bills; I never attended a meeting

---

42 See Seckler (2010), 340–348.

43 McMurtry to Wasserman, September 24, 1976. SWC.

44 Wasserman (2012), 150.

nor witnessed a degree."[45] According to Starr, the reason for S.O.T.O.'s existence was to publish Crowley's writings, "drawing from the erroneous belief that Crowley's will vested his copyrights in the O.T.O., to which the S.O.T.O. claimed to be the successor organization."[46] Since McMurtry had laid claim to the O.T.O., Motta attempted to usurp this claim by creating S.O.T.O. Yet Starr remembers S.O.T.O. only after it fell apart. According to Gunther, the lodge did, in fact, function for a short period of time. He says, "The first initiation was in the U.S.A. [...] Richard Gernon was Lodge Master [...] Motta managed to effectively dismantle the lodge [...] After I left, the fledging Lodge of S.O.T.O. fell apart—or was driven apart by Motta's insanity."[47] Although S.O.T.O. may have functioned in some capacity as a Lodge for a period of time, it nevertheless was primarily Motta's attempt to further legitimize himself as the rightful heir to Crowley's writings.

Under Motta's supervision, the first publication of his Thelema Publishing Company went to press in 1979 as *The Equinox*, Volume V, Number 2.[48] It included a new O.T.O. Manifesto, as well as *LXV Commented*, which had been pulled from Samuel Weiser since the falling out in 1976. He began his *Equinox* in the tradition of Crowley's original 1909 publication with an A∴A∴ Præmonstrance. However, unlike Crowley, Motta's Præmonstrance resembled less of a verbal declaration of the A∴A∴, and more of Motta's own virulent attacks on publishing houses and those involved with the Thelemic movement, including Samuel Weiser, Inc., Regardie, Seckler, and McMurtry, among others.

Not long before Motta's *Equinox* went to print, Daniel Gunther was forced to break with his teacher. Despite Motta's later claims that Gunther was "demoted for planning to murder his hierarchic superior" and that he "withdrew voluntarily from the A∴A∴,"[49] letters reveal that Gunther's departure in 1978 happened quite differently. While he

---

[45] Starr (2003), x.

[46] Ibid.

[47] Personal email correspondence with J. Daniel Gunther, July 13, 2015.

[48] See Motta (1979).

[49] Crowley and Motta (1981), xi.

never planned to murder anyone, nor withdrew from anything, paranoia and violent ideation were overarching themes for all involved with Motta at this time. Gunther recounted many years later that "it wasn't what I had signed up for."[50] Gernon left shortly thereafter in 1980, eventually followed by Martin P. Starr in 1985. Motta continued publishing his writings with the help of his few disciples up to his death in 1987. It is clear from his later writings that whatever erudition he had previously possessed as a Thelemic teacher had been lost. His writings degenerated more and more into the ranting of an ever-increasing psychologically unstable, paranoid, and hostile personality. Reflecting on his time as a student of Motta, James Wasserman recalls, "Motta was a very difficult teacher, and we were a bunch of young and stupid, undisciplined kids who needed adult supervision. On the other hand, as time went on, Motta became more unbalanced."[51] Wasserman explained further regarding Starr's leaving, "Motta's abusive behavior was a symptom of his deepening psychological instability and alcoholism [...] Gurney, Daniel, and I had all previously reached the same conclusion about his treatment of each of us."[52]

The Thelemic Movement, Publication, and O.T.O. (1977–1979)

After the explosive episode with Motta, Grady McMurtry continued his work with the O.T.O., increasing membership across the United States and pursuing his own publishing efforts. Although he and Phyllis fell into disagreement, they continued to work together to further the movement. Grady continued to initiate people into the O.T.O. and started a newsletter that was offered to its members. The contents included various articles about Thelema, rituals, and poetry. These early newsletters formed the foundation for the newsletters and periodicals released by the O.T.O. today. Meanwhile, Phyllis Seckler continued her *In the Continuum* under the auspices of the College of Thelema.

---

[50] Interview J. Daniel Gunther by author, Murfreesboro, Tennessee, February 22, 2015.

[51] Wasserman (2012), 207.

[52] Ibid.

In 1978, McMurtry traveled to New York to increase O.T.O. membership on the East coast of the United States. James Wasserman, who had since left Samuel Weiser in 1977 to pursue his own entrepreneurial efforts, was given the I° by McMurtry in August. Wasserman describes this moment as being timely for that period of his spiritual life, stating that it "helped heal the wounds of my rift with Motta, and deepened my relationship with Grady."[53] He had refused to take the I° initiation back in 1976 when it was first offered to him because of problems that arose between himself, Seckler, and Motta. Two years had now passed since the upheaval, and Wasserman was now assured of his path. "I realized, in no uncertain terms, that the O.T.O. was my last option. It was the only fraternal organization on the planet that accepted *The Book of the Law*."[54] McMurtry continued his East Coast travels to Syracuse, New York, where he initiated William Breeze of 93 Publishing—and, later, Grady's successor—into the Minerval degree. In the following year of 1979, McMurtry worked with Breeze and Peter Macfarlane in publishing Thelemic material—establishing the first proper notices of O.T.O. copyright since Crowley's day.

In 1979, the O.T.O. under McMurtry began to grow exponentially, gaining legitimacy through renewed legal efforts. According to long-time member Bill Heidrick, "O.T.O. was incorporated under the laws of the State of California on March 26, 1979," converting from an association to a corporation.[55] The O.T.O. was now in full swing in McMurtry's home state of California, as well as New York. James Wasserman assumed leadership in what came to be TAHUTI Lodge in New York in 1979.[56] There was plenty to accomplish on the road ahead but, for the moment, the Thelemic movement, as established by Grady McMurtry's O.T.O. organization, was quickly gaining steam and becoming a recognizable entity in the world of contemporary occultism.

---

[53] Ibid., 138.

[54] Ibid.

[55] See Bill Heidrick, "Ordo Templi Orientis: A Brief Historical Review," http://hermetic.com/heidrick/oto_history.html (accessed June 6, 2015).

[56] See Wasserman (2012), 157–178.

༃༅

The Law Within the Law (1980–1985)

The story as it has been explored thus far can, in many ways, be considered only the beginning of a long battle towards legitimacy. The Thelemic movement suffered many growing pains in the first half of the 1980s as well. While the problem over copyrights on Crowley's works was raised by the late 1970s because of the disputes with Motta, it wasn't until the first half of the 1980s that the O.T.O. began to extend its legal precedent into the secular sphere. In 1982, the O.T.O. secured a United States Federal Tax exemption as a religious entity under IRS code 501(c)3. As important as this was for the longevity of the O.T.O., there were more pressing matters at the time. Marcelo Motta was taking action to secure copyrights to Crowley's literary legacy. In a later case, it was the O.T.O. that took the offensive towards Motta in court. The outcome of these hearings would help to solidify the legitimacy of O.T.O. as it existed under McMurtry.

Motta first took action against Samuel Weiser, Inc. for copyright infringement of Crowley's work in 1982. The trial itself began on March 1, 1984, in the United States District Court of Maine, the state in which Samuel Weiser, Inc. was then located.[57] In order to make his case for copyright infringement, Motta had to prove that he was the sole legitimate inheritor of Crowley's literary estate, meaning that he was the O.H.O. Motta relied heavily on the statement in his 1962 letter from Sascha Germer telling him that he was "the Follower." The court was less convinced by the vague statement, which held no parlance in any O.T.O. language concerning "O.H.O." Grady's credentials, however, proved to be more substantial.

The second court hearing placed Motta in the position of defendant. Court proceedings were held at the United States District Court of the Northern District of California, in San Francisco. In this trial, Motta was accused of violating the names and trademarks of the O.T.O. in his own Society Ordo Templi Orientis, and committing

---

[57] Motta v. Samuel Weiser, Inc., 633 F. Supp. 32 (D. Me. 1986).

libel against certain named individuals including McMurtry, Seckler, Wasserman, Heidrick, et al.[58] By this time, Motta was essentially alone in his testimony, while those who took the offensive with Grady were plentiful. Wasserman, who had for many years prior suffered the abusive treatment of Motta, recounts feeling sympathy for him: "I was deeply troubled by Motta's isolation. There was Grady, surrounded by a group of adoring friends—people who looked up to and after him and enjoyed his company. Marcelo, who had such a wealth of information to contribute, was all alone. It was thoroughly depressing."[59] Word that the Ninth Circuit Federal District Court in San Francisco ruled in favor of the O.T.O. and the libel claimants came on July 12, 1985. It was a resounding victory for the Ordo Templi Orientis—at least in court. That same day, Grady McMurtry died. Marcelo Motta died two years later on August 26, 1987. A new leader had to be chosen.

⁓🜃⁓

Election of a New Caliph (Autumn 1985)

It was Grady's wish that an election among the IX° take place to determine his successor after his death. The Grand Treasurer General at the time, Bill Heidrick (b. 1943), assumed interim control of O.T.O. Along with the Grand Secretary General at the time, James Graeb (1954–2012), an election for a new Caliph was scheduled on September 21, 1985. This event was later called "The Meeting of the Elector IX°s" and took place at a hotel in Concord, California. Among those present were eleven IX° members of the O.T.O. including, Bill Heidrick, James Graeb, Phyllis Seckler, Helen Parsons Smith, Lon DuQuette,

---

[58] The original California libel suit began with a phone conversation between William Breeze and Kenneth Anger, both of whom had been attacked in print by Motta. Breeze brought in McMurtry, who brought in Regardie, and the list continued to grow. When the case was moved from the State to the Federal court, however, the litigant roster had to be trimmed to conserve funds. Breeze quipped in an email that the speed with which the suit expanded was a testament to "Motta's ability to unite people." Email from William Breeze, June 11, 2018.

[59] Wasserman (2012), 208.

and James Wasserman. The initial nominees for the position were Bill Heidrick and James Eshelman (b. 1954), who was at that time a V° member. Eshelman's name had been put forward by Phyllis Seckler. However, Helen Parsons Smith nominated William Breeze just as the September 7 deadline for nominations approached. After eight hours of deliberating and questioning candidates, Breeze was unanimously elected "Caliph" and the "Acting Outer Head of the Order" at 11:11 p.m., taking the name "Hymenaeus Beta."[60]

James Wasserman recalls that the immediate period following the election was a difficult and uncertain time for the O.T.O. due to the changes in tide. "There was a suspicion of Bill as a young and unknown member thrust into a position of leadership after the death of the person who was a father figure to us all."[61] Yet, since Breeze was elected to his position in 1985, the O.T.O. has grown significantly in membership around the world, establishing an International Headquarters and a total of five Grand Lodges at the time of this writing. New policies have been instituted in the Order, aiming to strengthen cohesion within the organization as a whole, and to gain recognition as a legitimate religious body.

Despite the O.T.O. formalizing itself with regulations and policies, Breeze has insisted on allowing the Order to remain organic in its development, granting the leadership in local areas the freedom to experiment with tactics for growing the organization. After the election of the Caliph in 1985, a new volume of *The Equinox,* being Volume III, Number 10, was published in 1986. In the introduction, Breeze comments on the O.T.O.'s "experimental design," noting that the intention of the O.T.O. *is not* to formulate a "cult of Thelema," but rather a "culture" that is Thelemic:

---

[60] Caliph Election Minutes. Unpublished. It has been only recently, in October of 2014, that Breeze officially achieved the title of "Outer Head of the Order." He was unanimously elected by five X° members, the "Supreme and Holy Kings," representing O.T.O. in the United States, England, Italy, Croatia, and Australia. O.T.O. International Headquarters News, October 10, 2014, http://oto.org/news1014.html (accessed July 1, 2015).

[61] Wasserman (2012), 213.

While it has never been necessary to join the O.T.O. to be a Thelemite, it is central to the Order's "experimental design" that being a Thelemite never becomes a bar to membership. In this important sense, the O.T.O. is a crucible for the development of the social models necessary to a Thelemic culture, as opposed to Thelemic cult.[62]

In remarking on his efforts to grow the O.T.O. in Australia under Breeze's leadership, Grand Master General Shiva X° of Australia Grand Lodge remarks that Hymenaeus Beta has "taught us, his direct Representatives—by example more than by instruction—to take the high road in the Order's dealings, defense, aims and purposes."[63] According to Shiva, Hymenaeus Beta's "publishing blitz" of the 1990s ushered in the Order's renaissance, not only with sound and meticulous editorial work of Crowley's literature, but also in the U.S. O.T.O. newsletter, *The Magical Link*, which "provided the much needed news and archives, especially in the days before email and the web [...] The *Link* was our education!" Indeed, under Breeze, the publishing efforts have undergone a process of standardization, and many previously unpublished works have been made available, newly typeset in authorized format with exhaustive editorial work, usually by Breeze himself, along with the assistance of other O.T.O. and A∴A∴ members.

Yet, the resurgence of the O.T.O. was not in publication and academic matters alone. Shiva notes that Hymenaeus Beta (also known as H.B.) advocated for an open and creative spirit that allows for a rich and diverse O.T.O. culture, which has developed around the world:

I was soon aware of O.T.O. microtones coming out of New Zealand, Japan, Canada, Yugoslavia, Norway, the UK, and Germany; and later on in the adventure, Italy, Serbia, Croatia, Slovenia, South Africa, Sweden, Macedonia, and Poland; and, later still, Russia, Brazil and the South Americas. There are many others.

---

[62] Hymenaeus Beta (1986, 1990), 10.

[63] Shiva X°, in O.T.O. (2015), 13.

Each tuned in turn and tone by H.B. and his Representatives, with improvisation and experiment, or if you prefer, Peace, Tolerance and Truth.[64]

Indeed, "Peace, Tolerance and Truth" has been the tripartite welcoming of O.T.O. members into the fold of Thelema's core principles of fraternity and cooperation. And it is done, Shiva says, with fervent creativity and passion: "If there's one thing that H.B. not so much taught us but *let us*, it was to be artist—to get intimate and be intimate with the highest reality."[65]

Legitimacy for the O.T.O. within the legal sphere has extended beyond the United States. Since the late 1980s and into the 1990s, concerns were raised in the United Kingdom over the unauthorized reproduction of sensitive materials related to the O.T.O. A former member was distributing such papers through a local bookshop. Other issues had arisen regarding the unauthorized use of the name O.T.O. and its trademarks by small publishers in England. While these activities might be considered equivalent to "putting out small fires," in 2002 the High Court of the United Kingdom ruled in favor of copyright for the O.T.O. in a case against John Symonds and Mandrake Press.[66] The O.T.O. has continued to establish itself and its legal rights across Europe and beyond.

⛧

The journey thus far has taken us to the modern manifestation of the O.T.O. What then became of the A∴A∴? The administration of the A∴A∴ was essentially dismantled once the court battles with Motta began, and the Order has taken time to legitimize itself, particularly within the O.T.O. community. When Gunther broke with Motta,

---

[64] Ibid., 17–18.

[65] Ibid., 20.

[66] Ordo Templi Orientis v. John Symonds, Mandrake Press, Ltd., HC 99 04477 (May 2, 2002).

contact with students under him who were associated with the O.T.O. was also severed (i.e., Breeze and Wasserman), and the A∴A∴ went silent for many years. Amidst this breakdown, a power vacuum emerged creating the popular discourse of "A∴A∴ lineages" that many Thelemites know today. The phenomenon of "A∴A∴ lineages" will be discussed in chapter eleven: however, the remainder of this chapter will present the reformulation of the A∴A∴ as it functions alongside the O.T.O. today.

The O.T.O. was in need of rebuilding. H.B. spent the years immediately following his election with his sole attention given to the O.T.O. The first indicators of the appearance of renewed A∴A∴ activity occurred in the summer of 1992. In a letter dated August 16, on a letterhead from the Teitan Press, Inc., one Frater A.T. wrote to Fratres K.N. and N.Tz. addressing points from a meeting that had occurred shortly prior. "Let me reiterate my entire satisfaction with our recent meeting. I thought it was an important first step in our generation toward the expansion of the Work of the Outer College along the lines set out by the founding Adepti."[67] Frater A.T. continued by setting out the immediate work of the newly-formed triad of officers, including the building of a Temple of Initiation, establishing a source for robe procurement, manufacturing Seals of the founding Adepti, republishing "Liber Collegii Sancti," and republishing the three volumes of "ΘΕΛΗΜΑ." The administrative triad and the presence of the A∴A∴ were shortly thereafter publicly announced with the publication of *Magick: Liber ABA, Book Four* in 1994, which bore the traditional A∴A∴ Imprimatur, with Frater V. as Præmonstrator, Frater V.V. as Imperator, and Frater S.U.A. as Cancellarius. The alliance between the A∴A∴ and the O.T.O. was officially announced in 1996 with the publication of *The Equinox*, Volume IV, Number 1, known as *The Commentaries on the Holy Books and Other Papers.* "The O.T.O. has a long history of close alliance with the A∴A∴, having jointly published *The Equinox* virtually since its inception."[68]

---

[67] A.T. letter to Fratres K.N. and N.Tz., August 16, 1992. Private Collection.

[68] "Præmonstrance," in Crowley (1996b), ix.

J. Daniel Gunther has been involved exclusively with the A∴A∴ curriculum, and has worked diligently to further develop Thelemic doctrine through his writings and lectures.[69] Gunther and Breeze's work in the A∴A∴ has been met with criticism from schismatic groups (both inside and outside the O.T.O.). Yet, their unmistakable high standards in publication include exhaustive editorial notes, critical apparatus, and comprehensive theological and doctrinal analyses of Thelema.[70] Gunther expresses an optimistic vision for the future of the movement, noting that "[Thelema] is no longer a local thing, unless 'local' is defined as 'global.'"[71] Gunther remarks that in his travels, "I get to meet people who have incredible talents in Sanskrit, Chinese, Japanese, psychiatry, history, and so on. All these people being Thelemites, they're able to apply those talents and those skills, and they're interested in taking the next step forward, and to see what we can add to the corpus of knowledge that we already have." When asked if he thought his current work was the "key to that transmission," Gunther humbly replied, "the answer to that question is one that history is going to write. I am just trying to do what I can with what I have. That's all we can do."[72]

⊰ਃ⊱

With the O.T.O. publication of *The Equinox* Volume III, Number 10, first privately by the O.T.O. in 1986, and again by Weiser in 1990, under Hymenaeus Beta, and the subsequent A∴A∴ issuances of *The Equinox*, Volume IV, Numbers 1 and 2,[73] the Thelemic movement has enjoyed steady growth. With the appointment of Grand Master

---

[69] See J. Daniel Gunther's website (accessed April 25, 2018).

[70] See, for example, Crowley (1996b) and editorial notes by Hymenaeus Beta and the comprehensive discussions on Thelema offered in Gunther (2009) and (2014).

[71] J. Daniel Gunther, "The Revival of Thelema," Episode 4, White Rabbit Podcast.

[72] Interview with J. Daniel Gunther by Frater Puck [ps. of Peter Seals], released June 9, 2015 on Thelema Now! Podcast (accessed June 14, 2015).

[73] See the aforementioned Crowley (1996b) and Crowley (1998a).

General Sabazius X° in the United States Grand Lodge in 1995, the O.T.O. in the U.S. has witnessed a further development of its Ecclesiastical branch, the Ecclesia Gnostica Catholica. Grand Lodges have also been established in the United Kingdom (2005), Australia (2006), Italy (2014), and Croatia (2014). The O.T.O. has more recently sought entrance into the academic sphere with the formation of Academia Ordo Templi Orientis, or A.O.T.O. It holds frequent academic-style conferences, with its chairs held by O.T.O. members who are established researchers in the field of religious studies and Western esotericism.

Before drawing Part II to its conclusion, it is important to bring the reader up to speed on more contemporary manifestations of the Thelemic movement. We will next review the modern phenomenon known as "A∴A∴ lineages." Considered a controversial subject in some circles, it has been a matter of some debate now for at least three decades.

CHAPTER ELEVEN

Hydra Lernaia: "Lineages" of A∴A∴

THE MODERN CONTROVERSY over A∴A∴ "lineages" is tied to the uncertainty created by Germer's failure to either designate a successor or propose a means by which others could choose their leader after his death. The conflict that resulted was played out three decades ago in venues as high as the United States Supreme Court, which passed on hearing Motta's challenge to the Ninth Circuit ruling of 1985. Thus, while Grady McMurtry of O.T.O. and Marcelo Motta of A∴A∴ once lit up the heavens with their claims and counterclaims, we are fortunate today to have—at least, within the bonds of the O.T.O.—benefitted from a proper solution to their quandary.

We will here explore a short history of A∴A∴ "lineages" and show how that notion permeated the modern thinking of the Thelemic movement. Before doing so, however, let us first take a brief detour to discuss how discursive methods of narrative construction are often used by religious groups as ways to legitimize themselves. Let us then distinguish between history and what is known as "mnemohistory," or history as it exists in memory.

※

Historical Narrative and Religion

History vs. Mnemohistory

It is common practice throughout the history of religion for followers to construct historical narratives. This practice is intended to present adherents with more meaning and purpose in their religious identity, whatever that may be, and often at the expense of historical accuracy. For example, Jan Assmann argues that, although there is little to no historical evidence of an Exodus led by Moses occurring the way it has been described in the Torah, the story was successful in constructing a narrative for the Semitic culture. He claims, "All cultural distinctions need to be remembered in order to render permanent the space which they construct. Usually, this function of remembering the fundamental distinctions assumes the form of a 'Grand Narrative,' a master story that underlies and informs innumerable concrete tellings and retellings of the past." Assmann calls this constructed historical narrative, "Mnemohistory." Even if the biblical account of the Exodus is not accurate, the story nevertheless provided a history for the people and helped form their religious identity:

> Unlike history proper, mnemohistory is concerned not with the past as such, but only with the past as it is remembered. It surveys the story-lines of tradition, the webs of intertextuality, the diachronic continuities and discontinuities of reading the past. Mnemohistory is not the opposite of history, but rather is one of its branches or subdisciplines, such as intellectual history, social history, the history of mentalities, or the history of ideas. But it has an approach of its own in that it deliberately leaves aside the synchronic aspects of what it is investigating [...] Mnemohistory is reception theory applied to history. But "reception" is not to be understood here merely in the narrow sense of transmitting and receiving. The past is not simply "received" by the present. The present is "haunted" by the past and the past is modeled, invented, reinvented, and reconstructed by the present.[1]

Yet, the emergence of a mnemohistory is simply a by-product of the attempts at legitimization. As Olav Hammer has pointed out, religion in the modern era, especially new religious movements, have employed a number of methods in an effort to legitimize themselves. The appeal to science, for example, has been a significant part of religious discourse, especially in esotericism, since the late modern period. Hammer argues that this isn't the practice of real science; rather, it is a belief

---

[1] Assmann (1997), 8–9.

he calls "scientism."[2] This method of legitimization essentially negoti-
ates spiritual ideas with scientific terminology. This was evident in the
nineteenth century with the Society for Psychical Research, an organization that believed it could use scientific practices to prove para-
psychological phenomena.[3] We even find this method being employed
in the works of Crowley, who was at pains to make occultism scientific.[4] More recently, in the post-1960s New Age milieu, a "spiritualized
science" has emerged in popular culture. Examples of this are found
in Fritjof Capra's *The Tao of Physics*, Amit and Maggie Goswami's *Science and Spirituality*, and the *What the Bleep Do We Know!?* films by
proponents of Ramtha's School of Enlightenment.[5] While these latter
examples of "legitimizing with science" are a far cry from the occultism
of Crowley, they are mentioned to show how widespread this tactic is
implemented in religious discourse today.

More important for the present discussion is the discursive method
that Hammer identifies as the appeal to tradition. In this method, a

---

[2] Hammer defines scientism: "Scientism is the active positioning of one's own claims
in relation to the manifestations of any academic scientific discipline, including, but
not limited to, the use of technical devices, scientific terminology, mathematical cal-
culations, theories, references, and stylistic features—without, however, the use of
methods generally approved within the scientific community, and without subsequent social acceptance of these manifestations by the mainstream of the scientific
community through e.g. peer reviewed publication in academic journals." Hammer
(2004), 206.

[3] For a history on psychical research, see Alan Gauld (1968) *The Founders of Psychical
Research*, (London: Routledge).

[4] In distinction to the "psychologization" of magick in Israel Regardie, Crowley
insisted upon a naturalization of magical practice, putting into place testable methods of the student's success. A detailed discussion of this can be found in Egil Asprem
(2008).

[5] See Fritjof Capra (1975) *The Tao of Physics: An Exploration of the Parallels Between
Modern Physics and Eastern Mysticism* (London: Fontana/Collins), and Amit Gos-
wami and Maggie Goswami (1998) *Science and Spirituality: A Quantum Integration*
(Delhi: Project of History of Indian Science, Philosophy and Culture). The Ramtha
School was founded in 1988 by J. Z. Knight, claiming to channel communications
from a 35,000-year old inner-plane intelligence of that name.

movement constructs a cohesive narrative to provide a plausible historiography for legitimization purposes. Hammer notes there are many "examples where emic historiography contrasts sharply with etic history."[6] Hammer further states that these historical narratives are often more or less an attempt at myth-making—fragmentary elements that are put together to give a sense of an unbroken line of succession. Indeed, the source of transmission of esoteric wisdom becomes the leading factor for recognition as a source of authority. Andreas Kilcher similarly remarks:

> "The questions of heritage and tradition, of origin and genealogy are crucial to the foundation of any esoteric knowledge. It defines, and moreover legitimates itself, through its origins, its ancestry, and its means of esoteric transmission. In so doing, esotericism seeks to invent its own tradition, to map its master narratives, to construct its myths of origin and its myths of transmission."[7]

One example of narrative construction lies in the story of the "cipher manuscripts" that prompted the formation of the Hermetic Order of the Golden Dawn, as mentioned in chapter three. One of the founders of the Golden Dawn, W. Wynn Westcott, came into possession of curious manuscripts written in cipher. This cipher proved to be written from right to left in a cryptic alphabet originally published in the 1561 Paris edition of *Polygraphia,* a book written by Johannes Trithemius. The cipher manuscripts gave an outline for the five outer grades of a magical order, along with associated mystical diagrams, sketches of magical weapons, and knowledge lectures. Among the pages of the cipher manuscripts Westcott discovered a paper upon which was written the name and address of a Fräulein Sprengel, proclaimed to be a prominent Rosicrucian Adept residing in Germany. He wrote to her

---

6 Hammer (2004), 91. "Emic" refers to the "insider's" point-of-view, whereas "etic" is an observer on the outside. Academia refers to its methods of critical evaluative research as etic, and the participants of the movement or movements they study as having emic interpretations of their group.

7 Kilcher (2010), ix–x.

and she authorized him to found an English branch of *Die Goldene Dämmerung*, or The Golden Dawn. While this story has been challenged by various historians, it created one of the most successful and well-known esoteric societies in history.

From an objective historical standpoint, even Crowley constructed a narrative of transmission. In "Liber LXI vel Causæ," he describes how the link to the Secret Chiefs was lost with the schism that occurred in the Golden Dawn, only to be re-established through himself and George Cecil Jones:

> The ordeals were turned into contempt, it being impossible for any one to fail therein. Unsuitable candidates were admitted for no better reason than that of their worldly prosperity.
>
> In short, the Order failed to initiate.
>
> Scandal arose and with it schism.
>
> [...]
>
> Thereupon these two adepts conferred together, saying: May it not be written that the tribulations shall be shortened? Wherefore they resolved to establish a new Order which should be free from the errors and deceits of the former one:
>
> [...]
>
> In the fullness of time, even as a blossoming tree that beareth fruit in its season, all these pains were ended, and these adepts and their companions obtained the reward which they had sought— they were to be admitted to the Eternal and Invisible Order that hath no name among men.[8]

It is not the place here to inquire into the *legitimacy* of "transmission." Crowley's ingenium and insight with what he left the world speaks for itself. The reader of his work must judge whether or not a link to the Secret Chiefs was successfully established. I simply bring these narratives into the discussion to make the reader aware of the distinction between objective history and constructed historical narratives. As we will soon see, stories of "A∴A∴ lineages" are mnemohistorical. That

---

[8] See Crowley (1983), xlv.

is, they are "history as it is remembered," or constructed narratives that aim for legitimacy within a circle of adherents.

⌘

A∴A∴ "Lineages": A Short History

The concept of "lineage" in terms of religion may very well be traceable to the beginning of religiosity itself. One would be hard-pressed to find a single religious tradition which has not splintered off into another group or groups. The centuries-old conflict between Sunni and Shi'ite Muslims can be traced back to a disagreement in lineal descent from the prophet Muhammad. Christianity split into the Catholic Church of Rome and the Eastern Orthodox of Constantinople. Even later, the Reformation generated the Protestant movement, which in turn has witnessed a wide variety of denominations and sects. New religious movements in particular are prone to fractioning and schism from their original source:

> [New religious movements] form a number of distinctive religious traditions of their own [...] [NRMs] too are subject to schisms. That is, the "church-sect" process operates within any religious tradition, not just in dominant traditions. Thus, a large number of American [NRMs] form by fission. However, having broken off from the "parent" body, they also remain [NRMs] if they remain within a novel tradition. Moreover, [NRMs] tend to form lineages even when they did not originate via schism. Many [NRM] founders engage in wholesale borrowing from other [NRMs]. Indeed, often a[n] [NRM] founder serves an apprenticeship in an established [NRM] group before leaving to found a new group with a slightly modified version of the established [NRM]'s teachings and ceremonies. The result of such modes of [NRM] formation is that [NRMs] form quite distinctive families, or similarity clusters.[9]

---

[9] Stark, Bainbridge, and Doyle (1979), 351–352. "New Religious Movement" ("NRM") is a term in sociological research that has replaced the dated and often pejo-

The concept of "A∴A∴ lineages" within the Thelemic community is similarly a dispute over succession, yet another indication that Thelema is better understood within the context of "religion" and not simply as a "philosophy" or "a way of life." Yet the subject of "A∴A∴ lineages" is also a recent development in the Thelemic movement. Contrary to popular belief, the phenomenon of lineage within the A∴A∴ dates no further back than the 1980s.

What is important to note at the start of this discussion is that all the discourse relating to succession in the Thelemic movement prior to 1975 was exclusively regarding the O.T.O. Hermann Metzger in Switzerland, Kenneth Grant in the United Kingdom, and Grady McMurtry in the United States were claiming successsorship in the O.T.O. Any mention of the A∴A∴ is suspiciously absent. In fact, the only mention of the A∴A∴ following Germer's death seems to lie with Marcelo Motta, who, as we have seen, was always more A∴A∴–centric in his approach to Thelema. This peculiarity should give us pause as we move forward.

Before exploring the various lineage claimants, it is important to address why this has become an important factor within the Thelemic community, particularly the O.T.O. The significance of the problem is most likely because the O.T.O. currently acknowledges only one governing triad; that is, the O.T.O. works alongside a singular administration of the A∴A∴. This has been the case since the re-emergence of the A∴A∴ in the early 1990s, and the subsequent announcement of its alliance with the O.T.O. in *The Equinox*, Volume IV, Number 1. Additionally, this publication seems to have anticipated the problematic nature of "lineages":

> Since its establishment, the many, whose name is legion, have sought to profit by the reputation of the A∴A∴, and some have been deceived thereby. How can one tell the false from the True?

---

rative phraseology of "cult" used by social theorists in the 1970s. Although "cult" is often used in popular culture with a negative connotation, it was simply used in sociological literature as a term for a new and small religious movement. "Cult" has therefore been replaced with "NRM" by this author in the quoted extract above.

The principles of the Order of A∴A∴ are clear and unequivocal; those who act in a manner contrary to them are automatically excluded from its fold [...] The Order is One, unbroken in its Chain of succession from V.V.V.V.V. through its senior living Adepti.[10]

More recently, the reason for an alliance with a singular A∴A∴ was succinctly explained by USGL Grand Master Sabazius X°:

Within A∴A∴ all services are rendered free of charge, and no social activities are held. A∴A∴ is not incorporated, holds no copyrights or trademarks, and charges no dues or fees. It has no monetary income, and it operates no dues-collecting front groups. It is largely dependent on O.T.O. for assistance with practical matters that lie outside its primary mission, which is purely spiritual in nature. For example, it is O.T.O., not A∴A∴, which holds the Crowley copyrights, O.T.O. and A∴A∴ jointly issue the journal The Equinox, and A∴A∴ initiation events and lectures are often hosted by local O.T.O. bodies.[11]

Sabazius concluded his remarks by stating that, "it is also not the case that O.T.O. can have a 'close alliance' and working relationship with a multiplicity of A∴A∴ administrations. For its purposes, O.T.O. recognizes a single administration of A∴A∴." Along with Sabazius' explanation, there are other factors to consider, which will be further examined in Part III. However, let us return to the reason this topic has remained controversial. It comes down to the factors discussed in chapter six. The popular opinion is that affiliation with the A∴A∴ is personal and private, and concerns one's spirituality. The implication of a singular A∴A∴ suggests that other lineages or claimants aren't legitimate. Hence, we return to the centuries-old rivalry that characterizes religion in every era. Some particularities of humanity never

---

[10] "Præmonstrance," in Crowley (1996b), x.

[11] Grand Master General Sabazius X°, July 17, 2015. http://invisiblebasilica. blogspot.nl/2015/07/oto-and-aa.html (accessed November 20, 2016).

change. To assert the existence of A∴A∴ lineages admits the reality of religious schism. Thus, to discuss A∴A∴ lineages, we must do so by placing them within the context of religious "faction," "schism," or simply "sectarianism."

With regard to the breadth of coverage related to this subject, the reader might be disappointed that it is beyond the scope of this book to analyze each of these "lineages" at length. According to one website, there are at least twelve groups operating under the pretense of the A∴A∴, but this number could easily be double or triple. To discuss each of these groups in depth would take a book of its own. The groups herein reviewed are the most salient of A∴A∴ "claimant groups."

❀

Besides the A∴A∴ as reformulated under Gunther and Breeze, there have been a number of branches headed by former students of Motta, mostly those who held membership in the aforementioned S.O.T.O. These include David Bersson, Ray Eales, and William Barden, among other groups in Motta's home country of Brazil. While the activities of these groups lie outside of the modern O.T.O. almost entirely, they warrant mention as they share history with Motta and the S.O.T.O. David Bersson took over S.O.T.O. after Motta's death in 1987, and has operated a small group out of Pittsburgh, Pennsylvania, for many years. Ray Eales, also a former member of S.O.T.O., later formed his "Holy Order of Ra-Hoor-Khuit" (H.O.O.R.) in Tampa, Florida. William Barden's group has operated out of Australia.

The variations of descended A∴A∴ lineages have become exhaustive. One group derives their lineage through the aforementioned Solar Lodge, tracing its line from Jane Wolfe, through Ray Burlingame and Jean Brayton. Another claims a "composite" pedigree through Marcelo Motta, Grady McMurtry, and C.F. Russell. Another that was headed by British revisionist historian Gerald Suster has claimed connection through Israel Regardie. It is unknown to the author to what extent all of the above mentioned groups are active, as their respective websites often change domain names, are not in service, or there is simply no trace of them besides a vague mention on internet forums. While it is ultimately unknown for certain the degree to which they operate, it is probable that these groups, if active, are relatively small in number. A thorough study of these A∴A∴ lineages, if one were to take the time, would require a great deal of resourcefulness. The researcher would have to be: (1) successful in making contact with these groups; and (2) successful in convincing them to cooperate with such a project.

The "Soror Estai Lineage" (Part One): Phyllis Seckler

The most significant A∴A∴ claimant group that requires attention and has been operating within the O.T.O. since the 1990s, and perhaps the 1980s, was developed by Phyllis Seckler—at least in part. Soror Estai was Jane Wolfe's magical motto. Its successful mnemohistory involving Phyllis Seckler was meticulously crafted by former O.T.O. member James Eshelman. In fact, a closer look at the history of the Estai/Seckler A∴A∴ lineage will exemplify how a carefully constructed narrative can take the place of actual history in a religious tradition. Later, it will be shown how this has played out in the recent development of the O.T.O. community.

As we have learned, Phyllis Seckler was a member of Agape Lodge, taking the O.T.O. degree of Minerval in 1939. She was later received as a Probationer by Crowley's student Jane Wolfe sometime in the early 1940s. Phyllis' formal advancement in the A∴A∴ past the grade of Probationer, however, is rather elusive, and no documentation seems to exist. Having been responsible for singularly raising three children and putting herself through college, she admitted to not having worked through the system until sometime in 1975:

> I was absolutely bewildered by the material set before me which had to do with Thelema. This was so new to my soul that it took about 30 years of the Probationary period of the A∴A∴ to get some sort of idea about what was involved in Thelema.[12]

---

[12] See Seckler (1996), *In the Continuum*, Vol. V, no. 10, 1.

Seckler continues that from the year 1975, "I had a great deal of time to fill in the blanks and so took up the practices and studies [...]"[13] Despite her "30 years of the Probationary period," spanning the years from 1940 to 1975 (thirty-plus years, then), the reader should recall that Seckler's July 1952 correspondence with Karl Germer indicated that she had an experience of the Holy Guardian Angel. We will return to this shortly, but, for the present, the reader is reminded that it was the 1952 exchange of letters that would play a significant role in the Eshelman narrative.[14]

As we saw in chapter ten, one of the contenders for the position of acting Outer Head of the Order in 1985 was James A. Eshelman, whom Seckler had nominated for Caliph. Phyllis met Eshelman in 1975, recalling:

> I needed a person with similar goals and interests to monitor my progress and confirm if I had done the work as thoroughly as possible [...] Jim [Eshelman] immediately found an interest in what I was doing and opted to travel to my home in Dublin in Northern California for instructions and conferences. He was visiting only for about the third time when I knew he was to be my successor. In the many years that followed we helped each other to do the mandated A∴A∴ work and, here was the person to monitor what I was working on and to give me encouragement and also advice. I did the same for him, of course [...] The College of Thelema grew and Jim put the A∴A∴ on a clear footing as to instructions and work.[15]

Eshelman left the O.T.O. half a decade after the Election, having served for a time as Deputy National Grand Master General, as appointed by H.B. He would continue his Thelemic work with Seckler. It seems the two began assisting one another through the A∴A∴ curriculum around 1979 by way of self-initiation, and they would later begin

---

[13] Ibid., 4.

[14] See a memorandum written June 26, 2000, published in Seckler (2012), 276–277.

[15] Seckler (1996), V:10, 4.

taking students of their own in the early 1980s. This seems consistent with *In the Continuum* at the time, as Seckler released a document entitled "Official A∴A∴ Exam for Probationers," signed as "Soror Meral, Neophyte of the A∴A∴."[16]

Together, Seckler and Eshelman advertised the College of Thelema as a training ground for entrance into the A∴A∴ in the biannual *In the Continuum*. "The College asks that students attend both Seminars and private sessions of teachings. Should the student prove competent, and should he desire it, he or she may ask to join the A∴A∴."[17] Fees were asked of students for course instruction, to pay for materials, and to prepare them for the A∴A∴ work ahead of them. The requirement of fees made it particularly problematic with regard to the tradition of A∴A∴, as Crowley made it explicitly clear early on that no fees were to ever be charged for spiritual instruction.[18] This dilemma was cleverly circumnavigated, however, by claiming that it was the College of Thelema, and not the A∴A∴, asking for the fees. The College was merely preparing people for its "Student of the Mysteries" grade.[19]

The journal *In the Continuum* had been in print since 1973. While later issues published in the 1980s began recounting Phyllis' involvement with the A∴A∴, the full lineage narrative was outlined in an article entitled "The Legacy of Jane Wolfe," written by James Eshelman and published in the final issue of *In the Continuum* in September of 1996. The article told the story of Jane Wolfe, an A∴A∴ student of Crowley's during the Beast's Cefalù period from 1920–1923. Eshelman recounted Phyllis Seckler being received as a Probationer under Wolfe in 1940. According to Eshelman, Wolfe was allegedly reluctant to take on Phyllis as a student because she was never notified by Crowley that she had advanced beyond Probationer and was eligible

---

[16] Seckler (1980), "Official A∴A∴ Exam for Probationers," in *In the Continuum*, Vol. II, No. 9.

[17] Seckler (1982), III:2, 2.

[18] See "Editorial," in Crowley (1972a), originally published 1909. Also see "One Star in Sight."

[19] The instructors in the College were, of course, the same people bringing students into their A∴A∴ group.

to take students. Crowley is said to have responded by telling Jane that she had been a Neophyte since "God knows how many years ago," and giving Wolfe permission to take Seckler as a Probationer.

The article continues by stating that Seckler's A∴A∴ work was later supervised by Karl Germer, quoting their correspondence in 1952 as evidence of her attainment to the grade of Adeptus Minor. While she busied herself with life for many years after, Eshelman states that when Seckler eventually returned to the Work she established the College of Thelema "as a teaching vehicle, to prepare individuals, so far as they are able, to undertake the deeper work of the A∴A∴."[20] Eshelman concludes the article by reinforcing to the reader that the legacy of Jane Wolfe is that of an "unbroken chain" of transmission of the A∴A∴, and he states, "Some have fallen away. Some have persevered. And, of those, some have attained. The legacy continues, passed from generation to generation in an uninterrupted chain."[21]

By 1987, Seckler and Eshelman had taken on a number of students, and with Eshelman's effort they established another new teaching order involving initiatory rituals in the style of both the A∴A∴ and the Golden Dawn, called the "Temple of Thelema."[22] Between the College of Thelema, the newly formed Temple of Thelema, and the Jane Wolfe lineage of the A∴A∴, Eshelman effectively manufactured his own Thelemic movement. He only needed a link back to Crowley, and essentially used Seckler as a means to legitimize his narrative.

Now, let us take a closer look at some of the claims within this story. The first point that should be raised is the timing of the article itself. "The Legacy of Jane Wolfe" was published in the very last issue of *In the Continuum* (September 1996). Eshelman's self-published *The Black Pearl* began to run shortly thereafter. Why this is important is because this essay publicly announced the full lineage narrative, promoting it beyond his own circle of acolytes at the time. Being the final issue of Seckler's journal and the beginning of Eshelman's, the article also marked a transference of power from Seckler to Eshelman.

---

[20] Seckler (1996), V:10, 9.

[21] Ibid., 9.

[22] Seckler (1989), IV:5, 2.

While Seckler would remain the figurehead of the Jane Wolfe lineage, Eshelman gained full control over its message.

Secondly, the actual timeline of events, according to the story, is incorrect—an indicator to the acute historian that there is some level of intentional myth-making in process. For example, Eshelman claimed that Jane Wolfe was initially unsure whether she was eligible to take Phyllis as a Probationer, and so asked for Crowley's permission first. Crowley wrote Jane back the following: "Lord! You were passed to Neophyte God knows how many years ago. In any case Do Things!" According to Eshelman, Jane took this as permission to receive Seckler as a Probationer in 1940. Only, the letter that is referred to by Eshelman and Seckler in their writings was not written in 1940. The original letter exists in the O.T.O. archives and is dated March 25, 1934, placing Crowley's permit to Wolfe to receive students three years *before* Phyllis even met Jane. The only letter in which Wolfe refers to Phyllis by name in such a context is dated September 1943, to which Wolfe says that Phyllis "is my Probationer, has been for 1½ years," placing Seckler's reception as Probationer around spring 1942.

Another problem exposed in the correspondence concerns Seckler's "5°=6° attainment," supposedly recognized by Germer in 1952. In this regard, it is less likely that Germer *conferred* the grade of Adeptus Minor to Seckler, and more likely that he genuinely wanted to believe she was in contact with the Holy Guardian Angel. Germer wrote to Jane Wolfe on June 24, 1952, expressing that he was "sure" that Phyllis had "gone through 5°=6° some time ago."[23] Yet, it should be noted that the experience of the Knowledge and Conversation of the Holy Guardian Angel is not the same as holding the grade of Adeptus Minor (5°=6°).[24] Stating that Seckler has "gone through 5°=6°" or that she had "risen to or above Tiphareth" is not the same as officially recognizing the Grade. Germer often used "5°=6°" or "8°=3°" as a short-hand to refer to the experiences attributed to Tiphareth or

---

[23] Karl Germer to Jane Wolfe, June 24, 1952. Shoemaker, Ferrell, and Voss (eds.) (2016), 272.

[24] Recall Motta's criticism, mentioned earlier, that she had confused the Vison of the Angel with the Knowledge and Conversation.

Binah, respectively.[25] Furthermore, it is clear from a careful reading of the correspondence that Phyllis didn't actually believe the experience was authentic at the time, and it was only after Germer encouraged her that she began to accept it.

Finally, when one considers Volume II, Number 9, of *In the Continuum* (September 1980), we find a document entitled "Official A∴A∴ Exam for Probationers," in which Seckler signs off as "Soror Meral, Neophyte of A∴A∴," and ends that the materials are available "due to the invaluable work of Frater Yod [Eshelman]."[26] Gathering from this source and Seckler's previously-mentioned account of meeting Eshelman, I have surmised that Eshelman impressed Seckler upon their initial meeting, and persuaded her to admit him as a Probationer, so that she could now advance beyond her "30 years of the Probationary period" to Neophyte. As time passed, Eshelman self-initiated through the grades and took control of the whole lineage.

Seckler broke with Eshelman by the year 2000. Eshelman continued his A∴A∴ group, while Seckler turned her attention to another promising new student, David Shoemaker. She is recorded to have said in an interview, "When I die, David will probably be in charge of the C.O.T. [College of Thelema] and the A∴A∴ up here in this area."[27] Shoemaker indeed succeeded Phyllis in her A∴A∴ group in 2004. Given his seasoned involvement and recognition within O.T.O., he has found the latter to be an effective vehicle for the promotion of his A∴A∴ efforts.

The "Soror Estai Lineage" (Part Two): Grady McMurtry

Although Seckler admitted to only being a Probationer and not having worked with the curriculum of the A∴A∴ until after 1975, there is

---

[25] In other words, the grades were used as shorthand in Germer's letters to refer to the experiences of "Knowledge and Conversation" and attaining to Master of the Temple.

[26] Seckler (1980), "Official A∴A∴ Exam for Probationers," II:9, 4.

[27] Heather Des Roche interview with Phyllis Seckler, 2000, printed and published in Seckler (2010), 373.

some indication that she admitted Grady McMurtry as a Probationer in 1969. She claimed in an interview that, "He [Grady] took the [Probationer Grade of] A∴A∴ from me, when I didn't know him too well." However, after their relationship collapsed, she recalled:

> He never did the work of the Probationer. Never [...] I threw him out of the A∴A∴.. He has no A∴A∴ background. None. However, he went around pretending that he did have, and telling people he was such-and-such a Grade. And then, of course, [...] Oh God, he made trouble for other people [...] Grady had no right to say he was A∴A∴ after I threw him out. He had no right to initiate anybody because he had never done the Probationer work.[28]

As mentioned in chapter ten, despite being given the title of Caliph and charged with emergency orders to re-establish the O.T.O., Grady's official association with the A∴A∴ remains obscure. Judging from existing records it does not appear that he signed the Oath and Task during Crowley's lifetime. In later personal correspondence with Regardie, Motta, and Wasserman, he was always elusive about his involvement. He once insisted to Israel Regardie that, "one thing we won't discuss is anyone's grade in A∴A∴, since that is a matter for discussion only between pupil and superior."[29] Similarly, when writing to Motta in 1976, as discussed earlier, he essentially repeated his statement to Regardie, "choosing to obey A.C.'s injunction [...] that 'Theoretically, a member knows only the superior who introduced him, and any person whom he himself has introduced'."[30] While McMurtry remained ambiguous about his personal association with the A∴A∴, he would remark on it in the spring 1979 *O.T.O. Newsletter*:

> First of all, just who is a member of A∴A∴? In as much as this is an Inner Order, there can be only one person who can answer such a question in a particular case the claimant herself. When some-

---

28 Ibid, 367.

29 McMurtry to Regardie, April 30, 1970. MRSC.

30 McMurtry to Motta, July 21, 1976. SWC.

one tells me that he or she [...] is a member of A∴A∴., I believe it. I also often wonder what business it is of mine. A∴A∴. is not a school of outer initiation, like O.T.O. in some of its aspects. A∴A∴. is a body of individuals who have attained particular grades of self-initiation in accordance with particular standards [...] Some persons have direct lineage from Crowley as proctors for A∴A∴. work [...] Anyone of sufficient judgment and intelligence can apply themselves diligently to the Great Work along this course. An Inner Order should be free from politics. If an aspirant to A∴A∴. would enter one of the several surviving direct lines of instruction, they can be found only through great effort.[31]

This statement appears to be an endorsement for the lineage concept if there ever was one. However, the case for Grady's involvement in the A∴A∴. is, frankly, baffling. Did he misunderstand some key differences between the O.T.O. and the A∴A∴.? For example, his Charter to Thelema Lodge in Berkeley, California, in 1977 reads, "Let all Thelemites know that I, Hymenaeus Alpha, 777, IX° O.T.O., 9°=2□, Caliph of Ordo Templi Orientis of Aleister Crowley, Baphomet 666 do hereby Charter Thelema Lodge as Grand Lodge of O.T.O."[32] Was Grady here claiming the A∴A∴. grade of Magus, or did he simply equate "9°=2□" to the IX° of O.T.O.? Was he confusing the Orders, as some believe, or was he affirming his attainment?[33] Perhaps he felt the need to assert A∴A∴. credentials to counter the claims of others like Phyllis Seckler, for example, who discredited his claims to the A∴A∴. in a 1977 open letter to O.T.O. members. She later stated after his death that he never

---

31 Grady McMurtry, "A∴A∴. or, Who Has the Right to the Star?" in *O.T.O. Newsletter*, Vol. III, nos. 7 & 8 (Double Issue) (Berkeley: O.T.O., Winter-Spring, May 1979), 104-105.

32 Charter for Thelema Lodge, Berkeley, California, as United States Grand Lodge, O.T.O. UC.

33 Alternatively in his biography of Grady, Jerry Cornelius provides an account of Grady taking the "Oath of the Abyss," McMurtry's tribulations therefrom, and attainments thereafter. See J. Edward Cornelius (2005) *In the Name of the Beast,* Vol. 2 (Berkeley, published by author).

went beyond the grade of Probationer. Yet, the reader may recall the intense bitterness that transpired between them since the mid-1970s, so Seckler may prove to be less than a reliable resource.

As Grady continued his efforts to actively reconstitute the O.T.O. in the late 1970s, he began to travel fairly regularly. He made visits to various areas to begin the process of chartering local O.T.O. bodies and conduct initiations. He later sent out "kits" that included forms and certificates needed to establish local camps, oases, and lodges. In 1981, this packet began to include printed copies of the A∴A∴ "Oath and Task of the Probationer." During Grady's visit to Montreal in the summer of 1981 to help William Breeze establish Phoenix Lodge, Breeze recalls inquiring of Grady why the Oaths were included in O.T.O. paperwork. Grady explained that he had no authority in the A∴A∴, but that the Oaths were included to get the whole program going again. Breeze explained, "I told him that he had to stop sending those out to new O.T.O. bodies—that he was confusing two very different organizations and that it would lead to nothing but trouble."[34] After that meeting Grady made a call to headquarters in Berkeley and subsequently stopped the copies of the Oath of Probationer from being included with the O.T.O. "starter kits."

However, some years later, Gerald Edward (Jerry) Cornelius of Brocken Mountain Lodge in Connecticut pressed Grady for the IX°. Grady instead decided to advance him to VIII°, making it a condition that Cornelius swear the "Oath of the Abyss." Was he confusing VIII° O.T.O. with 8°=3▢ A∴A∴? According to Cornelius' account, he swore the Oath of the Abyss in Grady's presence in April of 1984, after which McMurtry granted him the VIII° of O.T.O.[35] Cornelius has promoted a "Grady McMurtry lineage" of A∴A∴ for some time. Furthermore, his website has been one of many sources of eristic diatribes directed at the O.T.O. administration—to which we will return shortly.

* * *

---

[34] Email correspondence between the author and William Breeze, March 10, 2018.

[35] Jerry Cornelius, "An Open Epistle on Lineages of the A∴A∴," on Cornelius' *Red Flame* website (accessed July 29, 2018).

It is worth noting that each of these "lineages" or "claimant groups" holds a characteristic tone that is distinct from one another. The A∴A∴ as it is aligned with the O.T.O., coming from Motta, tends to have a "traditionalist" approach. That is, the curriculum and administration follows the original vision put forth by Crowley in his lifetime. Also, publications under this group remain within the scope of primary Thelemic literature, referencing ancient and classical texts as secondary sources. In distinction, the groups deriving through Seckler and Eshelman appear to be particularly "variated" in the way that Stark, Bainbridge, and Doyle describe schismatic groups to be, borrowing from other traditions and presenting modified versions of the original movement's teachings and ceremonies.[36] The Seckler version of the "Soror Estai Lineage" has created one "Thelemic" organization after another over the years. Since the advent of the "College of Thelema," the "Temple of Thelema" was established. These were followed by Shoemaker's "The Temple of the Silver Star," and, later, Gregory Peters' "Ordo Sunyata Vajra," which appears to import Eastern tantra into the Thelemic system. The Estai lineage then has incorporated a more contemporary "New Age" approach, blending elements of pop-psychology, Golden Dawn magic, and modern tantra.[37] Cornelius' writing is best understood within the context of polemics aimed against the O.T.O.[38]

❄❧

---

[36] Stark, Bainbridge, and Doyle (1979), 351–352.

[37] It should be noted that the element of Jungian psychology is present in both Gunther's and Seckler's writings, though from different angles. Gunther references the works of Carl G. Jung and Eric Neumann to discuss the vast periods of history known to Thelemites as "Aeons." The works of Seckler and Shoemaker appropriate Jungian psychology to interpret magical practices. The phenomenon of psychological explanations for occult concepts has been explored thoroughly in Hanegraaff (2003) "How Magic Survived the Disenchantment of the World."

[38] See, for example, his most recent work, J. Edward Cornelius (2018) *Memoirs of an A∴A∴ Initiate: Being the True Story of the Struggles for Freedom in the 1990s Against the Restrictionists* (Berkeley: Published by author).

The Battle for Legitimacy

It is here that we arrive at the discourse of A∴A∴ lineages within the
O.T.O. With so many groups of A∴A∴ splintering off, it is surprising
that it has only been a few that have become problematic to O.T.O. The
trouble stems from their attempt to create factions within the O.T.O.,
thus disturbing continuity in administrative leadership and disrupt-
ing group cohesion. While the leaders of some of the lesser known
"A∴A∴ groups" have been critical of O.T.O.'s administration, most of
them have maintained distance or remained altogether outside of the
O.T.O. Most of the discord that has emerged within O.T.O. has come
from proponents of the Eshelman/Shoemaker "Seckler lineage," and
the Cornelius "McMurtry lineage."

As we have seen, Phyllis Seckler had clearly been a mover and shaker
in re-establishing the O.T.O., despite her efforts to: (a) undermine
Grady's leadership, and (b) sequestering (and ultimately losing) the
library. In any case, she has appeared to many in the Thelemic community to have a legitimate claim to the lineage she helped formulate.

On the other hand, we have the A∴A∴ efforts led, in part, by
William Breeze. He was unanimously elected by a committee of
Grady's existing IX° members of O.T.O. (including Seckler) in 1985,
and is now the de jure O.H.O. of the O.T.O. He has sought to rebuild
the A∴A∴ so that both orders can once again operate in the way
Crowley intended.

* * *

The feverish and often hostile debate over A∴A∴ lineages can be
linked to the premier issue of Eshelman's journal, *The Black Pearl*, in
the spring of 1997. It included a review of the then-recent publication of *The Commentaries of the Holy Books* (1996). It criticized the
"A∴A∴ Publication in Class D" entitled "Liber Vesta vel פרכת sub
figurâ DCC."[39] This was a new document issued by the Great Order of
the recently established Administrative Triad, which gave a description

---

[39] In Crowley (1996b), 53–58.

of the robes and emblems in the Outer College (First Order). Eshelman wrote:

> The one serious embarrassment of the volume is a new paper titled *Liber Vesta*, which claims to give "the correct designs (with color illustrations)" of the robes for each A∴A∴ grade. This paper is new, created for the A∴A∴ lineage served by the individuals who lent it their imprimatur. Except for the Probationer robe, these designs do not at all match those which have come down to us from the A∴A∴'s founders. They do not even distantly resemble the many published photographs of A∴A∴ robes which embellish Crowley's writings.[40]

Eshelman critiqued the document, believing it did not follow any traditional scheme as laid out by Crowley in the original founding of the A∴A∴. He then outlined his own understanding of the robe designs as given in his book, *The Mystical and Magical System of the A∴A∴* (first edition 1993).[41]

Eshelman's article precipitated an article titled "Consider the Source," written by Hymenaeus Beta in the 1998 edition of *The Magical Link*. He revealed a letter from Crowley to J. F. C. Fuller dated November 9, 1909, describing each of the Grades of the Outer College. These accurately conformed with the instructions given in "Liber Vesta." H.B. continued:

> I am usually sanguine about negative or stupid reviews, but when they make pretensions to knowledge and authority and are actively misleading, I take spiritual offense, and feel obligated to respond. This instance also happens to be farcical.
>
> *Black Pearl* is the magazine of the Temple of Thelema, an occult group in Los Angeles founded comparatively recently by a resigned O.T.O. officer. It purports to act as a training group for

---

[40] Eshelman (Spring 1997), 18.

[41] See revised edition in Eshelman (2000), 237.

the A∴A∴ and seeks to foster the erroneous notion of A∴A∴ "lineages," as they reject the traditional authority of the Order.[42]

In the article, Hymenaeus Beta produced original sketches of the Robes that Crowley had sent to J. F. C. Fuller in the early formulation of the A∴A∴.

The misinformed attack by Eshelman, however, would only prove to be the beginning of the battle for legitimacy of a unified A∴A∴ administration. The controversy took an especially hostile tone when Jerry Cornelius published his virulent criticism of Breeze in his journal, *The Red Flame*, Number 7, in 1999. He wrote:

> Since the death of our beloved Grady Louis McMurtry a new branch of the A∴A∴ has been guiding the Ordo Templi Orientis. This branch is run by some of Marcelo Motta's students. In a recent issue of *The Magical Link* they have come out rather boisterously proclaiming that they, and they alone are the undisputed "traditional authority" of the A∴A∴ [...] What infuriated me most was the sarcastic condemnation of the idea of "lineages" and an "erroneous notion" of our beloved Soror Meral's [Phyllis Seckler] bloodline which, in fact, it is not. Here and in other places they have publicly attacked her and her lineage, trying hard to find "discrepancies" with this gentle woman's claims, in an attempt to drag her down and discredit her and her students [...] before Motta's students start throwing stones they should remember that if the shoe were on the other foot would they like someone *publicly disclosing* their dirty little laundry?[43]

The tirade continued for several pages, and eventuated in Cornelius exposing a number of higher O.T.O. degree-sensitive materials which had originally been given to him after his taking an oath of secrecy. Cornelius claims to have later been put through a trial of expulsion from the O.T.O. According to Cornelius, Phyllis Seckler came to his

---

[42] "Consider the Source," in *The Magical Link*, new series, No. 2, 10.

[43] Cornelius (1999), xi–xii.

defense. In a purported letter to Breeze, she lodged a number of complaints, including a similar attitude regarding his stance on lineages. She also made demands that Breeze "not sue either me or my successors over the use of the name of the A∴A∴."[44] In the same year, Seckler wrote to her own students, "To the best of my knowledge, upon Karl's death [in 1962], I was 'the member of the A∴A∴ highest in rank (and then in seniority).' The office fell to me." She continued:

> I very much dislike claiming things, and I dislike people who go around claiming this and that high title. All they do is make themselves look ridiculous to anyone who really has eyes to see. I wouldn't come out and lay claim to this title or office at all except to protect the A∴A∴ from those who would try to own it as their private property [...] Recently, one group has tried to do this, building on the claim that Marcelo Motta was the Head of the Order of Thelemites after Germer's death, and that they have somehow inherited it from him.[45]

Like McMurtry before her, Seckler confused the conditions of succession. Only, in this case, she confused the beneficiary of the Order of Thelemites with heirship in the A∴A∴, quoting from the Constitution of the former: "the member of the A∴A∴ highest in rank (and then in seniority) shall assume Our present functions, and govern the Order in Our Place."[46] Seckler died in 2004, not long after writing the above memorandum. Breeze appears to have been diplomatic with Phyllis', and now Shoemaker's followers, treating the group with a relative amount of tolerance over the last decade.

However, the conflict was enflamed again with the publications of J. Daniel Gunther's *Initiation in the Aeon of the Child* (2009) and *The Angel and the Abyss* (2014). Both books were listed with the traditional

---

44 Phyllis Seckler to William Breeze, June 27, 2000, printed in Cornelius (2018), 157–163.

45 Memorandum written by Phyllis Seckler, signed June 26, 2000. Published in Seckler (2012), 276–277.

46 Point 14, "Constitution of the Order of Thelemites," UC.

seal of the A∴A∴ and designated as an "A∴A∴ Publication in Class B" under the Imprimatur of "N. Fra: A∴A∴ and V. 7°=4▫ R.R. et A.C."

It was also around this time that the idea of "Duplexity," advanced by several Thelemic writers, became a subject of much discussion.[47] Proponents of Duplexity argue that there is an inherent doctrinal alliance between the O.T.O. and the A∴A∴, and that the two orders should work in cooperation with one another. Australian Grand Master Shiva X° recently noted that, "AUGL [Australia Grand Lodge] has explicitly affirmed the close alliance with the A∴A∴ and made A∴A∴ both visible and accessible to our members."[48] Following the publication of his memoir, *In the Center of the Fire*, long-time O.T.O. member James Wasserman was interviewed in the 2012 summer issue of the O.T.O. newsletter, *Agape*. When asked what he thought the single greatest misstep of the O.T.O. had been in the last thirty years, he replied:

> I think the greatest failure of O.T.O. has been our unwillingness to publicly criticize the modern fallacy of A∴A∴ "lineages." I appreciate the thinking behind this—allowing people maximum freedom to make choices, including bad choices. But I believe we have a doctrinal obligation to point out pretenders, misguided spiritual interpretations, and erroneous behavior.[49]

The debate was once again ignited, and threads on social media websites were filled with impassioned discussions about what this meant for the O.T.O. Many were worried it implied that one A∴A∴ group

---

[47] See, for example, AISh MLChMH (2004).

[48] "Interview with the King Shiva X°," interview with Grand Master General of Australia Grand Lodge O.T.O. by Frater S.D.S. and Soror N.R., in *OZ: The Quarterly Publication of the Australian Grand Lodge of Ordo Templi Orientis*, No. 3, Fall 2014, 12.

[49] Robert Brett Sherry and Terry Murdock "Centennial Interviews with Richard Kaczynski and James Wasserman," *Agape: The Official Organ of U.S. Grand Lodge, O.T.O.*, Summer 2012, Volume XIII, No. 2, pg. 12.

was going to govern the O.T.O. The conflict reached its boiling point in December 2014, just a few months after Gunther's *The Angel and the Abyss* was published. Hymenaeus Beta reached out personally to David Shoemaker in an effort to put the issue to rest, pointing out that it would be better for David to cooperate than to allow history books to focus on senseless quibble.[50] It would appear from Shoemaker's subsequent public post on Facebook that the correspondence did not conclude in an agreement. He wrote:

> Since much of the recent turbulence has taken place within the bounds of O.T.O., let me also make it clear that none of these comments are in any way intended to undermine or devalue the work of Hymenaeus Beta in his official capacity within O.T.O. I fully support his leadership and I appreciate his long history of service to O.T.O. [...] We have disagreement on the foundational issue of succession from Germer, and the validity of our respective claimant groups. [...] Furthermore, some A∴A∴ claimants may even be promoting certain spiritual doctrines that are at variance with those of other organizations [...] In any case, hundreds and hundreds of aspirants, within O.T.O. and without, have made choices to affiliate with the A∴A∴ organization I administer as a matter of personal conscience, and deep reflection on their affinity with the available options [...] I believe the best way to avoid [a potentially harmful] outcome is for the two most visible and populous A∴A∴ organizations to issue a joint statement of mutual respect and tolerance, coupled with a strongly worded request for everyone in our care to cease any expressions of negativity toward aspirants in alternate organizations [...] Several days ago, we proposed such an arrangement to the administrators of the A∴A∴ claimant group led by J. Daniel Gunther, and I dearly hope they take us up on the offer, for the sake of all Thelemites—especially those within O.T.O.[51]

---

50 This correspondence occurred over private email, and is not available to the general public.

51 David Shoemaker, public Facebook post, December 16, 2014.

What was initially an extension of an olive branch from Hymenaeus Beta to Shoemaker in private correspondence became a public "peace offering" on social media.

In the following May of 2015, O.T.O. celebrated its centennial existence in North America in Vancouver, British Columbia, with an academic-style conference held by Academia Ordo Templi Orientis. After a series of presentations, Hymenaeus Beta addressed nearly one hundred O.T.O. members in attendance, many of whom were in the "Lovers" and "Hermit" triads.[52] His talk primarily outlined many of the inspiring cultural and historical factors that have nurtured the two orders over the last one-hundred years, while addressing the lessons that might be learned as the O.T.O. and the A∴A∴ move forward in the future. One segment of his conclusive remarks relayed the history of Seckler and Eshelman as a cautionary tale for the audience. He told the attendees that he had been received as a Probationer under J. Daniel Gunther in 1975, and proceeded to describe his disagreements with Seckler over the years concerning A∴A∴ matters. During the months leading up to the election of Grady's successor in 1985, Seckler had nominated Eshelman to become O.H.O. Similarly, Eshelman had self-initiated through the A∴A∴ system and put Phyllis through the grades afterward. Half-jokingly, Hymenaeus Beta recounted, "Phyllis and Jim were seeking to gain control of the O.T.O. just as they were trying by other means to gain control of the A∴A∴ [...] Talk about Duplexity!" He continued by noting that the situation had always been treated with tolerance, which, according to H.B. "is a great O.T.O. tradition." He concluded with a cautioning note to the audience on this point: "O.T.O. organizers who front also for other organizations have to be kept from positions of any real influence in O.T.O." He continued:

> History shows us that they can't be relied upon to refrain from diverting other O.T.O. members. These dangers have brought

---

[52] Hymenaues Beta, "Hundred Years of the O.T.O. in North America: Inspirations and Lessons."

down O.T.O. groups in entire major cities and have crippled some others. We have a long tradition, and one I really hope to develop further, and that is the tradition of tolerance. I will tolerate almost anything, but I will not tolerate a threat to the O.T.O. [...] Our traditional openness, our lack of dogma, our unwillingness to engage in cult recruitment techniques [...] these leave us vulnerable [...] We'll always be vulnerable in ways other groups are not. We're vulnerable to what I call false flag recruitments, people recruiting under our name and diverting them into something else. We have to learn the necessary lessons from our past and ensure that our efforts are not compromised in the future nor [being] diverted for purposes that were not intended by our founders.[53]

The following July, Grand Master Sabazius X° released a statement on his blog:

We have received an increasing number of inquiries regarding the relationship between O.T.O. and A∴A∴. [...] Despite their close relationship (as well as certain structural similarities and a strong, mutual interest in the life and works of Aleister Crowley), O.T.O. and A∴A∴ are distinctly separate organizations with their own curricula, customs, rituals, spheres of operation, means and methods; and neither is subordinate to the other [...] In recent years, a variety of individuals and groups have asserted themselves as legitimate successors to the administration of A∴A∴ that existed under the external leadership of Aleister Crowley. It is not the place of the O.T.O. to judge the spiritual merits or ultimate "validity" of these various claimants, but it is also not the case that O.T.O. can have a "close alliance" and working relationship with a multiplicity of A∴A∴ administrations. For its purposes, O.T.O. recognizes a single administration of A∴A∴.[54]

---

53 Ibid.

54 "O.T.O. and A∴A∴," Sabazius X°, July 17, 2015.

This position was reinforced within the O.T.O. leadership by Grand Master Phanes X° stating that, "the time is over for such inconsistent hogwash as 'lineages.'"[55]

In the loquacious and unquiet environment of social media, the debate over A∴A∴ lineages continues to surface from time to time, despite the O.T.O. administration's public stance on the matter.[56] In Part III of this book, I will explore this topic within the context of a cost-benefit inquiry with regard to the O.T.O. At present, it is important that we consider a more contemporary manifestation of the Thelemic movement. We will next look at the online world of cyberspace and how it both aids and hinders Thelema's growth in the twenty-first century.

---

[55] Phanes X°, quoted in O.T.O. (2015) *Success is Your Proof*, 82.

[56] For example, a series of threads debating the lineage phenomenon has surfaced again in August of 2018 following the electronic publication of an essay entitled "Three Common Myths about Phyllis Seckler," which discusses much of the mnemohistorical narratives outlined here. See http://www.thelema101.com/three-common-myths-about-phyllis-seckler (accessed August 20, 2018).

CHAPTER TWELVE

The Digital Magus

Thelema in the Age of Information

> Consider the popularity of the cinema, the wireless, the football
> pools and guessing competitions, all devices for soothing fractious
> infants, no seed of purpose in them.
>
> —Crowley, "The New Aeon," Introduction to *The Book of the Law*

IT IS NO MYSTERY that the world has changed and become smaller
because of internet technology. Communication is nearly instant,
access to information is immediate, and many everyday tasks that were
previously time-consuming can now be executed in a matter of seconds,
allowing more leisure for the general populace than ever before. Just as
the world wide web and social media have facilitated growth in communities in general, it has done the same for the Thelemic community,[1]
allowing it to become more connected through a number of online
channels. We will see in this chapter some of the ways in which the
internet has initiated change in the group dynamics of Thelema.

In addition to social shifts, the world wide web has made source
Thelemic literature readily available. Much of this online material
may or may not be under copyright of the O.T.O., and some of it is
reproduced without the Order's permission. However, the fact remains
that many people can access core materials who would otherwise be
unable to obtain them, whether that is because they are currently out of

---

[1] In this chapter, I refer to the "Thelemic community" as the total participants that
engage in all of the online channels of the internet and World Wide Web, including
social media, blog forums, discussion groups, etc. While a great number of these individuals are members or former members of one or both orders discussed in this book,
the following discussion is not exclusive to the O.T.O. and the A∴A∴.

print, or simply unaffordable and rare. Much of the A∴A∴ curriculum is now accessible online. The availability of these materials may not make them any easier to comprehend without formal guidance from an Instructor, but it does at least lend the practitioner access to learning. Unfortunately, many of these online materials are incorrectly edited, therefore readers should take caution when utilizing these versions. For example, several of the digital copies of the Holy Books of Thelema have incorrect words and punctuation, thus violating the injunction of not changing "as much as the style of a letter." Probationers of the A∴A∴, for example, would be at risk of learning their chapter of "Liber LXV" incorrectly when performing Point 4 of their Task.[2] Group readings of incorrectly worded texts in the O.T.O. would be similarly problematic, teaching groups of people corrupted versions of Class A literature.

There is also a growing number of online secondary literature on Thelema appearing in the form of blogs and websites. Some of these sources are official, being statements from representatives of the O.T.O. or digital newsletters that are released at various intervals.[3] Most of this secondary online Thelemic literature remains unofficial with regard to the O.T.O. Some of it appears to be quite useful for beginning students, especially when considering that the content attempts to translate Thelemic concepts in a popular and approachable way. Yet the reader of such material runs the highest risk of being misled. Many of these online writers offer pop-Thelemic literature which advances stripped-down rudimentary analyses of otherwise complex ideas. Then there are the discussions offered by self-appointed experts.

Grand Master Shiva X° has remarked on this, particularly with regard to the subject of the Holy Guardian Angel, one of the central mysteries of the A∴A∴. "In the forums and pages of cyberspace and Thelemic social media, these attainments are often commented upon,

---

[2] See the Probationer Oath in "Liber Collegii Sancti sub figurâ CLXXXV," where it reads, "He shall commit a chapter of Liber LXV to memory [...]" See Crowley (1996b)

[3] U.S. Grand Master General Sabazius X°, for example, has a personal blog, and *Oz* is the Australian Grand Lodge Newsletter distributed electronically each quarter.

yet the ease and lure of popular comment can result in them being mischaracterized and misrepresented, potentially misleading new students and confusing even experienced practitioners."[4] The question then remains: how may one distinguish the true from the false in the busy world of the internet? It is a question that individuals will have to answer for themselves, yet it is hoped that our continued discussion may shed some light on the factors needed for consideration in coming to the best conclusions possible.

⛤

Cyberspace as a Thelemic "Egregore"

In the post-Chaos magick paradigm of the contemporary occult milieu,[5] many participants in the magical community (including many Thelemites) utilize the technology of the internet as a magical tool for their group work, despite living vast distances from one another. Whether they meet up on Google video to discuss the Gnostic Mass, or dress in full magical regalia over Skype to perform a group ritual in their respective home temples, the internet has brought the astral to closer physical awareness; at least, this has been the belief of many contemporary occult practitioners. Author John L. Crow has remarked on this phenomenon, stating, "With the emergence of computer technology, and the Internet specifically, various groups of people began to transfer the imaginative quality of the astral environment to cyberspace, and language that was previously used to refer to the astral was now used to describe cyber realms."[6] Crow notes that esotericists have now implemented internet technology as a way of extending their magical

---

[4] Shiva X°, "Preface," in Gunther (2014), 11.

[5] A general overview of the history of Chaos Magick is found in Colin Duggan (2013) "Perrenialism and Iconoclasm," in Egil Asprem and Kennet Granholm (eds.) *Contemporary Esoterism* (Sheffield: Equinox Publishing, Ltd.), 91–112.

[6] John L. Crow (2013) "Accessing the Astral with a Monitor and Mouse: Esoteric Religion and the Astral Located in Three-dimensional Virtual Realms," in Asprem and Granholm (2013), 159–180.

identities into the virtual world, creating profiles and avatars that allow
the practitioner to take on a "polymorphic identity," assuming images
of gods and goddesses with wings, animal features, and alternate gen-
ders. This phenomenon is more than just occult fantasy-making; rather
it "forms a larger context for identity exploration."[7] This factor of identity and the online occult world will feature more prominently in a
later discussion. For the moment, let us see how cyberspace creates the
possibility of a "Thelemic egregore."

What is meant by the term "Thelemic egregore"? I use this phrase
in the most simplistic of ways. Essentially, I am referring to a Thelemic
"group think," "seminar" or "discussion." Services such as YouTube,
Google Hangouts, and Periscope have opened new ways for classes
and seminars to be broadcast online. I once led a discussion on the
Thoth Tarot through Google Hangouts—myself in Amsterdam, and
several other Dutch O.T.O. members tuning in from other areas of the
Netherlands. Similarly, I delivered a talk on *The Vision and the Voice.*
The audio and video were broadcast live from Sekhet-Maat Lodge in
Portland, Oregon, through Periscope, a free video-streaming service
offered on tablet technology. The Lodge Master at the time simply
linked the Periscope internet address to social media, and anyone in
the world with the link could watch the lecture. Many other individuals
around the world are using similar internet tools to present classes,
lectures, and seminars in much the same way.

The ability to conference call with services like Skype and Google
has provided outlets for executive meetings to take place with relative
ease, including between members of the Electoral College of O.T.O.,
who occasionally meet online. This presents timely and hassle-free
options for several members to meet and discuss a range of issues,
whether on a local or national level. With the ability to conference
call through Skype and Google Hangouts, and live stream through a
multitude of services, Thelema has entered a new era in which classes,
discussions, seminars, and meetings can happen anywhere, anytime,
and involve anyone who is interested and invited.

---

[7] Crow (2013), 180.

⁓⚹⚶⁓

Social Media: Identity, Alterity and Power

O generation of gossipers! who shall deliver you from the Wrath that is fallen upon you?

O Babblers, Prattlers, Talkers, Loquacious Ones, Tatlers, Chewers of the Red Rag that inflameth Apis the Redeemer to fury, learn first what is Work! and THE GREAT WORK is not so far beyond!

— *The Book of Lies*, "The Bull-Baiting"

It is the opinion of the author that the online Thelemic community today appears to be a microcosmic reflection of the greater social community that surrounds it. To clarify, the Thelemic community, although relatively small when compared to other religious groups, is by no means homogenous. Its membership is diverse, both culturally and politically. Each geographical region of the Thelemic community is culturally unique. The American O.T.O. and American Thelemites are culturally *American*, while Thelema in the UK, Italy, or Australia may be characteristically *British*, *Italian*, or *Australian*. Thelema in the Pacific states of the United States (i.e., California, Oregon, and Washington) can be regionally distinguished in many ways from Thelema in the Southeastern states of the country. While this fact of local variation may be due simply to the cultural plurality of the United States in general,[8] this nuance is worth examining especially with regard to

---

[8] In his detailed analyses of American culture, Colin Woodard has pointed to eleven different cultural regions of the United States, tracing their respective histories from the seventeenth century to the twenty-first century. For example, the Northeastern "Yankeedom" holds culturally distinct values and customs when compared with the "Deep South" and "Appalachia" regions. As these regions became populated and spread westward, so too did their respective cultures and values. Woodard implies that these "American nations" have repeatedly come into conflict for more than two centuries, and that the individual states in America that are markedly identified as "red," "blue" or "purple" are so by virtue of the cultural nation that dominates the region. Woodard's compelling argument explains a number of events in United States

online social forums. It might help to explain many of the cultural and political clusters that meet in the world of cyberspace and find themselves either in agreement or disagreement about the ways in which Thelema could be or *should* be applied in the world. That said, a fundamental fact remains apparent: members of the Thelemic community are human, and human beings tend to disagree with one another about many social and political issues.[9] It may be that the human element demonstrates there is not much difference in social media in general and social media specific to Thelema, the only difference, of course, is that the latter appropriates a niche spiritual philosophy into its discussion forums.

The following section will explore some of the more problematic social mechanics that have been created by social media within the small group dynamics of the Thelemic community. This will be examined through the conflict that arises through the relations of identity, alterity, and power. While some of these features can be explained simply by the ways in which people behave within the social dynamics of online forums in general, other idiosyncrasies are indicated by the religious,

---

history, ranging from reasons why some states were more involved than others during the revolutionary period, to how the republican and democratic parties in the U.S. have perceivably switched over the last century as being categorically identified as "Liberal" and "Conservative." Woodard further implies that, since these regional cultures have come into frequent conflict on fundamental issues (i.e., between diametrically opposed principles of individual liberty and the common good), there is no one single value that can be identified as "American." See Woodard (2011) *American Nations; A History of the Eleven Rival Regional Cultures of North America* (New York: Penguin Books) and (2016) *American Character: A History of the Epic Struggle Between Individual Liberty and the Common Good* (New York: Penguin Random House).

[9] One political factor that is worth mentioning that has extended beyond America is the United States presidential election of Donald Trump in November of 2016. Since this event, the Western world has witnessed an insurmountable level of social upheaval. Political ideologies have compounded between "left" and "right," and factions across the United States have formed into pockets of extremities. As a result, the Thelemic community (being one of thousands of sub-groups in America) seems to have become politicized to some degree, with several group identities on social media emerging, either contesting or supporting Trump's presidency and policies.

spiritual, and occult elements that characterize Thelema. In short, we will see how the online Thelemic community has been affected by factors in the greater social sphere.

It should be noted from the outset that some of the following may appear to the reader as an exhortation. This is perhaps a by-product of what is otherwise intended to be an investigative inquiry into a noticeably contemporary phenomenon. It is the aim of all critical inquiry in the humanities—whether in the disciplines of philosophy, history, or social theory—to raise questions and propose solutions, if and when possible. As such, the following discussion aims to touch on sensitive topics and speculate on hypothetical outcomes.

Identity, Alterity, and Power

It was implied earlier that the internet has been utilized as a way for people to reconstruct identity. This is particularly the case with social media services such as Facebook, Twitter, and Google+, among others. The ability to create a personal profile allows one to extend oneself in a selective way within the greater social sphere. A person can easily create a description about him or herself, use a chosen image to represent how they can be viewed by others, join groups that reflect their own interests, and follow pages and individuals with whom they find affinity. In short, social media allows people the freedom to construct a public image that extends into any number of social circles with which they associate.

The formation of identity online is a phenomenon that is not easily explained, and the use of social media with regard to the eccentricities of self-image only complicates the wide spectrum of behavioral variances in any given individual. Recent studies in psychology have associated the frequent use of social media to certain nuances of identity formation. For example, negative personality traits such as narcissism have been linked to frequent use of Facebook,[10] while

---

[10] Studies are now beginning to link Facebook Addiction Disorder (FAD) with negative behavioral patterns such as depression, anxiety, and narcissism. Coincidentally, these studies have reported a lack of positive variables (i.e., overall life satisfaction,

other studies have produced evidence that visitation of one's own Facebook profile momentarily increases self-esteem, but decreases overall task performance.[11] These peculiarities of social media use and its effects on human psychology are only beginning to be explored in scientific studies. While more studies are needed to determine if the normal distribution of individuals posting on Facebook actually have any correlation to those who carry such personality traits or not, it is arguable that social media use is intrinsically linked to one's image of self and identity. It is this latter point with which we are herein concerned.

It is worthy to note the emergence of specialized group forums on social media platforms. Many groups on Facebook, for example, are specialized clusters of affiliated identities and number in the hundreds, thousands, or millions. They range from public pages and groups with no pre-approval for membership, to private groups which are not immediately accessible in search criteria and are "invitation only." Of particular interest for this discussion are groups that promote certain viewpoints regarding Thelema. Whether they do this explicitly or implicitly, these forums are constructing a particular group identity, or what can be understood in general as "identity politics." In short, these group forums are made up of individual users who support the group's specialized theme or cause.

As Gerd Baumann has noted, it is often assumed that "claims to identity, collective or individual, are inevitably tied to exclusions of alterity, that every 'us' excludes a 'them.'"[12] The inherent dichotomy of "self" and "other" and the conflict that arises from this distinction is

---

positive mental and physical health, etc.). See Julia Brailovskaia and Jürgen Margraf (2017) "Facebook Addiction Disorder (FAD) Among German students—a longitudinal approach," in *PLoS One*, Vol. 12, No. 12.

[11] Catalina L. Toma (2013) "Feeling Better but Doing Worse: Effects of Facebook Self-Presentation on Implicit Self-Esteem and Cognitive Task Performance," in *Media Psychology*, Vol. 16, No. 2. pp. 199–220.

[12] Gerd Baumann (2004) "Grammars of Identity/Alterity: A Structural Approach," in Gerd Baumann and Andre Gingrich (eds.) *Grammars of Identity/Alterity: A Structural Approach* (New York; Oxford: Berghahn Books), 18.

evident in every area of cultural studies. As Raymond Corbey and Joep Lerrssen note:

> All human cultures articulate, situate themselves by categorizing the world. Such a predicative act necessarily involves a distinction between that which is allowed into the sphere of culture, and that which is excluded; the circumscription of cultural identity proceeds by silhouetting it against a contrastive background of Otherness.[13]

"Otherness," or alterity, is a natural creation within a cultural sphere. A group of individuals with affinitive interests, whether cultural or ideological, will typically cluster, forming a group identity that is distinct. It is not an ethical case of whether or not this *should* happen, but a descriptive fact that this *does* happen in all aspects of human relations.

Naturally, a discussion on "Self," "Other," "Identity," and "Alterity" easily invokes the theories in any number of areas of study—including critical theory, conflict theory, post-structuralism, and many other sub-branches of sociology and philosophy that critique the relations of power in human structures—and would well exceed our purpose here.[14] We should, however, point out that where there are instances of the subject-object dichotomy in human relations (i.e., self-other and identity-alterity), there are factors involving the emergence of power that should be considered: self-constitution, self-assertion, and group-hegemony on the one hand, and estrangement, exclusion, and subordination on the other.

---

[13] Raymond Corbey & Joep Lerrssen (1991) "Studying Alterity: Backgrounds and Perspectives," in Raymond Corbey and Joep Lerrssen (eds.), *Alterity, Identity, Image: Selves and Others in Society and Scholarship* (Amsterdam: Rodopi), vi.

[14] Many of these social studies examine the mechanisms of the structures of human activities, for example, the relations of power and conflict within the social sphere. Such subjects have filled the contents of academic theses in the fields of philosophy, history, cultural studies, women's studies, gender theory, literary studies, and many more.

It is through a careful examination of these group identities and their relationships that we can find the emergence of such factors. This is especially the case when disagreement and conflict between groups arise. This is most explicitly observed in actual physical conflicts, such as the case of a political demonstration. Of particular interest to our present discussion is the conflict that emerges through discursive means—for example, in the form of a written polemic against one set of ideas or in a discussion thread on social media. The power relations that emerge through social media threads are fluid pronouncements of authority, and become present in the dynamic interchanges between the players involved. In this sense, "power" is never static for any substantial length of time. French philosopher Michel Foucault remarked on this fleeting characteristic of power expressed in discourse:

> Discourses are not once and for all subservient to power or raised up against it [...] We must make allowances for the complex and unstable process whereby a discourse can be both an instrument and an effect of power, but also a hindrance, a stumbling point of resistance and a starting point for an opposing strategy. Discourse transmits and produces power; it reinforces it, but also undermines and exposes it, renders it fragile and makes it possible to thwart.[15]

In the discursive world of cyberspace, power and authority are not permanent, but are pronounced at various moments. While one could characterize the content as rational discourse, social media seems to breed any number of fallacious behaviors including ridicule, appeal to emotion, and bandwagoning. The point to be made here is that the relations between group identities are best understood when they are placed within the dynamics of identity and alterity, and analyzed with respect to the presence or absence of power. These analytical tools are especially helpful when considering the often conflictual ground of

---

[15] Michel Foucault (1998) *The History of Sexuality: The Will to Knowledge* (London: Penguin), 100–101.

social media discourse in the Thelemic community, where discussions can unfold at a higher volume than we have previously witnessed in history.

The Digital Magi and Thelemic Group Gurus: the Occultist Factor

There is another factor related to identity that is exclusive to religious groups. It is what I refer to as the "guru" complex, or in the world of social media, the "digital magus" syndrome.

It has already been mentioned that scientific studies have revealed a degree of narcissism amongst excessive users of social media. It is also worth considering that narcissism has been linked to contemporary spiritualties that assert self-divinization.[16] Many currents of contemporary esotericism, including certain strains of occultism, can be placed within a "psychologized" form of spirituality which has been criticized for facilitating narcissistic dispositions. These modern currents of spirituality often assert a secular interpretation of religious experience, in which self-aggrandizement is disguised as "self-actualization," "self-awareness," or "self-apotheosis." Such psychologized spiritualties insist that the divine is equivalent to the "Higher-Self," and that the aim of religious practice is to apotheosize one's own ego.

These psychologized inclinations towards spirituality have been increasingly incorporated into a popular discourse about Thelema on social media. An example of this is the popular assertion that the Holy Guardian Angel is akin to the notion of the "Higher Self." Crowley remarked on this in his later life stating that, "He is not, let me say with emphasis, a mere abstraction from yourself; and that is why I have insisted rather heavily that the term 'Higher Self' implies 'a damnable heresy and a dangerous delusion.'"[17] Crowley is referring to the dangers of a narcissistic personality mistaking the mystery of the Knowledge

---

[16] See Paul Vitz (1977) *Psychology as Religion: The Cult of Self-Worship* (Grand Rapids: William B. Eerdmans Publishing Company) and A.H. Almaas (2001) *The Point of Existence: Transformations of Narcissism in Self Realization* (London: Shambhala).

[17] Crowley (1986) *Magick Without Tears*, 282.

and Conversation of the Holy Guardian Angel with the divinization of the ego—an idea that is prevalent in much of the popular literature on psychologized forms of spirituality, which features in numerous titles of books that fill the shelves in the "Self-help" and "New Age" sections of stores today,[18] and which might be called an omnipresent theme in much social media discourse.

The above argument is not claiming that all Facebook users are narcissists, nor is this an assertion that all occultists are self-aggrandizing. On the contrary, the internet and social media have offered many benefits to the Thelemic movement, as the discussion at the beginning of this chapter has outlined. What is being demonstrated here is that the personality traits that facilitate grandiosity and self-inflation are often present in online social forums, and that this same feature characterizes some individuals attracted to the occult. At the time of the writing of this book, there are many self-appointed internet experts on Thelema—Facebook group gurus and "keyboard warriors" who wish to make themselves known on social media forums, and who aim to prove themselves to be more knowledgeable than anyone else on Thelemic topics. In the digital age, these individuals have a platform to share their opinions in a way which was previously not available. Coincidentally, many of these "digital magi," as knowledgeable as they may appear to be, hold little to no authority in one or both orders. Many of them are former members of the O.T.O. who have either resigned or been placed on unfavorable membership status. It is also likely—based on the cognitive and emotional confusion exhibited—that the majority of such people have never passed the grade of Probationer. The result of the phenomenon of the "digital magus" is that many otherwise sincere

---

[18] The reader should take careful note that the mystery mentioned above known as the Knowledge and Conversation of the Holy Guardian Angel *is not* anywhere close to the aggrandizements of the self, and that the entirety of the curriculum of the Outer College of the A∴A∴, called the G∴D∴ (Golden Dawn) is specifically aimed to break down and control the ego, in an effort to prepare the aspirant for that Holy experience. It is also worth bearing in mind that Crowley's views on the nature of this mystery matured and developed during his lifetime, and that it is only in his later writing that he elaborated on this mystery with some clarity.

seekers looking for teachers are easily misled. It is an often overlooked point, both for novices and seasoned students of Thelema to consider: the fruits of the Great Work are revealed only in Silence, not through the garrulous chatter of discussion threads or the incessant banter of cults of personality.

Thelema in the Age of Information

It is at this point that we need to place this subject matter into some historical perspective, and remark on the nature of Authority where it concerns the Thelemic movement. In Crowley's lifetime, Authority in the two orders was straightforward. Crowley became the administrative head of the O.T.O. in 1925, and had held the office of Imperator of the A∴A∴ from 1907 until his death in 1947. His representative and later successor was Karl Germer. Wilfred T. Smith was the Grand Master General X° of the United States O.T.O. All matters of Thelemic doctrine and organization came from Crowley himself. If there were any concerns in the O.T.O., members would speak with the Lodge Master or direct their questions to Germer or Crowley directly. All matters of the A∴A∴ were handled in the way that the Great Order was established, and students dealt exclusively with their immediate superior.[19] However, again, in serious matters, Crowley, or later Germer, was only a letter away.

This authoritative structure fell into question upon Karl Germer's death, and it has only been since the election of Hymenaeus Beta that the two orders have been fully reconstituted along the lines originally envisioned. The O.T.O. functions very much in the way its founding documents have outlined, with a Frater Superior of the Order (the O.H.O.) acting as the executive administrator. This person is assisted by a Secretary General and a Treasurer General, and this triad of

---

[19] There were a number of contentions to Crowley's authority even within his lifetime. Several examples stand out, Charles Stansfeld Jones being the most salient case. Another instance is that of Cecil Frederick Russell, who broke from Crowley to start his own "Choronzon Club," later called the "Gnostic Body of God," which was advertised as a shortcut to initiation. See Martin P. Starr (2003).

executive officers oversees the O.T.O. as a whole on an international scale. Similarly, each national section has a Supreme and Holy King of the X°, who is assisted by a Grand Secretary General and a Grand Treasurer General. National sections also subsume other administrative bodies, such as a Supreme Grand Council and an Electoral College. The authoritative structure of the O.T.O. is designed in such a way that the administrative aspects are clear and distinct, and through the function of the offices they provide for balance in the running of the Order.

The A∴A∴ also functions in much the same way that Crowley designed it. A triad of officers in the Second Order (the Præmonstrator, Imperator, and Cancellarius) govern the Second Order and oversee the functions of the Outer College. Authority from the Third Order emanates and is manifested in each of these three officers, and a chain is formed through the successive links of aspirants who take up the initiatory journey of the Outer College through a student-teacher relationship, from Probationer to Adeptus Minor (within).[20]

In the digital age, a point of ambiguity has presented itself. While the authoritative chain of command in the O.T.O. and the A∴A∴ is clearly laid out with regard to the two orders' respective structures, the space that has been generated by the internet and social media is a free-for-all, between identity, alterity, and power. With all the benefits that the world wide web has offered us in the digital age, it is perhaps more important than ever to follow the maxim, *caveat emptor.*

The reader must make a careful note that the initiatory structures of both orders are designed in such a way so as to eschew such instances of grandiosity. If initiates of the O.T.O. live the Order's teachings, they are earnestly aware that the degrees aid in stripping away the negative aspects of the self and facilitate virtues of fraternity, responsibility, and tolerance, among other attributes. This process is no easy task, and often involves naturally occurring ordeals and tribulations in the initiate's life that agitate the ego so as to peel away the profane elements of the self. This is one reason why the Man of Earth degrees of the O.T.O. take no role in the governance of the Order. It is also why these degrees have a

---

[20] The true teacher at the grade of Adeptus Minor is the Holy Guardian Angel. One's Superior in the Outer College is simply an authoritative guide to this mystery.

high attrition rate, as these initiations tend to force new perspectives of reality upon the candidate. By the time one gets into the invitational degrees in the O.T.O., it is assumed he or she has been able to control the lower aspects of the ego and commit herself in service to fellow brethren.

The above similarly applies to the Grades of the Outer College of the A∴A∴. The First Order is that of "destruction," the *nigredo*[21] phase of alchemy in which the aspirant must begin to separate the false image of the self from the sacred divine center of the innermost nature. Each successive grade provides specific parameters that help aspirants to gain control of the appetitive and animalistic aspects of their nature, the parts where the ego thrives. Through the process of separating the higher and lower aspects of one's nature, referred to as the *separatio* phase of alchemy, the aspirant is prepared to be a vessel within which the God can indwell, participating in the world of humanity *through* the aspirant. J. Daniel Gunther explains this phase, saying:

> It is this separation (Separatio) that allows the human psyche to constellate aggregates of individual experience. Only a condition contrasting subject and object can support the differentiation of "I, me and mine,"—the hallmark of ego [...] The space between the opposites is the place where the human ego enjoys its existence. Uniting the opposites has an unavoidable conclusion; the ego, thriving in the spaces between, is destroyed. It is for this reason that most aspirants, at some level during their initial pursuit of the Great Work, experience an inexplicable fear of that Work. This arises from the ego, which senses its inevitable annihilation should the student persist in the work of Initiation.[22]

Gunther further notes that the true aim of the Great Work is service to humanity, "Genuine spiritual humility is gained by devotion to the Great Work, exalting that Work over self, and striving ever toward

---

[21] "Nigredo" means "blackening" and is the first phase of alchemy during which the dross material is burned away before the refining processes take place.

[22] Gunther (2014), 107.

the Beloved One, the Holy Guardian Angel."[23] For those who have remained chaste in their pursuit of the Great Work, Silence comes naturally, and the prattle of social media and internet blogging appears little more than the incessant ranting of Choronzon.

Solutions: Peace, Tolerance, and Truth on All Points of the Triangle

> I saw the petty, the quarrelsome, the selfish, —they were like men, O Lord, they were even like unto men. I saw Thee in these.
>
> —*Liber DCCCXIII vel ARARITA*, II:6

It is the opinion of the author that there exists no solution to the problem of agitated discourse and falsified information on social media and internet blogging. Not only does Thelema promote freedom of thought and speech, but there is no way to regulate the hundreds of thousands of discussion forums online. It is known to the author that a memorandum has been circulated in the Outer College of the A∴A∴ discouraging any such engagement in discussions on social media, and that policies for social media are being considered at certain administrative levels of the O.T.O. However, it will be the discipline that members of both orders are taught in their initiatory journeys that will determine to what degree this problem can be eschewed and to what level group cohesion can be maintained among its membership. While it may be a tall order to expect members to embrace the impassivity of an Adept when it comes to disquieting impressions from the world, it is nevertheless a fact that the members of the Thelemic movement can be anticipated to be more wholesome in character than the non-initiate still walking in darkness amongst the profane world. Just as Freemasonry makes a gentleman out of a normal man, Thelema—when applied correctly—creates an initiate out of an otherwise mundane individual.

That said, an embrace of daily mindfulness of the three points of the triangle may be the key: Peace, Tolerance, and Truth. These three points are realized and put in balance by the principles of fraternity

---

[23] Ibid., 178.

and universal brotherhood. Even at the initial degree of the O.T.O., Minerval, the candidate is shown that the pursuit of the Great Work is the pure and sincere desire for peace and the seeking of wisdom. It is through the work of the O.T.O. that candidates engage the work of *karma yoga,* finding peace in service to their brothers and sisters, in cooperation to promulgate the Law of Thelema.

Through the persistent reconciliation of all foreign elements that are "other" and not part of "self," the initiate learns tolerance. It is through the volitional engagement of experiences that are opposite to one's nature that the Thelemic maxim, "love under will" is exercised. As Crowley noted, "To refuse to unite oneself with any phenomenon soever is to deprive oneself of its value—even of life itself [...]"[24] The principle of tolerance is important, as it is most absent where the ego is most present. With this, I quote the post-structuralist philosopher, Emmanuel Levinas, who wrote about experiencing transcendence in the "other":

> The relation with the Other, or Conversation, is a non-allergic relation, an ethical relation; but inasmuch as it is welcomed this conversation is a teaching. Teaching is not reducible to maieutics; it comes from the exterior and brings me more than I contain. In its non-violent transitivity the very epiphany of the face is produced.[25]

In all the mundane truths and falsities uniquely experienced by each initiate's ego, it is in Truth—the principle which is above any one individual—that we are united in the spirit of fraternity and universal brotherhood. Through disciplined motion and impassive one-pointed-ness we can understand and do our pure will while allowing others to do theirs. There is indeed plenty of room for all. Through cooperation and service to the Great Work do we meet and march the war-engine

---

[24] "On Thelema," in Crowley (1998b), 173.

[25] Emmanuel Levinas (1991) *Totality and Infinity: An Essay on Exteriority* (trans. Alphonso Lingis) (London: Kluwer Academic Publishers), 51.

of Thelema forward—both internally within ourselves and externally in the world.

In closing this discussion, the author states his personal opinion that it is more productive to spend less time on the digital mediums related to Thelema, and more time being involved in one's local camps, oases, or lodges, where the O.T.O. is concerned. Furthermore, the practitioner of the A∴A∴ curriculum can advance quicker when the distraction of social media is replaced with constant study of the Holy Books, practicing the eight limbs of Yoga, and familiarizing oneself with the exercises in "Liber O" and "Liber E." Arguing whether or not Thelema is truly a conservative or liberal ideology to strangers on the internet may satisfy the ego, but it does very little to fortify one's own body of light or nurture the fraternal bonds that initiates have sworn solemn oaths to uphold. Let them who have the ears to listen, hear.

Aleister Crowley as world traveler, published poet, and student of mysticism. This picture was taken in New York City in May of 1906, two years after he had received *The Book of the Law.* He went on to found the A∴A∴ a year and a half later, and would become Baphomet X° O.T.O. within six years; "and blessing & worship to the prophet of the lovely Star!"

LEFT: S. L. MacGregor Mathers, one of the founders of the Hermetic Order of the Golden Dawn. RIGHT: Allen Bennett, an important friend and teacher in Crowley's life. BELOW: Rose Edith Crowley (*née* Kelly), the first Scarlet Woman, who assisted in the reception of *The Book of the Law*.

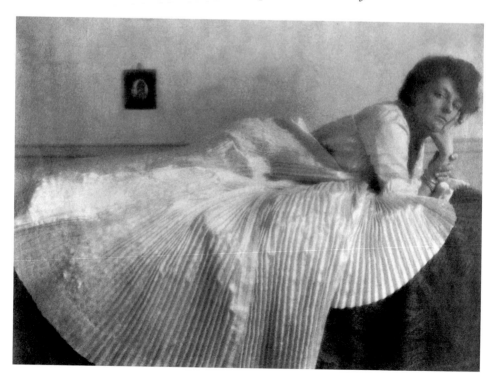

ABOVE: Victor Neuburg, one of Crowley's foremost students, who assisted with "The Vision and the Voice" and "The Paris Working." BELOW LEFT: Raoul Loveday, a young disciple who died at Cefalù. BELOW RIGHT: Major-General J.F.C. Fuller, one of the founding members of A∴A∴.

ABOVE LEFT: Theodor Reuss, a founder of the O.T.O., who rose to become its Outer Head. He initiated Crowley to the IX° in 1912. Crowley succeeded Reuss as the O.H.O. ABOVE RIGHT: A pre-performance publicity photo taken at the Equinox office before the Rites of Eleusis were presented at Caxton Hall in London in 1910. RIGHT: Charles Stansfeld Jones, Frater Achad, considered at one time to have been Crowley's "magical son." *Liber Aleph* was written for his instruction. He discovered the number 31 as a key to *Liber AL, The Book of the Law.*

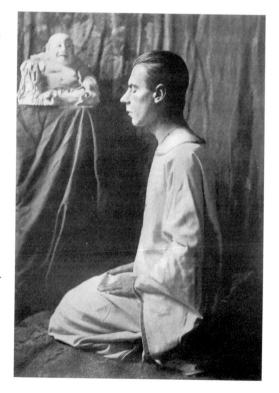

ABOVE LEFT: Jane Wolfe (left) and Leah Hirsig at Cefalù. Jane was an American actress and student of Crowley's to whom several of the letters in *Magick without Tears* were addressed. ABOVE RIGHT: Scarlet Woman Leah Hirsig (Soror Alostrael), posing beside Crowley's portrait of her. LEFT: Mary d'Este Sturges, the Scarlet Woman who served with Crowley during "The Ab-ul-diz Working," which manifested in his writing *Book Four,* Parts I and II, Meditation and Magick: Preliminary Remarks. She was also a close friend of dancer Isadora Duncan.

ABOVE: Wilfred T. Smith was the founder of Agape Lodge in California in 1933. LEFT: Jack Parsons was a rocket scientist, a co-founder of the Jet Propulsion Laboratory, and an inventor of solid rocket fuel. A crater on the Moon is named in his honor. OPPOSITE TOP LEFT: Karl Johannes Germer succeeded Crowley as head of the A∴A∴ and O.T.O. OPPOSITE TOP RIGHT: Grady Louis McMurtry, Caliph Hymenaeus Alpha, was responsible for reconstituting the modern O.T.O. OPPOSITE BELOW: Mildred Burlingame of Agape Lodge (left) with Israel Regardie and Phyllis Seckler.

OPPOSITE ABOVE: Jack Parsons and Marjorie Cameron. They met and were later married as a result of Jack's success in his Babalon Working, performed in 1946. Cameron is a well-known artist, whose work has been featured in numerous exhibits and books. She also appeared in a film by Kenneth Anger.

OPPOSITE BELOW: William Breeze was honored to have earned the friendship of both Cameron and Helen Parsons Smith. ABOVE RIGHT: Kenneth Anger visiting with Hermann Metzger, late head of the Swiss O.T.O. BELOW RIGHT: Metzger was succeeded by Annemarie Aeschbach, shown here during a visit from William Breeze that addressed past differences over O.T.O. leadership claims.

ABOVE: Kenneth and Steffi Grant. Kenneth met Crowley as a young man and later became a prolific writer. He focused on the Eastern Tantric roots of Thelemic sex magick. Steffi is a talented artist whose artwork and paintings have been published in several important works. BELOW: Rare photo of Grady McMurtry in Washington, D.C., in costume, during a Shakespearean play in the 1960s.

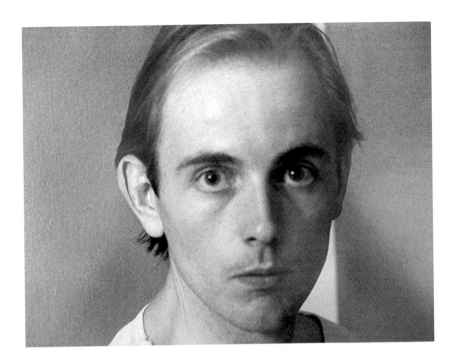

ABOVE: 1972 photo of Peter Macfarlane of 93 Publishing. He was responsible for several well-produced Thelemic works. RIGHT: 1970 photo of Llee Heflin with "The Universe" card superimposed. Heflin established Level Press. BELOW: Logo of Jerry Kay, founder of Xeno Press, whose simple, staple-bound, paperback edition of *The Book of the Law* in 1967 may have been the first Crowley publication since Germer's death in 1962.

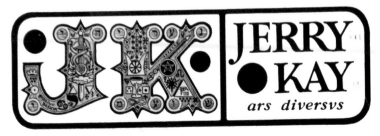

ABOVE: Harry Smith was consecrated a Bishop of E.G.C. by Hymenaeus Beta. He is shown here at Naropa Institute in Boulder, Colorado with a crown fashioned from extra covers of *The Holy Books of Thelema,* which featured his artwork on both the front, spine, and back. OPPOSITE ABOVE: Devoted Crowley student and avant garde filmmaker Kenneth Anger. OPPOSITE BELOW: Harry Smith and William Breeze in Brooklyn in 1987.

Helen Parsons Smith was responsible for advancing the candidacy of William Breeze in the IX° Election following the death of Grady McMurtry in 1985. A member of Agape Lodge, she was married to Jack Parsons and later Wilfred T. Smith. She published a number of elegantly-produced Crowley works through Thelema Publications.

Sister Regina Kahl
was an opera singer
and voice teacher. She
served for many years
as the High Priestess of
the Gnostic Mass, with
Wilfred T. Smith as
Priest, at Agape Lodge
in Southern California
beginning in the
1930s.

Sister Lola D. Wolfe
was a member of
Thelema Lodge in
Berkeley. She is a
Priestess of the Gnostic
Mass, rose to the IX°,
became an Elector
IX°, served as Grand
Secretary General, and
was the first Priestess
in modern times to
work in the Sixth
Degree Temple.

LEFT: Marcelo Ramos Motta was instrumental in reviving the A∴A∴ after the death of Karl Germer and the Interregnum period. His isolation in this photo seems in mute contrast to the photo of McMurtry. BELOW: Outside the Ninth Circuit Court in 1985. Standing (left to right): Helen Parsons Smith, James Wasserman, Patrick King, David R. Jones, Bill Heidrick, attorney Stuart Mackensie, Lola D. Wolfe, James T. Graeb. Seated: Martin P. Starr, Grady McMurtry, Andrea Lacedonia.

TOP: Publishing legend Donald Weiser in an iconic photograph by Don Snyder (*Aquarian Odyssey*). Donald is seen with the recently published Weiser edition of *The Book of Thoth,* Crowley's masterpiece on Tarot, originally published in 1944, reprinted in 1969. BOTTOM: William Breeze, Frater Superior Hymenaeus Beta, with Jimmy Page in the Yorke Collection stacks at the Warburg Institute (photo by Bradford Verter). Breeze has led the O.T.O. since 1985, and was elected as *de jure* O.H.O. by five X° members in 2014. He has been responsible for editing and producing some of the most important editions of Aleister Crowley's writings published to date.

ABOVE: James Wasserman (left) and J. Daniel Gunther in North Carolina at an A∴A∴ ceremony marking the reconstitution of the Outer College during the early 1990s. BELOW: The 1985 meeting of the late Caliph Hymenaeus Alpha's "Elector IX°s." They voted to appoint William Breeze as Caliph and Acting O.H.O. The election brought the Order through the ordeal of McMurtry's death with a unanimous vote. TOP ROW (left to right): *Lola D. Wolfe, Anthony W. Iannotti, James Eshelman, William Breeze, *Lon Milo DuQuette, *Bill Heidrick, *Mike Ripple, *James Wasserman. SECOND ROW: *Andrea Lacedonia, *James T. Graeb, *Mechelle Ripple. AT THE TABLE: *Helen Parsons Smith and *Phyllis Seckler. Grady's ashes sat on the table during the meeting. *Shirine Morton took the photo. (Asterisks designate Electors.) Breeze took the magical name of Hymenaeus Beta.

Richard Gernon and his wife, Deborah O'Melia, in Nashville during the late 1970s. "Gurney" was an enormously important part of Marcelo Motta and J. Daniel Gunther's efforts to rekindle the A∴A∴ spark. He was the Scribe for the magical workings recorded in Gunther's Ibis Press publication *The Visions of the Pylons.* He served for a time as Lodgemaster of Motta's Nashville S.O.T.O. until he resigned and moved to New York City in 1980. There he became an invaluable ally in the early years of TAHUTI Lodge, eventually succeeding James Wasserman as Lodgemaster in 1985, serving as E.G.C. Bishop, and being elevated to the IX° by Hymenaeus Beta.

Karl Germer and Marcelo Motta captioned this photo of Aleister Crowley, "In Hastings (with little left but pipe and wit)" in their 1962 first edition publication of *Liber Aleph*.

PART III

One Truth and One Spirit:

Aleister Crowley's Spiritual Legacy

CHAPTER THIRTEEN

"Duplexity" and the Mystic Marriage

"DUPLEXITY" IS A FAIRLY RECENT TERM in the lexicon of Thelema. It refers to the relationship that is shared between the O.T.O. and the A∴A∴ with regard to promulgating the Law of Thelema. It was first used in 2004 by O.T.O. member Frater AISh MLChMH, who has argued that the A∴A∴ and the O.T.O. are designed to work in close alliance. AISh MLChMH draws support for this claim from the 1915 diary entry, mentioned in chapter five, in which Crowley divined the word "Duplex" as the Word of the Vernal Equinox. "Duplex" was described by Crowley as "a word of mystic marriage of A∴A∴ and O.T.O."[1] In Part I, this subject was treated historically by discussing Crowley's vision of the two orders in his lifetime. Now, we will examine Duplexity both theoretically and practically with regard to the contemporary manifestation of the two orders.

It is first essential to define the term "Duplexity." The word, as used here, is a neologism constructed for convenience to describe the doctrinal crossover between the A∴A∴ and the O.T.O. *The Complete Oxford English Dictionary* defines "duplexity" as, "The quality of being double; doubleness"; while the meaning of "duplex" is given as "Composed of two parts or elements; twofold."[2] Thus it is that we conceive of A∴A∴ and O.T.O. as two parts of one whole.

When Crowley referred to the Word "Duplex" as the "mystic marriage of A∴A∴ and O.T.O.," he hints at the universal formula of the Rose and Cross. The Rose Cross will be discussed later in the context of the *Hieros Gamos* and the Gnostic Mass. Here, I will be referring to it with regard to Duplexity. The term "Mystic Marriage"

---

[1] Frater AISh MLChMH (Spring 2004).

[2] (1971) *The Compact Edition of the Oxford English Dictionary,* Oxford University Press.

is so broad it can indicate any number of points related to the Rose Cross—for instance, "The Knowledge and Conversation of the Holy Guardian Angel." However, "Mystic Marriage" remains the preferable term, since it was a key phrase Crowley used to describe the catholic unity[3] of the two orders upon receiving the Word "Duplex." "Mystic Marriage" and "Duplex" will thus be used interchangeably.

"Duplexity" is also used to describe a canopy of research that demonstrates the intricate levels of doctrinal coherence between the A∴A∴ and the O.T.O., and seeks to discover theoretical and doctrinal insights into Thelema. These studies involve the intricate mechanics of the two orders, their respective roles and functions, as well as their shared aims and goals. Such inquiries are historical, theoretical, and philosophical.

Duplexity has become a controversial topic among some in the O.T.O. today because of its practical import. This is because it has been linked to the O.T.O. administration being in alliance with the A∴A∴ administration. As noted in chapter ten, this was announced formally over two decades ago, in 1996, with the publication of *The Equinox*, Volume IV, Number 1.

Again, the issue is not related to disagreements over O.T.O. legitimacy. Apart from a handful of disgruntled former members, there is little disagreement about the legitimacy of a singular O.T.O. administration. The same is not yet the case for the A∴A∴ at this point in the history of the Thelemic movement. As such, Duplexity has become a political concern in the ongoing debates surrounding A∴A∴ "lineages," and is perceived as divisive by those who do not agree with the O.T.O.'s policy.

This chapter will be offering a critical discussion on Duplexity, presenting a possible explanation of the O.T.O.'s decision, and speculating on the future implications.

෯ఙ

---

[3] I am indebted in part to Kjetil Fjell, who referred to the phenomenon of Duplexity as such. The word "catholic" is used to indicate its Latin usage, *catholica,* meaning "universal."

As remarked above, a true understanding of the Mystic Marriage occurs on a doctrinal level. We have already seen some historical evidence of this in chapter five, where it was shown that the O.T.O. under Crowley became a Thelemic organization intended to be grounded in the principles of *The Book of the Law*. Crowley's American period is particularly important in this regard, as his understanding of himself as Magus of the A∴A∴ coincided with his reformulation of the O.T.O. along Thelemic lines. This can be exemplified in many ways and, as we continue, numerous points will come to light.

Symbolically, an overlap of the A∴A∴ system can be found even at the initial degrees of the O.T.O. within the Man of Earth Triad. Having already passed through most of the grades of the A∴A∴ by the time he came to America in late 1914, Crowley revised the Man of Earth initiations in the years that followed. It would only make sense that his initiatory insight through the A∴A∴ system helped inform these modifications. For example, an initiate of the Man of Earth degrees can find some relevance in the 6th Æthyr of *The Vision and the Voice*, which preceded Crowley's practical involvement with the O.T.O. by three years:

> Now I perceive the Temple that is the heart of this Aethyr; it is an Urn suspended in the air, without support, above the centre of a well. And the well hath eight pillars, and a canopy above it, and without there is a circle of marble paving-stones, and without them a great outer circle of pillars.[4]

The reader will also note the connection between Crowley's discovery of the "lost word" of Freemasonry and Thelema.[5] Just as "Thelema" is numerically equivalent to 93, so too is the restored Word of Freemasonry as explained in the III° of O.T.O. This is also evident in the "First Sketch of a Qabalistic Key to *Liber AL*," wherein "III°" is given the

---

[4] 6th Æthyr, *The Vision and the Voice*, in Crowley (1998a), 195. I would like to thank Dathan Biberstein for pointing out this particular connection.

[5] See Starr (2003), 42. Crowley discussed this discovery in *Confessions* in Crowley (1969a), 705–706.

numerological equivalence to 93.[6] The same text makes a reference to "M...M," adding to 93. This phrase refers to the Word of the Neophyte in the Outer College of A∴A∴, and provides yet another example of doctrinal crossover.

Those who have experience in officiating the O.T.O. degrees may find the words of "Liber A'ash" familiar. Written in the summer of 1911, it reads, in part, "I am Baphomet, that is the Eightfold Word that shall equilibrate with the Three."[7] As Grand Master Phanes X° states, it is yet another indication that "Crowley sought to back up his involvement in O.T.O. with permission from the Chiefs of the Third Order, in particular from that adept who would later be referred [to] as the Secret Master within our Order, whose utterances are enshrined in the Holy Books."[8]

The above examples offer some idea of the Mystic Marriage of the A∴A∴ and the O.T.O. We find evidence of this throughout Crowley's publications, diaries, and letters and, in turn, it enriches Thelema's philosophy and doctrine. The Mystic Marriage has relevance on a practical level with regard to the alliance shared today. Let us examine some of the practical implications of this phenomenon.

⛤

The A∴A∴ and the O.T.O.: Administrative Attitudes, Past and Present

As outlined in chapters four and five, Crowley intended for there to be a close cooperation between the A∴A∴ and the O.T.O, and, more often than not, this was the case during his lifetime. It is evident from historical accounts that it was very uncommon for anyone to hold membership in the O.T.O. who had not already started studying the curriculum of the A∴A∴.[9] It could then be surmised that O.T.O.

---

[6] Refer to Crowley (1997), 446.

[7] "Liber A'ash" v. 18, in Crowley (1983), 208.

[8] Phanes X°, in O.T.O. (2015), 73.

[9] The members who frequented Agape Lodge, for example, were also at least the grade of Probationer in most instances. See Starr (2003).

members in Crowley's day were expected to be working the system of the A∴A∴. Today, the opposite is more likely, with a majority of active O.T.O. members not officially affiliated with the A∴A∴. The reasons for this can only be speculative. It may be due to the troubled history of the two orders since Crowley's lifetime; the varying attitudes that have been held about their relationship and respective functions, or, perhaps, the lack of historical knowledge about the movement's past. It may also be a symptom of the superficiality and laziness of modern culture.

As we saw in Part II, Karl Germer and Marcelo Motta were both uninterested in the lodge work of the O.T.O., and both thought it was unnecessary if one had connection to the A∴A∴. Grady McMurtry held a very different, and, in some ways, opposite view of the A∴A∴. His belief that the A∴A∴ is self-initiatory, and that guidance from a Superior in the Order is not necessary, seems to be a common attitude today.[10] Several popular modern authors have expressed such a sentiment, writing that any student who is serious about A∴A∴ can begin the work simply by reviewing the curriculum, starting a regimented study and practice, and following self-initiated grade work. As such, they say that any person can make "inner-plane contact" with the Secret Chiefs directly and without an instructor in the Outer College. In this model, there is no temporal authority that represents the Order apart from the Third Supreme Order of the Secret Chiefs.

J. Daniel Gunther has remarked on such opinions in a private letter to one of these authors, writing "the statement that everyone is part of the A∴A∴ is totally incorrect. It is closer to the truth to say that the A∴A∴ is part of everyone, but the converse does not apply." Gunther remarked on "inner-plane contact" by way of example:

> many celestial bodies have been discovered by amateur astrono-
> mers. However, this one result, no matter how important to the

---

10 By "popular culture" of the Thelemic movement, I refer to the available platforms that are immediately accessible, such as social media discussion forums and the books of popular Thelemic writers.

world of science as a whole, does not confer a Ph.D. or make the amateur the equal of a professional Astronomer who has undergone the disciplines and rigors of training and who has dedicated his life to that line of work [...] While it is true that [inner-plane] contact with the Order can be made in that way, it is generally true only when a student has no possibility of making contact on this plane. [...] There is a means of entrance in place and functioning.[11]

Whether or not "self-initiation" through the A∴A∴ curriculum is sufficient for the aspirant to make inner-plane contact is indeed a problematic subject. Proponents of this idea hold the optimistic view that all can attain and will naturally have the self-evaluative tools for progress at their disposal. All that will be said on this subject here is that the gross must indeed pass through fire, and that the fine are tried in intellect. These are no easy tasks, even for the cognitively gifted. For the solitary practitioner, there is no substitute for the wisdom and guidance one may be given by a Superior who has already walked the path of Initiation—and suffered its ordeals, trials and tribulations. That said, it is important to say that the idea of self-initiation is not affinitive with how the Great Order functions.

Let us return to the relationship shared between the two orders, and how this is understood by the O.T.O. today. The attitude held by the O.T.O.'s current chief, Hymenaeus Beta, places value on both systems as did Crowley. He states that the A∴A∴ and the O.T.O. are complementary programs, while being exclusive to one another in their methodology:

"While the curricula of A∴A∴ and O.T.O. interpenetrate at points, this is more by nature than design, and the exception, not the rule. The respective systems and their methods are distinct. The O.T.O. does not teach or initiate in the same sense as the

---

[11] Gunther in a private letter, March 5, 1993. UC.

A∴A∴., nor does it have a definite curricula or set examinations in most degrees."[12]

He goes on to state that the initiatory journey into the Thelemic mysteries of the two orders is unique to each individual, and the insights that are drawn from their respective systems may be slightly different, as people approach Thelema from different angles. He remarks:

> "As the true curriculum of the O.T.O. is the life of each individual, so will each initiate's curriculum be unique. Also, the texts common to the curricula of both Orders may have a different emphasis; i.e., *Book 4* is the textbook for the magical theory and practice of the O.T.O. when read from the standpoint of its initiated tradition, just as it is for the A∴A∴ when read by that Light."[13]

More recently, other leaders in the O.T.O. have elaborated on Crowley's Duplex vision. Grand Master General Shiva X° has remarked that the O.T.O. in Australia works in cooperation with the A∴A∴:

> I think AUGL has explicitly affirmed the close alliance with the A∴A∴ and made A∴A∴ both visible and accessible to our members. This has brought with it, its own Blessings—unique doctrinal insights that we teach down here. And this alliance extends to practical support. This year as you may know we are bringing out Daniel Gunther, a senior instructor of A∴A∴, for a spiritual retreat—most attendees being OTO; this will be Daniel's second visit here; and next year Grand Lodge is actively answering the call to assist the Outer College with the resources to establish a Temple here in Australia. This gets to our core mission of making Initiation into Thelema accessible and operational in Australia, and our Asia-Pacific region.[14]

---

[12] Hymenaeus Beta, "O.T.O. Curriculum," in Crowley (1997), 476.

[13] Ibid.

[14] "Interview with Shiva X°," *Oz*, No. 3, Fall 2014, 12.

In his talk "Aspiring to the Holy Order," Shiva draws on a number of key doctrinal points to demonstrate that, in fact, the two orders are one Order. The A∴A∴ working on the inner plane and the O.T.O. on the outer.

Crowley describes the A∴A∴ in a number of places as "the Great Order," while in other places he refers to it as the "Holy Order."[15] In the central ritual of the O.T.O., the Gnostic Mass, the Priestess is introduced in the script as "specially dedicated to the service of the *Great Order*."[16] Yet, it is the "Holy Order" that members of the O.TO. know and swear by in their ceremonies of initiation. Shiva raises the question of whether the "Holy Order" referred to in O.T.O. ceremonies is the same as the "Holy Order" mentioned in "Liber LXI" and *Liber Aleph*, both of which refer explicitly to the A∴A∴. He believes so, and suggests that a key to understanding this is the fact that initiates of M∴M∴M∴ are held by Oath to acquire skills that are not part of the O.T.O. curriculum, but are offered in the A∴A∴. Shiva refers to a statement in Frater Achad's *The Alpha and Omega of Initiation*, where Achad refers to the O.T.O. as a "serious manifestation of the Great Order still working in the Outer."[17] Grand Master Phanes also notes the implication that the two orders are one, particularly when one looks at the O.T.O. pledge forms upon taking initiation into M∴M∴M∴. Phanes writes that, in 1925:

---

[15] See, for example, "Liber CXI," where it reads, "for once only does the *Great Order* knock at any one door." Crowley (1983), xxxix [emphasis added]. Again, in *Confessions* Crowley refers to the A∴A∴ as "the Great Order." Crowley (1969a), 832–833. Yet, in *Liber Aleph*, Crowley continuously refers to the A∴A∴ as the "Holy Order." See, Crowley (1991c). Coincidentally, *Liber Aleph* was written at the same time that Crowley was revising all the rituals for M∴M∴M∴, giving some evidence that Crowley had in mind the Duplex relationship since he used "Holy Order" to describe both orders.

[16] "Liber XV: The Gnostic Mass," emphasis added by author.

[17] Frater Achad (2010) *The Alpha and Omega of Initiation* (Greifswald: Reineke Verlag).

Crowley adopted the name Phoenix as O.H.O. and the cartouche of Ankh-f-n-khonsu as the O.H.O. seal. It is still in use, and displayed on our pledge forms along with the winged globe staff. The latter is the well-known caduceus, and is the Chief Adept's wand, the Præmonstrator or teaching adept of the A∴A∴. It was adopted as one of the symbols of the most mystical mysteries of O.T.O., showing that the authority is derived from the superiors, who are one."[18]

Phanes goes on to stress the doctrinal importance of this, noting that Crowley was authorized by the Secret Chiefs to take charge of the O.T.O. He reminds the reader that the Law of Thelema did not originate within the O.T.O., but that by the authority of Crowley as Baphomet, the O.T.O. was incorporated under the principles of *The Book of the Law,* and its rituals and teachings were revised accordingly. Phanes concludes by asserting that such an alliance between the two orders is of the utmost significance. He writes, "Without this authority and alliance the word has left the letter of truth, and as such we are no better off than the many profaned sanctums that the Great Order has authorized in the past and which are described in 'An Account of A∴A∴.'"[19]

⚜

It was mentioned in chapter six that the relationship to the A∴A∴ takes on an extremely personal nature, primarily because it is connected to one's individual spirituality. For those who hold membership in the O.T.O., but are members of A∴A∴ groups not officially recognized by the O.T.O., the subject concerning the Duplex alliance between the two orders may be interpreted as tacitly questioning the authenticity of one's spirituality. Such approaches to the debate often end in repeated

---

[18] Phanes X° (2015), 81.

[19] Ibid., 82.

disputes over authority. It is a question concerning schism and faction-alism. As I argued before, it is equivalent to why Catholics, Lutherans, and Calvinists exist within Christianity, or Shi'ias and Sunnis in Islam.

There are, in fact, some other key factors that make Duplexity controversial. First of all, the historical lines of succession are considered by critics to be tenuous. This is particularly the case with pedigrees being linked to an already controversial figure in Thelema's history, Marcelo Motta. Secondly, the question has been raised whether Duplexity is placing Thelema into a rigid dogmatism. Such accusations can only contribute to dissonance and alienation within a group. In the following section, I will address these points.

Succession

As discussed in chapter eleven, the "A∴A∴ lineage" debate is largely based on contention about historical succession. A number of websites have surfaced attempting to legitimize the "Soror Estai Lineage" while delegitimizing any claims that Marcelo Motta had upon Karl Germer's death, and subsequently discrediting J. Daniel Gunther and William Breeze.[20] The reasoning for such claims *seem* to make sense from the perspective of their mnemohistorical narrative. Their position is further supported by quoting a letter from Germer to Motta, where Germer tells Motta, "You are a Neophyte at best!"[21] Furthermore many critics reference Motta's spiral into insanity as evidence that he was not a wor-thy successor to leadership of the A∴A∴.

Admittedly, Motta has shown himself to be a problematic character in our story. Not only did he lose the court battles over O.T.O. copyright ownership to McMurtry, he did in fact exhibit increasing psychological instability as admitted to by his students Gunther, Wasserman, and Starr. While Motta may have also lost his bid for succession in the O.T.O., and while his mental health continued to degenerate in the years leading up to and following the court battles, the story painted by

---

[20] See for example the website, "The Truth about A∴A∴ Lineages," authored by Soror 33, Frater 49, Frater 120, Soror 156-93, and Frater 888. (accessed March 8, 2018).
[21] Germer to Motta, June 9, 1962. GMC.

his critics is not altogether accurate. There are many factors surrounding his relationship to Germer and his work in helping to re-establish the A∴A∴ that need mention.

As I discussed earlier, Motta was Germer's only formal student in the A∴A∴ and the two men became very close. Much of the correspondence between them (which still remains unpublished) demonstrates Germer's interest in Motta as a devoted student of Thelema. Germer would often remark positively on Motta's depth of knowledge about Thelemic literature. It is quite clear that Motta's interest in Thelema always lay exclusively with the A∴A∴ and not the O.T.O.[22] As historical documents show, Motta's claim to leadership in A∴A∴ was not contested at first, even by Phyllis Seckler. Despite her own ambitions and motives, she considered Motta heir to Germer and to the Thelemic library in letters prior to 1976, going so far as to recognize his claim to being Præmonstrator.[23] As James Wasserman points out, her contention began only after the battle over copyrights started in July of 1976.[24] It was later still that she wrote to Wasserman, "Frankly, I am quite convinced that Motta is not what he says he is and that his claims are spurious."[25]

Although one of the main ways critics attempt to invalidate Motta is to cite his evident mental instability, the reader must bear in mind that we are speaking about magical personalities and the agitating effects of Initiation. The reader will recall that Motta admitted in a letter to Wasserman in 1974 that he took the Oath of the Abyss,[26] and that this process may have been encouraged by Germer as early as 1957.[27] As Crowley once stated: "Now the rule is that if you claim to be 8°=3□, you are 8°=3□! And God help you! You accept the conditions. If there

---

[22] See Motta (1962).

[23] Referenced earlier in a letter from Seckler to Motta, April 19, 1976, SWC.

[24] See Wasserman (2012), 210.

[25] Seckler to Wasserman, September 24, 1976. SWC.

[26] "I underwent the Crossing of the Abyss, first on the emotional, then on the intellectual plane. Since then, Communication has occurred in a rather different manner." Motta to Wasserman, August 14, 1974. SWC.

[27] See chapter seven, letter from Germer to Motta, February 10, 1957. GMC.

is one drop of your blood that has not gone into the cup of 156, it corrupts the whole man."[28]

History has shown us many examples of the danger which the Great Oath can bring upon the initiate. Charles Stansfeld Jones, Wilfred T. Smith, and Jack Parsons were all living examples of just how treacherous that point of the journey can be. In Motta's case, it is quite possible this step is what inevitably led him to ruin. In what was an example of shining brilliance, discipline, and mastery in Thelema—as exhibited in his writings before that fateful summer of 1976—Motta's Initiation may have brought him to the end roads of tragedy. James Wasserman, who was well-acquainted with Motta, admitted in his memoir that despite Motta's dedication to, and erudite knowledge of, Thelema, "I believe he died a fallen adept in August of 1987."[29]

Yet, Motta, like many of the other figures who struggled with the Great Oath, is someone from whom we can learn. But Motta was also, as Wasserman points out, an example of the "Worthy Opponent." He forced the O.T.O. to get its act together, "to prove that we were the real O.T.O."[30] Is it not possible that Motta's loss of the legal case to a thoroughly reformed O.T.O. (because it had successfully responded to the threat he posed) may serve as the most subtle example of Duplexity in action?

As already demonstrated in chapter eleven, Phyllis Seckler's line to Crowley is even more tenuous. It is not clear when she became a Probationer under Jane Wolfe, the latter whom Crowley apparently advanced to Neophyte as an afterthought years later. Likewise, Phyllis admitted to not having worked the grade system until after she met James Eshelman. As it was shown earlier, the entire narrative is questionable.

It is the opinion of the author that succession should be measured with regard to the appointed leaders. Hymenaeus Beta was appointed unanimously by all the IX° members of the O.T.O. (i.e., those who

---

[28] Quoted from an undated note in the H.P. Smith Papers, ca. 1943. Quoted in Starr (2003), 50.

[29] Wasserman (2012), 211.

[30] Wasserman (2012), 209.

had been acknowledged to hold that degree by Hymenaeus Alpha). As O.H.O., H.B. participated in reconstituting the A∴A∴. The legitimacy of the officers must also be judged by the merits of their work. As Crowley described it, the work of the A∴A∴ is such "that when people become ripe, they are joined to the chain."[31] Attainment, then is demonstrated by the fruit of one's labors, forming a link in the "Catena" of transmission—a term to which we shall return.

Dogmatism

Another critique of the Duplexity argument is whether Thelema is becoming dogmatic and the O.T.O. is aligning itself within a confined set of teachings. On a surface level, this might seem to be a credible concern. The Class A Comment of 1925 (the "Tunis" or "Short Comment") is sometimes cited as a point of contention to Duplexity. Critics call attention to the apparent dogmatism which they say is implied by the concept. Crowley wrote in The Comment to *The Book of the Law*, "Those who discuss the contents of this Book are to be shunned by all, as centres of pestilence. All questions of the Law are to be decided only by appeal to my writings, each for himself."[32] Thus, no single interpretation of *The Book of the Law* can be claimed authoritatively, outside the word of The Master Therion. However, the "Preface" to *The Holy Books of Thelema* (1983) describes it thus:

> [The Comment] refers to the commentators that would otherwise revise and distort the original message of *Liber Legis* to their own ends, forming "schools of interpretation" with the conformist pressures and tendencies to schism that inevitably follow. *The Comment* warns against the dissemination of personal interpretations of the book, thus establishing a scriptural tradition resistant to the revisionism that plagued previous religions and mystery

---

31 Aleister Crowley to Charles Stansfeld Jones, February 7, 1919. CSJ Papers, O.T.O. Archives.

32 See Crowley (1983), 196.

schools. Yet it places supreme emphasis upon individual freedom of interpretation [...][33]

The Comment is of supreme importance for Thelema, because religious groups always run the risk of becoming obstinate and dictatorial. It is important that the interpretation of the foundational text of a religious movement be left to the individual. However, an authoritative claim in the interpretation of *The Book of the Law*—or for that matter any "A∴A∴ Publication in Class A"—and the expounding upon the large literary estate of Crowley with thoroughly-researched and well-argued theses is vastly different.[34] The editorial work of Hymenaeus Beta and the theological research present in Gunther's work can hardly be considered a prohibited commentary on the Class A literature.

It is also pertinent to clarify that membership or advancement in the O.T.O. has never been contingent on one's affiliation with the A∴A∴, or even affiliation with any claimant group referring to itself as A∴A∴. Treasurer General of O.T.O. Vere Chappell recently confirmed this:

> I would like to reaffirm for the record that being an aspirant to the A∴A∴ is not a requirement for O.T.O. advancement or appointment to office, at any level or in any Grand Lodge or O.T.O. International. Furthermore, membership in organizations using the name A∴A∴ which are not officially recognized as such by O.T.O. is not a bar to advancement or appointment to office in O.T.O., at any level or in any Grand Lodge or O.T.O. International.[35]

---

[33] Crowley (1983), viii–ix.

[34] The recent "Kill/Fill" debate is noteworthy. H.B.'s comment on this can be found at "Essay on Liber Legis" on the O.T.O. International website (http://oto.org/legis.html, accessed April 5, 2018), and a critique of the change can be found in Marlene Cornelius and R.L. Gillis (2013) *Liber AL: An Examination* (Berkeley: Conjoined Creations).

[35] Vere Chappell, "Official Ordo Templi Orientis – O.T.O. Facebook Group," January 29, 2018.

It may aid the reader to repeat Hymenaeus Beta's assertion that "the O.T.O. is a crucible for the development of the social model necessary to a Thelemic *culture*, as opposed to a Thelemic *cult*."[36] That is, the O.T.O. aims to formulate a society of individuals based on Thelemic values, not to establish a society of mindless acolytes.

Alienation

The last point of critique to address is the proclivity towards alienation among some in the O.T.O., given its closer alliance with the A∴A∴. One O.T.O. member expressed concern that his affiliation within the Order may be usurped by an entirely different organization. He wrote, "As I am NO flavor of A∴A∴, I resent tremendously the implications that my membership and my work here in the O.T.O. is solely to pay the way for a group that I am not directly affiliated with in any way."[37] Statements like these derive from the misinformed opinion that O.T.O. is somehow subsidizing A∴A∴ activities. The A∴A∴ charges no dues and accepts no monetary income, being an organization that is solely spiritual in nature. This edict is as true today as it was in Crowley's lifetime.[38]

Following Grand Master Sabazius X°'s official statement on O.T.O.'s stance regarding A∴A∴, another more seasoned member in the O.T.O. said, "I'm not an A∴A∴ member, so I have no personal dog in this fight. But this topic has been creating a lot of disharmony between Brethren, and I believe any public stance at all will end up ultimately helpful."[39]

It is the opinion of the author that alienation from the O.T.O. as

---

[36] Hymenaeus Beta, in O.T.O. (1990), 10.

[37] Facebook user, December 18, 2014.

[38] In some cases, where expenses are incurred, such as for Temple equipment, funds are raised directly from A∴A∴ members. It could be asserted that since O.T.O. owns the copyrights to Crowley's literary legacy (which includes the A∴A∴ materials), the money acquired from these publications actually helps fund the O.T.O., in the form of royalties for example.

[39] Facebook user, July 18, 2015.

a result of its alliance with A∴A∴ is unfortunate. There is really no easy solution to this problem if cooperation between the two orders is rejected on a significant scale. It will be a decision that individuals must make for themselves: whether they continue to work with the O.T.O. administration and remain active, or to resign for this or other reasons.

⛤

Given the tumultuous history of the O.T.O., the battles for succession in the past, the subsequent re-establishment of the Order, and its relative success following all of these events, O.T.O. members must ask themselves: what has caused events to transpire in the way that they have? It is arguable that, had the O.T.O. made a few different turns, it would be much different today. Had Motta been in closer proximity to Sascha Germer when she invited him to visit after Karl Germer's death, he may have secured the library for himself. Had William Breeze not been nominated by Helen Parsons Smith shortly before the election for O.H.O., the O.H.O. may have been Bill Heidrick or James Eshelman. Had Eshelman, as nominated by Phyllis Seckler, been elected, the Secret Chiefs might have been seen as "choosing" Seckler's "line" to take charge of the A∴A∴ and the O.T.O. Yet, it was not Eshelman who was elected. Rather, Breeze assumed the burden of raising the O.T.O. to greater heights, of reconstituting the A∴A∴, and of re-establishing the two orders in the tradition that Crowley originally envisioned.

The secular, academic argument would state that this was all simply a matter of small-group politics. However, if the reader chooses to assume that the Secret Chiefs continue to guide the Great Work of Thelema, then it must be considered that "They," or perhaps V.V.V.V.V., chose the person best suited at the right time to lead the two orders.

Hymenaeus Beta once described the instructional model he believes the Secret Chiefs acted upon. By way of analogy, using a diagram of the Harvard architecture of microprocessing design which specifies that instructions and data must be kept separate,[40] the Frater

---

[40] It is discussed at https://en.wikipedia.org/wiki/Harvard_architecture (accessed August 1, 2018).

Superior described the A∴A∴ as the set of spiritual instructions sent to the O.T.O., which represents the memory data, i.e., the practical implementation in history. "A∴A∴ are the instructions. We [O.T.O.] get the instructions from the Secret Chiefs [...] They vouchsafed them to Crowley but we have been entrusted as his successors."[41]

With this in mind, the above lends itself to Crowley's original idea of "Catena." As one Sovereign Grand Inspector General of O.T.O. has noted:

> I have long held that the notion of lineages is deeply problematic and (if you excuse my usage of the word) unconstitutional as far as the A∴A∴ goes. As H.B. [Hymenaeus Beta] notes concerning the fallacious notion of the Bishopric lineages, it is not your spiritual pedigrees that grants authority in Thelema, it is one's work and the fruit that is the witness thereof. From the beginning, the A∴A∴ was never meant to be organized as a lineage wherein members trace their spiritual pedigree back to one of the founding three of the Order.
>
> Rather, the inaugural word of the Equinox that marked its reconstitution in the Outer [was] CATENA, or chain [...] Consequently as I have always maintained, the Order was always from the beginning organized as a Chain of brethren from the highest to the lowest, going back to V.V.V.V.V. as the chain of the old systems are falling away from you.[42]

"Catena" indicates a line of transmission rather than concern for temporal origin, or, more parochially, a "paper trail" back to Crowley. Much more important to revealing the chain of transmission is the fruit of the Work being produced by aspirants to the A∴A∴. The question left to the reader is: who has been shown to produce work of a significant caliber?

---

[41] "One Hundred Years of the O.T.O. in North America: Inspirations and Lessons."

[42] Kjetil Fjell, June 21, 2015.

Breeze's contribution to the Thelemic movement has already been described at some length. As Grand Master General Shiva has remarked, Hymenaeus Beta has "raised high the roof beam of Ordo Templi Orientis, gradually (you could say silently) transforming it from countercultural fringe to the worldwide social laboratory, literary estate, and research institute that it is today."[43]

Grand Master Shiva similarly remarks on J. Daniel Gunther's contribution to Thelema with regard to the A∴A∴:

"He just said to me one day on his first Australian visit that we should go and 'light a fire in the East together.' So, with our close Brother Hiroyuki-san and the good brethren of Japan, we organized some joint lectures in the East. In Tokyo, to be precise. And we lit a fire! It was during that process that the whole Duplexity thing came down and we both lectured about that from the distinct perspectives of the O.T.O. and the A∴A∴."[44]

Gunther expresses a great deal of enthusiasm going forward:

"I never thought that in my lifetime I would be invited to the Land of the Rising Sun, Japan to give lectures on Thelema. I saw that as a harbinger of things to come, that there are no borders. It is up to us to produce our work, and produce it in a scholarly way, a scientific way, an intelligent way, and also in a way that is keeping with the doctrine that we have embraced. I think what we see now is a period of great success before us."[45]

⛤

---

[43] Shiva X°, in O.T.O. (2015), 13.

[44] "Interview with the Shiva X°," *OZ*, No. 3, Fall 2014, 13.

[45] J. Daniel Gunther, "The Revival of Thelema," Episode 4, White Rabbit Podcast (accessed March 8, 2018).

Some Closing Thoughts on Duplexity

It should be clear by now that Crowley intended the O.T.O. to be the social engine for Thelema; and that, at least from October of 1915 onward, the O.T.O.'s mission was to promulgate and establish the Law of Thelema in the world, as set forth by the Secret Chiefs. By 1919, with the publication of *The Blue Equinox*, both the A∴A∴ and the O.T.O. were expounded upon and dually promoted. In terms of succession, it is more important to understand what was intended by Crowley receiving the word "Catena" in spring of 1907, when the A∴A∴ was announced. We must seek within the Thelemic community for a sufficient caliber of work being produced by its leadership.

As should also be clear, the "problem" of Duplexity is one that only exists within the O.T.O. Those who are affiliated with other A∴A∴ groups—who do not hold membership in the O.T.O.—have less of a conflict of interest in this regard.

I believe the existence of a unified administrative structure in both orders is crucial. As Frater AISh MLChMH points out, "the O.T.O. would not recognize duplicate copies of the A∴A∴ any more than it would recognize duplicate copies of itself."[46] One Thelemite pointed out on a social media thread that the point of contention in the lineage debate is whether "the structure of A∴A∴ admits the possibility of there being two living, spatiotemporal heads who are hierarchically disconnected from one another."[47] This begs the question that if the so-called "lineage groups" would effectively consolidate their respective efforts under the rubric set forth by the current A∴A∴ administration, could the issue be resolved at long last?

There is a further insight into the doctrine of Duplexity when we consider the weapon of the Imperator, the phoenix wand or Egyptian *uas* sceptre. We again refer the reader to the discussion in chapter four, but add here that the *uas* sceptre was traditionally attributed to the Egyptian god Set and later morphed into the phoenix-headed wand. Grand Master Phanes X° writes, "Crowley would make a connection

---

[46] AISh MLChMH (2004), 11.

[47] Facebook user, December 16, 2014.

between Set and Baphomet, stating that, 'this again is connected with the wild ass of the wilderness, the god Set [...]'"[48] That the seal of Ankh-f-n-khonsu—the ring of whom is traditionally worn by the Imperator—is affixed to each applicant's paperwork in M∴M∴M∴ is another point for consideration, as is the fact that the winged globe staff of the Præmonstrator accompanies this seal.

It is necessary to keep in mind that the administrative consideration I have put forth about the identity of the Imperator and the O.H.O. is a theoretical construct based on Crowley's example. It has only recently been re-established:

> It is important to underline that we are speaking on an archetypal plane, which needs to readjust itself from time to time upon incarnation, according to circumstances. The former Imperator, Marcelo Motta, was never O.H.O., nor did past Frater Superior Grady McMurtry hold authority with the A∴A∴. But this archetypal template is at work and I believe the doctrinal and practical importance of this is of an immense proportion, as it stresses that the true authority of O.T.O. rests on the authority that Crowley gained from the Secret Chiefs.[49]

From an administrative point of view, the alliance between our two orders is critical. Again quoting Phanes X°, "We [the O.T.O.] know how to manage cash flow, furniture, and real estate; the A∴A∴ system does not include this, and this is one of the many reasons why the Prophet endowed us with an invaluable resource, his literary legacy."[50] This leads us back to the spiritual consideration discussed in chapter six. The A∴A∴ needs the O.T.O.'s assistance to promulgate Thelema, just as the O.T.O. relies on the A∴A∴ for its Word of Truth.

---

[48] Phanes X° (2015), 78.

[49] Ibid., 82.

[50] Ibid., 83.

CHAPTER FOURTEEN

The Ecclesia Gnostica Catholica and the Gnostic Mass

Virtue through the Sacrament of the Mass of the Holy Ghost

Human nature demands (in the case of most people) the satisfaction of the religious instinct, and, to very many, this may best be done by ceremonial means.

—Aleister Crowley, *Confessions*

THE ECCLESIA GNOSTICA CATHOLICA, or Gnostic Catholic Church (herein referred to as the E.G.C.) has a long history, being rooted in the French Gnostic Revival of the nineteenth century and making its way into Thelema via the O.T.O. Today, the E.G.C. serves as one of the fundamental ways in which Thelema can be introduced to the public, primarily through the performance of the church's central rite, the Gnostic Mass. With regard to Thelema, the E.G.C. was first established as the "Church of Thelema" in the 1930s by Agape Lodge Master Wilfred T. Smith. Very little E.G.C. activity occurred in the interregnum years until it was reignited by Grady McMurtry in the late 1970s. The E.G.C. has taken a much larger role since the 1990s, expanding its rites to include marriage ceremonies, last rites, and other sacramental activities. It has a novitiate program that trains clergy in the Mass, and in some parts of the world it offers workshops such as "Pastoral Counseling."

We will review the E.G.C. as the ecclesiastical branch of Thelema. It will be shown that its enterprises are of a communal and unifying nature: encouraging cooperative participation from O.T.O. members; promoting the truths of A∴A∴ in the public domain with its sacramental mysteries; and facilitating community and social harmony through its activities. Whereas membership in the A∴A∴ is asocial, and membership in the O.T.O. is confined to dues-paying initiates, the E.G.C. offers lay membership to the public by administering baptism and confirmation ceremonies. Let us begin with a historical overview of the E.G.C.

The Gnostic Church: A Brief History[1]

The Gnostic Church can be traced back to the milieu known as the "French Occult Revival."[2] The Church's founder was the nineteenth century spiritualist and Grand Orient Freemason, Jules-Benoît Doinel du Val-Michel (1842–1903). Before the establishment of the Gnostic Church, Doinel had been involved in a number of occult circles, engaging in activities such as spiritualism and the Swendenborgian Church. His masonic activities began in 1884. In 1885, he was initiated a Master Mason with the encouragement of Albert Pike.[3] He became Worshipful Master of Orléans Lodge in 1892, and entered the Rose-Croix a year later in the Parisian chapter, "L'Étoile Polaire."

It was through a series of séances held in 1889 at the home of Lady Caithness (1830–1895)[4] that the Gnostic Church began to take

---

[1] A history of the Gnostic Catholic Church has been examined in some depth by United States Grand Master General Sabazius X° in *Mystery of Mystery*. This synopsis is but a summary of Sabazius' well-recounted history. His authoritative essay is recommended to the reader for a more detailed analysis. It can be found in Ordo Templi Orientis (2014) *Mystery of Mystery: A Primer of Thelemic Ecclesiastical Gnosticism* (Berkeley: O.T.O.).

[2] In English, see Christopher McIntosh (1972) *Éliphas Lévi and the French Occult Revival* (London: Rider & Co.) and Tobias Churton (2016) *Occult Paris: The Lost Magic of the Belle Époque* (Rochester: Inner Traditions). There is another, more difficult, text on the subject in French, Jean-Pierre Laurants (1992) *L'ésotérisme chrétien en France au XIXe siècle* (Lausanne: L'Age d'Homme).

[3] Ladislaus Toth, "Gnostic Church" in Hanegraaff (ed.) (2006) *Dictionary of Gnosis & Western Esotericism* (Leiden: Brill), 401.

[4] Maria de Mariategui, or Marie Sinclair, Countess of Caithness, was an aristocratic supporter of spiritualism, Theosophy, and occultism in the *fin-de-siècle* of the nine-

shape for Doinel. He believed he had contacted a number of figures from the Gnostic tradition. Noteworthy here is Guihabert de Castres, a twelfth century Cathar Bishop of Toulouse, who instructed Doinel to re-establish the Gnostic doctrine. Doinel soon setup the Nouvelle Église Gnostique Universelle (New Universal Gnostic Church); its assembly was made up of presiding male Bishops and female "Sophias." The Gnostic Church would aim to be a spiritually elite group, tying itself to Freemasonry and eventually Martinism, the latter organization becoming intrinsically tied to the Gnostic Church after Papus (Gerard Encausse, 1865–1916) was consecrated Bishop.[5] The Gnostic Church, then, was a blend of the Gnostic doctrines of Simon Magus and Valentinus, and the mysticism of Freemasonry and Martinism.

A propaganda campaign against esotericism advanced by Gabriel-Antoine Jogand-Pages in 1881 resulted in negative attention being

---

teenth century. Described by historian Joscelyn Godwin as a "remarkable woman who quarrelled with no one, not even the Roman Catholic Church, who fraternized with French socialists and English peers, believed in esoteric Buddhism and in esoteric Christianity, entertained mediums and cardinals [...]" She served as a financial support to many esoteric groups of this period, placing her as an important female figure in Western esotericism. She contributed writings to the Theosophical Society and later befriended Anna Kingsford (1846–1888) and Edward Maitland (1824–1897), who formed the Hermetic Society (1884–1887). Marco Pasi has recently noted in his lecture, "Liquid Magic: Materials Towards a Cultural History of Bodily Fluids," delivered at the Academica Ordo Templi Orientis Conference in Ascona, Switzerland, August 26, 2017 that Lady Caithness was involved in the development of sexual magic, pointing to her *L'Ouverture des Sceaux*. Pasi has shown that Caithness' work is evidence of sexual magical writings in the nineteenth century which predate even the occultism of Paschal Beverley Randolph, often believed to be one of the pioneers on the subject. See Toth in Hanegraaff (2006) above and Joscelyn Godwin (1994), 304–305 and 338–339.

[5] Originating in 1740 by Martinez de Pasqually (d. 1774), Louis Claude de Saint-Martin (1743–1803) and later Papus, Martinism is an esoteric form of Christian mysticism that was developed through currents of the aforementioned French gnostic revival and high-grade Freemasonry. Its teachings therefore find affinity with Freemasonry, Illuminism, and Rosicrucianism. See Jean-François Var, "Martinism: First Period" and Massimo Introvigne, "Martinism: Second Period," in Hanegraaff (2006), 770–783.

directed towards the Gnostic Church, and Doinel in turn defected. Leonce-Éugène Fabres des Essarts was then elected Patriarch by the Synod of Bishops in 1886. In 1901, Fabres des Essarts consecrated Jean Bricaud (1881–1934), who would break from the Gnostic Church in 1907 to form the l'Église Catholique Gnostique (Gnostic Catholic Church), along with Encausse and Louis-Sophrone Fugairon (b. 1846). In 1908, at the "International Masonic and Spiritualist Conference," Theodor Reuss presented Encausse with a charter to establish a "Supreme Grand Council General of the Unified Rites of Antient and Primitive Masonry for the Grand Orient of France and Dependencies in Paris." Reuss would subsequently gain episcopal authority in the Gnostic Catholic Church from Encausse. The Church eventually branched into other variations, including l'Église Gnostique de France (via Fabres des Essarts), l'Église Gnostique Universelle (via Encausse and Brichaud), and later l'Église Gnostique Apostolique, headed by Robert Ambelain.

Pertinent to the present discussion is the development of the Gnostic Catholic Church in Thelema. Aleister Crowley received consecration as a Bishop of E.G.C. through Reuss in 1910 when he was conferred the VII° of O.T.O. Crowley wrote the Gnostic Mass three years later, in 1913, in Moscow, and he performed parts of it in Cefalù. The first known full public performance of the Gnostic Mass was held at Agape Lodge on Sunday, March 19, 1933, at 1746 Winona Blvd. in Hollywood, California. Wilfred T. Smith officiated as Priest, Regina Kahl as Priestess, and Oliver Jacobi as Deacon. Crowley was delighted with the news and even told Smith at the time to "not bother with the O.T.O. stuff: You ought to concentrate absolutely on the Mass."[6] The Gnostic Mass, also called "Liber XV," thence became a regular performance at Agape Lodge. After Crowley's death in 1947, and the subsequent dissolution of Agape Lodge, the performance of the Mass ceased almost entirely, except for Herman Metzger's O.T.O. group in Switzerland. When the O.T.O. was revived by Grady McMurtry, the Gnostic Mass was performed again for the first time in July of 1977.

Grand Master Sabazius X° notes:

---

6 Crowley to Smith, undated (ca. April 1933), quoted in Starr (2003), 194.

"When Hymenaeus Beta took office, he perceived that the divergence of the paths of E.G.C. and O.T.O. would ultimately be unhealthy for the development of Thelema. The O.T.O. required the focus and open social structure provided by the regular celebration of the *Gnostic Mass*, and the E.G.C. required the perspective and esoteric teachings of the O.T.O. initiatory system."[7]

In 1987, bylaws were established within the O.T.O. to define "Ecclesiastical Membership," which included consecrated Bishops of the E.G.C. In 1991, more policies were instituted to add ordained Priests, Priestesses, and Deacons in Ecclesiastical Membership. These required Deacons to hold at least the II° in O.T.O. membership, and Priests and Priestesses to be K.E.W. (Knight of the East and West). The E.G.C. has since undergone a great deal of development in its rites and the clerical services offered to laity. Sabazius has helped in the development of the church, and has placed the E.G.C. as part and parcel of activities of the O.T.O. in the United States, while other Kingdoms and O.T.O. International have adopted similar models.

Structure of the E.G.C. and its Functions

The structure of the E.G.C. is loosely modeled along a traditional administrative episcopate. The Frater (or Soror) Superior of the O.T.O. (the O.H.O.) is the Patriarch (or Matriarch) of the Church. The Grand Master Generals of the O.T.O. preside over their Kingdoms as Primates of the Church. The E.G.C. Bishops act as the Episcopate, overseeing church activities. Bishops are representatives of the Primate (or Patriarch in areas absent a Primate), administering ordinations of clergy in the priesthood and diaconate, and performing sacramental rites such as baptism and confirmation. One is consecrated a Bishop in the E.G.C. upon being conferred the VII° of O.T.O. and becoming a Sovereign Grand Inspector General (SGIG). In the O.T.O., an SGIG acts as an administrative assistant to the Supreme and Holy King, so there is an implicit overlap between the O.T.O. and the E.G.C.

---

[7] Sabazius X°, "The History of the Gnostic Catholic Church," in O.T.O. (2014), 13.

The Priesthood is composed of Priestesses and Priests. These individuals act as representatives of the church and may be delegated clerical responsibilities under the supervision of a Bishop. The diaconate will assist the priesthood. Both the priesthood and diaconate are required to have held membership within the E.G.C. as laity prior to their ordination. According to current E.G.C. policy under United States Grand Lodge, members of the diaconate are not considered official representatives of the E.G.C.[8] The novitiate are lay members of the church and initiate members of the O.T.O. who wish to undergo training as clergy under the supervision of a Bishop. Finally, laity members are conferred through the ceremonies of baptism and confirmation in the E.G.C.

Functionally speaking, the E.G.C. operates differently in comparison to the traditional mainstream understanding of clerical church services. As Sabazius points out, the Roman Catholic Church is traditionally understood as performing its rites miraculously. For example, the Catholic Mass is based on faith in the Grace of God for its efficacy. In this traditional sense, the priesthood is an intermediary between God and the congregants, and it is only through him, and the powers invested in him through the church (i.e., from its Cardinals, Bishops, and Pope), that the sacraments can be effectively administered to the congregation. In distinction, the function of the E.G.C. is *Gnostic*. This means that clergy are not the sole arbiters of religious experience, but "teachers, facilitators and counselors [...] to see that the rituals are 'rightly performed with joy & beauty.'"[9] As a Gnostic Church, the E.G.C. seeks primarily to bring its congregants into direct personal experience with the divine, rather than ask its congregation for their faith in sacerdotal rites. Similar to a traditional church, this is primarily performed through the administering of sacraments.

According to Sabazius, sacraments are the "specific religious rites used by a church in the activation, maintenance, and nurturing

---

[8] The USGL diaconate policy is under review as this book heads to press.

[9] Sabazius X°, "The Role and Function of Thelemic Clergy in Ecclesia Gnostica Catholica," in O.T.O. (2014), 280.

of the spiritual community."[10] The E.G.C. currently administers seven different sacraments, attributed Qabalistically by Sabazius to the seven traditional planets of astrology: (1) Baptism (Moon), (2) Confirmation (Mercury), (3) Marriage (Venus), (4) Ordination (Sun), (5) Will (Mars), (6) the Eucharist (Jupiter), and (7) Last Rites (Saturn).[11] Marriage and Last Rites need no explanation. Baptism and Confirmation are voluntary rites offered to the laity, while Ordination concerns clergy. "Will" may be considered the Thelemic equivalent of saying "Grace" before meals, yet it is distinguished by the fact that it is an affirmation of one's intentions to fortify oneself with nourishment and sustenance. Of particular concern for this chapter is the sacrament of the Eucharist, also known as the "Mass of the Holy Ghost." It may be performed in any number of ways by an individual Thelemite. This rite is best known, however, through "The Gnostic Mass," to which we turn our attention.

꓿꓿

Liber XV: The Gnostic Mass

Crowley unambiguously defines the place of the Gnostic Mass in the O.T.O. as "the central ritual of its public and private celebration."[12] Written in Moscow in 1913, and inspired by the Eastern Orthodox Mass, Crowley later recalled that he had wished to devise a ritual, "through which people might enter into ecstasy as they have always done under the influence of appropriate ritual." He continued, "I resolved that my Ritual should celebrate the sublimity of the operation of universal forces without introducing disputable metaphysical theories."[13] The Mass is the central ceremony of the E.G.C. because it displays in dramatic form the mysteries of Thelema. By "mysteries

---

[10] Ibid., 283.

[11] See Ibid., 291–295.

[12] Crowley (1969a), 714.

[13] Crowley (1969a), 713.

of Thelema," I am referring to both the systems of the O.T.O. and the A∴A∴. In this sense, the Gnostic Mass can be seen as the single most important example of Duplexity, and the bridge between the two orders. However, it is first important to review what the Mass exhibits on a fundamental level, esoterically speaking. We must, therefore, look closer at the operation of the Mass of the Holy Ghost, its process known as the Rose and Cross, and its result, which is the *Hieros Gamos*, or "Holy Marriage."

The Mass of the Holy Ghost, the Rose and Cross, and the Hieros Gamos

The Mass of the Holy Ghost is discussed by Crowley most openly in *Magick in Theory and Practice,* in the chapter entitled "Of the Eucharist; and of the Art of Alchemy."[14] He describes the operation as "the simplest and most complete of magick ceremonies."[15] The Mass can be understood plainly as a transmutative operation of alchemy. The individual practitioner, then, is the *prima materia*, and the Mass of the Holy Ghost is the procedure which transforms the basic material into "gold." The success of this operation requires that the elements in the ceremony be consecrated as talismans and prepared as a eucharist, whereby the practitioner takes "a substance symbolic of the whole course of Nature, make[s] it God, and consume[s] it."[16]

The Mass of the Holy Ghost itself is comprised of a number of rites that are enacted through the formula of the Rose and Cross.[17] The

---

[14] In Crowley (1997), 267–274.

[15] Ibid., 267.

[16] Ibid.

[17] The reader should note that the Mass of the Holy Ghost and its formula, the Rose and Cross, encompass an entire canon of magical operations. Some of these rites are intended as an "act of creation" to produce a "magical child" and others are reserved for different aims: the consecration of talismans, spiritual health and rejuvenation, or the redistribution of magical force. That said, the reader should not mistake more specific magical formulae, such as Tetragrammaton, as being distinct from the Rose Cross; rather, Tetragrammaton is one of many ways in which the Rose and Cross formula is implemented to successfully perform the Mass of the Holy Ghost. For the names of the rites that make up the canon, see Gunther (2014), 61.

primary operation of the Mass is the "Rite of the Lion and the Eagle." It is this rite that we are concerned with presently, as it is displayed in dramatic form in "Liber XV, The Gnostic Mass." To put it simply, this operation celebrates the two fundamental and universal elements of nature that are necessary for the generation of life, the spermatozoon and the egg. These principles symbolize essential aspects and are represented by the motif of the *mysterium oppositorum* (the mystery of opposition): *yin* and *yang, lingam* and *yoni,* and rose and cross, among other examples. Though contrasting by nature, the respective qualities of the Lion and Eagle are necessary ingredients. When combined, they are the recipe for creation. In short, the Rite of the Lion and the Eagle is a basic function of our world, the interplay of polarities actively partaking in the creative force of the universe.

The execution of the Mass of the Holy Ghost is localized in a set of component parts known as a magical formula. Like a chemical formula or a mathematical formula, a magical formula consists of elemental parts that interact with one another and produce results according to a set of specific parameters. In Crowley's definition of "Magick," the "Science and Art of causing Change to occur in conformity with Will," he illustrates this with the postulate of the magical formula, noting, "Any required Change may be effected by the application of the proper kind and degree of Force in the proper manner through the proper medium to the proper object." He continues:

> I wish to prepare an ounce of chloride of gold. I must take the right kind of acid, nitrohydrochloric and no other, in sufficient quantity and of the adequate strength, and place it, in a vessel which will not break, leak, or corrode, in such a manner as will produce undesirable results, with the necessary quantity of Gold; and so forth. Every Change has its own conditions.[18]

An example of the use of the magical formula of the Gnostic Mass is given by Archbishop of E.G.C. and Deputy Grand Master of the United States Grand Lodge of O.T.O. Lon Milo DuQuette and his

---

[18] *Magick in Theory and Practice,* "Introduction," in Crowley (1997), 126.

wife and E.G.C. Bishop, Constance DuQuette. In their lecture series "The Miracle of the Mass," they note that the Supreme Secret of the O.T.O., which is housed in the Sovereign Sanctuary of the Gnosis in the IX°, is exemplified in dramatic ritual form in the Gnostic Mass. As Crowley alludes to in his writings, Lon and Constance remark that the Secret is an operation of nature itself. In the Gnostic Mass, the ritual is performed and the operation is accomplished by one Priest and one Priestess. They compare the various elements of the ceremony to the ingredients that make up the recipe of an apple pie. "If you don't follow the essentials of the recipe, it won't be an apple pie, and if you don't follow the essentials of Liber XV, it won't be a Gnostic Mass."[19]

This is the nature of a magical formula in theory. If the practitioner properly applies the necessary components to the magical formula, then a certain result will be achieved. In terms of the Mass of the Holy Ghost, it is through the processes of purification, consecration, and invocation that the Priest and Priestess of the Gnostic Mass (i.e., the Lion and Eagle) produce a *conjunctio* through their interaction. By contributing their respective elements, they produce a "child," a eucharistic sacrament which will fortify the spiritual well-being of the congregation. The result of the operation is the Eucharist itself, the *Hieros Gamos,* or "Holy Marriage." It represents many things. On a spiritual level, it is the marriage between Earth and Heaven, and the aspirant with the Holy Guardian Angel. Quite literally, it is the spermatozoon and egg which produces flesh and blood, life and human consciousness. This result of the Lion and the Eagle is the production of the Mercurial Serpent, the Holy Spirit, or the Holy Ghost; that is, it is the essence of the divine which can be awakened and realized in the individual. This is the central mystery of creation that is displayed in dramatic form in "Liber XV."

The above description is but a brief overview of the operation. This rudimentary glance however should provide the reader with enough information to grasp the ensuing discussion on the Gnostic Mass. It

---

19 Lon Milo and Constance DuQuette, "The Miracle of the Mass, Part II," on The Speech in the Silence Podcast, Episode 15.

should be noted that the technique needed to perform the operation successfully—that of the formula of the Rose and Cross—is taught in both the O.T.O. and the A∴A∴. Within the O.T.O., initiates are introduced to this in theory even at the entering degree of Minerval (0°). Initiates are presented with it more clearly at the degree of the Sovereign Prince(ss) of the Rose Croix in the V°. The full disclosure of the technique and the method of putting it into practice is reserved for initiates of the Sovereign Sanctuary of the Gnosis in the IX°.

Aspirants to the A∴A∴ are introduced to the formula of the Rose and Cross at the grade of Zelator (2°=9□). This is because Zelators are expected to begin equilibrating themselves in Yesod on the Tree of Life, establishing their foundation upon *The Book of the Law*, and beginning to discipline and control their bodies and minds with yoga. Gaining awareness of the subtle mechanisms of consciousness and movement is imperative at this stage, for the aspirant will have to be prepared to withstand the experience of the Holy Guardian Angel, and the temple (the body) must be sufficiently strong and cleansed. It is further necessary to begin disciplining the body so as to be able to efficiently perform the technique of the Mass of the Holy Ghost when the aspirant is conferred the title of Dominus Liminis, at which stage the practical application of the Rose Cross is taught. The Dominus Liminis is expected to work the method of the Rose and Cross and perform it regularly. By consolidating all they have learned in the Outer College, and incorporating the Rose and Cross into their daily lives, they equilibrate and fortify themselves to enter into the mystery of the Adeptus Minor and the Knowledge and Conversation of the Holy Guardian Angel.

The relationship shared by the two orders regarding the enactment of the Mass of the Holy Ghost—and the incorporation of the Rose and Cross to formulate the *Hieros Gamos*—is exemplified perfectly in the Gnostic Mass. However, besides the obvious, there are many other doctrinal aspects regarding Thelema present in the Gnostic Mass.

⊰❀⊱

Liber XV, The Gnostic Mass: A Doctrinal Analysis

What follows is the author's personal interpretation of the Gnostic Mass, given from the viewpoint of the limited scope of his experience as a member of the E.G.C. laity, diaconate and priesthood. The author holds no official episcopal positions in the E.G.C. such that a Bishop would assume, and is making no authoritative claims to the truth of the doctrinal exegesis that follows. Aleister Crowley himself never put forth any interpretive text on the ceremony. E.G.C. Bishops today are reluctant to discuss the Mass' doctrinal meaning. The Gnostic Mass is a ceremony that expresses in symbolic fashion the creative elements of nature. It is intended to bring each participant into a mystical, Gnostic experience that is unique for each individual. The following section offers my own insights into the ceremony and its relationship to the systems of the A∴A∴ and the O.T.O.

I understand the Mass as being the Rite of the Lion and the Eagle proper. I thus believe the Gnostic Mass can be seen as utilizing the magical formula of Tetragrammaton.[20] In short, the formula of Tetragrammaton is a fourfold elemental process that describes: (a) the creation of the universe, and (b) the human being's return back to God. While Tetragrammaton can, in theory, be any combination of four Hebrew letters, it is usually represented by the Hebrew name of God, YHVH (יהוה), and concerns the four traditional elements in Western esotericism: Fire (△), Water (▽), Air (△), and Earth (▽). This scheme is taken Qabalistically: Fire (Father, Chokmah) and Water (Mother, Binah) produce two offspring, Air (Son, Tiphareth) and Earth (Daughter, Malkuth). This describes the creation of the universe, from Kether, at the top of the Tree of Life, to Malkuth, the material world. The reverse of this, the process of reuniting with God, is called the Path of the Great Return in the writings of J. Daniel Gunther.

---

[20] See "The Formula of Tetragrammaton," in Crowley (1997), 153–154. For a more detailed discussion on its relation to the Gnostic Mass, see Sabazius X°, "The Formula of Tetragrammaton in the Gnostic Mass," in O.T.O. (2014), 108–111.

The Daughter (Aspirant in Malkuth) is wedded to the Son (the Holy Guardian Angel in Tiphareth), and is then exalted to the throne of the Mother (in Binah as the Master of the Temple), who rekindles the primordial Fire of the Father (Chokmah). This Path of Return signifies the initiatory structure of the A∴A∴.

The Temple of the Gnostic Mass may be understood as depicting the Tree of Life, with a tomb for Malkuth in the West and a High Altar representing Kether in the East. The High Altar is draped in red cloth and is adorned with flowers and a candle on either side. Atop the High Altar is affixed a Super-Altar with the Stele of Revealing with four candles on each side. There is a space below upon which sits *The Book of the Law* flanked by six candles on either side.[21] Upon the High Altar is the chalice of wine (elemental Water) and the vestments of the Priest. Two elemental altars are stationed along the central corridor of the Temple, the first representing the active elements of Fire and Air and the second the passive elements of Water and Earth.

The Priest begins unseen in the tomb in the West (the place of death in Egyptian religion, called Amenti). The Priest in the tomb is enclosed in the darkness of the profane world. He has not yet been awakened. He begins therefore as Asar (Osiris), the Lord of the Dead. He bears a Lance, the elemental weapon of Fire, the Yod (י) of Tetragrammaton, and a symbol of aspiration.

---

[21] As for the number of candles, I offer one interpretation. The Stele of Revealing, surrounded by eight candles, represents Thelema, the Word of the New Aeon. The Word is communicated through the exalted form of Mercury/Thoth in the number eight. *The Book of the Law,* delivered by Aiwass, whose number is 93, is surrounded by twelve candles (93=9+3=12). Furthermore, these twelve may represent the starry heaven of the zodiac, the crown of the Holy Guardian Angel, through whom the influence of Thelema is transmitted. See "Liber LXV," I:28: "My head is jewelled with twelve stars; My body is white as the milk of the stars; it is bright with the blue of the abyss of stars invisible." In Crowley (1983), 55. J. Daniel Gunther points out that the number twelve is also that of the important word הוא, "He," a title of Kether, identifying it with the zodiac, the home of the twelve Stars. Also, הוא conceals the Trinity of Kether, Chokmah and Binah: ה = Binah the mother, ו = Chokmah the father, and א = Kether the Crown. See Crowley, "An Essay Upon Number," Section IV, and *Sepher Sephiroth,* under the number twelve.

The People (the congregants) are admitted to the Temple. Being the "body" of the Gnostic Church, I consider them representative of elemental Earth. The Deacon, symbolizing elemental Air, is adorned with yellow, the color of Tiphareth (and of Mercury, the communicator). The Deacon prepares the ceremony with an opening, places *The Book of the Law* on the Super-Altar, and subsequently turns to the congregation and proclaims the Law of Thelema. Initiated by a symbolic act of penance (i.e., a penal sign),[22] the Deacon leads the congregation in the recitation of the Creed of the E.G.C. This Creed affirms the Qabalistic elements of creation from Kether to Malkuth and the transmission of Gnostic truth to generations of humankind through the saints of the Church. It serves as a confession of the efficacy of the transmutative power of the ceremony, and is an assertion of the Thelemic precept that "every man and every woman is a star"—one, individual, and eternal within the body of Nuit.[23]

The Priestess, according to the rubric of the Gnostic Mass, "should be actually Virgo Intacta or specially dedicated to the service of the Great Order."[24] That the Priestess should actually be a virgin to perform the ceremony is unlikely. I interpret the clause as a reference to the Tarot Card, Atu II, The High Priestess, a virginal goddess who embodies the divine influence of the Supernal Triad on the Tree of Life downward to Microprosopus, the seven Sephiroth below the Abyss. Speculative as it may seem to analyze occult symbols in this fashion, this interpretation finds some backing in the fact that the Priestess greets the congregation with the words, "Greeting of Earth and Heaven"—implying the path of Gimel (ג), which descends from Kether to Tiphareth.

The virginal aspect may be further elucidated in the phrase "Virgo Intacta," which could imply that the Priestess is ideally an initiate of the VI° of the O.T.O., a "Dame Companion of the Holy Grail," who has been "shown how to consecrate [herself] to the particular Great

---

22 Called the "Step and Sign of a Man and a Brother."

23 The reader may wish to consult Sabazius X°'s discussion on the Creed of the Gnostic Catholic Church in O.T.O. (2014), 66–77.

24 "Liber XV, The Gnostic Mass," in Crowley (1997), 584–597.

Work which [s]he came to Earth in order to perform."[25] This degree precedes that of VII°, in which the inmost Secret of the O.T.O. begins to be openly revealed to the candidate. The Secret being the nature of sexual magic, the VI° has attained the highest initiated standpoint in the O.T.O. system, while still remaining "virginal."

Another clause that is worth some attention is "specially dedicated to the service of the Great Order." Crowley commonly referred to the A∴A∴ as "the Great Order." In his essay, "The Alpha and Omega of Initiation," AISh MLChMH interprets this to signify that the O.T.O. is dedicated to the work of the A∴A∴.[26] While this is true from a doctrinal point of view, it requires further explanation. The reader should note that in *The Book of Lies*, in the chapter wittily titled "The Oyster" (referring to a symbol of the *yoni*), Crowley writes, "The Brothers of A∴A∴ are Women: the Aspirants to A∴A∴ are Men." In the commentary that follows the chapter Crowley writes, "this chapter gives the initiated feminine point of view."[27] The "initiated feminine point of view," is that of Atu II, The High Priestess, "Virgo Intacta," who is located *above* the Abyss. Furthermore, the phrase "The Brothers of A∴A∴ are Women" is not referring exclusively to a biological female, but to the attainment of the grade of Master of the Temple (8°=3▢)— those aspirants who have become "Scarlet Women" by pouring their blood into the Cup of Babalon. J. Daniel Gunther remarks on this:

> The Order of A∴A∴ corresponds to the Third Order that is above the Abyss. All Brothers of A∴A∴ have therefore attained to the grade of Master of the Temple, which is attributed to the Sephira Binah on the Tree of Life [the Great Mother] [...] All Masters of the Temple are Women, being one with the Mother

---

[25] Crowley (1969a) *Confessions*, 702.

[26] AISh MLChMH, "The Alpha and Omega of Initiation: Aleister Crowley, Charles Stansfeld Jones and the Way of Duplexity," in O.T.O. (2015), 114.

[27] *The Book of Lies*, "The Oyster," in Crowley (1981), 16–17.

of the Child. Therefore also, all Masters of the Temple are Scarlet Women.[28]

While it is of course ideal that any clergy officiating the Gnostic Mass hold some level of sufficient initiated understanding of both A∴A∴ doctrine and the system of the O.T.O., the above is not implying that those who serve as Priestesses in the E.G.C. have to be VI° of O.T.O. or Masters of the Temple of A∴A∴. It is interesting, as a side note, that the male perspective described in "The Oyster" is one, not of *member-ship* in the A∴A∴ (i.e., the Third Order), but of aspiration *towards* (i.e., upward) the A∴A∴. This seems to be another key doctrinal aspect, as it is the Priest who bears the Lance that is a symbol for aspiration.

The Formula of ALHIM in the Gnostic Mass

As already mentioned, most of "Liber XV" exemplifies the primary operation of the Rite of the Lion and the Eagle in terms of the formula of Tetragrammaton and the Path of the Great Return. However, before this can occur, aspiration must be activated in the dead man, Asar, who has until now been trapped in darkness. He must undergo a ceremony of consecration to become a Priest of the Holy One. This is done by the Priestess through another magical formula, that of ALHIM.

The Priestess enters the Temple in full regalia of blue and gold, girt with a Sword, the weapon of elemental Air. She also bears the Paten, symbolic of elemental Earth. By the powers latent within her, and in service to the Great Order, she greets the Congregation and places the Paten with the Cakes of Light upon the High Altar in adoration. She then begins a serpentine circumambulation about the elemental altars in the Temple consisting of "3 and a half circles," said to be the number of coils of the *kuṇḍalinī* at the base of the spine.[29] The Priestess' gesture

---

[28] Gunther (2014), 104–105.

[29] The likely earliest mention of the *kuṇḍalinī* residing as a coiled serpent within the body is a tantric text dating to the eighth century CE, the *Tantrasadbhāva*. See David Gordon White (2003) *Kiss of the Yoginī: "Tantric Sex" in its South Asian Contexts* (Chicago: University of Chicago Press), 230.

then is considered to be a preliminary invocation of the *kuṇḍalinī* energy, a theme that features heavily in the M∴M∴M∴ degrees of the O.T.O., not to mention the opening of the Holy Book "Liber LXV Cordis Cincti Serpente":

> I am the Heart; and the Snake is entwined
> About the invisible core of the mind.
> Rise, O my snake! It is now is the hour
> Of the hooded and holy ineffable flower.
> Rise, O my snake, into brilliance of bloom
> On the corpse of Osiris afloat in the tomb![30]

After invoking with the serpentine movements, the Priestess approaches the tomb of Osiris and opens it. As the sole representative of the Temple, she breathes life into him with the martial power of iron (the sword, the weapon of severity), and in the name of the Lord that is visible and sensible to us on Earth, the Sun.[31] Asar issues forth from the tomb with three steps and presents three penal signs, gestures that assure the Priestess and the Gods that he is worthy of consecration and is dedicated to pursue the Work of the Mass, under the penalty of obligation. He then kneels and worships the Lance, expressing his willingness to administer the sacraments to the Church if he be worthy of such an act. An intricate process of purification with passive elements, consecration with active elements, and dedication with vestments follows, duly preparing him as a "Man among Men," qualified to serve as Priest of the Holy One. Bishops Tahuti and Mara (James and Nancy Wasserman) make an interesting observation about Crowley's vision of the magical roles of Priest and Priestess:

> The [. . .] Priestess is regarded quite differently from the Priest. She enters the Temple, is saluted by all, approaches the High Altar, energizes the Sacred Space with her walk, and is now in

---

[30] "Liber LXV" I:1, in Crowley (1983), 53.

[31] There is also a hint of the Secret and Invisible Lord whose name is Mystery in her line, "and of our Lord ✠ . . . ."

a position to elevate the Priest from his darkened condition. [. . .] The fact that the Priestess is viewed as of sufficient spiritual purity to conduct these actions prior to her own purification by the Priest [. . .] is strong evidence that the common slurs directed against Thelema and O.T.O. as being either male-centric, anti-feminine, or paternal, are a misunderstanding of our doctrine and symbolism.[32]

These preliminaries in the Gnostic Mass performed by the Priestess are preparations using the formula of ALHIM (אלהים), a Pentagrammaton.[33] The formula of ALHIM is an act of *Consecration,* whereby the Priestess sanctifies the Priest for his service.[34] The feminine component is here the active force. Crowley writes that it "represents Śakti, or *te*; femininity always means form, manifestation. The masculine Śiva, or *Tao* is always a concealed force."[35] Furthermore, he states that ALHIM, "is the breath of benediction, yet so potent that it can give life to clay and light to darkness."[36] As such, the Priestess represents the active side

---

[32] James and Nancy Wasserman (2013) *To Perfect This Feast: A Performance Commentary on the Gnostic Mass,* (West Palm Beach: Sekmet Books), 65–66.

[33] A Pentagrammaton (a five-lettered Name), in distinction to Tetragrammaton (a four-lettered Name), is a formula by which the fifth Element of Spirit enters into the four Elements, giving life to a component of ritual so that it may be executed appropriately.

[34] Its image is that of the Stélé of Revealing with Nuit arched over Hadit. In the formula of אלהים, the juxtaposition of ה and ׳ indicates a modification of the formula expressed in יהשוה (YHShVH) where the male ׳ precedes the feminine ה. With א as the initial letter and ם as the final letter (forming the word אם "mother"), we should expect to see ש in the midst as the letter of Primal Fire. (Thus forming א ש ם, the Primal Elements reflected from Kether, Chokmah, and Binah). Yet we have ה in the center, the letter of Breath, and thus representing Spirit. Likewise, instead of Earth being represented by ה (which together with א would form the word ATh "Essence," and the Hebraic equivalent of the Greek ΑΩ), there is ל for Earth, with Aleph forming the word "God." In practical function, this shows the Woman ה elevated above the ׳. See AL I:14. (My thanks to J. Daniel Gunther for this footnote.)

[35] "The Formula of ALHIM, and that of ALIM," in Crowley (1997), 155.

[36] Ibid.

of formation. It is a process that gives form and manifestation to the Priest-to-be, who has at this point been the passive, "concealed force."

It is implied from a commentary to the Holy Book "Liber A'ash vel Capricorni Pneumatici," that this text presents the formula of ALHIM. Charles Stansfeld Jones said:

> Let us suppose however that [verse 0] refers to the *yoni*. The position indicated would then seem to be one in which the female is above the male; and this idea is more or less confirmed in "Energized Enthusiasm," when after placing the Priest in position the priestess takes her appointed place.[37]

Through the process of awakening the Man from the darkness of the tomb of the profane world—purifying him with Water and Earth, consecrating him with Fire and Air, and adorning him with the proper vestment of a Priest—she has with the divine powers latent within her given "life to clay and light to darkness." In one final act of preparation, the Priestess kneels and delivers eleven strokes to the Lance before invoking the presence of the Lord.

The Priestess' invocation complete for now, the Priest exclaims, "Thee therefore whom we adore, we also invoke!" By the power now invested in him, he raises the Lance, takes the Priestess to the East, and places her upon the Altar.

The Sun, and the Lion-Serpent

> Our religion therefore, for the People, is the Cult of the Sun, who is our particular star of the Body of Nuit, from whom, in the strictest scientific sense, come this earth, a chilled spark of Him, and all our Light and Life.
>
> —Commentary to *The Book of the Law*, III:22.

The solar-centric quality of "Liber XV" is explicit throughout the ceremony. The Priestess adorns the Priest with his robe as the "Priest of

---

[37] "Comment on Liber A'ash sub figurâ CCCLXXI," in Crowley (1996b), 351–352.

the Sun." During the "Ceremony of the Opening of the Veil," the Priest reaches the third step exclaiming, "Thou that art One, our Lord in the Universe the Sun!" Upon hearing the Priestess announce, "There is no law beyond Do what thou wilt," the Priest pierces the Veil and offers ecstatic litanies to Gnostic solar deities, such as Mithras and Abrasax. The first Collect is attributed explicitly to the Sun. When later consecrating the elements of the Eucharist, the Priest presents them as an offering to "be borne upon the waves of Æthyr to our Lord and Father the Sun." Finally, in "The Anthem" the invocation includes, "Thee, centre and secret of the Sun." James and Nancy Wasserman specifically identify the first ten lines of the Anthem as a description and invocation of the Holy Guardian Angel, thus designating the Mass as a perfect example of Duplexity—a ritual appropriate to both the A∴A∴ and the O.T.O.[38]

The doctrinal importance of the Sun in Thelemic spirituality cannot be overstated. The Sun is the giver of light and provides many of the basic necessities to sustain life on Earth. It is the visible and sensible heavenly body that we can identify as directly responsible for our well-being and continued existence. From a spiritual standpoint, the Sun holds Qabalistic significance in its association with Tiphareth, the sixth sephira on the Tree of Life. The number six indicates consciousness, awareness, and knowledge of oneself. It is for this reason that Tiphareth has been linked to the Serpent of Genesis—who brought humankind to self-knowledge and the wisdom of God (i.e., Baphomet and the "Lion-Serpent").[39] Tiphareth is also the Heart of Man wherein the

---

[38] Wasserman (2013), 104.

[39] "The Name Jesus" in Hebrew, "שם יהשוה," enumerates to 666. This number, apart from its usual association with the Beast of Revelation, is a mystical number of the Sun. The Serpent in Genesis, although typically associated with the Devil, Satan, and evil, was considered by the Gnostics to be the initiator of humankind. He was the being who brought Adam and Eve to self-understanding and individual consciousness where the knowledge of good as well as evil exists. For Qabalistic analyses on this, see "Sepher Sephiroth," 57, in Crowley (1977) *777 and Other Qabalistic Writings of Aleister Crowley* (York Beach: Samuel Weiser, Inc.) and *The Equinox* Vol. I, nos. 5 and 7. For a discussion on the Serpent as initiator, refer to Gunther (2014), 170–192.

Kingdom of God dwells, and it is in this sephira where union with God is experienced, thus it is the home of the savior gods such as Osiris and Christ. Lastly, the expansive energy of the Sun is representative of our own spiritual Will, our "solar-phallic" center of purpose. The Sun then refers to the initiate's omni-directional extension into the world by way of the four rays of the Law of Thelema: Light, Life, Love, and Liberty— encapsulated in the phrase "Khabs am Pekht."[40]

The outward expansive quality of the Sun features heavily in the thematic scheme of the O.T.O. The reader will recall that the A∴A∴ has been referred to as the "Path of Night," and the O.T.O. as the "Path of Day."[41] Along similar lines, the A∴A∴ may be understood as being inward, mystical, and averse, and the O.T.O. as outward, magical and upright. The A∴A∴ follows the Path of the Great Return: the initiate begins in Death, travels through Life, and re-enters the Womb of the Mother, and becomes a "Babe in the Egg" and Master of the Temple. The O.T.O. is known as the Path in Eternity, where the candidate experiences the attraction to incarnation, birth, life, death, annihilation into the infinite, and the subsequent spiritual life. The initiatory structure of the O.T.O. guides the candidate in motion with the diurnal path of the sun, the formula of I.A.O.[42] In the Path in Eternity, the candidate is instructed in lessons in the natural world through the processes of birth, life, and death.[43] In the A∴A∴, this process is reversed through

---

[40] "Light in Extention." See "De Lege Libellum" on the four rays and "Khabs am Pekht," both in Crowley (2007b) *The Blue Equinox*.

[41] See chapter six.

[42] "Iao" is the Gnostic name for God, but also refers to a formula by which death is overcome through resurrection. This was the supreme attainment in the Old Aeon, in which the initiate experienced salvation through the cross of suffering in order to attain the Grace of God. This formula is synonymous with the formula of L.V.X. (Light in Extension). In the New Aeon, the formula of I.A.O. is no longer associated with vicarious atonement of sin through the cross of suffering, but instead as the individual identification with the Sun and the Inner Sanctum.

[43] Qabalistically, "O.T.O." equates with the Sun. Shiva X° has noted that the letters "O.T.O." taken in its Hebrew equivalent (עתע) and spelt in full (עין תו עין, "Ayin Tau Ayin") enumerates in Gematria to 666.

(**Figure 12.1**) **Showing the paths** of Ayin and Nun that lead to Tiphareth

the formula of O.A.I.[44] Where the O.T.O. describes infinite expansion from the center outward, the A∴A∴ involves infinite contraction inwards towards the center. [45]

It is for this reason that I associate the two paths on the Tree of Life leading to Tiphareth, "ע" and "נ" with the paths of the O.T.O. and the A∴A∴, respectively (see figure 12.1).[46] The path of Ayin (ע), attributed to the Tarot card "The Devil," represents the ecstatic outward formula of the O.T.O. Crowley's description of The Devil card exemplifies this:

> The formula of this card is then the complete appreciation of all existing things. He rejoices in the rugged and the barren no less than in the smooth and the fertile. All things equally exalt him.

---

[44] In O.A.I., destruction comes first, followed by resurrection and finally Life.

[45] This is not to imply that the O.T.O. is sun-worship and the A∴A∴ is lunar worship. Rather, the two systems are both "solar" insofar as recognizing the Crowned and Conquering Child Horus as a solar deity. The difference lies in their respective formulas. The O.T.O. instructs its members on the spiritual properties of the Sun as the Lord, sensible and visible, where the initiate of the Outer College worships the Sun in its hidden form, that is the Khabs and the Secret-Self.

[46] Initiates of the Minerval degree of the Man of Earth will note that these two letters add up in Gematria to 120, which holds special significance to the Sun and to their Initiation. Likewise, will initiates of M∴M∴M∴ in general note that the three Mems of Mysteria Mystica Maxima also add to 120.

He represents the finding of ecstasy in every phenomenon, however naturally repugnant; he transcends all limitations; he is Pan;
he is All.[47]

The path of Nun (נ) characterizes the inward journey of the A∴A∴,
wherein the candidate willingly submits to discipline, quieting the
mind and listening to the inner voice of God within. The candidate
becomes the self-slain Ankh-f-n-khonsu, wilfully bringing Death to
himself in an effort to understand the True Life of Initiation. As Atu
XIII, "Death" is interpreted by Crowley as the element which "willingly
subjects itself to change; thus, potassium thrown upon water becomes
ignited, and accepts the embrace of the hydroxyl radicle."[48] We can see
from the above then that the two orders share their own orientation to
the Sun. Two horizons: one is of Life, the other of Death.[49]

This equilibration between Life and Death—and their relationship
to the Sun—is found in the solar figure known as the Lion-Serpent. In
"Liber XV," when the particulate (the spermatozoon) drops into the
chalice of wine (the *yoni*), the "Mystic Marriage" has occurred and the
Eucharist is duly prepared for consumption. The Priest exclaims thrice,
"O Lion and O Serpent that destroy the destroyer, be mighty among
us!" The Lion-Serpent is a composite symbol taking on a number of
meanings. In terms of the "Mystic Marriage," the Lion-Serpent refers
to the union between God and the human being, the descent of spirit
into matter, and the completion of the Rite of the Lion and the Eagle.
The Hebrew letter Teth (ט), meaning "serpent," is attributed to the
zodiacal sign of Leo (a lion) through the Tarot card, Atu XI, "Lust."
The Serpent is linked to the watery sign of Scorpio, whose symbol is
also an Eagle. Leo is, of course, elemental Fire, hence the Lion-Serpent
is an expression for the Rite of the Lion and the Eagle. Furthermore,
Atu XI depicts the conjoining of Babalon and the Beast, referring to

---

[47] Crowley (2007a) *The Book of Thoth* (Newburyport, MA: Weiser Books), 106.

[48] Ibid., 100.

[49] The reader should note that the Hawk-headed Lord of the New Aeon, Ra-Hoor-
Khuit in Egyptian is "Ra-Horakhty" meaning "Horus of the Horizons." These are the
horizons of East and West, of Life and Death. See Gunther (2009), 61–74.

the sexual formula of the operation, again demonstrating the theme that features the interplay of polarities. Finally, the serpent refers to Death and the Lion to Life, two forces equilibrating to produce the phenomenon of existence.

The Communion of Saints

The office of the Collects is meant to invoke a number of positive elements into the ceremony. Each of these short prayers are blessings and bestowals upon the myriad facets of existence, granting them each their sacred place in the lives of Church laity. While all of the Collects are significant and deserve a complete discussion in and of themselves, we limit our discussion here to the fifth Collect, "The Saints."

First of all, what does "sainthood" mean for Thelema? In the Christian tradition, we understand saints to be members of the Christian community whose works exemplify beyond doubt their service to the Church, and who are deserving of veneration for such acts. They are thought to be selfless, reverent, and holy figures in Church history and often recognized for sacrificing a great deal of themselves, sometimes their lives in martyrdom for the sake of faith. Lawrence Cunningham provides a succinct overview of the history of sainthood in the Christian tradition:

> [B]y the waning years of the late antique period, the cult of the saints was already well lodged in the practice of Christianity. Born out of the experience of martyrdom, and furthered by the example of the ascetics and the spread of the monastic life, the veneration of the saints was part of the fabric of Christian piety. In the late antique and early medieval period there was no formal procedure by which one entered the list (canon) of the saints. All that was required to achieve the reputation of being a saint after death was a body or something identified with the person to be venerated, a shrine of some sort, a narrative of the person's life and deeds (it could be something as brief as the acts of the person's condemnation in the case of a martyr), and people who would come to pray at the place where the shrine was located.

The overarching criterion marking the desirability of such signs was a continuing indication of the miraculous. The most formal recognition that a person could hope for in addition to those conditions was being placed in the calendar(s) of those who were commemorated publicly in the liturgy of the great centers of the church like Rome or Jerusalem.[50]

The criteria for sainthood in Thelema has an obviously less developed tradition, but this does not invalidate its genuineness. As Sabazius notes, the Saints Collect "proclaims our historical current throughout its various phases [...] These men were keepers of the sacred flame, whether they knew it (or desired it) or not. In a personal sense this Collect represents the acknowledgement of our own magical currents, our own past lives, ancestors, teachers, and heroes."[51] It would seem that Crowley identified sainthood with an unwavering level of devotion to one's spiritual path—to a point that one's work has contributed to the gnostic enlightenment of humanity. Some of these figures are indeed religious prophets, though there are also authors, artists, poets, philosophers, and past masters of the O.T.O. listed as well. In short, sainthood constitutes those who have "transmitted the Light of the Gnosis to us their successors and their heirs."[52]

A key doctrinal point concerning the A∴A∴ emerges once again in the Gnostic Mass when discussing sainthood. Crowley seems to imply that all those who become members of the Third Order, having attained to the grade of Master of the Temple, are included amongst the saints. They are, as Sabazius notes, the "Great World Initiators, Magistri Templi and Magi of the Great White Brotherhood of the Silver Star, sent to enlighten civilization and initiate historic periods."[53] This is because these initiates have given themselves fully to the Great

[50] Lawrence S. Cunningham (2005) *A Brief History of Saints* (Oxford: Blackwell Publishing), 26.

[51] Sabazius X°, "The Collects," in O.T.O (2014), 81.

[52] Collect V, "The Saints," "Liber XV: The Gnostic Mass," in Crowley (1997), 591.

[53] Sabazius X°, in O.T.O. (2014), 81.

Work, completely and without condition.[54] Such, of course, are the seven Magi described in Chapter I of this book, and listed elsewhere in *The Book of Lies*[55] and *Liber Aleph*.[56]

Although Crowley may have not explicitly referred to them as "Masters of the Temple," it is possible that the list of figures in the fifth Collect of the Gnostic Mass may include those generally referenced in *The Vision and the Voice* when it describes the "Blood of Saints" being "mingled" in the "Cup of Babalon." In such a case, we may extend the terminology more broadly to include the poets, mythic heroes, mystics, gnostics, martyrs of papal oppression, alchemists, romantics, philosophers, and other esotericists listed among the Saints who have continued "knowledge from generation unto generation" and who "did of old manifest" the glory of the Lord unto the world.

The analytical levels of the Gnostic Mass are fractal; every corner of its rubric produces gradient degrees of doctrinal insight into Thelema, the A∴A∴, and the O.T.O. A thorough examination of the ceremony could easily fill a bookshelf. That said, it is hoped that the above discussion has provided a few examples of the complexity of "Liber XV."

E.G.C. in the Present Day

Today, the Gnostic Mass is performed all over the world: in North America, South America, the United Kingdom, much of Europe, Oceania, and Japan. Because the Gnostic Mass is so well-practiced, it

---

[54] See references to such in Crowley (1998a) *The Vision and the Voice with Commentary and Other Papers*, 23, 149, and 210.

[55] Crowley (1981), 24–25. Interestingly, in *The Book of Lies* these prophets are only referred to as Masters of the Temple ($8°=3^□$), whereas in *Liber Aleph* they are Magi ($9°=2^□$). This is a doctrinal nuance that can probably be explained historically. Crowley wrote *The Book of Lies* in 1912, having already attained to the grade of Master of the Temple, and *Liber Aleph* after he attained to Magus. It would seem that Crowley may not have considered these saints to be Magi until he came to understand what the grade entailed.

[56] Crowley (1991c), 68–74.

is a flourishing time for the Ecclesia Gnostica Catholic and the O.T.O. Members enjoy the fact that the Thelemic current can be experienced with their brothers and sisters in many travel destinations, giving them a sense of a global community. From a magical standpoint, the E.G.C. and the O.T.O. have both gained a tremendous level of momentum in this regard. There are many variations in the performance of the ceremony. Anyone with experience in attending a Gnostic Mass more than once will realize that it is unique in every combination of participants, whether as Priestess, Priest, Deacon, Children, or Congregant. It is another example of the pluralistic platform embraced by the O.T.O., and a mark of unity in diversity.

The E.G.C. is not without its challenges. In the wake of postmodern trends of Western society the Gnostic Mass has received critical inquiry. Very recent academic work has commented on the Mass' perceived "heteronormativity" and has sought to examine gender dynamics within the O.T.O.[57] Other critiques have questioned Collect V: "The Saints" as exclusively male, and some recent works have argued for

---

[57] See Manon Hedenborg-White (2013) "To Him the Winged Secret Flame, To Her the Stooping Starlight: The Social Construction of Gender in Contemporary Ordo Templi Orientis," in *The Pomegranate*, Vol. 15, Issue 1-2:102–121. Hedenborg-White writes, "The ritual has a heterosexual structure; it shows the union of the divine feminine as Nuit, embodied by a female priestess, and the divine masculine as Hadit, represented by a male priest, uniting to create their magical offspring. However, heteronormativity also entails that the correlation of physical body with gender performance (specific personal traits, abilities, appearance and characteristics) and sexual orientation is seen as preferable to other combinations." (109). Hedenborg-White here incorporates Judith Butler's performativity theory of gender, which asserts that gender is not determined at birth, but fluid and socially constructed. Yet, Hedenborg-White admits the limitations of her method, when she notes that the subjects of her study refer to the perceived "heteronormativity" of the Gnostic Mass as being a magical formula of universal import. She writes, "a scholar of religion cannot enter into discussions about magical formulae, and as such can only observe the surface level of the mass, which is heteronormative." (112). As such, Hedenborg-White's study reveals how an academic approach to this subject remains narrow in scope. As is common with the "etic" methodology of Western esotericism, any analysis of a magical ritual from a purely academic standpoint remains "surface level."

gender-bending performances of "Liber XV."[58] In 1997, Hymenaeus Beta presented some of these problems at the Women's Conference:

> The Gnostic Mass was written by a man, and is a celebration of the sexual polarities and their cosmic and natural interplay from that standpoint. The male has the largely active role, and the goddess, speaking initially the words of Nuit, is veiled on the altar. The Saints are paternal, but this is intentional. It is a list of the small handful of men and man-gods who, in the opinion of the author of the Mass, understood the divinity of woman. I've heard the Mass criticized as sexist, and frankly think that stupid. Who, when the Mass was first introduced to America during World War I, was worshipping the goddess? Especially in the context of a religious ceremony of Western origin? Who understood the divinity of the feminine at all? Someday, perhaps not soon, but who knows, a woman adept in the O.T.O. Sovereign Sanctuary will manifest the genius to compose a Mass in which the female takes the more active role, and the male the more passive (as with Śiva and Śakti in Hinduism)—in which the Deacon, speaking for the Priestess, can claim communion with women in history that perceived the divinity of man.[59]

Remember Lon and Constance DuQuette's advice on apple pie, quoted earlier.[60] The Mass is a dramatic ritual performed by one Priest and one Priestess. It offers one recipe for creating one result: "If you don't follow the essentials of the recipe, it won't be an apple pie, and if you don't follow the essentials of 'Liber XV,' it won't be a 'Gnostic Mass.'" On the other hand, a well-made cherry cobbler can be a very tasty dish indeed!

---

[58] See Michael Effertz (2013) *Priest/ess: In Advocacy of Queer Gnostic Mass* (Hollywood: Luxor Media Group, LLC.).

[59] Hymenaeus Beta, "Women's Conference Address," in *The Magical Link,* New Series, No. 1, Fall 1997. 8–10.

[60] See aforementioned note on "The Miracle of the Mass, Part II," on The Speech in the Silence Podcast, Episode 15.

As also previously mentioned, the Mass of the Holy Ghost comprises a number of rites, not all of which are heteronormative. It is historically evident that Crowley did not constrain sexual magical ritual primarily to traditional gender relations. In fact, significant doctrinal insights were produced by Crowley through non-heteronormative sexual relations. The problem then lies not with the Gnostic Mass' formula being "heteronormative," but with the as yet unrealized potential for more rituals.

The Ecclesia Gnostica Catholica is one of the most progressive ecclesiastical institutions on earth. O.T.O.'s non-discriminatory policy recognizes members of all sexual orientations.[61] The E.G.C. ordains its clergy into the Priesthood and Priestesshood regardless of sexual preference. In short, the O.T.O. and E.G.C. stand among the most open religious institutions in the world today.

---

[61] In 2004, the E.G.C. introduced a policy, issued by the O.H.O., in which transgender individuals may be ordained Priests or Prietesses according to the gender with which they identify, regardless of their sex at birth.

CHAPTER FIFTEEN

Brilliance

By the Unity Thereof

He hath ploughed with the seven stars of his Plough, that the Seven
might move indeed, yet ever point to the unchanging One.

—*Liber ARARITA,* VI:7

IN THE LAST SEASON of Crowley's life, he divined his final Word of
the Equinox in the autumn of 1947. "Brilliance" was delivered from
V.V.V.V.V. The Word was announced on O.T.O. letterhead and
signed with Crowley's signature as To Mega Therion, Magus of the
A∴A∴—Duplexity in action. The historian can only speculate as to
the meaning of the Word. Yet the mystic may consider it to refer to the
illuminated Eye in the Triangle, the sigil of the A∴A∴, the symbol
for the Holy One whose utterances are enshrined in the Holy Books
of Thelema, and that to which the Great Work of both orders is dedicated. If such is the case, Crowley's final divination of the Word of the
Equinox is an indication that, even in the closing year of the Beast's life,
there was a unity of purpose to Thelema—to promulgate the Word of
Truth for the New Æon, the message from the Secret Chiefs to liberate
humanity.

The spiritual legacy of Aleister Crowley remains as a singular
unwavering Thelemic message that is united in Truth and in Spirit
by its two orders. This may seem like a questionable conclusion from
an empirically historical vantage point. The history of religion, as we
have noted, reveals that religious and spiritual groups are especially
prone to splintering and schism. Admittedly, Thelema is not different
in this regard. Yet, limiting the scope of this book to the activities of
those groups in closest proximity to Crowley and his followers, we find

that the historical Thelemic movement and its modern development remains both consistent and continuous.

Thelema, even as a religious phenomenon, extends beyond my purposefully circumscribed definitions of the Thelemic movement. Despite its syncretic occult philosophy, the secularizing influences of the modern world, the proclivities towards schism that characterize all religious movements, and its own unique and perplexing history, Thelema has nonetheless been established most identifiably through the two orders that were forwarded in Aleister Crowley's lifetime. Furthermore, these organizations as they exist today have contributed to Thelema having a defined and verifiable presence in the world. They are truly living representatives of One Truth and One Spirit. As Thelema continues to grow in popularity, it is demonstrating that it is a spiritual movement in affinity with our contemporary world; it is inexorably penetrating ever-larger spheres of society and culture.

Thelema as an Academia

Nearly all academic work on Crowley has been confined to the discipline of Western esotericism, which is almost exclusively tied to the history of religion. The fact that academic work on Thelema has thus far been confined in this way exemplifies: (1) that it has often been neglected by other fields, and (2) that the field of Western esotericism may be limiting Thelema's scope of inquiry. At this point, Western esotericism is a relatively new discipline within academia and has yet to effectively break into other fields of research. However, as Western esotericism grows, and more scholarship on Thelema is put forth, I hope its study will expand to include academic work in philosophy, sociology, psychology, political science, behavioral and cognitive sciences, and even environmental studies.

A recent statement of aims from the president of Academia Ordo Templi Orientis (A.O.T.O.) expressed such goals to its membership:

[I]n order to escape being perceived as an insular group of individuals engaged in our own internal monologue, we need to address, interrogate, criticize, invoke, debate, and show cognizance of the larger, "outside" academic discourse related to our field of research [...] Without showing familiarity and engagement with the larger world of academic writing on OTO, Thelema, and Western Esotericism [...], we run the risk of becoming insignificant as an Academia, even if our research is excellent as such.[1]

Similarly, a number of guilds have been formed so that professionals in various fields who hold membership within the O.T.O. can implement their respective disciplines for the benefit of other members. One example of this is the Psychology Guild, which holds seminars on topics related to psychology and mental health.

With regard to philosophy, there have been some efforts to establish a Philosophy Guild within the O.T.O., though this prospect is still in need of attention. Yet, recent academic work has been produced utilizing contemporary philosophical methods of phenomenology and cognitive sciences to investigate the embodied experience of Thelemic practices.[2] The author's own research has explored the history of philosophy by tracing England's reception of Friedrich Nietzsche and how Crowley may have been influenced by him.[3] In time, Thelema will witness sound academic scholarship in all branches of philosophy: including metaphysics, epistemology, ethics, aesthetics, political science, philosophy of mind, cognitive science and phenomenology, post-structuralism, and gender theory among many other fields. It is without a doubt an exciting time for scholarship on Thelema.

---

[1] "A.O.T.O. vs Research Lodge," presidential statement on the current aims of the A.O.T.O. to its membership.

[2] See Damon Lycourinos (2013) "Sex Magick and the Occult Body of the Mega Therion: A Study of Ritual Body Techniques, Applied Occultism, and Aleister Crowley's Sex Magick," 4th International ESSWE Conference, University of Gothenburg, Sweden, June 28, 2013.

[3] Keith Readdy (2014) "The Antichrist and the Beast: Friedrich Nietzsche's connection to Aleister Crowley," Universiteit van Amsterdam, unpublished.

Thelema as a Religious Phenomenon:

Authority and Legitimacy in Religious Tradition vs. Occulture

In chapter six, Thelema was defined within a sociological framework as a religion, whose activities typify those of groups with spiritual and religious aims. Yet Thelema as a religious phenomenon complicates, even problematizes, the sociological study of religion. This is because Thelema has elements that seem to stand in direct contrast—sharing aspects of both "tradition" and "fringe."

Syncretism, Deviance, and Religion

Thelema spans the boundaries between occultism and religion. On the one hand, it is characterized by the syncretic blending of various religious elements and the oppositional deviant fringe that typically qualifies the occult. The occultist tradition, in general, can be identified by the two aspects of syncretism and sociological deviance from mainstream society. However, as distinct from normal occultism, Thelema shares traditional elements of established religion—for example, sacramental rites through its clerical activities in the E.G.C., the teaching of prayer and meditation in its instructive branch the A∴A∴, and the offering of fellowship and community in its social and fraternal organization the O.T.O. In short, there is an implicit overlay between the syncretic and deviant elements of occultism, and the clearly defined and established Thelemic religious tradition.

Syncretism is typified by the practice of blending various elements from a number of traditions and appropriating them under one branch of thought. We can link this practice to what Western esotericism scholar Antoine Faivre calls "concordance." Faivre has argued that a common practice in esoteric currents of religion is to discover sympathies with other traditions to uncover a core mystical element inherent in all religion. He explains:

> "The type of concordance meant here [...] concerns individual
> at least as much as collective illumination and manifests the will

not only to eliminate some differences or to uncover harmonies among diverse religious traditions, but to acquire above all a gnosis embracing diverse traditions and melding them in a single crucible."[4]

As Faivre notes, syncretism has long been an aspect of esotericism, but it is particularly featured in the modern discourse on the subject.[5] Occultism is but one of these modern esoteric currents that is syncretic.

Thelema derives its syncretic elements from its ancestral roots in the Hermetic Order of the Golden Dawn, which blended the mystical Christian currents of Rosicrucianism; the Hermetic magical tradition (deriving its influence as far back as Hellenistic Egypt, later rediscovered and developed in the Renaissance writings of Marcilio Ficino and others); and the Jewish and Christian Qabalah. Beyond this, Crowley later incorporated elements from many religious traditions including Judaism, Christianity, Islam, Taoism, Hinduism, and Buddhism, among others. These strands are woven together to give Thelema a unique quality of universality. It is a diverse, accessible, and attractive form of spirituality for contemporary society.

As discussed in chapter six, modern manifestations of esoteric and occult currents gained the attention of sociologists in the 1970s. We will recall that they classify the occult and the "cultic milieu" as "deviant," in other words, opposed to mainstream society. The occult has long been associated with forbidden practices, magical power, and devil worship. This has in turn earned occultism considerable negative attention in mainstream media and has subsequently attracted alternative music and art. As such, contemporary manifestations of occultism carry an

---

[4] Faivre (1994) *Access to Western Esotericism*, 14.

[5] Syncretism was one of the primary factors that facilitated the removal of esoteric discourse from the academy in the early modern era. In his *Schediasma historicum* (1655), Jakob Thomasius blamed the central element of syncretism, which he identified with "pagan philosophy," for corrupting Christian theology. Thomasius, along with a handful of other Protestant historians of philosophy, used such logic to polemicize the Catholic Church, and in doing so effectively marginalized esoteric discourse for over three centuries. See Hanegraaff (2012).

element of intentional aberrance from societal norms. As Jeffrey Kaplan and Heléne Lööw remark on the "cultic milieu" (which includes the occult):

> The cultic milieu is oppositional by nature. The cultic milieu is a zone in which proscribed and/or forbidden knowledge is the coin of the realm, a place in which ideas, theories and speculations are to be found, exchanged, modified and eventually adopted or rejected [...] The sole thread that unites the denizens of the cultic milieu [...] is a shared rejection of the paradigms, the orthodoxies, or their societies.[6]

The above is best illustrated by using the example of a contemporary occult organization that has drawn influence from Thelema and the O.T.O. In chapter six, we discussed the neologism "occulture," coined by Genesis P-Orridge, who used performance art, music, and ritual as devices to challenge social convention as early as the mid-1970s.[7] By the 1980s, P-Orridge established the occult organization "Thee Temple ov Psychick Youth" (TOPY), drawing inspiration from the work of Aleister Crowley and Austin Osman Spare. Yet, TOPY was not simply a juvenile attempt at polemicizing mainstream culture through occultist philosophy. At its root, it sought to question the very nature of identity in consensus reality, and to actively decondition people from the restrictions imposed by the dominant establishment, be it oppression

---

[6] Kaplan and Lööw (2002), 3–4.

[7] These early art experiments, called COUM Transmissions were further developed in the musical act, Throbbing Gristle, and later still in the audio-visual project known as Psychic TV. Psychic TV became the artistic medium for TOPY, whose antinomian ideology would find a magical and spiritual outlet, attracting thousands of collaborators at its height in the 1990s. Finally (and most recently), Genesis has challenged societal conventions through h/er on-going art experiment, *Pandrogyny*, intended to bring into question the very nature of identity. For an exhaustive history on the early days of Genesis P-Orridge with COUM and Throbbing Gristle, see David Keenan (2003) *England's Hidden Reverse: A Secret History of the Esoteric Underground* (London: SAF Publications Ltd.).

towards sexual orientation, political persuasion, or otherwise. TOPY used art, media, and magick to oppose the normative structure.

TOPY exemplifies the implicit countercultural element of occultism with which Thelema is intrinsically bound. An inquiry worth raising is whether or not Thelema will always be associated with the oppositional, deviant, countercultural fringe of society. If it is, how does this affect it as a movement? Does unrestrained syncretism run the risk of misappropriating inconsistent components that dilute an established tradition? How do we determine what is and is not "Thelemic"?

Thelema as Tradition

Despite its elasticity due to its embrace of syncretism, Thelema maintains its own doctrine and tradition, making it a unique religious phenomenon.[8] I am using the term "tradition" as it is commonly understood: "The transmission of customs or beliefs from generation to generation, or the fact of being passed on in this way."[9] The initiatory scheme in Thelema utilizes its own specific symbol set. From initiation equipment to robes and insignia, each aspect of its ceremonies holds

---

[8] The "Thelemic tradition" bears no relation to "Traditionalism," a specific esoteric current in the first half of the twentieth century. Traditionalism sought to reorient Western culture to spiritual principles that were believed to have been corrupted or lost due to the disenchanting and secularizing processes of modernity. As Mark Sedgwick points out, "The Traditionalist movement [...] takes 'tradition' primarily in this sense, as belief and practice transmitted from time immemorial—or rather belief and practice that *should* have been transmitted but was lost to the West during the last half of the second millennium AD. According to the Traditionalists, the modern West is in crisis as a result of this loss of transmission of tradition." See Mark Sedgwick (2004) *Against the Modern World: Traditionalism and the Secret Intellectual History of the Twentieth Century* (Oxford: Oxford University Press). Traditionalism has been associated with the thought of René Guénon (1886–1951) and Julius Evola (1898–1974), both contemporaries of Crowley, and both of whom held poor opinions of him. See Pasi (2014), 117–136 and Hans Thomas Hakl, "Some Additional remarks on Julius Evola and Aleister Crowley," in Pasi (2014), 141–152.

[9] "Tradition," Oxford Dictionary

significant import. Thelema also has a defined trinity of Egyptian-derived gods in its theology, marking its own doctrine and teachings. While Nuit, Hadit, and Ra-Hoor-Khuit signify cosmic and universal principles of the universe, they nonetheless have their own imagery. Thelemic cosmology has its unique way to explain the universe. In short, Thelema has a developed tradition with its singular symbolism, theology, and cosmology that distinguishes it from other movements.

Thelema also employs a set of regular practices that set it apart, although grounded in the great religions of the past. The recitation of "Will" before a meal, for example, replaces the Christian practice of saying "Grace."[10] In the Ecclesia Gnostica Catholica, the central ceremony administers the sacramental rite of the Eucharist in a similar way to the tradition of the Catholic Church. The fourfold daily prayers of "Liber Resh vel Helios" may be likened to the daily practice of *Salah* in Islam. The O.T.O. also tends to promote fellowship and community in the way a traditional temple or church functions.

Where, then, shall we place Thelema? Is it part of a deviant counter-culture, or is it a clearly identified religion with laity, practices, customs, and ceremonies? The answer is that it is *both*. It is the opinion of the author that "Thelemic tradition" lies within the structure and organization of the Thelemic movement (i.e., the A∴A∴, the O.T.O., and the E.G.C.), while more fluid currents of Thelema are present in the Thelemic community at large, by which I refer to the varying and emergent "Thelemic occulture" localized in other organizations, online forums, and art and media channels in popular culture. The first

---

[10] Quoting *Magick in Theory and Practice:* "In an Abbey of Thelema we say 'Will' before a meal. The formula is as follows. 'Do what thou wilt shall be the whole of the Law.' 'What is thy Will?' 'It is my will to eat and drink' 'To what end?' 'That my body may be fortified thereby.' 'To what end?' 'That I may accomplish the Great Work.' 'Love is the law, love under will.' 'Fall to!' This may be adapted as a monologue. One may also add the inquiry "What is the Great Work?" and answer appropriately, when it seems useful to specify the nature of the Operation in progress at the time. The point is to seize every occasion of bringing every available force to bear upon the objective of the assault." 102–103. *Diary of a Drug Fiend* adds a battery of eleven knocks: three, five, three. 313–314.

is characterized by structure and organization, the second by fluidity and syncretism. Let us now describe each in turn.

Thelema and the Discipline of Hierarchy

Thelemic tradition has been developed in the movement's three structured organizations.[11] Each of these has contributed to establishing the Thelemic tradition by developing its teachings, formulating cultural customs, and systematizing practices that distinguish it from the more general Thelemic occulture.

Over the last several decades since its reconstitution, the A∴A∴ has published new documents and monographs that have introduced comprehensive analyses of Thelema's theology and doctrine. These publications have utilized rigorous and exhaustive research methods and primary source materials to advance Thelema's spiritual teachings. Furthermore, the A∴A∴ continues to observe its method of instruction through the original syllabus as put forth by Crowley. Through disciplined motion, the A∴A∴ gradually leads the initiate through the Outer College, assisted by the guidance, wisdom, and ingenuity of a teacher who has trodden the path. Eventually, the candidate enters into communion with the Holy Guardian Angel. Even before the initiate becomes a newly-made Adept, he or she is bound by Oath and Deed to serve humanity in accomplishing the Great Work.

Through its hierarchical chain of command and its procedures and policies, the O.T.O. aims to establish Thelemic principles in the world, while creating an environment for a Thelemic culture to flourish. The initiatory ceremonies in the M∴M∴M∴ and the ecclesiastical activities in the E.G.C. are not only spiritual experiences for initiates and laity, but bonding experiences for participants. The customs of holding feasts, taking communion in the Gnostic Mass, or participating in a group ritual are all examples of common practices today. The

---

[11] In defining the A∴A∴ as a "Thelemic organization," I refer particularly to the Outer College, as it exists as an entry point for guided and tested instruction into the mysteries of the initiatory system generally encompassed by the term, "A∴A∴." The E.G.C. is the third, although often treated as "within" the O.T.O.

O.T.O. shares such interests through fraternal bonds—yet each person can contribute his or her own individual skills and abilities in helping the O.T.O. to establish Thelema in the world. Each local initiate body discovers its own unique methods of doing this by holding events in affinity with the local area. O.T.O. culture is characteristically diverse, not only from country to country, but from town to town, and city to city. Still, all members are bound by the same oaths of fraternity and follow the same ceremonies, rituals, policies, and procedures to help keep the Order functioning.

The need for policy and procedure in a religious organization is straightforward, yet the importance of its principle often escapes those who are less inclined to commit to a group effort. Even at the entering degree of Minerval, the candidate member of the O.T.O. is provided a meditation on the importance of the principles of discipline and structure. Similarly, Crowley outlined the need for discipline, structure, and organization in *Liber Aleph,* describing their importance by an allegory on the course of nature herself. It is worth quoting at length:

> Consider the Bond of a cold Climate, how it maketh Man a Slave; he must have Shelter and Food with fierce Toil. Yet hereby he becometh strong against the Elements, and his moral Force waxeth, so that he is Master of such Men as live in Lands of Sun where bodily Needs are satisfied without Struggle. Consider also him that willeth to exceed in Speed or in Battle, how he denieth himself the Food he craveth, and all Pleasures natural to him, putting himself under the harsh Order of a Trainer. So by this Bondage he hath, at the last, his Will. Now then the one by natural, and the other by voluntary, Restriction have come each to greater Liberty. This is also a general Law of Biology, for all Development is Structuralization; that is, a Limitation and Specialization of an originally indeterminate Protoplasm, which latter may therefore be called free, in the Definition of a Pedant.[12]

---

[12] "On Cultivating Strength through Discipline," in Crowley (1991c) *Liber Aleph,* 35.

Such are the reasons why administrative authority, policy-making, and procedural processes are necessary for the two orders. Just as a flower needs the planting of seeds, watering, and careful attention to bloom, the seeker of the mysteries needs physical, mental, and emotional preparation to function properly. True spiritual service requires discipline, observance of rules, and spiritual humility. When asked what advice he would give members of the Man of Earth degrees who wish to traverse through the difficulties of group power dynamics in the O.T.O., Grand Master General Shiva X° replied, "Meditate on the Holy Books of Thelema. Observe our Oaths. Walk humbly. Walk humbly. Walk humbly. And stick around."[13]

As the O.T.O. grows in popularity and membership, so too will its influence as a Thelemic society. Many experimental and innovative approaches to operating the O.T.O. are being implemented at local levels in an effort to bring the Order's presence into new ground. Workshops and classes offer readings and study groups on Thelemic literature. Dinner feasts, art collectives, dancing, music, wine tastings, board games, and group rituals are frequently held at O.T.O. Camps, Oases and Lodges. Discourse on blogs and internet group forums deliberate on how to retain membership, avoid attrition, initiate public and community outreach, and increase E.G.C. laity. The O.T.O. in its second century is indeed an exciting time for its membership.

Many challenges accompany such growth and influence. Being a hierarchical organization—whose foundation is based upon an individualistic philosophy—there is no shortage of membership expressing disagreement with its administration, whether on local, national, or even international levels. The existence of various schismatic claimant groups to A∴A∴, and the more vocal critical members on social media, have further contributed to disunity in the Order. It is the opinion of the author that problems arising from such disruptive factors may perhaps be eschewed by: (a) efforts on behalf of the administration to maintain a more visible presence of leadership among its lower-tiered membership, especially the Man of Earth Triad;

---

13 "Interview with Shiva X°," *Oz*, No. 3, Fall 2014, 14.

(b) clear and distinct statements of purpose for the organization as a whole; and (c) encouraging a culture of self-disciplined and fraternal cooperation—rather than unconstructive criticism—among all members.

Other Thelemic Movements and the Thelemic "Occulture"

If we consider Thelema as a religious phenomenon in general, it is evident that it extends beyond the exclusivity of the O.T.O. and the A∴A∴. Thelema is the spiritual movement of which the O.T.O. and the A∴A∴ are its most recognizable organizations. Thelema is a spiritual philosophy that many incorporate into their daily lives without any formal affiliation with the A∴A∴ and the O.T.O. And many other Thelemic organizations have emerged since Crowley's death, especially in recent decades.[14] It is unclear how populated these groups have become or to what degree they are active. Many are present primarily on the internet, while others seem to hold varying numbers of members in a physical organization. Some identify exclusively as "Thelemic," while others promote claimant A∴A∴ groups. A number of groups may be peripherally Thelemic, blending in elements of other spiritual and occult traditions. Their respective teachings may or may not be at variance with the current administrations of the A∴A∴ and the O.T.O., yet these organizations remain distinct and unaffiliated, even though some members of the O.T.O. may share membership.

---

[14] The reader should note that by "other Thelemic organizations" I am referring to any group that does not operate under the auspices of the O.T.O. or the A∴A∴ but which claims to represent Thelema. These include actual organizations that have been formed, as well as visible online Thelemic communities. At the time of this writing, several examples of physical Thelemic organizations can be named, whether they exist presently or have in the past. They include the Typhonian Order, the Fraternitas Saturni, the Gnostic Body of God, the Temple of Thelema, the Temple of the Silver Star, Society Ordo Templi Orientis, the Order of Thelemic Knights, the Holy Order of Ra-Hoor-Khuit (H.O.O.R.), the Thelemic Order of the Golden Dawn, the Temple of Babalon, the Ordo Astri, Ordo Sunyata Vajra, the Invisible House Society, The Gnostic Church of L.V.X., Horus-Maat Lodge, Cor Lucis, Thelemic Union, and Technicians of the Sacred. These are just a few.

As noted in chapter twelve, Thelema has extended substantially into the world of cyberspace. Discussion forums on social media have incorporated Thelemic thought into social and political platforms at an increasing frequency—ranging from topics such as individual liberty and social justice, to Thelemites who enjoy outdoor activities. Additionally, it is evident that Thelemic symbolism has become more prevalent in art, visual media, and music.

As Thelema continues to unfold outside the boundaries of the A∴A∴ and the O.T.O., it is likely that it will diversify, blend with other religious and occult movements, and branch off into other areas of the more general syncretic milieu of occulture. As such, anyone who wishes to research this trend may uncover more about the sociology of Thelema by examining the artistic and discursive currents of its effects throughout the wider ranges of its popular influence.[15]

Authority and Legitimacy

There are two interrelated points to be made about legitimacy. The first concerns the legitimacy of the Thelemic occulture—if it has any authoritative claims on Thelema. The second involves the legitimacy of the Thelemic movement itself. First of all, this research cannot remark on the "legitimacy" of any of the trends, currents, movements, and organizations that are herein described as part of the Thelemic occulture. As noted in chapter twelve, the groups and individuals within the Thelemic occulture exist primarily in a vacuum of anarchy, similar to the way international relations theory asserts that there is no hierarchical superior outside any one nation-state.[16] Authority and legitimacy

---

[15] It has been suggested that occulture can be utilized as a method for the study of art, culture, and religion. See, for example, Tessel Baudin (2013) "Introduction: Occulture in Modern Art," in *Aries: Journal for the Study of Western Esotercism*, Vol. 13, No. 1. (Leiden: Brill), 1–6. Also, Nina Kokkinen (2013) "Occulture as an Analytical Tool in the Study of Art," in *Aries: Journal for the Study of Western Esotercism*, Vol. 13, No. 1 (Leiden: Brill) 7–36.

[16] It is assumed that nation-states hold their own rule over their citizens as sovereign entities who can exact the legitimate use of force. Anarchy is the idea that no single power exists in the international sphere, and nation-states are therefore constrained

are intrinsically bound up within the dynamics of identity, alterity, and power. What can be said with certainty is that such claims remain outside the boundaries of the Thelemic movement. Any conclusions of legitimacy must ultimately derive from the reader's own critical analysis.

As we have seen, the Thelemic movement itself has undergone its own struggles with legitimacy. In Part II, we noted that the O.T.O. passed through many challenges on its way to establishing legitimacy. Although the absence of copyright to its literature helped disseminate published material in the 1970s, and therefore facilitated a growth of interest, it also allowed for the distortion and vitiation of its message, as well as discrepancies over authority. These factors motivated O.T.O. representatives to work within the secular sphere to sanction copyrights to the Thelemic literature.

Legitimacy in the A∴A∴ has been more controversial to date because of the schismatic discourse over "lineages." More recently, however, discussions on Duplexity and the Mystic Marriage, the subject of chapter thirteen, have advanced the legitimacy of the A∴A∴ and exposed the fallacy of the lineage discourse. What organization would allow multiple authoritative chains of command within its own borders?

Crowley understood the fundamental doctrinal precept—that he was under the command of the Secret Chiefs to follow out their mission in promulgating Thelema, and to do this through both the A∴A∴ and the O.T.O. It is clear from the current administrations of both orders today that this design has been reconstituted and set in place in a way that closely resembles Crowley's model.

O.T.O. in the Wider Context

There exists another set of challenges for the O.T.O. as it extends into larger spheres of influence in society. I refer to public opinion and social

---

to act out of self-interest (Realism), security (Neo-realism), or co-operative institutional measures (Liberalism and Neo-liberalism). See Kenneth Waltz (1979) *Theory of International Relations* (Reading: Addison-Wesley Pub. Co.).

standing. In his talk on the centenniel of O.T.O. in North America, Hymenaeus Beta outlined the struggles that the O.T.O. has faced concerning its reputation ever since Crowley's lifetime. One of the lessons to be learned from the past, according to the Frater Superior, is to "fight bad press." The press often took the offensive towards Crowley and his teachings. Such behavior has left a lasting negative cultural impression of Thelema and the O.T.O. The image of a drug-addicted, sex-crazed, murderous, devil-worshipping cult is an all-too-familiar stereotype. Any misconduct that arises within our membership only reinforces this negative portrait. Hymenaeus Beta recalled the struggles during the "Satanic Panic" of the 1980s, during which the O.T.O. fought hard to litigate through its publishers. Even more recently in 2004, the Grand Lodge of Australia filed a complaint case of religious vilification against people who breached the country's Racial and Religious Tolerance Act and slandered the Order on the internet. The case was won in the O.T.O.'s favor in 2006 in the Victorian Civil and Administrative Tribunal of Melbourne.[17]

The fact of the matter is that Thelema could not be further from the clichéd evil satanic sex cult. Its principles are based on individual liberty. Its teachings promote freedom from all forms of oppression— be they political, spiritual, social, or otherwise. While O.T.O. policies, procedures, and mission statements may vary depending on where they are issued, the Order universally upholds principles that promote diversity and harmony, facilitate cooperation and fraternity, and forbid criminal activities. As an example, the United States Grand Lodge has presented its mission statement as "cultivating the ideals of individual liberty, self-discipline, self-knowledge, and universal brotherhood," and to "foster harmonious and constructive relationships with the academic, business, civil, and greater social communities within which we operate."[18]

Despite such efforts to foster positive relations, the reader must be aware that even an organization based upon the highest level of spiritual principles will still find an unscrupulous percentage of its populace

---

[17] See the "Legal" tab on Grand Lodge of Australia Ordo Templi Orientis website.

[18] "Mission & Planning," United States Grand Lodge, Ordo Templi Orientis website.

seeking to exploit its more libertine themes and manipulate others. It is beyond doubt that some people come to Thelema and the O.T.O. for the wrong reasons: seeking power or prestige; believing "Do what thou wilt" can justify personal misconduct or the unleashing of character defects; or simply misunderstanding the O.T.O.'s philosophy of sexual magick and approaching the organization as if it were some kind of sex club. Vetting processes, such as requiring sponsorship for members to join and advance, seek to eschew such personalities; however these maladies can often go undetected until misconduct transpires. It is then required that the O.T.O. be swift and sure in upholding its behavioral standards.

Another factor challenging the O.T.O.'s reputation is the clamor from disgruntled members (or ex-members) whose animosities and hostilities produce negative impressions about the Order—especially with the reach offered by social media to aggressive keyboard warriors. In the disquieted environment of social media, it is apparent that an irritable and restless lay membership has surfaced in the Thelemic occulture and created its own online outlets to voice grievances. Whether these people are envious of others whose positions or degrees they seek, have had negative experiences with other members and wish to blame the Order as a whole, or simply do not respect the policies and procedures of the Order, the harm they cause—whether intended or not—strains our reputation. Perhaps such "knights and dames," self-resplendent in their shining armor, would like to think of themselves as the new Martin Luthers of Thelema. Instead, history may remember them as a collection of modern Cotton Mathers. They often seem to forget they have sworn oaths of fraternal bonds to their brothers and sisters. O.T.O. initiates must never forget that the Order is based upon oaths of service, fraternity, and fidelity—not on self-aggrandizement or public pronouncements of moral superiority.

It is today's initiate members who are responsible for upholding the Order's reputation. The O.T.O. may have policies that promote harmony and cooperation and rules that prohibit misconduct. The Order may have procedures to follow in the event that disagreements or transgressions occur between members. Yet, the whole is only as strong as the sum of its parts. As Hymenaeus Beta has remarked, "we always have to be prepared to fight for our reputation, or we will lose it."[19] It is therefore important as the O.T.O. goes forward that its members defend and act upon the spiritual principles taught to them during their initiations.

⋇

Conclusion

We have reached a critical point in the history of Thelema. It is one in which the Thelemic movement (O.T.O. and A∴A∴) and the Thelemic occulture have both witnessed an unprecedented growth. At points they intersect, yet they have developed their own respective subcultures. A rich and diverse social interaction is desirable for many reasons, and is a sign of marked growth. Yet, as a religious movement, Thelema faces the same threats that religions of the past have always had: schism, sectarianism, and factionalism. We have explored this, at length, within the modern discourse of A∴A∴ lineages. Regardless of those who oppose their alliance, the two orders rely on one another for reasons already outlined extensively in this book. With regard to membership in the O.T.O. on this point, the author anticipates a number of possible scenarios:

1. The remaining dissident A∴A∴ groups will decide to ally with the O.T.O. administration and begin to work to achieve unity in vision.

2. The administrators of the remaining dissident groups will continue to maintain a distinct identity within the O.T.O. (i.e., in the form of forwarding their "co-legitimacy" discourse by taking advantage of the promotional channels offered by membership), thus fanning factionalism, with members remaining largely divided.

---

[19] "One Hundred Years of the O.T.O. in North America: Inspirations and Lessons."

3. The administrators of the remaining dissident groups will resign from involvement in the O.T.O., and their respective "lineages" will continue outside of the O.T.O., as has been the path of several other A∴A∴ administrations.

4. The worst option, in my opinion, is that the O.T.O. could drift away from its association with the A∴A∴ and become a secularized fraternal organization with a Thelemic identity, but with less spiritual content—like a "Thelemic" Odd Fellows or Raccoon Lodge.

History may look back upon these years and see a "Council of Nicaea" moment. As we have explored in chapter thirteen, the tension between the O.T.O.'s administrative policies regarding its relationship to the A∴A∴—and whether or not this policy is accepted by its overall membership—is based upon fundamental spiritual principles. The O.T.O. has much to learn from the history of religion about schismatic movements. It is left to the Order's membership as to whether it will have the ability to execute its missions alongside the teachings, philosophy, and theology forwarded by the A∴A∴. I believe the full cooperation between the two orders should be sustained, and that those who seek to advance Thelema will find Duplexity—the "Mystic Marriage"—to be the surest means to realize that they are united in One Truth and One Spirit.

Yet, the proclivity towards schism is no longer relegated exclusively to the A∴A∴. We now see a conflict emerging between the O.T.O. and the more variant and deviant Thelemic occulture on social media. Although its most vocal members are still relatively few, their idiosyncratic approach to Thelema has been made accessible through internet forums. I speak here of the lines of distinction that have formed along political and secular viewpoints, rather than the strictly spiritual ones of the lineage problem. The self-proclaimed authority of the loudest voices stems not from any seasoned initiated involvement with the O.T.O., but from the transient dynamics of power expressed through identity and alterity politics in public forums.

Perhaps from this dynamic a different sort (or sorts) of Thelemic movement(s) may emerge. It may be that history will witness the surfacing of a "Thelemic Protestantism" or even a "Thelemic Puritanism." This will be recalcitrant to authoritative structure, and instead wanting to foster a more secular, non-hierarchical interpretation of Thelema in which traditional forms of spiritual initiation within the O.T.O. and the A∴A∴ hold less importance than that of political consciousness. Whatever the case may be, we hope to be able to trust in the safeguard of contemporary Western democratic society to never again plunge into the bloody physical conflicts that typified religious wars of the past. This does not mean that freedom cannot still be threatened on the mental, emotional and spiritual planes. Thelema indeed remains a safeguard for these as well, as long as it remains strong.

* * *

Thelema's history is not just a story of a new religious movement. It is a story of human beings and all the complicated nuances of what it means to experience the journey of life together, both in prosperous and in difficult times. In the closing of *The Book of the Law*, Ra-Hoor-Khuit reminds the Thelemite that, to arrive into His fold, His adherents must pass through the "tribulation of ordeal, which is bliss."[20] The challenges that face a new religious movement in its early years are plentiful. Some of these challenges, like schismatics, are as old as religion itself. The secularizing conditions of modern society are a new obstacle. With that said, a religion today must survive under the same conditions as, perhaps, a business does. A new religious movement must meet the demands of its seekers in the contemporary "marketplace of spiritualties."

While Thelema has been subject to many power struggles, both in the past and at present, the "war-engine" thunders forward. As is the case in any dynamic involving human beings, cooperation, clarity, and unity of purpose will realize greater achievements toward the intended goals. Observance and scrutiny of the oaths of fraternity and fidelity will only build a stronger Thelemic movement.

---

[20] AL III:62.

The Thelemic path is not meant to be an easy one. Thelema will not sugarcoat one's spiritual path with promises of the "feel-good" life. For those courageous enough to work this path, it will deliver the seeker to Truth. Thelema promises a unique journey among the stars of heaven.

The three forms of the Thelemic movement—A∴A∴, O.T.O., and E.G.C.—offer the chance of union among them. They serve distinct yet specific functions, and characterize Thelema as a highly diverse, comprehensive set of practices and activities that brings its adherents to heightened states of consciousness and spiritual freedom. Thelema as a religious phenomenon is a spiritual expression of Eternity set within a new condition of humankind ushered in by the Aeon of Horus. The individual drive for self-awareness, autonomy, and freedom from tyranny and oppression is the hallmark of Aleister Crowley's spiritual legacy. One can hope that the Thelemic movement will continue to move forward. Indeed, "Success is your proof."[21] May it remain informed by the Chiefs of the A∴A∴, organized and executed by the leaders of the O.T.O., and advanced and promulgated by the E.G.C. There is plenty of room for all.

---

[21] AL III:46.

Acknowledgments

I WOULD LIKE TO THANK the many persons who made this work a reality. First and foremost, I must humbly thank my editor-in-chief and project manager of this entire endeavor, Brother James Wasserman. Jim provided source material, including letters and out-of-print newsletters and journals when I initially wrote much of this material as my Master's thesis, and he has been a fundamental element in the editing, arranging, and managing this publication. Without his support and encouragement, this work would most likely never have come to fruition.

My wife, Kyra Readdy, has been a continual source of inspiration, support, and influence throughout. Much of the work in Part I was initially inspired by her, especially chapter five, "The War Engine." She has made many other contributions throughout. This work would surely not be what it is without her initiated insight and her feedback on the material as I was developing the book.

I am very grateful to Yvonne Paglia and the staff at Ibis Press for trusting and believing in me to produce this work. I am eternally grateful for this opportunity to step into the world as a published author with such a respected house in esoterica.

I wish to extend my gratitude to J. Daniel Gunther for his feedback, guidance, and friendship throughout my endeavors, both in this work and over the years I have known him. Daniel provided a great deal of insight in a number of areas explored here: including, but not limited to, linguistics, history, and the finer points of Crowley's philosophy of magick. I am also thankful for the cooperation and assistance of Frater Superior Hymenaeus Beta, who provided a number of unpublished source materials, including many rare photographs, and offerred much insightful feedback throughout. An early manuscript draft was reviewed and commented upon by the Supreme and Holy King of Australia, Frater Shiva X°, and I am thankful for his constructive feedback. Furthermore, it is a great honor to be introduced by Brother

Vere Chappell, who has also offered a great degree of assistance, help, and support throughout this project. Thanks to Scott Hobbs of the Cameron Parsons Foundation for generously allowing us to use the photos of Jack Parsons and Cameron, and to Mikki Maher of the Don Snyder Estate for permission to use Don's photo of Donald Weiser and *The Book of Thoth*.

I would further like to thank all those who dedicated their time to read proofs and make comments which helped improve this work tremendously, including: Nancy Wasserman, Frater Spiritus, James Strain, Richard Batchelor, Douglas Brown, Franc O'Shea, Patrick Everitt, Marko Milenovic, Craig Leifsol, and Leopold Vasquez. Special thanks to Douglas Brown and Franc O'Shea for taking on the arduous task of assisting with reading over Crowley's hand-written letters. Many readers and Crowley scholars can empathize with your suffering in these matters! Both James Strain and Richard Batchelor provided exhaustive editorial notation and errata throughout the proofing process. Nancy Wasserman provided abundant feedback and consistent encouragement, as did Brother Kjetil Fjell. Thank you to Richard Kaczynski for his meticulous scrutiny editing later drafts.

This work would not be what it is without the professional guidance over the years from my professors at the University of Amsterdam, and the University of Central Florida's department of philosophy. Although they were not directly involved in the current publication, I would like to acknowledge them, for it is under their tutelage that I had the opportunity to learn and develop the skills necessary for the research I have put forth herein.

I would also like to express my appreciation to those from whom I have learned and been supported in the Thelemic movement. To my instructor in the Outer College, whose guidance over the years has unquestionably led me ever closer to the Inner Guide—perhaps I would not have written this otherwise. To those chartered initiators and officers who have brought me into the mysteries of the O.T.O., please accept my gratitude. I would also like to thank the local bodies in which I have had the pleasure to serve over the years, including: Hidden

Spring Oasis in Orlando, Florida; Solve et Coagula in Amersfoort, Netherlands; Sekhet-Maat Lodge in Portland, Oregon; and AMeTh Lodge in London, United Kingdom. My sisters and brothers within these O.T.O. bodies have been sounding boards over the months and years leading up to this publication. You have helped me develop many of the ideas that are presented here, and have been supportive of my efforts, even when we may have disagreed.

Lastly, I would like to thank my friends and family for all of your support over the years. I so appreciate your endless encouragement to follow my path—whether it concerned my studies in Thelema, or simply the life choices that led to the materialization of this book.

Bibliography

Unpublished papers, letters, etc.

O.T.O.   O.T.O. Archives. Unpublished documents not immediately accessible to the public or scholars.

GYC   Gerald Yorke Collection. Unpublished documents located at the Warburg Institute, London, UK.

GMC   Karl Germer and Marcelo Ramos Motta Correspondence. Private collection.

GM-PSC   Grady McMurtry and Phyllis Seckler Correspondence. Private collection.

MSC   Marcelo Motta and Phyllis Seckler Correspondence. Private collection.

SWC   Samuel Weiser Correspondence. Private collection.

MRSC   Grady McMurtry, Israel Regardie, and Phyllis Seckler Correspondence. Private collection.

UC   Unpublished, Unsorted and Miscellaneous Correspondence. Private Collection.

Works by Aleister Crowley

Crowley, Aleister (1905–1907) *The Collected Works of Aleister Crowley*. Volumes I–III. Des Plaines, IL: Yogi Publication Society.

_____ (1909–1913) *The Equinox: The Official Organ of the A∴A∴: The Review of Scientific Illuminism*. Volume I, Numbers 1–10. London: Various publishers (See also 1972a).

_____ (1919) *The Equinox: The Official Organ of the A∴A∴, The Official Organ of the O.T.O.: The Review of Scientific Illuminism*. Volume III, Number 1 (*The Blue Equinox*). Detroit: Universal Publishing Company.

_____ (1936) *The Equinox of the Gods*. London: O.T.O. (See also 1974a, 1991a, 1991b).

_____ (1938) *The Book of the Law*. London: O.T.O.

_____ (1952a) *The Vision and the Voice*. Barstow: Thelema Publishing Company.

_____ (1952b) *777 Revised*. London: Neptune Press.

_____ (1954) *Magick Without Tears*. New Jersey: Thelema Publishing Company.

_____ (1961) *Liber Aleph vel CXI: The Book of Wisdom or Folly*. West Point: Karl Germer.

_____ (1962) *The Book of Lies*. New York: The Haydn Press (See also 1981).

_____ (1969a) *The Confessions of Aleister Crowley: An Autohagiography*. Edited by John Symonds and Kenneth Grant. London: Jonathan Cape, and New York: Hill & Wang.

_____ (1969b) *The Book of Thoth*. New York: Samuel Weiser, Inc.

_____ (1971) *Shih Yi*. Oceanside: Thelema Publications.

_____ (1972a) *The Equinox: The Official Organ of the A∴A∴: The Review of Scientific Illuminism*. Volume I, Numbers 1–10. New York: Samuel Weiser, Inc.

_____ (1972b) *The Equinox: The Official Organ of the A∴A∴: The Review of Scientific Illuminism*. Volume III, Number 1 (*The Blue Equinox*). New York: Samuel Weiser, Inc.

_____ (1972c) *The Magical Record of the Beast 666: The Diaries of Aleister Crowley 1914–1920*. Edited by John Symonds and Kenneth Grant. London: Duckworth.

_____ (1973a) *Magick*. Edited by John Symonds and Kenneth Grant. London: Routledge & Kegan Paul.

_____ (1973b) *Cocaine*. San Francisco: Level Press.

_____ (1973c) *The Heart of the Master*. Montreal: 93 Publishing.

_____ (1973d) *Khing Kang King*. Kings Beach: Thelema Publications.

_____ (1974a) *The Equinox of the Gods*. New York: Gordon Press.

_____ (1974b) *On Magick: An Introduction to the High Art*. Edited by Llee Heflin. San Francisco: Level Press.

_____ (1974c) *The Magical and Philosophical Commentaries on the*

Book of the Law. Edited by John Symonds and Kenneth Grant. Montreal: 93 Publishing.

_____ (1974d) *The Soul of the Desert*. Kings Beach: Thelema Publications.

_____ and Motta, Marcelo Ramos (1975) *The Commentaries of AL*. New York: Samuel Weiser, Inc.

_____ (1976) *Leah Sublime*. South Stukely: 93 Publishing.

_____ (1977) *777 and Other Qabalistic Writings of Aleister Crowley*. New York: Samuel Weiser, Inc.

_____ (1981) *The Book of Lies*. New York: Samuel Weiser, Inc.

_____ and Motta, Marcelo (1981) *The Equinox: The Official Organ of the A∴A∴: The Review of Scientific Illuminism*. Volume V, Number 4 *(Sex and Religion)*. Nashville: Thelema Publishing Company.

_____ (1986) *Magick Without Tears*. Edited by Israel Regardie. Tempe, AZ: New Falcon Publications.

_____ (1983) *The Holy Books of Thelema*. New York: Samuel Weiser, Inc.

_____ (1990) *The Rites of Eleusis*. Thame, Oxon: Mandrake Press Ltd.

_____ (1991a) *The Equinox of the Gods*. Scottsdale, AZ: New Falcon Publications.

_____ (1991b) *The Equinox of the Gods*. New York: 93 Publishing.

_____ (1991c) *Liber Aleph vel CXI: The Book of Wisdom or Folly*. York Beach: Samuel Weiser, Inc.

_____ (1992) *The Heart of the Master*. Edited by Hymenaeus Beta. Scottsdale, AZ: New Falcon Publications.

_____ (1996a) *The Law Is for All: An Authorized Popular Commentary to The Book of the Law*. Edited by Louis Wilkinson and Hymenaeus Beta. Tempe, AZ: New Falcon Publications.

_____ (1996b) *Commentaries on the Holy Books and Other Papers: The Equinox*. Volume IV, Number 1. York Beach: Samuel Weiser, Inc.

_____ (1997) *Magick: Liber ABA: Book Four*. Edited by Hymenaeus Beta (ps. of William Breeze). York Beach: Samuel Weiser, Inc.

_____ (1998a) *The Vision and the Voice with Commentary and Other Papers*. York Beach: Weiser Books.

_____ (1998b) *The Revival of Magick and Other Essays (Oriflamme 2)*. Tempe, AZ: New Falcon Publications.

_____ (2007a) *The Book of Thoth*. Newburyport, MA: Weiser Books.

_____ (2007b) *The Equinox: The Official Organ of the A∴A∴, The Official Organ of the O.T.O.: The Review of Scientific Illuminism*. Volume III, Number 1 (*The Blue Equinox*). Newburyport, MA: Weiser Books.

_____ (Editor) (1995) *The Goetia: The Lesser Key of Solomon the King, Clavicula Salomonis Regis*. Translated by Mathers, Samuel Liddell MacGregor. 2nd edition. Hymenaeus Beta (Editor.). York Beach: Samuel Weiser, Inc.

Works by Other Authors

Achad, Frater (Charles Stansfeld Jones) (2010) *The Alpha and Omega of Initiation*. Greifswald: Reineke Verlag.

Åkerman, Susanna (1998) *Rose and Cross Over the Baltic: The Spread of Rosicrucianism in Northern Europe*. Leiden: Brill.

Almaas, A.H. (2001) *The Point of Existence: Transformations of Narcissism in Self Realization*. London: Shambhala.

Aryes, Lewis (2006) *Nicaea and Its Legacy*. Oxford: University of Oxford Press.

Asprem, Egil (2008) "Magic Naturalized? Negotiating Science and Occult Experience in Aleister Crowley's Scientific Illuminism." In *Aries: Journal for the Study of Western Esotericism*, 8. Leiden: Brill, pp. 139–165.

_____ (2012) *Arguing with Angels: Enochian Magic and Modern Occulture*. Albany: SUNY Press.

_____ (2014) *The Problem of Disenchantment: Scientific Naturalism and Esoteric Discourse 1900–1939*. Leiden: Brill.

Asprem, Egil and Granholm, Kennet (Editors) (2013) *Contemporary Esotericism*. Sheffield: Equinox Publishing, Ltd.

Assmann, Jan (1997) *Moses the Egyptian: The Memory of Egypt in Western Monotheism*. Cambridge: Harvard University Press.

Balfour-Clarke, Russell (1977) *The Boyhood of J. Krishnamurti*. Bombay: Chetana.

Balk, Antti P. (2018) *The Law of Thelema: Aleister Crowley's Philosophy of True Will*. London: Thelema Publications, LLC.

Bamberger, Joan (1974) "The Myth of Matriarchy: Why Men Rule in Primitive Society." In *Women, Culture, and Society*. Edited by Michelle Rosaldo and Louise Lamphere. Stanford: Stanford University Press.

Barber, Malcolm (1994) *The New Knighthood: A History of the Order of the Temple*. Cambridge: Cambridge University Press.

_____ (2001) *The Trial of the Templars*. Second Edition. Cambridge: Cambridge University Press.

Barton, Blanche (1990) *The Secret Life of a Satanist: An Authorized Biography of Anton LaVey*. Port Townsend: Feral House.

Baudin, Tessel (2013) "Introduction: Occulture in Modern Art." In *Aries: Journal for the Study of Western Esotercism* Volume 13, Number 1. Leiden: Brill, pp. 1–6.

Baumann, Gerd and Gingrich, Andre (Editors) (2004) *Grammars of Identity/ Alterity: A Structural Approach*. New York; Oxford: Berghahn Books.

Becker, Howard (1963) *Outsiders: Studies in the Sociology of Deviance*. London: Collier–Macmillan, Ltd.

Berkeley, George (2004) *A Treatise Concerning the Principles of Human Knowledge*. Mineola: Dover Publications, Inc.

Beta, Hymenaeus (Fall 1997) "Women's Conference Address." In *The Magical Link*, New Series, Number 1, pp. 8–10.

Bruce, Steve (2002) *God is Dead: Secularization in the West*. Oxford: Blackwell Publishing.

Bogdan, Henrik (2003) "Kenneth Grant: A Bibliography from 1948." Gothenburg: Academia Esoterica.

_____ (2014) "Kenneth Grant and the Typhonian Tradition." In *The Occult World*. Edited by Christopher Partridge. London: Routledge, pp. 323–330.

_____ (2016) "The Babalon Working 1946: L. Ron Hubbard, John Whiteside Parsons, and the Practice of Enochian Magic." In *NVMEN:*

International Review for the History of Religions. Volume 63. Leiden: Brill, pp. 12–32.

Bogdan, Henrik and Starr, Martin P. (Editors) (2012) *Aleister Crowley and Western Esotericism.* New York: Oxford University Press.

Bogdan, Henrik and Djurdjevic, Gordan (Editors) (2013) *Occultism in a Global Perspective.* Bristol: Acumen.

Booth, Martin (2000) *A Magick Life: A Biography of Aleister Crowley.* London: Hodder and Stoughton.

Brailovskaia, Julia and Margraf, Jürgen (2017) "Facebook Addiction Disorder (FAD) Among German students—a longitudinal approach" In PLoS One, Vol. 12, No. 12.

Campbell, Colin (1972) "The Cult, the Cultic Milieu, and Secularization" in M. Hill (Editor) *A Sociological Year-book of Religion in Britain.* Volume 5, pp. 9–36.

_____ (1977) "Clarifying the Cult." In *The British Journal of Sociology,* Vol. 28, No. 3, pp. 375–388.

Canagarajah, Suresh A. (2002) *A Geopolitics of Academic Writing.* Pittsburgh: University of Pittsburgh Press.

Capra, Fritjof (1975) *The Tao of Physics: An Exploration of the Parallels Between Modern Physics and Eastern Mysticism.* London: Fontana/ Collins.

Carter, John (2004) *Sex and Rockets: The Occult World of Jack Parsons.* Port Townshend, WA: Feral House.

Chaves, Mark (1994) "Secularization As Declining Religious Authority." In *Social Forces,* Volume 72, Number 3, pp. 749–774.

Churton, Tobias (2011) *Aleister Crowley: The Biography.* London: Watkins Publishing.

_____ (2014) *Aleister Crowley The Beast in Berlin: Art, Sex, and Magick in the Weimar Republic.* Rochester, VT: Inner Traditions.

_____ (2016) *Occult Paris: The Lost Magic of the Belle Époque.* Rochester, VT: Inner Traditions.

_____ (2017) *Aleister Crowley in America: Art, Espionage, and Sex Magick in the New World.* Rochester, VT: Inner Traditions.

Cluclas, Stephen (Editor) (2006) *John Dee: Interdisciplinary Studies in English Renaissance Thought*. Dordrecht: Springer.

Clulee, Nicholas H. (1988) *John Dee's Natural Philosophy*. London: Routledge.

Coontz, Stephanie (2000) *The Way We Never Were: American Families and the Nostalgia Trap*. New York: Basic Books.

Corbey, Raymond and Leerssen, Joep (Editors) (1991) *Alterity, Identity, Image: Selves and Others in Society and Scholarship*. Amsterdam: Rodopi.

Cornelius, J. Edward (1999) *The Magical Essence of Aleister Crowley. Red Flame: A Thelemic Research Journal,* Number 7. Berkeley: Publication by Author.

_____ (2005) *In the Name of the Beast*. Volume 2. Berkeley: Publication by Author.

_____ (2018) *Memoirs of an A∴A∴ Initiate: Being the True Story of the Struggles for Freedom in the 1990s Against the Restrictionists*. Berkeley: Publication by Author.

Cornelius, Marlene and Gillis, R.L. (2013) *Liber AL: An Examination*. Berkeley: Conjoined Creation.

Corydon, Brent and Hubbard, L. Ron Jr. (1987) *L. Ron Hubbard: Messiah or Madman?* Secaucus: Lyle Stuart.

Cremer, Herman (1895) *Biblico-Theological Lexicon of New Testament Greek*. Edinburgh: T, and T. Clark.

Cunningham, Lawrence S. (2005) *A Brief History of Saints*. Oxford: Blackwell Publishing.

D'Arch Smith, Timothy (1991) *The Books of the Beast: Essays on Aleister Crowley, Montague Summers and Others*. Oxford: Mandrake.

Dashu Max (2005) "Knocking Down Straw Dolls: A Critique of Cynthia Eller's *The Myth of Matriarchal Prehistory: Why an Invented Past Won't Give Women a Future*." In *Feminist Theology*, Volume 13, Issue 2, 185–216.

De Sainte Croix, Geoffrey Ernest Maurice (2006) *Christian Persecution, Martyrdom, and Orthodoxy*. Edited by Michael Whitby. Oxford: Oxford University Press.

Dehn, Georg (2015) *The Book of Abramelin: A New Translation* (Revised and Expanded Second Edition). Lake Worth: Ibis Press.

Descartes, René (1996) *Meditations of the First Philosophy with Selections from the Objections and Replies.* Translated by John Cottingham. Cambridge: Cambridge University Press.

Denton, M.L. and Smith, C. (2003) "Methodological Issues and Challenges in the Study of American Youth and Religion." Chapel Hill, NC: National Study of Youth and Religion.

Deveney, John Patrick (1997) *Paschal Beverley Randolph: A Nineteenth-Century Black American Spiritualist, Rosicrucian and Sex Magician.* Albany: SUNY Press.

Eckartshausen, Karl von (1896) *The Cloud Upon the Sanctuary.* Translated by Isabel de Steiger. (Reprinted 2003) Lake Worth: Ibis Press.

Effertz, Michael (2013) *Priest/ess: In Advocacy of Queer Gnostic Mass.* Hollywood: Luxor Media Group, LLC.

Eliade, Mircea (1959) *The Sacred and the Profane: The Nature of Religion.* Translated by Willard R. Trask. London: Harcourt, Inc.

Eller, Cynthia (2000) *The Myth of Matriarchal Prehistory: Why an Invented Past Won't Give Women a Future.* Boston: Beacon Press.

Ellwood, Robert S. (1994) *The Sixties Spiritual Awakening: American Religion Moving from Modern to Postmodern.* New Brunswick: Rutgers University Press.

Embley, Peter (1966) *The Origins and Early Development of the Plymouth Brethren.* Ph.D. dissertation. Cheltenham: St. Paul's College.

Eshelman, James A. (Editor) (Spring 1997) *The Black Pearl.* Volume I, Number 1. Los Angeles: The College of Thelema.

_____ (2000) *The Mystical & Magical System of the A∴A∴.* Los Angeles: The College of Thelema.

Evans, Dave (2004) "Trafficking with an Onslaught of Compulsive Weirdness: Kenneth Grant and the Magickal Revival." In *Journal for the Academic Study of Magic: Issue 2.* Oxford: Mandrake, pp. 226–259.

_____ (2007) *The History of British Occultism after Crowley.* Harpenden: Hidden Publishing.

Evans, M. Stanton (2007) *Blacklisted by History: The Untold Story of Senator Joe McCarthy and His Fight Against America's Enemies*. New York: Three Rivers Press.

Faivre, Antoine (1994) *Access to Western Esotericism*. Albany: SUNY Press.

Fjell, Kjetil (2014) "The Vindication of Thelema." In *The Fenris Wolf*. Issue 7. Stockholm: Edda.

Flowers, Stephen E. (2018) *The Fraternitas Saturni*. Rochester, VT: Inner Traditions.

Forman, Robert (Editor) (1998) *The Innate Capacity: Mysticism, Psychology, and Philosophy*. Oxford: Oxford University Press.

Fowden, Garth (1986) *The Egyptian Hermes*. Princeton: Princeton University Press.

Fried, Albert (1997). *McCarthyism, The Great American Red Scare: A Documentary History*. Oxford: Oxford University Press.

Foucault, Michel (1998) *The History of Sexuality: The Will to Knowledge*. London: Penguin.

Fuller, Jean Overton (1990) *The Magical Dilemma of Victor Neuburg: A Biography*. Oxford: Mandrake.

Gallagher, Shaun and Zahavi, Dan (2008) *The Phenomenological Mind: An Introduction to Philosophy of Mind and Cognitive Science*. New York: Routledge.

Gauld, Alan (1968) *The Founders of Psychical Research*. London: Routledge.

Gerth, H.H. and Mills, C. Wright (Translators) (1946) *Max Weber: Essays in Sociology*. New York: Oxford University Press.

Gilbert, Robert A. (1983) *The Golden Dawn: Twilight of the Magicians*. Wellingborough: The Aquarian Press.

_____ (1986) *The Golden Dawn Companion: A Guide to History, Structure, and Workings of the Hermetic Order of the Golden Dawn*. York Beach: Samuel Weiser, Inc.

_____ (1998) *Golden Dawn Scrapbook: The Rise and Fall of a Magical Order*. York Beach: Samuel Weiser, Inc.

_____ (January 2005) "Independent Witnesses: Observers of English Occultism in the Victorian Era." In *Theosophical History*, Volume XI, Number 1.

Gimbutas, Marija (1991) *The Civilization of the Goddess: The World of Old Europe*. San Francisco: Harper.

Gilly, Carlos (2004) *Adam Halmayr*. In de Pelikaan: Amsterdam.

Giudice, Christian (2014) "Ordo Templi Orientis." In *The Occult World*. Edited by Christopher Partridge. New York: Routledge.

Godwin, Joscelyn (1994) *The Theosophical Enlightenment*. Albany: SUNY Press.

Godwin, Joscelyn; Chanel, Christian; Deveney, John Patrick (1995) *The Hermetic Brotherhood of Luxor: Initiatic and Historical Documents of an Order of Practical Occultism*. York Beach: Samuel Weiser, Inc.

Goodman, Paul (1956) *Growing Up Absurd: Problems of Youth in the Organized System*. New York: Random House.

Goodrick-Clarke, Nicholas (2008) *The Western Esoteric Traditions: A Historical Introduction*. Oxford: Oxford University Press.

Goodwin, Charles Wycliffe (Translator) (1852) *Fragment of a Græco-Egyptian Work Upon Magic from a Papyrus in the British Museum*. Cambridge: Deighton, Macmillan and Co.

Goswami, Amit and Maggie (1998) *Science and Spirituality: A Quantum Integration*. Delhi: Project of History of Indian Science, Philosophy and Culture.

Grant, Kenneth (1973) *The Magical Revival*. New York: Samuel Weiser, Inc.

Greer, Mary K. (1994) *Women of the Golden Dawn*. Rochester: Park Street Press.

Gunther, J. Daniel (2009) *Initiation in the Æon of the Child: The Inward Journey*. Lake Worth: Ibis Books.

_____ (2014) *The Angel and the Abyss*: *Comprising The Angel and the Abyss and The Hieroglyphic Triad, Being Books II and III of The Inward Journey*. Lake Worth: Ibis Books.

_____ (2018) *The Visions of the Pylons: A Magical Record of Exploration in the Starry Abode*. Lake Worth: Ibis Press.

Hakl, Thomas (Trans.) (2014) "The Magical Order of the Fraternitas Saturni." In *Occultism in a Global Perspective*. Edited by Henrik Bogdan and Gordan Djurdjevic. New York: Acumen, pp. 37–56.

Hammer, Olav (2004) *Claiming Knowledge: Strategies of Epistemology from Theosophy to the New Age*. Leiden: Brill.

Hanegraaff, Wouter J. (1998) *New Age Religion and Western Culture: Esotericism in the Mirror of Secular Thought*. Albany: SUNY Press.

_____ (1999) "Defining Religion in Spite of History." In *The Pragmatics of Defining Religion: Contexts, Concepts, and Contests*. Edited by Jan G. Platvoet and Arie Leendert Molendijk. Leiden: Brill, pp. 337–378.

_____ (2003) "How Magic Survived the Disenchantment of the World." In *Religion*. Volume 33, Number 4, pp. 357–380.

_____ (2012) *Esotericism and the Academy: Rejected Knowledge in Western Culture*. Cambridge: Cambridge University Press.

_____ (2013) *Western Esotericism: A Guide for the Perplexed*. London: Bloomsbury Publishing Plc.

Hanegraaff, Wouter and Pijenburg, Joyce (Editors) (2009) *Hermes in the Academy: Ten Years' Study of Western Esotericism at the University of Amsterdam*. Amsterdam: Amsterdam University Press.

Hardwick, Charley D. (1973) "The Counter Culture as Religion: On the Identification of Religion." In *Soundings; An Interdisciplinary Journal*, Vol. 56, No. 3, pp. 287–311.

Harkness, Deborah (1999) *John Dee's Conversations with Angels*. Cambridge: Cambridge University Press.

Hedenborg-White, Manon (2013) "To Him the Winged Secret Flame, To Her the Stooping Starlight: The Social Construction of Gender in Contemporary Ordo Templi Orientis." In *The Pomegranate*, Vol. 15, Issue 1–2, pp. 102–121.

Heelas, Paul (1996) *The New Age Movement: Religion, Culture, and Society in the Age of Postmodernity*. Cambridge: Blackwell Publishing.

Heelas, Paul and Woodhead, Linda (Editors) (2000) *Religion in Modern Times: An Interpretive Anthology*. Oxford: Blackwell.

_____ (2005) *The Spiritual Revolution: Why Religion is Giving Way to Spirituality*. Malden: Blackwell.

Heselton, Philip (2012a) *Witchfather: A Life of Gerald Gardner, Vol. I: Into the Witch Cult*. Loughborough, Leicestershire: Thoth.

_____ (2012b) *Witchfather: A Life of Gerald Gardner, Vol 2: From Witch Cult to Wicca*. Loughborough, Leicestershire: Thoth.

Heflin, Llee (1973) *The Island Dialogues*. San Francisco: Level Press.

Heidegger, Martin (2010) *Being and Time*. Translated by Joan Stambaugh. Albany: SUNY Press.

Higgs, John (2006) *I Have America Surrounded: The Life of Timothy Leary*. Fort Lee: Barricade Books, Inc.

Howe, Ellic (1978) *The Magicians of the Golden Dawn: A Documentary History of a Magical Order 1887–1923*. York Beach: Samuel Weiser, Inc.

Hoyt, Sarah F (1912) "The Etymology of Religion." In *Journal of the American Oriental Society*, Volume 32, Number 2, pp. 126–29.

Hume, David (2007) *An Inquiry Concerning Human Understanding*. Oxford: Oxford University Press.

Huss, Boaz; Pasi, Marco; von Stuckrad, Knocku (Editors) (2010) *Kabbalah and Modernity: Interpretations, Transformations, Adaptations*. Leiden: Brill.

Husserl, Edmund (2001) *Logical Investigations*, Volumes I–II. Translated by J.N. Findlay. New York: Routledge.

Hutton, Ronald (1999) *The Triumph of the Moon: A History of Modern Pagan Witchcraft*. New York: Oxford University Press.

Inman, Thomas (1875) *Ancient Pagan and Modern Christian Symbolism*. Second Edition. New York: J.W. Bouton.

James, Geoffrey (1998) *The Enochian Magick of Dr. John Dee: The Most Powerful System of Magick in Its Original, Unexpurgated Form*. St. Paul: Llewellyn Publications.

Jorgensen, Danny L. and Lin (1982) "Social Meanings of the Occult." *The Sociological Quarterly*, 23:3 (Summer), pp. 373–389.

Kaczynski, Richard (Spring 2006) "Panic in Detroit: The Magician and the Motor City." In *Blue Equinox Journal*, Number 2. Royal Oak, MI: O.T.O.

_____ (2010) *Perdurabo: The Life of Aleister Crowley*. Berkeley: North Atlantic Books.

_____ (2012) *Forgotten Templars: The Untold Origins of Ordo Templi Orientis*. N.p.: Published for the Author.

Kahn, Charles H. (1960) *Anaximander and the Origins of Greek Cosmology.* New York: Columbia University Press.

Kant, Immanuel (2007) *Critique of Pure Reason.* Translated by Marcus Weigelt. Oxford: Penguin Books, Ltd.

Kaplan, Aryeh (1997) *Sefer Yetzirah; The Book of Creation In Theory and Practice.* York Beach: Samuel Weiser, Inc.

Kaplan, Jeffrey and Lööw, Heléne (2002) *The Cultic Milieu: Oppositional Subcultures in an Age of Globalization.* New York: Rowman & Littlefield Publishers, Inc.

Kaufmann, Walter (Translator) (2000) *Basic Writings of Nietzsche.* Toronto: Random House, Inc.

Keenan, David (2003) *England's Hidden Reverse: A Secret History of the Esoteric Underground.* London: SAF Publications, Ltd.

Kellner, Carl (1986) *Yoga Eine Skizze über den psycho-physiologischen Teil der alten indischen Yogalehre.* Munich: International Congress of Psychology.

Kilcher, Andreas (2010) *Constructing Tradition: Means and Myths of Transmission in Western Esotericism.* Leiden: Brill.

King, Francis (1970) *Ritual Magic in England.* London: Neville Spearman.

_____ (Editor) (1973) *The Secret Rituals of the O.T.O.* London: C.W. Daniel Company Ltd.

King, Stephen J. (2014) "Interview with the King, Shiva X°." By Frater S.D.S. and Sr. N.R. In *OZ: The Quarterly Publication of the Australian Grand Lodge of Ordo Templi Orientis.* Number 33, pp. 12–15.

Klehr, Harvey and Haynes, John Earl (1999) *Venona: Decoding Soviet Espionage in America.* London: Yale University Press.

Knecht, Robert (2002) *The French Wars of Religion: 1559–1598.* Oxford: Osprey.

Kokkinen, Nina (2013) "Occulture as an Analytical Tool in the Study of Art." In *Aries: Journal for the Study of Western Esotercism.* Volume 13, Number 1. Leiden: Brill, pp. 7–36.

Laurants, Jean-Pierre (1992) *L'ésotérisme chrétien en France au XIXe siècle.* Lausanne: L'Age d'Homme.

Leary, Timothy (1968) *The Politics of Ecstasy.* Oakland: Ronin Publishing.

Leibniz, Gottfried W. (1991) *Discourse on Metaphysics and Other Essays.* Translated by Daniel Garber and Roger Ariew. Indianapolis: Hackett Publishing Company, Inc.

Lévi, Éliphas (1896) *Transcendental Magic.* Translated by Arthur Edward Waite. London: Rider.

Levinas, Emmanuel (1991) *Totality and Infinity: An Essay on Exteriority.* Translated by Alphonso Lingis. London: Kluwer Academic Publishers.

Lingan, Edmund B. (2006) "Contemporary Forms of Occult Theatre." *PAJ Journal of Performance and Art*, 28:3 (September), pp. 23–38.

Luck, Georg (2000) "Theurgy and Forms of Worship in Neoplatonism." In *Ancient Pathways and Hidden Pursuits: Religion, Morals and Magic in the Ancient World.* Georg Luck (Editor). Ann Arbor: University of Michigan Press.

Lycoyrinos, Damon (2013) "Sex Magick and the 'Occult' Body of the Mega Therion: A Study of Ritual Body Techniques, Applied Occultism, and Aleister Crowley's Sex Magick." 4th International ESSWE Conference. Gothenburg: University of Gothenburg.

Lyons, Arthur (1970) *The Second Coming: Satanism in America.* New York: Dodd, Mead and Company.

Magee, Bryan (2001) *The Story of Philosophy.* London: Dorling Kindersley.

Martin, David (1979) *A General Theory of Secularization.* New York: Harper & Row.

McIntosh, Christopher (1972) *Eliphas Lévi and the French Occult Revival.* London: Rider & Co.

_____ (1992) *The Rose Cross and the Age of Reason: Eighteenth-Century Rosicrucianism in Central Europe and its Relationship to the Enlightenment.* Albany: SUNY Press.

_____ (1997) *The Rosicrucians: The History, Mythology, and Rituals of an Esoteric Order.* York Beach: Weiser Books.

Miller, Russell (2014) *Bare-Faced Messiah: The True Story of L. Ron Hubbard.* London: Silvertail Books.

MLChMH, AISh (2004) "Duplexity: A Cursory Glance at the Relationship Existing Between the Orders O.T.O. and A∴A∴." In *The Laughterful Caress: The Journal of Leaping Laughter Oasis, O.T.O.*, Volume V, Number

1, Spring Equinox Anno IV: xii. Minneapolis: Leaping Laughter Oasis, O.T.O., pp. 7–11.

Mondlin, Marvin and Meador, Roy (2003) *Book Row: An Anecdotal and Pictorial History of the Antiquarian Book Trade*. New York: Carroll & Graf.

Morrisson, Mark (Winter 2008) "The Periodical Culture of the Occult Revival: Esoteric Wisdom, Modernity and Counter-Public Spheres." In *Journal of Modern Literature*, Vol. 1, No. 2, pp. 1–22.

Motta, Marcelo Ramos (1962) *Chamando os Filhos do Sol, da Parte da Ordem do Rubi e Oro*. Rio de Janeiro.

_____ (1979) *The Equinox: The Official Organ of the A∴A∴: The Review of Scientific Illuminism*. Volume V, Number 2. Nashville: Thelema Publishing Company.

Neitzsche, Friedrich (1999) *The Birth of Tragedy and Other Writings*. Translated by Ronald Spiers. Cambridge: Cambridge University Press.

Neumann, Erich (1995) *The Origins and History of Consciousness*. Translated by R.F.C. Hull. Princeton: Princeton University Press.

Nilsson, Martin Persson (1950) *The Minoan-Mycenaean Religion and Its Survival in Greek Religion*. New York: Biblo & Tannen Publishers

Otto, Rudolph (1958) *The Idea of the Holy: An Inquiry into the Non-Relational Factor in the Idea of the Divine and Its Relation to the Rational*. Translated by John W. Harvey. Oxford: Oxford University Press.

O'Rourke, Fran (1992) *Pseudo-Dionysius and the Metaphysics of Aquinas*. Leiden: Brill.

Ordo Templi Orientis (2014) *Mystery of Mystery: A Primer of Thelemic Ecclesiastical Gnosticism*. Edited by Sabazius X° [Pseudonym David Scriven]. Berkeley: O.T.O.

Owen, Alex (2004) *The Place of Enchantment: British Occultism and the Cult of the Modern*. Chicago: The University of Chicago Press.

Parsons, John Whiteside (1990) *Freedom is a Two-Edged Sword*. Scottsdale, AZ: New Falcon Publications.

Partridge, Christopher (2004) *The Re-Enchantment of the West: Alternative Spiritualities, Sacralization, Popular Culture, and Occulture*. Volume I. London: T. and T. Clark International.

Pasi, Marco (1998) "L' anticristianesimo in Aleister Crowley (1875–1947)." In *Aleister Crowley: Un Mago a Cefalù*. PierLuigi Zoccatelli (Editor). Rome: Edizioni Mediterranee.

_____ (2003) "The Neverendingly Told Story: Recent Biographies of Aleister Crowley." In *Aries: Journal for the Study of Western Esotericism*, 3:2, pp. 224–245.

_____ (2005) "Occultism." In *Dictionary of Religion*, 3. Edited by Kocku von Stuckrad. Leiden: Brill, pp. 1364–68.

_____ (2005) "Ordo Templi Orientis." In *Dictionary of Gnosis and Western Esotericism*. Edited by Wouter J. Hanegraaff. Leiden: Brill, pp. 898–906.

_____ (2014) *Aleister Crowley and the Temptation of Politics*. Bristol: Acumen Publishing, Ltd.

Pendle, George (2005) *Strange Angel: The Otherworldly Life of Rocket Scientist John Whiteside Parsons*. London: Weidenfeld & Nicolson.

Perl, Eric David (2007) *Theophany: The Neoplatonic Philosophy of Dionysius the Areopagite*. Albany: SUNY Press.

Popiol, Alexander and Schrader, Raimund (2007) *Gregor A. Gregorius– Mystiker des Dunklen Lichts*. Bürstadt: Esoterischer Verlag.

Rabelais, François (1952) *Gargantua and Pantagruel*. Translated by Sir Thomas Urquhart and Peter Motteux. Chicago; London: William Benton / Encyclopedia Britannica.

Readdy, Keith (2014) "The Antichrist and the Beast: Friedrich Nietzsche's Connection to Aleister Crowley." Universiteit van Amsterdam. Unpublished.

Regardie, Israel (1937) *The Golden Dawn: An Account of the Teachings, Rites, and Ceremonies of the Hermetic Order of the Golden Dawn*. Four Volumes. Chicago: The Aries Press.

_____ (1938) *The Middle Pillar: A Co-Relation of the Principles of Analytical Psychology and the Elementary Techniques of Magic*. Chicago: The Aries Press.

_____ (1970) *The Eye in the Triangle: An Interpretation of Aleister Crowley*. St. Paul: Llewellyn (see also 1982).

_____ (1982) *The Eye in the Triangle: An Interpretation of Aleister Crowley*. Las Vegas: Falcon Press.

_____ (1984) *The Complete Golden Dawn System of Magic*. Tempe, AZ: New Falcon Publications.

Richmond, Keith (Editor) (2009) *The Progradior Correspondence: Letters by Aleister Crowley, Frank Bennett, C.S. Jones, and Others*. York Beach: The Teitan Press.

_____ (Editor) (2011) *Aleister Crowley, the Golden Dawn, and Buddhism: Reminiscences and Writings of Gerald Yorke*. York Beach: The Teitan Press.

Rorem, Paul (1993) *Pseudo-Dionysius: A Commentary on the Texts and an Introduction to Their Influence*. Oxford: Oxford University Press.

Roszack, Theodore (1969) *The Making of a Counter Culture: Reflections on the Technocratic Society and Its Youthful Opposition*. Garden City: Doubleday & Company, Inc.

Sanders, Ed (1971) *The Family: The Story of Charles Manson's Dune Buggy Attack Battalion*. New York: Dutton.

Seckler, Phyllis (1973–1996) *In the Continuum*. Volumes I–V. Oroville: The College of Thelema.

_____ (2010) *The Thoth Tarot, Astrology, and Other Selected Writings*. Edited by David Shoemaker, Gregory Peters, and Rorac Johnson. York Beach: The Teitan Press.

_____ (2012) *The Kabbalah, Magick, and Thelema: Selected Writings Vol. II*. Edited by David Shoemaker, Gregory Peters, and Rorac Johnson. York Beach: The Teitan Press.

Sedgwick, Mark (2004) *Against the Modern World: Traditionalism and the Secret Intellectual History of the Twentieth Century*. Oxford: Oxford University Press.

Seligman, Paul (1962) *The Apeiron of Anaximander: A Study in the Origins and Function of Metaphysical Ideas*. London: The Atholone Press University of London.

Scholem, Gershom (1946) *Major Trends in Jewish Mysticism*. New York: Schocken Books.

Schrecker, Ellen (1998). *Many Are the Crimes: McCarthyism in America.* New York: Little, Brown and Company.

Shepherd, William C. (1972) "Religion and the Counter Culture: A New Religiosity." In *Sociological Inquiry*, 42:1.

Shiva, Frater (2007) *Inside the Solar Lodge, Outside the Law: True Tales of Initiation and Adventure.* York Beach: The Teitan Press.

_____ (2012) *Inside the Solar Lodge, Behind the Veil: True Tale of Initiation and Adventure.* Los Lunas: Desert Star Temple.

Shoemaker, David; Ferrell, Andrew; and Voss, Stefan (Editors) (2016) *Karl Germer: Selected Letters 1928–1962.* Sacramento: International College of Thelema.

Spence, Richard (2008) *Secret Agent 666: Aleister Crowley, British Intelligence and the Occult.* Port Townsend, WA: Feral House.

Spinoza, Benedict de (1996) *Ethics.* Translated by Edwin Curley. London: Penguin Books, Ltd.

Stace, W.T. (1960) *Mysticism and Philosophy.* London: Palgrave Macmillan.

Stanley, Thomas (2010) *Pythagoras: His Life and Teachings.* Edited by James Wasserman and J. Daniel Gunther. Lake Worth: Ibis Press.

Stark, Rodney (Fall 1999) "Secularization, R.I.P." In *Sociology of Religion,* Volume 60, Number 3, 249–73.

Stark, Rodney; Bainbridge, William Sims; and Doyle, Daniel P. (Winter 1979) "Cults of America: A Reconnaissance in Space and Time." In *Sociological Analysis*, Volume 40, Number 4, "Sects, Cults and Religious Movements," 347–359.

Starr, Martin P. (2003) *The Unknown God: W. T. Smith and the Thelemites.* Bolingbrook: The Teitan Press, Inc.

_____ (2012) "Aleister Crowley—Freemason?!" in *Aleister Crowley and Western Esotericism.* Edited by Henrik Bogdan and Martin P. Starr. New York: Oxford University Press.

Steinberg, S.H. (1961) *Five Hundred Years of Printing.* Harmondsworth: Penguin Books, Ltd.

Sutin, Lawrence (2000) *Do What Thou Wilt: A Life of Aleister Crowley.* New York: St. Martins Griffin.

Symonds, John (1951) *The Great Beast: The Life of Aleister Crowley*. London: Rider.

_____ (1971) *The Great Beast: The Life and Magic of Aleister Crowley*. London: Macdonald & Co.

Szönyi, György E. (2004) *John Dee's Occultism*. Albany: SUNY Press.

Thatcher, David (1970) *Nietzsche in England: 1890–1914*. Toronto: University of Toronto Press.

Tiryakian, Edward A. (1972) "Toward the Sociology of Esoteric Culture." *American Journal of Sociology*, 78:3 (November), pp. 491–512.

Toma, Catalina L. (2013) "Feeling Better But Doing Worse: Effects of Facebook Self-Presentation on Implicit Self-Esteem and Cognitive Task Performance." In *Media Psychology*, Vol. 16, No. 2, pp. 199–220.

Troeltsch, Ernst (1992) *The Social Teaching of the Christian Churches*. Volumes I–II. Westminster: John Knox Press.

Truzzi, Marcello (1972) "The Occult Revival as Popular Culture: Some Observations of the Old and Nouveau Witch." *The Sociological Quarterly*, 13:1 (Winter), pp. 16–36.

Unknown (June 1972) "The Occult: A Substitute Faith." *Time Magazine*. 99 (25), p. 68.

Van den Broek, Roelof (2013) *Gnostic Religion in Antiquity*. Princeton: Princeton University Press.

Vernon, Roland (2000) *Star in the East: Krishnamurti, the Invention of a Messiah*. New York: Palgrave.

Vitz, Paul (1977) *Psychology As Religion: The Cult Of Self-Worship*. Grand Rapids: William B. Eerdmans Publishing Company.

Wallis, Roy (1974) "Ideology, Authority, and the Development of Cultic Movements." In *Social Research*, Vol. 41, No. 2 (Summer), pp. 299–327.

Waltz, Kenneth (1979) *Theory of International Relations*. Reading: Addison-Wesley Publication Co.

Wasserman, James (2004) *The Slaves Shall Serve: Meditations on Liberty*. New York: Sekmet Books.

_____ (2012) *In the Center of the Fire: A Memoir of the Occult, 1966–1989*. Lake Worth: Ibis Press.

Wasserman, James and Nancy (2013) *To Perfect this Feast: A Performance Commentary on the Gnostic Mass.* (third edition) West Palm Beach: Sekmet Books

Wax, Dustin M. (2008) *Anthropology at the Dawn of the Cold War: The Influence of Foundations, McCarthyism and the CIA.* London/Ann Arbor: Pluto Press.

Weber, Max (1922) "Wissenschaft als Beruf," *Gesammlte Aufsaetze zur Wissenschaftslehre.* Tubingen: J.C.B. Mohr.

Weinstein, Allen (1997) *Perjury: The Hiss-Chambers Case.* New York: Random House, Inc.

White, David Gordon (2003) *Kiss of the Yoginī:"Tantric Sex" in its South Asian Contexts.* Chicago: University of Chicago Press.

Willard, Thomas (1983) "The Rosicrucian Manifestos in Britain." *The Papers of the Bibliographical Society of America.* Vol. 77, Fourth Quarter, pp. 489–495.

Williams, Raymond (1958) "Culture is Ordinary." In *The Everyday Life Reader.* Edited by Hen Highmore. London: Routledge.

Wolfe, Burton H. (1974) *The Devil's Avenger: A Biography of Anton Szandor LaVey.* Salem: Pyramid Books.

Woodard, Colin (2011) *American Nations; A History of the Eleven Rival Regional Cultures of North America.* New York: Penguin Books.

_____ (2016) *American Character: A History of the Epic Struggle Between Individual Liberty and the Common Good.* New York: Penguin Random House LLC.

Index

Contact Information

To contact O.T.O. worldwide

Ordo Templi Orientis
www.oto.org

To contact A∴A∴

Chancellor
BM ANKH
London WC1N 3XX
ENGLAND
www.outercol.org

For more information on this book:

https://www.one-truth-one-spirit.com/